Population and Development in North East India

About the Editor

Bimal J. Deb is Professor and Head, Department of Political Science, North Eastern Hill University, Shillong, He is also the President of North-East India Council for Social Science Research.

Population and Development in North East India

Edited by

Bimal J. Deb

CONCEPT PUBLISHING COMPANY PVT. LTD.
NEW DELHI-110059

ISBN-13-978-81-8069-688-6

First Published 2010

Published and Printed by

Concept
Since 1974

Concept Publishing Company Pvt. Ltd.
Regd. Office:
A/15-16, Commercial Block, Mohan Garden
New Delhi-110059 (India)
Phones : 25351460, 25351794, *Fax* : 091-11-25357109
Email : publishing@conceptpub.com,
Website: www.conceptpub.com

Editorial Office:
H-13, Bali Nagar, New Delhi-110 015, India.

Cataloging in Publication Data--*Courtesy:* D.K. Agencies (P) Ltd. <docinfo@dkagencies.com>

Population and development in North East India / edited by Bimal J. Deb.
p. cm.
Contributed articles.
Includes bibliographical references.
Includes index.
ISBN 13: 978-81-8069-688-6

1. India, Northeastern--Population--Economic aspects. 2. India, Northeastern--Economic conditions. 3. India, Northeastern--Social conditions. 4. Quality of life--India, Northeastern. 5. Sustainable development--India, Northeastern. I. Deb, Bimal J.

DDC 304.609541 22

Foreword

Population and development in North East India is yet another pioneering venture of North East India Council for Social Science Research. As many as twenty eight sections in the book are devoted to providing an explanatory framework for understanding population dynamics and issues of population and development in the context of North East India. One can only confidently hope that this volume would be of immense help to the administrators, policy makers and researchers who are keen to understand the issues highlighted in proper perspective. On behalf of the Council I take this opportunity of expressing our gratitude to Professor Bimal J. Deb who, with his vast experience in the field of developmental politics and administration, has carefully edited the book for the benefit of all concerned.

Dr. S. Sharma
Secretary
North-East India Council for
Social Science Research
Shillong

Contents

List of the Contributors

Dr. A.K. Neog	A Senior Member of Indian Economic Service, New Delhi
Prof. J.B. Ganguly	Former Vice-Chancellor, Tripura University
Dr. Madhushree Das	Department of Geography, Cotton College, Guwahati
Dr. Bimal Kumar Kar	Department of Geography, Gauhati University, Guwahati
Dr. P.C. Dutta	Department of Statistics, Hailakandi College, Assam
Dr. A.K. Borah	Reader, Department of Sociology, Dibrugarh University
Dr. J. Borbora	Reader, Department of Sociology, Dibrugarh University
Dr. S.V. Borbora	Reader, Department of Sociology, Dibrugarh University
Dr. Subrata Purkayastha	Lecturer, Department of Geography, NEHU, Shillong
Mr. Somnath Hazra	Research Associate, ICFAI, Research Centre, Kolkata
Prof. Raj Kumar Sen	Professor of Economics, Rabindra Bharati University, Kolkata
Dr. Reema Choudhury Chakrabarty	Lecturer, Department of Economics, Barooah College, Guwahati
Mrs. P.K. Ryngnga	Anthropological Survey of India, Shillong
Mrs.Chaiti Sharma Biswas	Economic Research Unit, Indian Statistical Institute, Kolkata
Dr. Arup Kumar Hazarika	Lecturer, Cotton College Guwahati

Dr. Utpal Kumar Dey	Reader, Department of Economics, NEHU, Shillong
Prof. K. Alam	Former Professor and Head Department of Economics, Gauhati University, Guwahati
Prof. Lakhyahira Datta	Professor, Department of Geography Gauwahati University, Guwahati
Dr. Gorky Chakraborty	Lecturer, Department of Economics, Doom Dooma College, Tinsukia, Assam
Dr. Jayasree Borah	Lecturer, Department of Geography Cotton College
Mr. Aditya Ch. Deka	Lecturer, Pub Kamrup College, Assam
Dr. Zona Bhuyan	Research Scholar, NEHU, Shillong
Prof. Malabika Das Gupta	Honorary Associate, Centre for Urban Economic Studies, Department of Economics, Calcutta University, Kolkata
Prof. Suchintya Bhattacharya	Professor, Tripura University, Agartala
Dr. Mithilesh Kumar Sinha	Reader, Department of Economics, Nagaland University,
Dr. Manoj Kumar Singh	Lecturer, People's College, Mokokchung (Nagaland)
Dr. R.P. Athparia	Sr. Anthopologist, Anthropological Survey of India
Dr. B.F. Kalirani	Superintending, Anthropologist, Anthropological Survey of India.
Dr. R.P. Bhattacharjee	Secetary, Social Science Research Institute of Arunachal Pradesh, Itanagar and Deputy Registrar, NERIST
Dr. Surojit Sen Gupta	Lecturer, Department of Sociology, St. Edmund's College Shillong
Dr. Elangbam Nixon Singh	Lecturer, D.M. College of Commerce, Imphal

Prof. G.P. Prasain	Professor and Head, Department of Commerce, Manipur University, Imphal
Dr. Rajmani Singh	Associate Professor, Department of Commerce, Manipur University, Imphal
Mr. A. Ratan Sharma	Research Fellow, Department of Commerce, Manipur University
Prof. Tapan Kumar Chattopadhyay	Professor of Political Science, Calcutta University, Kolkata

1 Introduction

It has long been recognized that population issue should not be seen in isolation, but within the larger context of sustainable development of the planet for the betterment of humankind. The perimeter of this approach includes within its fold economic activity that increases the quality of life for all people through curbing excessive consumption and generating productive growth, alleviating poverty, achieving sustainable agricultural and industrial production and improving health care and access to education. At the same time, population issues need to be resolved in such a way that cultural identity, values and tradition are not in stake. The empowerment of women and the improvement of their political, social, economic and health status are highly important ends in themselves. The Cairo Declaration on Population and Development way back in 1994 had underlined the strategy of fully integrating population issues in all development planning policies and programmes encompassing environment, human rights, social development and role of women. It is, therefore, essential that population and development problems are resolved keeping in view the formulation of new and wide-ranging economic policies supportive of sustainable development. The issue of reproductive health and family planning may also be addressed by national governments and constituent units keeping in view national and cultural identity, values and tradition. At the same time, efforts must also be directed to provide universal access to family planning information and services. It has also long been recognized globally that human development cannot be sustained unless women are guaranteed equal rights and equal status with men. As Cairo Declaration mentions :

"In this process, women should be seen not merely as the

beneficiaries of change but as the agents of change as well". Education was rightly viewed as the single most important element on the road to equality and empowerment of women. Equally, disparities in health conditions and mortality risks widely prevalent in developing countries need to be reduced by means of global commitment. As a matter of fact, the elected representatives of the people have a great role to play in translating public support for population and development activities into "the most beneficial distribution of budgetary, human and administrative resources". It goes without saying that international consensus on the need to mobilize significant domestic and external financial resources and proper implementation thereafter will hold the key in strengthening population and development programmes. While emphasizing allocation of adequate financial resources in the implementation of population policies and programme, one cannot but mention the non-performance of the role the parliamentarians had undertaken around the world to monitor and evaluate the progress in the fields of legislation, policy making and global commitment. What is needed is greater awareness among policy makers and the general public alike about population and development issues, within the global context of sustainable development.

In this book, as many as twenty eight papers cover the various dimensions of population dynamics in North East India which will strengthen our understanding of population and sustainable development and facilitate adoption of corrective measures aimed at improving the quality of life.

2 Population of Agricultural Workers in the North East India and their Work Participation

A.K. Neog

The term 'population of agricultural workers' as used in this paper refers to agricultural workers, which include cultivators and agricultural labourers, which are so classified in the population census by the census organization. In the census, work is defined as participation in any economically productive activity with or without compensation, wages or profit. It also includes part-time help or unpaid work on farm. All persons engaged in 'work' are workers. They are classified into main workers and marginal workers. The 'time criteria' of employment has been used to classify workers. Workers who used to work for six months or more during the reference period (period of census enumeration was 9th to 28th February, 2001) are main workers, and those working for less than six months are marginal workers. The magnitude of marginal workers is a measure of underemployment though its intensity cannot be gauged from the census data. It may be mentioned that as per coverage in population census, cultivation does not include cultivation of tea, coffee, rubber, coconut and betel nuts (areca nuts). It may also be mentioned that the census classifies the total workers into four categories, viz. cultivators, agricultural labourers, household industry workers and 'other' workers. On the other hand, non-workers are those who did not work at all during the reference period. Students, beggars, vagrants, person not engaged in productive work, dependent, pensioners etc. are examples of non-workers. However, the census results do not furnish the age of workers. The aim of this paper is to explore the dynamics of work force in the population with special reference to draw some inferences having bearing on policy for development.

2. Methodology, Data, Coverage and Reference Period

The implicit methodology introduced in this exercise is a worker participation identity, which can be enunciated as follows:

$$(a/b)= (a/c)(c/b)(d/a).........(1)$$

where a, b, c and d denote respectively total workers, total population, main workers and marginal workers in an economy.

Identity (1) implies that the ratio of total workers to total population is a combined product of four ratios. There are the ratio of total workers, and total workers to total population, marginal workers to total workers, and total workers to marginal workers. Given the population data, Table 2.1 is a reflection of the above identity.

Another analogous identity is used to examine the distribution of workers in the form of cultivators and agricultural labourers. This can be stated as follows:

$$(F/W)=(F/L)(L/W)................(2)$$

where F, L and W denote respectively cultivators, agricultural laboures and agricultural working population. Identity (2) implies that the ratio of cultivators to total agricultural workers is a product of the ratio of cultivators to labourers, and the ratio of labourers to total workers. Table 2.2 is a reflection of this identity.

Correlation coefficient (r) and linear regression are used for data in respect ofTable 2.5 while examining the relationship between Gross Domestic Product and agricultural workers.

Data used in our analysis are secondary data, which are published by the Government sources. Reference period for the workers data is of 2001, while for the employment data the same is of 1993-94 and 1999-2000, and for agriculture census and Gross State Domestic Product it is of 2000-01. Unless stated otherwise, the geographical coverage in the paper is the eight States of North East India, viz. Assam, Arunanchal Pradesh, Manipur, Meghalaya, Mizoram, Nagaland, Tripura and Sikkim *vis-a-vis* all-India.

3. All-India Scenario

As per 2001 Population Census, India has more than 12.73 (10.36 main +2.37 marginal) crore cultivators (accounting for 31.7 per cent of the total workers) and about 10.68 crore agricultural labourers (accounting for 26.5 per cent of the total workers in the economy). These two category of workers account for 31.53 per cent of the total rural population. In 1991, there were 12.47 crore cultivators and 8.60 crore agricultural labourers. The number of cultivators, during the decade 1991-2001, rose by 2.08 per cent and of agricultural labourers by 24.19 per cent. The agriculture sector directly employs 58.2 per cent of the workers at the all-India level. The proportion of agricultural labourers to cultivators is 0.84. However, in the country the State with the highest percentage of total cultivators to its total workers is found to be Himachal Pradesh with 65.3 per cent closely followed by Nagaland with 64.7 per cent. Himachal Pradesh also tops in the percentage of female cultivators (85.8 per cent) to total female workers, closely followed by Uttarakhand (77.8 per cent) and Nagaland (77.5 per cent) compared to all-India average (32.9 per cent). The State with the lowest percentage of total cultivators is Kerala (7 per cent), with female cultivators 4.8 per cent. On the other hand, the State with the highest percentage of agricultural labourers in its workforce is Bihar at 48.0 per cent, with female agricultural labourers at 62.6 per cent of its female workers. Himachal Pradesh has the lowest percentage of agricultural labourers at 3.1 per cent, female labourers 2.9 per cent.

4. Size and Composition of Main and Marginal Workers

As per 2001 Census, the number of main workers (rural+urban) in India as a whole stood at 31.3 crore (i.e. 24.01 crore male and 7.29 crore female) and marginal workers at 8.92 crore (i.e. above 3.48 crore male and 5.44 crore female). The main workers accounted for 77.82 per cent of the total (main+marginal) workers in the entire economy while the marginal workers were 22.18 per cent of the total. Of the main workers, 22.92 crore (i.e.16.19 crore male and 6.01 crore female) were rural, i.e. 73.23 per cent, while 8.38 crore (i.e.

7.10 crore male and 1.28 crore female) were urban, i.e. 26.77 per cent. The proportion of workers in the rural areas is more than 2.74 times the urban workers.

In the regional economy of the North East India, the size and composition of the workers are as under. The total workers (rural+urban and of both genders) in Assam stood at 95.39 lakh (i.e. 68.71 lakh male and 26.68 lakh female). It accounted for 35.79 per cent of the total population (266.56 lakh) of the State, suggesting a dependency ratio of 64.21 per cent. Of the total workers in Assam, main workers declined in the State from the level of 86.4 per cent in 1991 to 74.6 per cent in 2001. During this period, the overall work participation rate, i.e. the percentage of total (main+marginal) workers to total population, in Assam fell from 36.1 per cent to 35.8 per cent compared to rise in the all-India average of 37.5 per cent in 1991 to 39.1 per cent in 2001. However, the male work participation rate in Assam rose marginally from 49.9 per cent while the same for female declined from 21.6 per cent to 20.7 per cent during the same period. The marginal workers stood at 24.24 lakh (i.e. 10.22 lakh male and 14.02 lakh female) accounting for 25.41 per cent of total workers. It may be mentioned that the female marginal workers in rural Assam is sizeable, at 58.53 per cent of the total rural marginal workers. Higher incidence of 25.41 per cent of marginal workers in Assam than the all-India average of 22.18 per cent indicates more underemployment in the State. It may be mentioned that of the main workers in the State, 60.51 lakh (i.e. 49.26 lakh male +11.25 lakh female) are rural, i.e. 85.06 per cent, while 10.64 lakh (i.e. 9.23 lakh male and 1.41 lakh female) are urban, accounting for 14.94 per cent. The above data for the States of North East India are given in Table 2.1.

The rural population in Assam stood at 232.16 lakh in 2001, which accounts for 87 per cent of the total population of the State. Total number of workers in the rural areas stood at about 83.97 lakh, accounting for 36.17 per cent of the rural population. However, the rural workers as a percentage of total (rural+urban) workers is 88.03 per cent.

Table 2.1: Spatial Distribution of Workers (In lakh numbers) North Eastern States

States	*Space*	*Main Workers*			*Marginal Workers*		
		Total	*Male*	*Female*	*Total*	*Male*	*Female*
Assam	Rural	60.51	49.26	11.25	23.46	9.73	13.73
	Urban	10.64	9.23	1.41	0.78	0.49	0.29
Arunachal Pradesh	Rural	3.40	2.07	1.33	0.62	0.23	0.39
	Urban	0.75	0.60	0.15	0.06	0.03	0.03
Manipur	Rural	4.95	3.20	1.75	2.28	0.78	1.50
	Urban	1.65	1.10	0.55	0.58	0.19	0.39
Meghalaya	Rural	6.27	3.93	2.34	1.96	0.75	1.21
	Urban	1.30	0.92	0.38	0.17	0.08	0.09
Mizoram	Rural	2.02	1.21	0.81	0.54	0.18	0.36
	Urban	1.61	1.05	0.56	0.50	0.19	0.31
Nagaland	Rural	6.08	3.49	2.59	1.33	0.58	0.75
	Urban	0.96	0.76	0.20	0.11	0.06	0.05
Tripura	Rural	7.48	6.06	1.42	2.35	0.81	1.54
	Urban	1.64	1.36	0.28	0.13	0.08	0.05
Sikkim	Rural	1.91	1.30	0.61	0.48	0.18	0.30
	Urban	0.22	0.17	0.05	0.018	0.013	0.05
All India	Rural	2291.86	1691.01	600.85	807.70	297.38	510.32
	Urban	838.18	710.46	127.72	84.60	5.129	33.31

Note : Figures are rounded of.
Source: Census of India 2001, Primary Census Abstract (Table-A-5).

5. Distribution and Participation of Agricultural Workers

As per 2001 Population Census, there are 1,273.13 lakh cultivators in the country as a whole. They account for 31.7 per cent of the total workers as against 39.7 per cent in 1991. Of the total cultivators, about 854.16 lakh (67.09 per cent) are male and 418.96 lakh (32.91 per cent) are female. The total number of agricultural labourers in the country stood at 1,067.75 lakh comprising 573.29 lakh (53.69 per cent) male and 494.46 lakh (46.31 per cent) female. The percentage of agricultural labourers to total workers in the country declined to 26.5 per cent from 27.4 per cent in 1991. As against this, the total number of cultivators in Assam stood at 37.31 lakh, of which 26.34 lakh (70.60 per cent) are male and 10.97 lakh (29.40 per cent) are female.

The cultivators and agricultural labourers together account for only 21.51 per cent of the rural population in Assam during 2001. But, they account for about 59.5 per cent of the total rural workers. However, the percentage of cultivators to total workers in 2001 in Assam sharply declined to 39.1 per cent from 54.8 per cent in 1991. On the other hand, the total number of agricultural labourers stood at 12,64 lakh comprising of 8.33 lakh male (65.90 per cent) and 4.31 lakh female. (34.10 per cent). The percentage of total agricultural labourers to total workers in the State has increased to 13.2 per cent in 2001 against 12.6 per cent in 1991.

Data in *Table 2.2* reveals that female cultivators as well as female agricultural labourers as percentage to total female workers in each category exceeds their male counterparts in all the States in 2001 (except of cultivators in Manipur). The female cultivators

Table 2.2 : Distribution of Agricultural Workers, 2001

States	*Cultivators*			*Agricultural Labourers*		
	Total (Lakh Nos.)	*Male (%)*	*Female (%)*	*Total (Lakh Nos.)*	*Male (%)*	*Female (%)*
Assam	37.31	38.3	41.1	12.64	12.1	16.2
Nagaland	5.49	55.4	77.5	0.31	3.3	4.2
Meghalaya	4.67	44.9	52.8	1.72	16.0	20.1
Manipur	3.80	40.6	39.6	1.14	9.5	15.2
Tripura	3.13	26.6	28.1	2.76	19.6	34.6
Arunachal Pradesh	2.79	46.4	75.5	0.19	3.5	4.5
Mizoram	2.56	49.6	61.6	0.27	4.9	6.9
Sikkim	1.31	42.3	62.8	0.17	5.3	8.5
All-India	1, 273.13	31.1	32.9	1,067.75	20.8	38.9

[NB: · Excludes Mao-Maram, Paomata and Rural Sub-divisions of Senapati District.

·· Male, female figures are in terms of percentage to all total workers in each category.]

Source : Census of India 2001.

(main+marginal) as a percentage of all total female workers (main+marginal) in Assam stood at 41.1 per cent as against 38.3 per cent for male. Likewise for agricultural labourers, it may be noted that the ratio of cultivators (male+female) to total workers drastically declined in Assam from 54.8 per cent in 1991 to 39.1 per cent in 2001 as stated earlier, while the ratio of total agricultural labourers to total workers rose marginally. This suggests consequent rise in open unemployment and dependency ratio.

From the above table (s) and analysis, one can make the following inferences:

(a) Emergence and pre-dominance of female labourers in agriculture in general, and particularly in North Eastern States.
(b) Increasing marginalisation of female workers particularly in the rural areas (as can be seen from column of Tables 2.1 and 2.2).

6. Results of Agriculture Census 2000-01

The process of marginalisation of farming is also evident from the provisional agricultural census data which are given in Table 2.3. At the all-India level about 82 per cent of the holdings are in the marginal and small farmers category owning about 39 per cent of the area under operational holdings. For Assam these data are 81.02 per cent and 42.54 per cent respectively. Data for the other States can be seen from the table. The average size of holdings at the national level came down to 1.32 hectare in 2000-01 from 1.41 hectare in 1995-96. Though the same for Assam stood at about 1.20 hectare against 1.17 hectare in 1995-96, the same is much below the national average.

7. Sectorial Distribution of Employment

Development theory hypothesizes that as an economy grows, the share of employment in the primary sector which comprises agriculture proper, animal husbandry, fishery, forestry, mining and quarrying tends to decline, that of the secondary, i.e. industrial sector and the tertiary sector, i.e. services go up. During the period 1993-94 and 1999-2000, the share of primary sector in employment in the country has gone

Table 2.3: Distribution of Holdings (thousand numbers) and Area Operated (thousand hectares) as per 2000-01 Agriculture Census (Provisional)

States	*Marginal*		*Small*		*Semi-Medium to Large*		*All Sizes*	
	Number	*Area*	*Number*	*Area*	*Number*	*Area*	*Number*	*Area*
Assam	1537	607	572	718	494	1790	2603	3115
Nagaland	5	2	9	11	130	1035	144	1048
Meghalaya	115	63	57	83	42	132	214	278
Manipur	75	40	49	63	25	69	149	172
Tripura	406	126	55	75	19	69	480	270
Arunachal Pradesh	15	7	20	27	72	360	107	394
Mizoram	34	22	28	36	14	35	76	93
Sikkim	28	12	12	17	11	51	51	80
All-India	76,122	30,088	22,814	32,260	21,886	97,555	120,822	159,903

Source: Government of India, Ministry of Agriculture.

down from 58.41 per cent to 52.43 per cent, while that of the other sectors have increased as can be seen from Table 2.4. In respect of Assam, even though the figure has gone down from 71.64 per cent to 57.90 per cent, it is still higher than the all-India average. On the other hand, the employment in the other two sectors have not gone up, particularly in the secondary sector. Except for Tripura, the primary sector is still dominant in the rest of the region.

Table 2.4 : Sectorial Distribution of Employment (Usual Primary Status) in Primary, Secondary and Tertiary Sectors (In percentage)

States	*1993-94*			*1999-2000*		
	Primary	*Secondary*	*Tertiary*	*Primary*	*Secondary*	*Tertiary*
Assam	71.64	3.04	25.32	57.90	3.81	38.29
Arunachal Pradesh	79.38	1.91	18.51	67.12	2.47	30.41
Manipur	55.19	9.11	35.70	63.49	6.33	30.18
Meghalaya	78.80	1.10	20.10	70.34	1.31	28.35
Tripura	41.20	5.50	53.30	38.20	3.87	57.93
All-India (Mean)	58.41	10.10	31.49	52.43	10.87	36.71

Note: Data for the remaining States of N.E. India are not available.
Source: Planning Commission, Tenth Five Year Plan document (2002-07), Vol-III.

8. Share of Agriculture in Gross State Domestic Product (GSDP)

One of the indicators of development is the income emerging from the agricultural sector and its relative share in the Gross State Domestic Product, particularly at constant prices. As per data available from the Central Statistical Organisation (CSO), the GSDP at constant 1993-94 prices originating from Agriculture (i.e. agriculture proper, forestry and logging and fishing) for the 2000-01 along with the share of the same in the total GSDP for the States for the region for which data are available are given in Table 2.5(a) along with the percentage of agricultural workers (cultivators+agricultural labourers) to the total rural workers and the estimated GSDP per head. It may be mentioned that since the share of agriculture SDP is coming down over time but the number of workers in agriculture still remains large, the annual per capita income of the agricultural workers is very low.

Table 2.5 : Percentage Share of Agriculture in GSDP, amount of Agriculture GSDP (at 1993-94 prices), number of Agricultural Workers and real GSDP per head for 2000-01

States	*Share (%) of Agriculture in GSDP or GDP*	*GSDP (Rs. Crore)*	*Percentage of Agricultural Workers*	*Amount (Rs.) of GSDP per head*
Assam	31.4	5,811	59.48	11,633.63
Arunanchal Pradesh	28.8	318	74.13	10,671.14
Manipur	20.1	442	68.33	8,947.37
Meghalaya	21.7	509	77.84	7,965,57
Tripura	23.5	669	59.58	11,358.23
All India	23.8	2,85,877	75.52	12,212.37

By using the cross-section data given in Table 2.5 it is found that there is a good negative correlation coefficient (denoted by r) between the percentage of agricultural workers (denoted by X) and share of Agriculture in total GSDP or GDP (denoted by Y). This indicates that higher percentage of agricultural workers are associated with lower share of income. The results are:

N (size of sample)=6; r=(-)0.35328
Y=38.21-0.19 X

In Table 2.5, the amount of real agriculture GSDP per head is estimated by dividing the State agriculture GSDP by the number of agricultural workers in each State. The correlation coefficient (r) between the number of workers (X) and real GSDP per head (Y) of the States and the regression equation is as under:

n (size of sample)=5; r=0.50959
Y=9549.35+40.33X

9. Some Inferences

From the analysis, the following inferences are inevitable, viz.

(i) Rural employment is still predominant.
(ii) Role of male workers in agriculture is declining.
(iii) Though female workers are emerging to be predominant in agriculture, they are increasingly in marginal workers category.
(iv) Underemployment (disguised employment) persists in agriculture.
(v) Agriculture is still predominant in the economy of the North Eastern region.
(vi) Share of agriculture in GDP is, however, declining over time.
(vii) Per capita income of the agricultural workers is considerably low.

In the context of North Eastern Region, the positive correlation between the number of workers and real agricultural GSDP per head gives a ray of hope to usher in a *renaissance* in agriculture. This opportunity should be seized for further growth of the region. The all-inclusive growth under the Eleventh Five Year Plan provides an added opportunity to achieve the same.

References

Registrar General and Census Commissioner, India (June, 2004): Census of India 2001, (Series-1) Primary Census Abstract.

Neog, A.K.: "Employment Potentiality in Agriculture" in P.C. Goswami (ed) "*Agriculture in Assam*", Assam Institute of Development Studies (1989), Guwahati.

Directorate of Economics and Statistics; *Agricultural Statistics at a Glance,* 2003, Government of India.

Barah, B.C.: "Strategies for Agricultural Development in the North East India: Challenges and Emerging Opportunities" in *Indian Journal of Agricultural Economics,* Vol. 62, No. 1, Jan. March, 2007.

3 Demographic Dividend as a Factor of Economic Development of North Eastern States

J.B. Ganguly

Demographic analysis of the trend of population growth in a country or region is now more concerned with the changing age-structure of population rather than the overall growth rate. If the relative size of the younger population of the working age group, i.e. belonging to 15 to 64 years of age compared to that of non-working age (children and older people) is higher than it will favourably impact on the growth of GDP given the favourable condition of skill development, employability and employment opportunities for the population entering into the working age. This factor of boosting economic growth is characterized as "Demographic Dividend".

For promoting growth investment of the surplus income over current consumption needs to be expanded. This is dependent on the magnitude of dependency ratio. "Since those outside the workforce would be consuming part of what is produced by currently employed workers, the ratio of those outside the workforce to those in it (the dependency ratio) would be among the factors influencing the surplus available for investment after current consumption. Hence, everything else remaining the same, the higher the proportion of workers to non-workers, the larger would be the surplus. For given unemployment rates, the higher the ratio of those in the labour force to those outside it, the larger would be the surplus."[1]

In Table 3.1 Decadal Variation in population and average exponential growth rate of population in the North Eastern States in 1971-81, 1981-91 and 1991-2001 have been shown. The average exponential growth rates have progressively fallen during those decades.

Table 3.1 : Decadal Variation in Population Change and Average Exponential Growth Rate of Population

States	*Decadal Variation in POP Per cent*			*Average Annual Exponential Growth Rate*		
	1971-81	*1981-91*	*1991-2001*	*1971-81*	*1981-1991*	*1991-2001*
Arunachal Pradesh	+35.15	+36.83	+26.21	3.01	3.14	2.33
Assam	+23.36	+24.24	+18.85	2.10	2.17	1.73
Manipur	+32.46	+29.29	+30.02	2.81	2.57	2.63
Meghalaya	+32.04	+32.86	+29.94	2.78	2.84	2.62
Mizoram	48.55	+39.70	+29.18	3.96	3.34	2.56
Nagaland	+50.05	+56.08	+64.41	4.06	4.45	4.17
Tripura	+31.92	+34.30	+15.74	2.77	2.95	1.46

Source: NEC Basic Statistics of NER, 2002, p. 7.

On the other hand net State Domestic Product's at current prices in 1980-81 through 2000-01 have consistently risen (Table 3.2). The main reason for this is presumed to be the increase in working population the estimate of which is available for 2001 and this is shown in Table 3.3.

Table 3.3 : Estmates of Working Population in North Eastern States

States	*Total Population*	*Total Workers*	*Total Workers as % of Total Population*
Arunachal Pradesh	1,096,702	482,206	44
Assam	26,638,407	9,557,064	38.87 Say 36
Manipur	2,388,068	1,069,578	44.76
Meghalaya	2,306,069	956,425	41.45
Mizoram	891,058	469,597	52.63
Nagaland	1,988,636	849,982	42.75
Tripura	3,181,168	1,151,190	36.18

Source: NEC Basic Statistics of NER, pp. 24, 25.

State-wise infant mortality rates for 1961, 2003 and 2005 as given in Table 3.4 show that these rates have fallen consistently. Table 3.5 reveals that both estimated annual birth and death rates have fallen from 1982 to 2000. Such demographic data point to the fact that NER population of youths who are the main sources of creation of wealth has been increasing; in other words, dependency ratio has been

Table 3.2 : Net State Domestic Product at Current Prices

New Series (*Rs. Crores*)

States	*1980-1981*	*1985-1986*	*1990-1991*	*1993-1994*	*1995-1996*	*1996-1997*	*1997-1998*	*1998-1999*	*1999-2000*	*2000-01*
Arunachal Pradesh	95	239	446	790	1067	1078	1192	1286	1533	NA
Assam	2365	5326	9775	13477	17170	18465	20211	21597	25051	NA
Manipur	197	367	714	1141	1410	1671	1945	2311	2554	2808
Meghalaya	207	394	884	1306	1689	1853	2149	2534	2806	3209
Mizoram	68	173	336	618	859	983	1022	1139	NA	NA
Nagaland	126	287	693	1251	1656	1849	2137	2184	NA	NA
Tripura	344	671	1193	1619	2073	2500	3015	3473	3813	4184

Note: "Estimates from 1993-94 onwards are as provided by the Directorate of Economics and Statistics of respective State Governments and Union Territories. Estimates prior to 1993-94 have been linked by using the method of splicing using the estimates as provided by the Directorate of Economics and Statistics of respective State Governments and Union Territories."

Source: NEC Basic Statistics of NER, 2002, p. 286 quoted from Economic Survery 2000-01.

falling. We are unable to make the projection of youth, population for the NER for want of required data. Therefore, we may go by the

Table 3.4 : State-wise Infant Mortality Rates

States	*1961*	*2003*	*2005*
Mizoram	69	16	20
Manipur	32	16	13
Arunachal Pradesh	126	34	37
Tripura	111	35	31
Meghalaya	79	57	49
Sikkim	96	33	30
Assam	NA	67	68
Nagaland	68	NA	18

Source: Government of India, Economic Survey 2006-07, p. s. 115

all-India data presuming that the direction of change would be the same, Registrar-General of India's projection of average annual increment in youth population stands as follows as quoted by Chandrasekhar and Ghosh[2].

2001-06	5406.2
2006-11	3532.4
2011-16	(-) 212.8
2016-21	(-) 1857.4
2021-26	(-) 1112

Estimates made by United Nations Population Division and that made by the Registrar General of India vary. According to the former, the youth population (15-24 age group) will 'begin to decline only by 2025' but the latter's projected decline will begin by 2011-16 as noted above.

From the above factual analysis we may conclude: first, growth of youth population of NER in the recent decades has been quite significant.

Secondly, the consistent growth of SDPs in the North Eastern States is partly attributable to the reaping of Demographic Dividend.

Finally, it may be projected that over the coming decades economic growth of these States will be boosted by this factor besides the recent initiatives taken by the Central Government to provide these States

Table 3.5 : Estimated Annual Birth Rates and Death Rates

States		*1982*	*1985*	*1990*	*1995*	*2000*	
Arunachal Pradesh	B.R.	34.2	35.5	30.1	23.8	22.3	
	D.R.	15.9	14.3	13.2	6.0	6.0	
Assam	B.R.	34.7	34.2	30.9	27.6	26.9	
	D.R.	12.1	12.6	11.5	9.6	9.6	
		(1983)					
Manipur	B.R.	28.0	28.5	21.1	20.6	18.3	
	D.R.	N.A.	7.7	5.9	6.7	5.6	
Meghalaya	B.R.	31.1	39.1	31.8	29.0	28.5	
	D.R.	8.9	12.7	7.8	8.9	9.2	
Mizoram	B.R.	-	-	-	-	16.0	1996: 15.1, 1997: 15.1
	D.R.	-	-	-	-	5.2	
		(1983)					
Nagaland	B.R.	23.1	25.3	18.5	N.A.	N.A.	
	D.R.	6.3	6.3	4.1	N.A.	N.A.	
Tripura	B.R.	24.4	27.3	24.9	18.9	16.5	
	D.R.	7.7	9.9	7.1	7.7	5.4	

Source: NEC Basic Statistics, 2002, pp. 37 & 38.

with sufficient amounts of grants under different heads for the development of the infrastructure, formulation and implementation of planned projects by streamlining the socio-political and economic governance systems. Also, a vitally important factor is the development of the human resource of the region through expansion of educational facilities helpful for skill formation and health care and food security measures. Expansion of range of areas of participation of local youths and leaders in influencing the policy formulation and execution of development schemes and projects will also push up the growth impetus. Of late some effective steps have been taken in subduing the violent insurgency operations which were inimical to the economic growth process. A 'climate conducive to investment and development' has been building up to reap the demographic divided by providing employment opportunities in both the public and private sectors besides making available inputs for self-employment.

References

1. C.P. Chandrasekhar, Jayoti Ghosh, Anamitra Roy Chowdhary (2006): "The Demographic Dividend" and Young India's 'Economic Future', *Economic and Political Weekly*, December 9-15, 2006, Vol. XLI No. 49, Mumbai, p. F5056
2. *Ibid*, p. 5058.

4 Population Growth and Changes in Demographic Structure in North East India

Madhushree Das and *Bimal Kumar Kar*

Introduction

With a long history of diverse population composition in respect of ethnicity, religion and language having varied economic and socio-cultural practices, the north-eastern region of India (also known as the land of seven sisters) is characterized by very high rates of population growth which have been even higher than the country's average growth all throughout the twentieth century.

At the beginning of the century the region's population was 4.27 million and it increased to 10.26 million in 1951and 38.44 million in 2001 by experiencing an average annual exponential growth not of 1.77 per cent during 1901-1951 and 2.68 per cent during 1951-2001 as against country's corresponding growth rates of 0.83 per cent and 2.11 per cent. As a consequence, the share of region's population to the country's total increase from 1.79 per cent in 1901 to 3.74 per cent in 2001. Most importantly, despite prevalence of almost similar trend of birth and death rates in the country, the 'considerably high growth rates of population in the region had been due to both natural increase and significant volume of migration from within and outside the country, (Sharma and Kar, 1997). Moreover, there exists a significant variation in population growth rates in the region in both spatial and social contexts. Thus, such a high and socio-spatially varied growth rates of population in the region are likely to have a number of far reaching demographic implications in the entire north-eastern region.

With the above background an attempt is made in this paper to analyse the pattern of population growth and its demographic implications including the changing pattern of population composition in North East India mainly during 1971-2001. This study bears significance because it would also help understand the emerging demographic character in near future.

Data Source and Methodology

The study is primarily based on secondary data taken from different Census of India publications for the period 1901-2001 in general and 1971-2001 in particular. The data so obtained have been analysed through some simple but meaningful statistical techniques including ratios/percentages and average annual exponential/decennial growth rates. The analysis of spatial pattern is made at State level. Conclusions of the study are drawn both on the bases of results derived from data analysis, available relevant literature and personal field experiences.

Trend of Population Growth

The north-eastern region of India, which constitutes country's 7.76 per cent area and 3.74 per cent population (2001 Census), has been witnessing an alarmingly high growth rate of population throughout the last century. It is striking enough to note that during the period of last hundred years (1901-2001) the region's population has increased from 4.27 million to 38.44 million (Table 4.1) by recording an increase of 9 times as against 4.3 times in the case of country's population. In fact, the population of the region has been always growing faster than that of the country as a whole throughout the last century. The population growth rate in the region, however, did not remain uniform throughout the century. The average annual growth rates in the region were 1.77 per cent during 1901-1951 (mostly pre-Independence period) and 2.68 per cent during 1951-2001 (post-Independence period). Accordingly, two distinct phases (1901-1951 and 1951-2001) with 1951 as a divide have been found in the demographic history of North East India.

During the first phase (1901-1951) of the demographic history, the region's population increased by 140 per cent as against the

Table 4.1: Trend of Population Growth in North East India during 1901-2001

Year	*Population*	*Average Annual Exponential Growth Rate (in per cent)*		*Percentage Share of Region's Population to India's Total*	*Population Density (Persons/Km²)*
		N.E. India	*India*		
1901	4,271,978	-	-	1.79	17
1911	5,058,699	1.70	0.56	2.00	20
1921	6,005,043	1.73	-0.03	2.39	24
1931	7,172,512	1.79	1.04	2.57	28
1941	8,618,116	1.85	1.33	2.70	34
1951	10,260,371	1.76	1.25	2.84	40
1961	14,500,572	3.52	1.96	3.30	57
1971	19,582,296	3.05	2.20	3.57	77
1981*	24,751,604	2.37	2.20	3.62	97
1991	31,547,314	2.46	2.14	3.73	124
2001	38,444,026	2.00	1.97	3.74	151

Assam's population is considered as per the estimation of the Census of India
Source: Census of India, Series 1, Primary Census Abstract, India, 1991 and 2001

country's 51 per cent. The decennial variation of the population growth was from 18.4 per cent to 20.2 per cent in the region, while it was 0.3 per cent to 14.2 per cent in the country (Table 4.1). Besides small volume of migration the relatively low and considerably uniform population growth in the region had been mainly due to the prevalence of comparatively high birth and death rates during the period. In the case of Assam, although migration had begun since the British annexation in 1926, it became active from the beginning of the last century. The main streams of migrants settled during this period in the then Assam are the peasants from erstwhile East Bengal (Now Bangladesh), tea garden labourers from Central India and the graziers from Nepal. Assam's immense economic potential coupled with cheap and plenty of virgin and fertile lands facilitated such migrations from both inside and outside the country. India's partition in 1947 had also been responsible for immigration of a large number of Hindu refugees from erstwhile East Pakistan to Assam and other parts of the north east region.

On the other hand, after Independence population in North East

India began to grow very rapidly by witnessing an increase of 275 per cent as against country's 185 per cent during the second phase (1951-2001) of the demographic history. This growth of population in the State contributed to a net increase of 28.18 million people. The decennial growth rates during the period 1951-2001, however, varied considerably between 21.9 per cent and 41.3 per cent in the region, while between 21.5 per cent and 24.8 per cent respectively in the country as a whole (Table 4.1). It is worth mentioning that among all the States of the country, the population growth rates in North East India and Sikkim have been the highest during 1951-2001. The sharp fall of death rates as compared to a very slow decline of birth rates and migration have contributed immensely to such increased rates of population growth in the entire region. Gradual disappearance of severe epidemics and famines coupled with improvement of health and medical facilities, among others, are responsible for the significant decline in death rates. On the other side, the measures to control birth rate could not make any significant headway until recently. A host of interrelated socio-economic factors such as universalisation of marriage, marriage at lower age, religious belief of child as the gift of god, illiteracy, poverty, high infant mortality, etc. might be responsible for keeping the birth rate still considerably high here as elsewhere in the country. Subsequently, however, the gradual expansion of family planning programme accompanied by progress in female education contributed to some extent towards bringing down the birth rate in many parts of the country (Gosal, 1993). This is also reflected in the steady fall of crude birth rates (per thousand) in the north-eastern region from around 38 to 26 and crude death rates (per thousand) from around 16 to 9 during 1971-2001. It means there had been a marginal decline in the natural growth rate of population from 22 to 17 during the period. One of the main reasons of decrease in the death as well as birth rates in the region during the period is the decline in Infant Mortality Rates (IMR) from around 135 in 1971 to around 68 in 2001 as against country's 129 and 66 (per thousand live births) respectively. Moreover, there exists a significant spatial variation of birth and death rates within the region due to a number of socio-economic factors.

From the above discussion it is almost clear that migration played a dominant role towards alarmingly high growth of population particularly during 1951-1991 in the region. The decades after Independence, in fact, witnessed a new stage of demographic development in the region. The period 1951-1971 experienced an unprecedented volume of immigration when annual population growth rate in the region shot up to 3.52 per cent and 3.05 per cent respectively during 1951-1961 and 1961-1971 (Table 4.1). The more important streams of migrants during this period consisted of Bengali Hindus and Muslim peasants in large volume from erstwhile East Pakistan. It may be mentioned here that the immigration of Muslims was more spectacular during 1951-1961. The Bengali Hindus from East Pakistan continued to pour largely into Assam and Tripura because of the recurrent communal disturbances there. Even after this, immigration from Bangladesh (mostly Muslims) and Nepal has been continuing unabated, though in reduced number, till today. On the other hand, immigration of people from other parts of India has also not been so insignificant. After Independence also, people mainly from Bihar, West Bengal, Uttar Pradesh, Rajasthan, Orissa and Punjab migrated in large number into Assam and other States of the region, more particularly to the urban areas for seeking economic opportunities in trade and commerce, industries, construction works, and many other occupations. The immigration of population having varied socio-economic levels have to a great extent influenced the very demographic scenario in the State. For instance, high total fertility rate and child-woman ratio as prevalent particularly among the Muslims of immigrant origin have been responsible for high rate of population growth among them in the region, as elsewhere in the country. In contrast, it is, however, important to note that as compared to the volume of immigation, the size of emigration from this region has been very insignificant because of relative absence of mobility of the indigenous people until the recent past. In a study it is justifiably estimated that the contribution of migration to the region's population increase would not be less than 7 million persons during 1951-1991 (Sharma and Kar, 1997). Nevertheless, the steadily declining birth rate and considerably checked infiltration from Bangladesh have been able to bring down overall annual growth rate of population in the region during 1971-2001 to such an extent that it becomes slightly higher than the national growth rate. Under this circumstance, if the population in the region continues to grow at the present rate it is likely to reach 46.8 million mark by 2011.

Spatial Pattern in Population Growth

An analysis of State-Level data for the period 1961-2001 reveals that there exists a significant spatial variation in population growth rates across the region depending on the nature and extent of migration, and a number of socio-cultural factors influencing the natural growth. The annual growth rates of population during 1961-1971 became quite high (above 3 per cent) in all the States of the region excepting Mizoram (2.25 per cent) and Meghalaya (2.77 per cent) (Table 4.2). However, the situation has improved considerably after 1971 when both Assam and Tripura have been able to check the natural growth rates and volume of migration. But population growth rates remained quite high in Nagaland (4.35 per cent), Mizoram (3.72 per cent) and Arunachal Pradesh (3.12 per cent) as against the regional average of 2.41 per during 1971-1991.

Table 4.2: Annual Growth Rate and Percentage Share of Population in the States of North-East India during 1961-2001

States	*Average Annual Growth Rate (%)*			*Percentage Share of Population to the Region's Total*	
	1961-1971	*1971-1991*	*1991-2001*	*1961*	*2001*
1. Arunachal Pradesh	3.34	3.12	2.42	2.32	2.00
2. Assam	3.04	2.16	1.75	74.74	69.33
3. Manipur	3.24	2.73	2.24	5.38	5.97
4. Meghalaya	2.77	2.85	2.71	5.30	6.03
5. Mizoram	2.25	3.72	2.56	1.83	2.31
6. Nagaland	3.41	4.35	5.10	2.55	5.18
7. Tripura	3.14	2.30	1.50	7.88	8.32
N.E. India	3.05	2.41	2.00	100.00	10.00

Source: Census of India, 1991, India, Brief Analysis of Primary Census Abstract; Census of India, 2001, India, Basic Results from Census 2001.

It is quite encouraging to note that the population growth rates in most parts of the region only excepting Nagaland have become significantly low during 1991-2001 (Table 4.2). As a matter of fact, the annual growth rate during this period has been as low as 1.5 per cent in Tripura and 1.75 per cent in Assam as against the regional and country's averages of 2.00 per cent and 1.97 per cent respectively. On the other hand, owing to considerably high birth rates as compared to death rates and rapidly declining infant mortality rates, the population growth rates have remained considerably higher in most of the tribal dominated States in the region. This is, however, more striking in the State of Nagaland (5.10 per cent) probably due to better enumeration unlike in the past. In any case, however, the prevailing growth rate of population in Assam which constitutes about 70 per cent of the region's population influences greatly the overall pattern of population growth in the region. Besides, it may be concluded that notably high population growth rate in recent time is largely confined to the areas where population density is quite low and fast development activities are going on.

Population Growth among Different Population Groups

The prevailing diversity in the population particularly in respect of ethnicity and religion makes the growth pattern of population in North East India quite varied and complex. In fact, depending on the ethno-religious background and associated socio-cultural practices and economic condition, the growth rate of population varies significantly from one community to another in the region. In the case of scheduled caste and scheduled tribe communities in the region, the average annual growth rates for the period 1971-2001 were as high as 2.64 per cent and 3.44 per cent respectively (Table 4.3) as against the total population growth rate of 2.27 per cent (Table 4.1). But it is quite interesting and surprising to note that excepting Assam and also unlike the regional and national averages, the annual growth rates of scheduled caste population during 1971-2001 have been higher than the corresponding growth rates among the scheduled tribes in all the States of the region (Table 4.3). Among the States, however, Arunachal Pradesh witnesses the highest growth rate of scheduled caste population (10.29 per cent) and Nagaland records

Table 4.3 : Growth Rates and Proportion of Scheduled Caste and Scheduled Tribe Population in North East India, 1971-2001

States	*Scheduled Castes*			*Scheduled Tribes*		
	Average Annual Growth Rate during 1971-2001 (in %)	*Proportion of S.C. Population out of Total Population (in %)*		*Average Annual Growth Rate during 1971-2001 (in %)*	*Proportion of S.T. Population out of Total Population (in %)*	
		1971	*2001*		*1971*	*2001*
1. Arunachal Pradesh	10.29	0.07	0.56	2.18	79.02	64.22
2. Assam	2.34	6.24	6.85	2.44	10.98	12.41
3. Manipur	4.42	1.53	2.77	2.69	31.18	34.20
4. Meghalaya	3.60	0.38	0.48	3.03	80.48	85.94
5. Mizoram	4.80	0.02	0.03	3.34	94.26	94.46
6. Nagaland	0.00	0.00	0.00	4.62	88.61	89.15
7. Tripura	3.59	12.39	17.37	2.67	28.95	31.05
North East India	2.64	5.75	6.40	3.44	19.17	26.93
India	2.42	14.82	16.20	2.75	6.82	8.20

Source: Census of India, Primary Census Abstract, 1971 and 2001.

the highest growth rate of scheduled tribe population (4.62 per cent) during 1971-2001.

However, in case of major religious groups like the Hindu, Muslim, Christian and Buddhist in the region, although there has been significant decline in the average annual growth rate of population among all of them since 1971, it is found to be still remarkably higher among the Muslims (2.67 per cent) and Christians (3.76 per cent) than that of the Hindus (1.31 per cent) and Buddhists (0.26 per cent) during 1991-2001 (Table 4.4). Again, in the period 1971-2001, the annual growth rates are found to vary between 1.33 per cent

Table 4.4 : Growth Rate among the Major Religous Groups during 1971-2001 and Percentage Contribution of each Group to the Total Population Increase in North East India

Religion	*Population Size*		*Average Annual Growth Rate (%)*			*Percentage of Contribution to Total Population Increase in the State*
	1971	*2001*	*1971-91*	*1971-2001*	*1991-2001*	
1. Hindus	13,001,136 (66.39%)	21,905,140 (56.98%)	1.98	1.75	1.31	47.21
2. Muslims	3,799,092 (19.40%)	8,850,940 (23.02%)	2.95	2.86	2.67	26.78
3. Christians	1,785,856 (9.12%)	6,224,348 (16.19%)	4.49	4.25	3.76	23.53
4. Buddhists	151,449 (0.77%)	371,458 (0.97%)	4.45	3.03	0.26	1.17
5. Others	844,763 (4.32%)	1,92.140 (2.84%)	0.04	0.86	2.51	1.31
Total Population	19,582,296	38,444,026	2.41	2.27	2.00	100

Figures within brackets indicate proportion of population among the respective religious group.
Source: Census of India, 2001, India, The First Report on Religious Data.

(Mizoram) and 4.45 per cent (Arunachal Pradesh) among the Muslims, and 3.22 per cent (Assam) and 14.34 per cent (Arunachal Pradesh) among the Christians in the region (Table 4.5). Similarly, during the period 1991-2001, among the north eastern States, the lowest annual growth rate has been -0.97 per cent among the Hindus

Table 4.5 : Growth Rates and Proportion of Population among the Major Religious Groups in North East India, 1971-2001

	States	Hindu			Muslim			Christian			Buddhist		
		Average Annual Growth Rate (%) During 1991-2001	*Proportion of Population out of Total Population (%)*		*Average Annual Growth Rate (%) During 1971-2001*	*Proportion of Population out of Total Population (%)*		*Average Annual Growth Rate(%) During 1971-2001*	*Proportion of Population out of Total Population (%)*		*Average Annual Growth Rate (%) During 1971-2001*	*Proportion of Population out of Total Population (%)*	
			1971	*2001*		*1971*	*2001*		*1971*	*2001*		*1971*	*2001*
1.	Arunachal Pradesh	4.45	22.00	34.60	11.26	0.18	1.90	14.34	0.79	18.70	2.86	13.13	13.00
2.	Assam	1.64	72.51	64.90	2.81	24.56	30.90	3.22	2.60	3.70	3.37	0.15	0.20
3.	Manipur	1.53	58.97	46.00	3.35	6.61	8.80	3.29	26.03	34.00	4.63	0.05	0.10
4.	Meghalaya	1.67	18.50	13.30	3.03	2.60	4.30	4.19	46.98	70.30	3.10	0.18	0.20
5.	Mizoram	1.33	6.39	3.60	5.76	0.57	1.10	3.37	86.08	87.00	3.86	6.81	7.90
6.	Nagaland	3.23	11.43	7.70	8.57	0.57	1.80	5.64	66.76	90.00	6.98	0.03	0.10
7.	Tripura	2.28	89.55	85.60	3.03	6.68	8.00	6.45	1.00	3.20	2.87	2.72	3.10
	N.E. India	1.75	66.39	56.98	2.86	19.40	23.02	4.25	9.12	16.19	3.06	0.77	0.97
	India	2.03	82.72	80.50	2.74	11.21	13.40	1.77	2.60	2.30	2.48	0.70	0.80

Source: Census of India, 2001, India, The First Report Religion Data.

in Mizoram, 2.60 per cent among the Muslims in Assam, and 1.64 per cent among the Christians in Manipur. Although the occurrence of high growth rate in recent time mainly among the Muslims is largely associated with poverty and illiteracy, the contribution of migration, religious influence and religious conversion can never be ruled out. For instance, the literacy rate (as per 2001 Census) among the Muslims is still as low as 49.02 per cent as compared to 70.83 per cent among the Hindus in the region. On the other hand, prevalence of considerably high fertility rate especially among the tribes and religious conversion has been responsible for the high growth rate of population among the Christians in most parts of the region (1.64 per cent in Manipur to 8.73 per cent in Arunachal Pradesh during 1991-2001). It means the considerably high literacy rate (67.20 per cent) as prevalent among them does seem to have much impact towards lowering the population growth rate in most parts of the region. In any case, the prevailing significant variation in population growth rates among different communities in the region contributes differently to its total growth of population. This phenomenon certainly has a remarkable bearing on the prevailing population structure with far reaching demographic implications in near future.

Changing Population Structure

The variation in population growth pattern largely caused by differential fertility behaviour and migration, particularly among the Scheduled Castes (SC) and Scheduled Tribes (ST), and also among the Hindus, Muslims and Christians in North East India, as revealed in the foregoing analysis, has been significantly changing the demographic structure including the composition of scheduled and religious population groups in the region.

Age Structure

Due to the prevalence of considerably high fertility rate the age composition of population in North East India still remains almost similar to that of many less developed countries of the world with higher burden of children population. Although the proportion of children population (0-14 age group) in the region has witnessed a decline from 45.72 per cent to 36.98 per cent during 1971-2001, it is still far from satisfactory (Table 4.6). The proportion of children of age group 0-6 in the region has witnessed a very negligible fall from

Table 4.6 : Percentage Distribution of Population in Different Age Groups in North East India at State Level in 1971 and 2001

States	*Age Groups*					
	0-14		*15-59*		*60+*	
	1971	*2001*	*1971*	*2001*	*1971*	*2001*
1. Arunachal Pradesh	38.28	40.40	57.07	54.90	4.65	4.70
2. Assam	46.95	37.40	48.34	56.60	4.71	6.00
3. Manipur	42.50	32.60	51.41	60.50	6.09	6.90
4. Meghalaya	43.55	42.30	51.78	53.10	4.67	4.60
5. Mizoram	43.26	35.20	51.57	59.10	5.17	5.70
6. Nagaland	37.98	36.50	55.32	58.57	6.70	4.80
7. Tripura	44.19	33.60	49.77	58.90	6.04	7.50
North East India	45.72	36.98	49.30	57.12	4.98	5.90
India	42.03	35.30	52.00	56.90	5.97	7.80

Source: Demographic Profile of North East India, S.C. Srivastava, Mittal Publications, New Delhi, 1987; and Census of India, 2001, Report and Tables on Age, India.

19.5 per cent during 1991-2001. But, what is more important here is the prevailing variation in the proportion of children in age group 0-6 among different population groups in the region (Table 4.7). Being influenced by considerably high population growth rates with slight variation among the SC, ST and General in the region, the proportion of children in age group 0-6 (as per 2001 Census) is found to vary from 15.7 per cent (SC population) to 17.1 per cent (ST population) though 16.5 per cent (Total population). There is, however, spatial variation in this respect, with 8.1 per cent (Mizoram) to 17.1 per cent (Arunachal Pradesh) among the SC; 14.0 per cent (Manipur) to 20.9 per cent (Meghalaya) among the ST; and 13.6 per cent (Tripura) to 20.2 per cent (Meghalaya) among the total. The variation in the proportion of children in 0-6 age group is even more glaring among the Hindus (14.3 per cent), Muslims (21.6 per cent), Christians (17.1 per cent) and Buddhists (18.5 per cent) in the region (Table 4.7). In the case of spatial variation, the proportion ranges between 9.2 per cent (Mizoram) and 21.8 per cent (Assam) among the Muslims; between 14.0 per cent (Manipur) and 21.1 per cent (Meghalaya) among the Christians; and between 11.9 per cent (Nagaland) and 20.5 per cent (Mizoram) in the region. Hence, it is quite clear that the population groups witnessing higher growth rates of population have recorded, as expected, higher proportions of children population.

Table 4.7 : Percentage Distribution of Children in Age Group 0-6 among Different Communities in North East India, 2001

States	*Total Population*	*Scheduled Castes*	*Scheduled Tribes*	*Hindus*	*Miuslims*	*Christians*	*Buddhists*
1. Arunachal Pradesh	18.8	17.1	19.6	17.1	18.8	20.5	19.8
2. Assam	16.9	16.0	16.7	14.5	21.8	17.6	14.3
3. Manipur	14.2	14.6	14.0	13.2	19.8	14.0	18.4
4. Meghalaya	20.2	16.2	20.9	14.2	21.2	21.1	14.4
5. Mizoram	16.2	8.1	16.5	9.2	10.1	16.1	20.5
6. Nagaland	14.6	-	14.6	12.7	19.2	14.6	11.9
7. Tripura	13.6	13.3	16.4	13.0	18.6	15.7	17.9
N.E. India	16.5	15.7	17.1	14.3	21.6	17.1	18.5
India	15.9	17.4	18.5	15.6	18.7	13.5	14.4

Source: Census of India, Series 1, India, Primary Census Abstract, Total Population, Scheduled Castes and Scheduled Triebs; and Census of India, 2001, The First Report on Religion Data, India.

Composition of Scheduled Castes and Tribes

The contribution of varied and changing population growth rates among the SC and ST is clearly observed in the changing proportions of population among them in North East India during 1971-2001. It is found that due to higher annual growth rate among SC during 1971-1991 (3.03 per cent) the proportion of SC people in North East India increased from 5.75 per cent in 1971 to 6.85 per cent in 1991, and subsequently lowering down of annual growth rate during 1991-2001 (1.31 per cent) the proportion among them again decreased to 6.40 per cent in 2001 (Table 4.3). The ST people, however, witnessed a rise in the proportion from 19.71 per cent in 1971 to 26.93 per cent in 2001 through 25.81 per cent in 1991-2001. The rise in the proportion of population among the SC has been spectacular during 1971-2001 in Tripura and Manipur (Table 4.3). But in the case of ST, all the States excepting Arunachal Pradesh witnessed very low to moderate increase in the proportion during the same period (Table 4. 3). Arunchal Pradesh has witnessed a substantial decrease in the proportion of ST population from 79.02 per cent to 64.22 per cent during 1971-2001. This phenomenon may be largely due to considerable decline in the birth rate among the ST as compared to some non-tribal people including the Muslims and the onset of out-migration among the ST in the State.

Religious Composition

The impact of varied population growth rates among the major religious groups in the region has been clearly observed in the changing proportions of population among them and also the overall growth rates of population. It is worth mentioning that with considerably low and declining growth rate of population among the Hindus during 1971-2001, as mentioned already, the proportion among them has decreased from 66.39 per cent in 1971 to 56.58 per cent in 2001 in the region as a whole. Although all the north eastern States in the country excepting Arunachal Pradesh have witnessed the same phenomenon, it is found to be striking (more than 5 per cent decline) in Assam, Manipur and Meghalaya (Table 4.5). On the other side, with considerably high and rising growth rate of population the Muslims witnessed a significant increase of their proportion of population from 19.40 per cent in 1971 to as high as 23.02 per cent in 2001. In fact, the areas where there has been decline in the proportion of Hindus during 1971-2001 have experienced the increase in the proportion of Muslims, and in the process, for instance, the number of Muslim dominated districts in the State of Assam has increased from two (Dhubri and Hailakandi) in 1971 to as many as six (Dhubri, Hailakandi, Goalpara, Barpeta, Nagaon and Karimganj) in 2001, and another one (Morigaon) is going to be added during 2011 Census. It is found that the Muslims which constituted 19.40 per cent of the region's total population (as per 1971 Census) have contributed as high as 26.78 per cent of the region's population increase during 1971-2001 (Table 4.4). Although it is a national trend, it is found to be quite striking in the case of Assam and Manipur. Again, due to the prevalence of considerably higher growth rate the proportion of Christian population in the region has also increased from 9.12 per cent to 16.19 per cent during 1971-2001. Hence, if the same trend continues for some more time there would be even more remarkable change in the demographic structure in North East India.

Conclusion

The foregoing discussion reveals that the north eastern region of India has experienced a very high growth rate of population due to both high fertility and migration during the last century. Within the region again, the growth rates have been considerably higher in the States of Nagaland, Meghalaya, Mizoram and Arunachal Pradesh. Although the growth rate in the States of Assam and Tripura has been checked to a certain extent in recent time, their contribution towards region's overall population growth is still found to be very significant owing to large base population.

The causes behind prevailing spatial variation in population growth rate in the region, however, have become more clear when the pattern of growth rate is analysed separately for social groups like scheduled tribes, and major religious groups like Hindu, Muslim and Christian for the period 1971-2001. As socio-economically backward social groups, although growth rate was quite high among both SC and ST prior to 1971, it has come down significantly in recent time in most of the areas in the north eastern region. But, in the case of religious groups, unlike the Hindus, both Muslims and Christians have still been experiencing significantly high growth rates of population throughout the region. As a consequence, all the districts of Assam have been witnessing change in the proportion of Hindus, Muslims and Christians, though at varying pace, during the last few decades, and in the process the number of Muslim dominant districts in Assam has increased from two in 1971 to six in 2001. On the other hand, owing to declining growth rate among the Hindus, despite still being the largest religious group in terms of population in the region, the contribution made by them to the total growth of population in the region has not been so large. Besides, the proportions of children in age groups 0-14 and 0-6 have still remained very high in most parts of the region. Hence, it is clear that the prevailing varying pattern of population growth among different population groups in North East India is likely to bring about even more changes in the demographic structure in near future with far reaching socio-economic and political implications. In view of such a situation, every effort needs to be initiated to check the population growth rates among all the population groups in the region through equitable socio-economic development among them.

References

Census of India, 1901. Vol. IV, Assam, Part 1, Report by B.C. Allen.

Census of India, 1931. Vol. III, Assam, Part 1, Report by C.S. Mullan.

Census of India, 1951. Vol. XIII, Assam, Manipur and Tripura, Part 1-A, Report by R.P. Vaghaiwalla.

Census of India, 1971, *General Population Tables*, Series 1, India, Paper 1.

Census of India, 1991. Series 1, India, Paper 2, *Final Population Totals–Brief Analysis of Primary Census Abstract.*

Census of India, 1991. *Union Primary Census Abstract for Scheduled Castes and Scheduled Tribes*, Series 1, India, Paper 1 of 1993.

Census of India. *Primary Census Abstract, General Population, Scheduled Castes and Scheduled Tribes*, Assam Series 4, Part II-B.

Census of India, 1991. Series 4, Assam, Part IV-B (ii), *Religion* (Table 9).

Census of India, 2002. *Sample Registration Bulletin, India.*

Census of India, 2001. *Primary Census Abstract, Assam, Series 19.*

Census of India, 2001. *Basic Results from Census 2001. Census and You, Series–India.*

Census of India, 2001. *Assam at a Glance.*

Census of India, 2001. *The First Report on Religion Data, India.*

Directorate of Economics and Statistics, 2005. *Statistical Handbook, Assam.*

Gosal, G.S., 1993. India and the Demographic Transition Model. in A. Ahmad (ed.) *Social Structure and Religonal Development: A Social Geography Perspective.* Jaipur and New Delhi: Rawat Publications, pp. 105-119.

Kar, B.K., 1995. Population Growth Trend in Assam and its Socio-Economic Implications. *Geographical Review of India:* Vol. 57(4): 321-335.

Kar, B.K., 2002. Population in A.K. Bhagabati, A.K. Bora and B.K Kar (eds) *Geography of Assam.* New Delhi: Rajesh Publications, pp. 115-155.

North Eastern Council, 2002. *Basic Statistics of North Eastern Region,* Shillong.

Sharma, H.N. and Kar, B.K. 1997. Pattern of Population Growth in North-East India in A. Ahmad, D. Noin and H.N. Sharma (eds) *Demographic Transition: The Third World Scenario,* Jaipur and New Delhi: Rawat Publication, pp. 73-93.

5 Population Growth and Development in North Eastern Region of India

P.C. Dutta

The concept of change and development is a dynamic one apprehending each and every aspect of human existence. In the era of globalisation rapid socio-economic transformation has been taking place in the economy at international level. The development of an area is best reflected in the quality of life of its people. The planners and policy makers in India are trying to cope with it. Population is a very important factor in the whole process of socio-economic development. The world has a population of more than six billion and knocking at the door of seven billion while India alone has a population of more than one billion, in spite of the fact that India was the first country in the world to have a population policy. This large population is causing alarm. Population growth is the reason for every environmental problem facing India today, and many of their economic and social dilemmas as well. India, with a current estimated population of 1.4 billion and a population growth rate of 2.52 per cent., has specifically staggering population-related problems, as one-third of the total population are forced to live below the poverty line. Excessive population growth in the region of North Eastern States of India not only adversely affects the increase in per capita income, but also causes serious difficulties in food supply, housing, education, employment and environment, and it may even disrupt the social balance and stability of the system. The people of NER now realize that the population problem is vital in determining whether we shall be able to accomplish the task of modernization of agriculture, industry, defence, science and technology by 2020. In addition, Region's natural and environmental resources are shrinking day by day. The land area is prone to soil erosion; dense and closed forests have been declining considerably and widespread water scarcity and water pollution subsist. North East India which is also called as mini-India is of striking demographic diversity. Substantial differences are visible between States in the achievement of basic demographic indices. This has led to significant disparity in current population size, pattern and the potential to influence population increase during the last few decades. There are wide inter-state, male-female and rural-urban disparities in outcomes and impacts. These differences stem largely from poverty, illiteracy, and inadequate access to health and family welfare services, which coexist and reinforce each other. In many parts, the widespread health infrastructure is not responsive.

Keeping in view the above facts, the present study is an attempt at studying certain aspects of socio-economic develoment affected due to rapid population growth in the region. Efforts are also being made to examine the impacts like suicides, crimes, economic disparity, expenditure made to control insurgency etc. which in turn affects the overall socio-economic development of the region. The study has been concluded with some suggestions for future planners and policy-makers of the country to resolve the issues. For the purpose, the study is based on secondary sources of data relating to socio-economic and demographic variables for the North Eastern Region of India.

The study brings out considerable regional variations in overall socio-economic development amongst the States of NER and India as a whole, despite some efforts being made by the Central and the State governments for balanced regional development. However, the Governments of the States of NER and at the Centre, with greater co-ordination, should envisage a major programme in human resource development through education, technical training, family welfare etc. which would not only help in removing poverty and unemployment but also reduce the regional disparities and which will ultimately upgrade the overall socio-economic development in the region. At the same time they should implement the reform policies with extreme caution so that it would not arouse the people's emotion and sentiments by interfering in the social laws, customs, traditions etc. hence the slogan should be '*Globalisation within limits or reform in a controlled manner.*'

The World Summit on Sustainable Development (WSSD) in Johennesburg, South Africa (26 August-4 September, 2002) was called by the United Nations to consider strategies towards sustainable development in all its dimensions. Its mandate was broader than that of the 1992 United Nations Conference on Environment and Development (the Rio Conference). Population issues have previously been discussed in a separate series of World Population Conference (Bucharest, 1974, Mexico City, 1984, Cairo, 1994). Sustainable development aims at improving human well-being, particularly through alleviating poverty, increasing gender equity, and improving health, human resources, and stewardship of the natural environment. Because demographic factors are closely linked to these goals, strategies that include consideration of population have a better chance of success. The International Conference on Population and Development in Cairo in 1994 recognized that population policy should be oriented towards improving social conditions and expanding choices for individuals. In Johennesburg, consideration of sustainable development policies included population growth and distribution, mobility, differential vulnerability, and the empowerment of people, especially women.

Rapid population growth has exacerbated freshwater depletion, climate change, bio-diversity loss, depletion of fisheries, and degradation of agricultural lands. It can also have important economic benefits by reducing the number of children relative to the working-age population, creating a unique opportunity to increase investment in health, education, infrastructure, and environmental protection. Before the end of this decade, a majority of the world's population will live in urban areas. Urbanisation can improve people's access to education, health and other services. It also creates environmental health hazards, such as water and air pollution, and by increasing consumption levels, can have environmental impacts in distant rural areas also.[1]

The modern theory of human capital came to prominence in economics only in recent decades, but its antecedents can be traced back to the earliest economic writings. The notion that human skills represent economic value comparable to that of capital was clearly articulated by the classical economists, notably by William Petty and Adam Smith. That improvement of skills and increase in the number of persons in whom skills are embodied are sources of economic progress follows from their conceptual clarification. The economic value of the population depends very much on their command over the powers of nature; which they acquire by education.

Addressing an international conference of Islamic Scholars (ulema) on '*Population and Development*' on 6th May, 2005 in Islamabad, General Pervez Musharaf, President of Pakistan stressed the need for population politics based on a realistic assessment of socio-economic conditions in Pakistan and more broadly, in the Muslim World (Umah). He was of the opinion that there should be no doubt in his mind that the main factor retarding economic growth, poverty alleviation and action on joblessness is population growth. Those who do not understand this are living in a world of their own. In the case of Pakistan, from 1951 to the mid-1980s population grew roughly at an average of 3 per cent per year; from mid–1980s to 2000 it grew at an average of 2.5. ; from 2000 to 2005, the growth rate at an average of 2.0 per cent. In his view, "Had we grown at 2 per cent per year from 1951 onwards our per capita income today would have been $920- much more than China's– instead of $650 which we are at now. This is the negative impact and effect of population growth on our economy and on our poverty level. However, history cannot be undone but we must wake up..... So our plan is to reduce our population growth rate from 1.9 per cent to 1.3 per cent by 2020. We must do it for the sake of our future generation, who will otherwise be poorer." He feels that the Ulema can play an extremely important role in controlling population. But unfortunately, some Ulemas are playing a negative role by giving a *fatwa* against population control. He acknowledged the role of the Ulema in Iran, Turkey, Indonesia, Egypt and Bangladesh, where they are for population control.[2]

The Russian President Vladimir Putin's 2005 annual address to the Federal Assembly of the Russian Federation, delivered on 25th April was widely noted in the World Press. The President expressed confidence that by creating conditions to "encourage people to have children, lower the mortality rate and bring order to immigration", the size of the Russian population will gradually stabilize. He was also of the opinion that increase in the population should be accompanied by a carefully planned immigration policy. It is in our interest to receive a flow of legal and qualified workers......... without any rights, after all, illegal immigration are convenient in that they can be exploited endlessly. They are also a potential danger from the point of view of breaking the law.[3]

China's one-child policy is a major example of social engineering and the subject of human rights concerns. Given the significance of the policy, it is important to ascertain the attitudes of Chinese citizens. Announcing in 1980, China's one-child-per-couple policy was formulated in the wake of the Cultural Revolution (1966-76) as an emergency measure to slow rapid population growth and to facilitate modernization goals (Wang, 2005; Croll, 1984). This draconian policy met with strong resistance, especially in China's vast rural areas where the peasant family remains the primary locus of economic activity and old-age support. A few years after the announcement of the policy, a quiet but significant retreat took place to modify the radical and unrealistic stance. In China's privileged urban sectors, the population continued to be subject to the one-child policy. Couples in rural China were allowed to have two children if they met certain criteria, most notably if they lived in a poor area or had only a daughter. Exemption to the one-child rule often came with a spacing requirement, stipulating a minimum of four or six years between the first and second birth. Modifications to the State policy of population control have been left to each province, under the general principle of slowing down population growth and encouraging only one child per couple.[4]

The latest United Nations Population Projections to 2050 (UN 2005) indicate that the deceleration of world population growth may be even faster than thought only a few years earlier. According to Nikos Alexandratos (2005), the realization that world is probably on a fairly smooth path of transition towards a near-stationary population in the not-too-distant future influencing the debate on the interrelationship between population, development, and sustainability. The notion that the trend towards an ever-growing population, the so-called population explosion, threatens our welfare and the sustainability of our existence (or, at least, the prospect that all people can achieve "acceptable" living standards) seems to be losing currency among the public.

India has for centuries had rich intellectual tradition concerning both the quantitative and qualitiative aspects of population, as well as practical experience in controlling fertility since time immemorial.[5] In fact, Indians have for many years been participating in International Debates about population. Following Independence, and after the 1951 Census showed continued population growth despite a decade of war, famine, and sectarian strife, Nehru called for the new Planning Commission to convene another population committee. Their report recommended fertility limitation both for the sake of mothers' and children's health and to stabilize population "consistent with the requirements of national economy." It called for free sterilization and contraception when recommended on medical grounds, and suggested that where feasible these methods should be adopted for social and economic reasons as well.[6]

Officials were still concerned about population "quality". To control population growth, family planning as a measure for achieving faster economic development has its supporters as well as opponents, of course, supporters are more numerous. India was the first country to obtain family planning advice from the World Health Organization. However, India's Government was slow to implement a family planning programme. In 1960 Indian Officials elevated the family planning programme to "the very centre of planned development."[7] India committed to the goal of reducing the birth rate by 40 per cent by 1972. It becomes clear that there were always some individuals who fought to defend family planning as a means to promote individual dignity and welfare, rather than to control population growth. The correct consensus is not, therefore, just faddish or politically current, but the fruit of a long struggle, one that is far from over (Connelly, 2006).

The concept of development has been defined as a stage of growth or advancement of a society and the different countries of the world have broadly been classified into two categories, viz. 'developed' and 'developing'. The primary object of development is to satisfy the essential material needs of the society, but not at the cost of local environment and people's culture. When people change, the society to which they belong also change, and the country moves with them too. But the North Eastern Region (NER) is not an exception while this region is endowed with rich resources of land, water, forests, minerals etc. It appears that it is difficult to establish any relationship between expressed opinion on family size, actual family size, and family's economic achievement. The economic development not only brings about changes in the socio-economic and cultural life of population but it also influences the consumption pattern in the long run. The development is a complex process and has multi-dimensional structure depending upon its resources in general and infrastructural facilities in particular (Dutta, 1966).

In the era of globalisation rapid socio-economic transformation has been taking place in the economy at international level. The planners and policy-makers in India are trying to cope with it. Economic welfare does not merely depend upon the level of development but also on its distributive aspects. In the pluralistic nature of the country, differences in natural resources, climate, topography, vegetation and density of population can be identified easily and the North Eastern Region of India (NER) is no exception to it. Unequal distribution of wealth and resources caused regional disparity in the country as a result of which the States of NER are lagging behind.

One must realize that north-east is a mini-India. There are more than 75 major population groups and sub-groups, speaking approximately 400 languages and dialects, of which there are about 168 in Arunachal Pradesh, 95 in Nagaland, 87 in Manipur, 100 in Tripura and 200 in Assam, Meghalaya and Mizoram (Madhab, J, 1999). Thus, the whole north eastern India is a place with people of diverse races, cultures, languages and various dialects with different traditions. Besides the heterogeneity of geographical and socio-cultural factors, the more striking view of the north eastern scenario is the co-existence of the extreme forms of both tradition and modernity.

It is a fact that urbanisation is most essential for all-round development of the developing nations, as it increases employment, income and standard of living in these countries. But it simultaneously creates a number of socio-economic and environmental problems. Urbanisation disturbs the ecological balance by creating air, water and noise pollution through industrialisation. Haphazard growth of urban centres and their ill-planned urbanisation aggravated the pollution problems and deteriorated the environment.

Therefore, environmentalists aptly say that urbanisation-environment relationship is not complementary but contradictory with each other. The increasing urbanisation has led to a number of socio-economic problems like crime, suicides, drug abuse, unemployment and poverty, alcoholism, overcrowding, housing shortage, slums, traffic control and pollution etc. At the same time they are also centres of civilisation and culture by helping a lot in the process of modernisation (Dutta, 2002).

It is in this context, an enquiry is deemed to be necessary to examine the multi-dimensional and complex relationships among some socio-economic and demographic variables of the north eastern region of India as it is physically located in a backward and disadvantageous position due to its physical geography as well as the social and political conditions prevailing in the region. One of the purposes of the present study is to examine whether or how urbanisation creates the hazardous situation in socio-economic aspects. Further, the study shows how population growth affects overall environment of the region. The study has been concluded with some valuable suggestions. The study is based on secondary sources of data relation to socio-economic and demographic variables for the North Eastern Region of India. Different rounds of NSS Data and Census Data, Rural Health Statistics, Ministry of Health and Family Welfare, Government of India and other published and unpublished secondary data are used in the present study.

Population Growth and Socio-Economic Characteristics

The total population of the region is about 38.5 million representing 3.75 per cent of India's total population in 2001 and 40.02 million in the mid-year of 2003. It is of great interest to note that India's population exceeded the population of Europe (729 million) comprising 47 countries and was equal to Europe and Northern America including United States of America (310 million). We live in a world of unprecedented demographic change. Global population increased by 2 billion during the last quarter of the 20th century, reached 6 billion in 2000. Changes in population growth, age structure, and spatial distribution interact closely with the environment and with development. Despite Government efforts to cut growth rates, India's population which was 238 million in 1947 touched, 1.012 billion in March 2001 and is expected to be 1.263 billion by 2016, according to India's Health Ministry.

The region's growth rate of population is much higher than the national average. It is striking to note that India's total population increased by 51.80 per cent in the period 1951-71, 54.39 per cent in 1971-91 and 21.35 per cent in 1991-2001. Whereas for the NER, respective growth rates are 90.86 per cent, 62.11 per cent and 22.02 per cent. At the same time share of population of NER, in comparison to all-India, increased from 2.84 per cent in 1951 to 3.75 per cent in 2001 (Table 5.1). As regards the decadal growth rate of population, the highest decadal growth rate (41.33%) was seen in the decade 1951-61. The decadal growth rate of population in NER were high as compared to all-India level. It is to be noted here that the percentage

Table 5.1 : Population Trend in North Eastern Region (In 000) Literacy Rate

Year States	*1951*	*1961*	*1971*	*1981*	*1991*	*2001*	*1991*	*2001*
ANP	–	337	468	632	865	1091	41.59	54.74
ASM	8029	10837	14625	18041	22414	26638	52.80	64.28
MNP	578	780	1073	1421	1837	2389	59.89	68.87
MGH	606	769	1012	1336	1775	2306	49.10	63.31
MZM	196	266	332	494	690	891	82.27	88.49
NGN	213	369	516	775	1210	1989	61.65	67.11
TRP	639	1142	1556	2053	2757	191	62.66	73.47
NER	10260	14501	19582	24752	31547			
India	361088	439235	548160	683329	846303	1027015	52.21	65.38
1*	---	41.34	35.04	26.40	27.45	22.02		
2*	2.84	3.30	3.37	3.62	3.70	3.75		

1* Decadal Growth Rate of NER.

2* Percentage of NER with respect to India.

of population in the region with respect to India was 1.70 in 1941. It can be concluded here that population is increasing faster in NER as compared to the country as a whole. It is observed that there is a large variation in the density of population among the States of NER (Table 5.2). Density of region's population (151) is almost half of the national density (324) in 2001 while it was only 34.19 in 1951. Again within the region it varies from 13 in Arunachal Pradesh to 340 in Assam. The bulk of population of the region (almost 70 per cent of total population of the region) is concentrated mainly of three sectors viz. Brahmaputra Valley and Barak Valley of Assam and Tripura. The large variation is caused by the geographical and economic factors, which vary greatly within the region. Population growth in the region has been unusually rapid, mainly due to inter-state migration in earlier decades and to immigration from other countries and relatively high fertility among some immigrant groups in recent decades.[8]

Table 5.2 : Female Literacy Rate, Female Work Participation, Gender Gap in Literacy and Density of Population (Per sq. km.)

States	*Female Literacy Rate (in p.c.)*		*Sex Ratio*			*Denisity of Population (Population per sq. km.)*			*Gender Gap in Literacy*	
	1991	*2001*	*1981*	*1991*	*2001*	*1951*	*1991*	*2001*	*1991*	*2001*
ANP	29.69	44.24	862	859	901	–	10	13	21.76	19.83
ASM	43.03	56.03	910	923	932	102	184	340	18.84	15.90
MNP	47.60	59.70	971	958	978	26	82	107	24.03	18.17
MGH	44.85	60.41	954	955	975	27	79	103	8.27	5.73
MZM	78.60	86.13	919	921	938	9	33	42	7.01	–
NGN	54.75	61.92	863	886	909	13	73	120	12.87	9.85
TRP	49.65	65.41	946	945	950	61	263	304	20.93	16.06
NER	–	–	921	925	937	40	124	151	–	–
India	39.29	54.16	934	937	933	117	273	324	24.84	21.69

The age-distribution in each State of NER is typical of high fertility populations, with a high proportion of the population in the younger age-groups. Manipur, Mizoram and Tripura have the lowest percentage of population below 15 years of age (37%) and this percentage is the highest in Arunachal Pradesh (43%). The proportion of the population of age 60 and above varies from just over 2 per cent in Tripura (Dutta, 2002).

The total number of tribal population is 81.42 lakh which is approximately 25.71per cent of the total population. The percentage of scheduled tribes varies from 13 per cent (Assam) to 91 per cent (Mizoram) which are above the country's figure (8 %). However, more than three-fourths of the household belong to scheduled tribes in the States of Mizoram, Nagaland (96 %) Meghalaya (89 %), Arunachal Pradesh (76 %) and while in Tripura (17 %), Manipur (35 %) and Assam, these are below 50 per cent (Dutta, 2002).

Sex ratio is an important determinant of population growth. This ratio in a population influences fertility rate. In all developed countries, the ratio is over 1000, while in most developing countries, it is below 1000. It is remarkable to note that the sex ratio in NER has consistently shown excess of males over females as noted for India. In India, there are only 933 females per 1000 males in the total population (Table 5.2). Amongst the States of NER, it is the highest in Manipur (978) followed by Meghalaya (975), Tripura (950) and Mizoram (938) while other States are lying below the national level. It seems that there is more male migrants in the region lowering the sex ratio of general population.

Education is the main instrument of social change. Normally it has been considered an agency helping economic production through the development of skills and efficiency highly necessary for the said production. "Education as an organic entity, changes, grows with the time, responds to the needs of the society and adopts to the environment. It was mostly an ornament in the agricultural civilizations, a tool in economic development in the industrial era and has become today all pervasive resource, a resource that can find substitutes for other resources, but has no substitute for itself." according to V.C. Kulandai Swami.

A minute look at Table 5.1, it is observed that there are some notable features of this region in regard to literacy rate. Except Arunachal Pradesh (41.59 %) and Meghalaya (49.1 %), the literacy level of the region's population is above the national level (52.12 %) according to 1991 Census while in 2001, percentage of literacy rate in the States of Arunachal Pradesh (54.74 %), Meghalaya (63.31 %) and Assam (64.28 %) are below the national figure of 65.38 per cent.

However, the female literacy rate is highest in Mizoram (86.13%) followed by Tripura (65.41 %) and lowest in Arunachal Pradesh (44.24%) which is the only State in NER below the national level (54.16.%) in this respect (Table 5.2).

The percentage of population of age 6 and above who are literate varies from 52 per cent in Arunachal Pradesh to 91 per cent in Mizoram. It is further to be mentioned that in every State of NER including India as a whole, a higher percentage of females has completed each level of schooling with few exception.

The SCR Committee Report shows clearly that the literacy and educational status of Muslims is particularly low. There is a significant disparity between the educational status of Muslims and that of other socio-religious categories (except SCs and STs). Muslim enrolment rates are showing steady increase. In 1999-2000, Muslims had the lowest enrolment rate among all socio-religious groups. However, in 2004-05, the Muslims enrolment had improved significantly. 25 per cent Muslims in the 6 to 14 age group have either never been to school or have dropped out at some stage.

There is a big gender gap in literacy (Table 5.2) which is one of the major obstacles in attaining total literacy. Enrolment in various stages of education is growing at a fast rate, but the proportion of girls is low and declines sharply at higher stages of education. The highest gender gap has been found in the States of Manipur (24.03% points), Arunachal Pradesh (21.76), Tripura (20.93) and lowest in Mizoram (7.01) followed by Meghalaya (8.27). However all the States of NER are below all-India (24.84 % points) level. Low female literacy has strong repercussions on other aspects like enrolment of children, population growth, child care and acceptance of family welfare measures.

Social liberalism and economic restructuring have given rise to two key changes for individuals: the provision of gender equity through an opening up of opportunities flow women beyond the household, and the rise of risk aversion among young people of both in an increasingly competitive labour market. These changes influence fertility. However, to some extent, education level for women increased and opportunities in paid employment opened to women to the extent that, in the institutions of education and market employment, considerable gender equity afforded to women individuals.

It is striking to note that per capita expenditure on education in 1997-98 is highest for smaller States of Mizoram (Rs. 1210), followed by Manipur (Rs. 984), Arunachal Pradesh (Rs. 951) and Tripura (Rs. 836) while it is lowest in Assam (Rs. 537) among the States of NER (Dutta, 2002). The Kothari Commission has laid special emphasis on higher education and research, as it strongly believed that it is higher education and research that will contribute to economic development, and to bridge the gap between the rich countries and India. It has also recommended a significant expansion in the allocation of resources to education to the level of 6 per cent of GNP (Gross National Product). Unfortunately, while the Commission recommended a package of reforms, the Government looked at the recommendations as piecemeal suggestions. It is thus a tragedy that the recommendations of the one commission which was directed to look comprehensively at education were considered mostly in a piecemeal fashion, Naik (1997, 1979) observed. While there can be several factors for the inaction of the Government, the lack of strong political will seems to be the most important one.

Population distribution according to religion (Table 5.3) reveals the fact that although NER is a small part of the country a great variation of demographic characteristics is seen during the period under consideration. The percentage of Hindu population is steadily decreasing in all the States of NER including India as a whole during the period 1951-2001 and the same trend has also been followed in the year 2011 as per estimated value. It is remarkable to note that during the same period, the percentage of Muslim and Christian population have shown their increasing trend in all the States of NER including India as a whole. The proportion of Hindu population have been declining mainly due to increase in proportion of population professing Muslim, Christian religion. As the Christian dominated States, viz. Nagaland, Mizoram and Meghalaya recorded a

Table 5.3 : Distribution of Population according to Religion (In per cent)

States	Year	Hindu	Muslim	Christan	Others
Arunachal Pradesh	1951	—	—	—	—
	1971	21.99	0.18	0.79	77.04
	1991	37.04	1.38	10.29	51.29
	2001	34.60	1.90	18.72	44.78
	2011*	32.61	2.41	26.67	38.31
Assam	1951	72.08	24.68	2.01	1.23
	1971	71.51	24.96	2.61	0.92
	1991	67.13	28.43	3.32	1.12
	2001	64.89	30.92	3.70	0.49
	2011*	62.12	33.01	4.02	0.85
Manipur	1951	60.11	6.44	11.89	21.56
	1971	58.47	6.11	26.03	9.39
	1991	57.67	7.27	34.11	0.95
	2001	46.01	8.81	34.04	11.14
	2011*	43.18	10.13	36.22	10.47
Meghalaya	1951	12.12	2.31	39.66	45.91
	1971	18.51	2.61	49.95	28.93
	1991	14.07	3.46	64.58	17.89
	2001	13.27	4.28	70.25	12.20
	2011*	11.89	5.14	74.51	8.44
Mizoram	1951	3.31	0.07	90.51	6.11
	1971	6.39	0.57	86.08	6.96
	1991	5.05	0.66	85.73	8.56
	2001	3.55	1.14	86.97	8.34
	2011*	2.81	2.08	88.34	6.77
Nagaland	1951	4.71	0.24	46.03	49.02
	1971	11.43	0.58	66.76	21.23
	1991	10.12	1.71	87.46	0.71
	2001	7.70	1.76	89.97	0.57
	2011*	6.31	2.22	91.21	0.26
Tripura	1951	75.92	21.43	0.82	1.83
	1971	89.55	6.08	1.01	3.36
	1991	86.51	7.13	1.68	4.68
	2001	85.62	7.95	3.20	3.23
	2011*	84.42	7.75	2.22	5.61
NER	1951	65.54	21.16	6.42	6.88
	1961	63.92	21.01	7.74	7.33
	1971	66.39	19.40	9.12	5.09
	1991	60.95	21.56	13.64	3.85
	2011*	58.35	24.08	14.82	2.75
India	1951	84.98	9.91	2.35	2.76
	1971	82.72	11.21	2.59	3.48
	1991	82.01	12.12	2.34	3.53
	2001	80.46	13.43	2.34	3.77
	2011*	78.03	14.91	2.87	4.19

* Estimated Figures.

Source: Census of India, various years.

comparatively higher growth rate of population during the last two or three consecutive decades that definitely resulted in an increase in proportion of population in Christian religion in North East of India. The same is true in case of Muslim population in the NER while Hinduism was seen as major religion in NER during 1991 as more than 60.95 per cent of population profess Hinduism followed by Muslim (21.56%) and Christian (13.64 %). According to 2001 Census figure, the percentage of Hindu population in the State of Assam decreased to 64.89 per cent while the per cent of population in case of Muslims increased to 30.92 and Christians to 3.70.

The decadal growth rate in NER recorded a very slow in case of population professing Hinduism during the study period. During 1971-91, proportion of Hindu population increased at the rate of 47.91 per cent against the growth rates of 140.89 per cent for Christian, 79.04 per cent for Muslims. As for the country (Table 5.3A), the decadal growth rate of Muslim population are 30.8 per cent, 22.9, 34.5 and 36.1 per cent against the Hindus population as 23.7 per cent, 21.3, 25.1 and 20.3 per cent during the period 1961-71, 1971-81, 1981-91 and 1991-2001 respectively. During the same period, the growth of Christians are 32.6 per cent, 13.7, 21.5 and 22.6 per cent which shows the fact that the decadal growth rate of Muslims is the highest throughout the period. This growth of

Table 5.3A : Decadal Growth of Population according to Religion (In per cent)

	Year	*Hindus*	*Muslims*	*Christians*	*Sikhs*	*Buddhists*	*Jains*
India	1961-71	23.7	30.8	32.6	32.3	17.1	28.5
	1971-81	21.3	22.9	13.7	26.0	23.8	23.1
	1981-91	25.1	34.5	21.5	24.3	35.3	4.6
	1091-01	20.3	36.0	22.6	18.2	24.5	26.0

population was mainly due to influx of people from the neighbouring countries as well as for better sex ratio. It is further to be noted here that for the country, the growth rate of Sikhs, Buddhists and Jains during the period 1991-2001 are 18.2 per cent, 24.5 per cent and 26.0 per cent respectively while during 1961-71, the respective growth rates were 32.3 per cent, 17.1 per cent and 28.5 per cent.

While the sex ratio in India as a whole is lower than 1000, it is not altogether surprising that Muslims show a better sex ratio as compared to other socio-religious groups. Further, Muslims have the highest child sex ratio of any social group in the country. Muslims constitute, at present, about 14.6 per cent of the total Indian population. A larger proportion of Muslims live in urban areas (36%) as compared to the population average (28 %). The community is also geographically concentrated in some specific areas. Fertility rates among Muslims are higher than average. The estimates show that the Total Fertility Rates (TFR) among Muslims declined from 4.3 to 3.6 in 1990s. During the same period the fertility rates for the population as a whole declined from about 3.4 to 2.9. Fertility among Muslims varies with socio-economic characteristics and there are significant inter-regional variations.

Since 2000 Christian population has grown exponentially in many regions due to massive conversions. The Christian population in India officially stands at 2.34 per cent which everybody including Christians do not trust. Majority of Christians do not report their religion as Christianity for 2 reasons, i.e. (1) loss of caste based reservation benefits and (b) Church leaders do not want to raise alarm bells about sudden increase in numbers. Indian Christian leaders conveniently use Census Data to portray minority status and pursue persecution strategy while using the church count data to show progress and request more funds from foreign donors. According to the Christian estimate collected by Joshua Project which is based on Church membership, Christians account for 6 per cent of Indian population. The Muslim population count is questionable as illegal Bangladeshi immigrants are not counted. According to Justice K.M. Yusuf, a retired judge of the Calcutta High Court and Chairman of the West Bengal Minority Commission, the true percentage is between 20-25 per cent (published in *The Hindu,* October 01, 1999). Further, it is remarkable to note that considering the percentage of Christian population in all the State capital towns of India, Aijawl stands at the top with 90.03 per cent followed by Kohima (85.03 per cent) and Shillong (41.02%), all belonging to NER.

In the developed economies, the process of urbanisation has been closely and positively related with the economic development, while in the third world developing countries is a consequential phenomenon. Besides, the pattern of urbanisation in the latter economies has been spatially and structurally imbalanced. The rates of urbanisation vary over time and space. In the later half of the twentieth century the developing countries have been urbanizing very fast and India is no exception. The rate of urbanization during the post-independence period has been quite rapid with highest rate, during 1971-81 decade, of 46 per cent The 1991 Census reveals a slowing down urban population growth (36.19 %) during 1981-91, and 32.61 per cent during 1991-2001. It is the quantum increase in urban population *vis-a-vis* total population growth which is of vital concern.

Coming the States of NER, the notable point is that the percentage of urban population to total population (urbanization) varies from 12.80 (Arunachal Pradesh) to 46.10 (Mizoram). It is striking to note that except Manipur (27.52 %) according to 1991 Census, urban population growth was always higher than total population growth during the 20th century. The slower tempo of urban population growth during 1981-1991 and longer perspective of guided urbanisation having been considered for future urban population growth. In 2001, the per cent of urbanization is the lowest in the State of Assam (12.90%) followed by Tripura (17.05 %) and Nagaland (17.74 %) while highest per cent observed in the State of Mizoram (49.63 %), which is the only State above national level (27.81 %), followed by Manipur (23.88%), Arunachal Pradesh (20.75 %) and Meghalaya (19.58%). As per the latest figure available only 15.51 per cent of the total population of NER resided in urban areas against the country's figure of 27.78 per cent in 2001 Census year. During the early period, i.e. 1951-61, the urban population of NER increased by 139.83 per cent and after that the decennial growth rate of urban population declined abruptly to 67.44 per cent in 1961-71, 57.49 in 1971-81, 50.67 per cent in 1981-91 and finally touched at 36.29 per cent in 1991-2001. The urbanization in India is structurally imbalanced and is going to maintain the same trend unless there is a policy intervention to reorient the urbanization trend in favour of small and medium size towns along with metropolitan decentralization.

Migration

Migration is the driving force of population growth. Migration has long been seen as a means of improving one's career prospects, particularly in developing countries where the distribution of economic opportunities is uneven. In contrast to migration, education has little effect on the rate of occupational change, but it gives a significant boost to the socio-economic level achieved after the change. The data base for a complete study of migration in India is weak, and official rigidity in respect of publication of certain information does not help the situation. It is a truism that, in developing countries, an accurate measurement of migration is grossly handicapped by the nature and lack of basic data on events. In most Third World countries today, population registers, an appropriate and key sources of data for migrants and migrations, are almost non-existent. In these countries, the most important sources of migration data in national censuses, usually conducted decennially. Again, in censuses, the information collected on migration is very limited, often restricted to lifetime migration only.

Hendrick and Henkeas (2007) concluded that age, education, income and social networks play key roles in triggering immigration. They are also of the opinion that economic considerations play a role in explaining the intent to immigration but the economic theory of migration is not sufficient to understand immigration. Needless to say, a significant number of migrants-refugees and asylum seekers are also sometimes forcefully driven by the quality of the public domain in their home country. They considered the perceptions of three aspects of the public domain, viz.

(i) societal problems such as crime, pollution and ethnic conflict,
(ii) environmental problems such as loss of natural environments and increasing population density, and
(iii) shortcomings in institutions that deal with welfare and social problems, that is the educational system, social security, health care, law and order and old-age pensions.

The assumption that population growth adversely affects economic growth and natural resources came under fire beginning in the late 1970s with the work of Julian Simon (1977, 1981). Simon's view was that moderate population growth is beneficial, not detrimental, because it induces technical innovation. Furthermore, market mechanisms insure substitution away from scarcer to more abundant resources, and thus prevent resource shortage. The report of National Academy of Sciences (NAS) concluded that population growth can have negative effects on some types of environmental outcomes, under particular social, economic and political conditions: Renewable resources, air and water quality, the climate, and species diversity may be harmed by rapid population growth. But the existence and size of these effects depend on the efficacy and efficiency of social institutions that regulate resource use and allocate the costs of externalities (NAS, 1986).

As NER is surrounded by four foreign countries, there is every possibility of influx from these countries in search of food, employment, business etc. The absolute number of the migrants was more than 91 thousand in 1901, since then it has been steadily increasing and reached at nearly 745 thousand in the Census Year 1991. The share of migrants from Bangladesh was between slightly more than 70 per cent to slightly more than 87 per cent in pre-Independence era. The post-Independence era, it reached at 94 per cent in 1951–the highest among the period, 1951-1991. From 1961 onwards the share started to decline and become around 89 per cent in the Census Year of 1991. It is also clear from the statistical information that Bangladesh was followed by Nepal in sending migrants to the NER of India. Again the number of migrants who come from other States of India varied between 0.5 million to around 0.8 million during the pre-Independence era. But it declined to around 0.4 million in 1951 and reaching slightly more than 0.5 million 1991. In the recent years the flow of immigration from the neighbouring countries shows an increasing trend. This heavy growth of population was mainly due to influx of people from the neighbouring countries or States in search of food, employment, business etc.

However, the share became around 89 per cent in the Census Year of 1991, the absolute figure is 745 thousand. Remaining 11 per cent of the migrants to this region are from Nepal, Myanmer etc. However, total migrants, from outside the country, to this region stands at 834 thousand during 1991. The proportion of foreign migrants from Bangladesh to Assam was around 85 per cent among the total foreign migrants in the State. The respective percentage for the State of Tripura was more than 99 per cent according to 1991 Census. This no doubt has some impact on the social, economic, cultural and political sphere of the North-Eastern Region.

It is to be noted here that from the pre-Independence period (Table 5.3B), the percentage of Muslim population in the State of Assam has been increasing steadily from 16.23 per cent in 1911 to 30.92 per cent in 2001 while in case of India it decreased from 22.39 per cent in 1911 to 9.91 per cent in 1951 but then again it has been

Table 5.3B : Proportion of Muslim Population in India and Assam (In per cent)

Years	*1911*	*1931*	*1951*	*1961*	*1971*	*1991*	*2001*
Assam	16.23	22.78	24.68	25.30	24.56	28.43	30.92
India	22.39	23.49	9.91	10.71	11.21	12.12	13.41

Source: Cenus of India, various years.

increasing steadily and reached at 12.12 p.c. in 1991. This is no doubt due to the effect of population migration from other States of the country and the neighbouring countries to this north-eastern States in general and Assam in particular. As a result, in 1951 Census, the rise in the population of Assamese-speaking people was substantial as the migrated Muslim population adopted Assamese as their language leaving their mother tongue Bengali. Meanwhile, the refugees from East Pakistan poured into the State. During that time the linguistic nationalism of the Bangalees in Barak Valley of Assam was at its peak against the Official Language Bill passed in the Assam Legislative Assembly. Besides, the leaders of the Indian National Congress encouraged Muslim infiltrators into Assam for their vote bank, which was clearly manifested in one of the election meeting in which a leading Congressman of Assam expressed "so long as Alis and Collies are with the Congress, we have nothing to fear". Lateron, the AGP Government of Assam continued to appease the Muslims by making them as their vote bank too. On the other hand, to reduce the Hindu

Bengalees into minority in Assam, the government of Assam is still trying to impose upon them the process of Assamization. Political vested interests have obviously played a decisive role in this development, which if allowed to go on unabated will worsen the situation and endanger India's unity and integrity.

In NER the expenditure to control insurgency has been increasing day-by-day. But ironically along with the expenditure to control insurgency, it has been increasing by leaps and bounds. During the period of seven years (1997-2003) the States of NER had sanctioned crores of rupees in their budget. Side by side an amount of 767 crores of rupees they have spent for police security out of the enhanced amount of Rs. 1,000 crores sanctioned by the Central Government. Among these seven States, Assam having an expenditure amounting to Rs. 487.8 crores, Tripura having 118 crores and Nagaland having 96 crores are on the top of the list. For the modernization of police force another 278 crores of rupees has been spent. In this sphere also Assam is on the top of the list along with the States of Tripura and Nagaland. The amounts spent for these States are Rs. 103 crores, Rs. 46 crores and Rs. 39 crores respectively. According to an official communique of the Home Ministry in the last 12 years only in the State of Assam, 1378 have been killed and 178 security personnel too have been murdered. This governmental information made it clear that despite high expenditure normalcy cannot be brought in the region. Here both the Central and the State Governments are a great failure (Dutta and Deb 2005) which ultimately affected overall socio-economic development of the region.

Economic Development and Environment

The main and foremost objective of all planning and policies of any country is human development and to improve the quality of life of the human resources of the country. As the second most populous country of the world, India has only 2.5 per cent of global land whereas it has to provide home for one-sixth of world's population. Thus, living in a country with a high population density and high growth rate of population, which increases pressure on the existing resources of the country, planners perceived that there was a serious threat coming up on the way to achieve developmental goals. Demographic transition is an important phenomenon in this regard. However, demographic pattern has already been studied in the previous sections of this paper.

Population pressure on farmland has long been a concern in the demographic literature. Foster *et al.* (1997) concluded that, in Indian villages, technological change in agriculture "reinforces the destructive effects of population growth on forests" (p. 13). But they also found that rural industrialization appears to preserve forest land. Population growth and its relation to economic development has been a matter of debate for over a century. For the developing country like India, population growth is likely to impede economic growth resulting in reduction of per capita income and resources. In addition to this the growth of labour force will add to the unemployment trends. The Tenth Five Year Plan (2002-07) was aimed at achieving the Gross Domestic Product (GDP) growth rate of 8 per cent, doubling the per capita income and creation of 100 million of employment opportunities in next 10 years (Planning Commission, 2002). These targets were formulated based on the past growth trends and the vision of making India as a developed country by 2020.

While one of the recognized strengths of demography is its powerful descriptive potential, the discipline also has a long history of causal analysis. Social Science problem often involves multiple causal forces operating within complex, interrelated networks. Complexity can probably be better handled by breaking up problems into separate components. However, several criteria can be used with reference to uncertain causal structures, such as the effect of historical changes on climate and population growth, the impact of legislation on demographic parameters (e.g. marriage and divorce), the economic consequences of migration, the demographic effects of particular social policies on the population and economic growth. Demographer's interest in the environment has generally been enmeshed in broader issues of population growth and economic development. Empirical research by demographers on environmental issues other than natural resource contraints is limited. In his first essay, more than 200 years ago, Thomas Malthus argued that unrestrained population growth would eventually be limited by fixed natural resources (Malthus,

1789). Human activity has radically altered the earth's surface, oceans, and atmosphere, especially over the last 200 years. On the 200th anniversary of this Essay, the relationships between population growth, human welfare, and the natural environment continue to be widely debated (Livernash and Rodenburg 1998; Lubchenco, 1998). Public and scientific concerns about population and the environment have, of course, varied over time. Vernoin Ruttan identified three waves of social concern about the environment since World War II (Ruttan, 1993). These waves, each of which focused on a different set of environmental issues.[9]

The first wave, in the late 1940s and early 1950s, centred on whether natural resources (such as land, water and energy supplies) could sustain economic growth and food production in the face of population increase. These issues are similar to Malthus' original concerns.

The second wave, in the late 1960s and early 1970s, added another focus—the environment's ability to absorb by-products of modern technology, such as air and water pollutants, asbestos, pesticides, radioactive waste, and household waste (Ruttan, 1993). This second wave was spured in part by rising incomes in industrialized countries, which, ironically, increased demand, both for the commodities producing these detrimental by-products and for a cleaner environment.

The third wave, in the late 1980s and early 1990s, added yet another focus—changes occurring on a global scale, including acid rain, global warming, and ozone depletion. The second and third wave issues involve public goods—air, water, and the atmosphere—which have a well-known tendency towards over-exploitation. As the 1997 Kyoto Conference on Global Climatic Change (UNFCCC, 1998; Warrick, 1998) suggests, third-wave problems will be particularly difficult to solve because they involve considerations of equity in the use of public goods among nations (Das Gupta, Folke, and Maler 1994; Najam,1996).

The interaction between economic development and female work participation has attracted attention amongst economists, social scientists etc. for more than fifty years. Female work participation is much higher in the States of North East except in Tripura. In a traditionally bound society like India where male predominates, the inferior image of women has become ingrained in the minds of men, and finds expression in their day-to-day life. Even though a woman can work proficiently as man she is considered inferior and subordinate to man. Bur with the advancement of time, more and more women are gainfully employed.

Food insecurity is a matter of great concern not only to the people of NER but also to the policy-makers and planners of NER. In the entire North East, the valley districts of Manipur are among the most productive zones of nation in the production of paddy. However, the same cannot be true about the districts of Assam and lack of assured irrigation seems to be the major factor behind it. The productivity of paddy in Manipur-Tripura Valley and Mizoram is higher than the regional average and also above Assam which alone accounts for more than 70 per cent of area and output in the region. Mizoram achieved a remarkable growth in the yield rate of paddy since around the middle of 1980 due to increase in fertiliser consumption and new land use policy in Mizoram. Although the paddy productivity is the lowest in Arunachal Pradesh, the yield of oilseed and pulses is the highest in the States of Meghalaya, Mizoram and the hill districts of Manipur. As the region is classified into hill areas and plain areas, the cropping patterns in the hill districts is more varied and not similar to that of plain areas. The development of infrastructural facilities like road and communications, banking, health are responsible for the above gaps. Further, corruption at the Government level and red-tapism of bureaucrats are responsible for this problem in the region. The expansion of irrigation facilities, operation and maintenance of irrigation system and distribution of water have not received due attention.

Irrigation sector is today facing twin issues of sub-optimal sector planning and financial management on the one hand and inadequate water management and maintenance on the other. Involving the farmers in the irrigation system is one obvious remedy for addressing the management problems. In comparison to all-India level only 1.4 per cent of area is under irrigation system in the NER and only 1 per cent in the State of Assam (5,39,000 hectares).

However, percentage of total irrigated area in Assam is 65 per cent with respect to total irrigated area in NER.

Since north eastern society is dominated by the tribal population, the reference may be made to the tribal method of cultivation. Out of 23.78 lakh hectare of land in the country as a whole 19.91 lakh hectare (83.73 %) of land in the North East is under shifting cultivation or jhuming which has now become an ecological menace. Rapid deforestation over the years 1987-1997 due to the shifting cultivation in the region have reduced the total forest cover amounting to 1312 sq. km (Table 5.2). An inevitable consequence of deforestation is increased runoff rain water, precipitation and extensive soil erosion resulting in unacceptable deterioration of top soil, degradation of land and sedimentation of water bases resulting in desertification and frequent flooding. The high rate of soil erosion in deforested area in our country ranges from 10 tonnes per hectare in the plains to about 30 tonnes per hectare in the North Eastern hilly rigion[10], 10 to 50 times larger than in the forest areas. Extensive deforestation in the region has resulted in increased carbon dioxide concentration in the atmosphere. The changes in climatic and rain pattern gradually set in because of deforestation. Water and soil erosion have affected the maximum lands used for agricultural purpose. The climatic fluctuation and changes in the rain pattern have further compounded the problem of providing adequate food security to our increased population. Gross neglect of environment also resulted in polluting not only river water but also surface water, making them fertile breeding grounds of many communicable diseases.

The Union Government sanctioned Rs. 68 crores to the eight North Eastern States during the past three years (2000-2003) for modernizing the forest protection force, forest protection system and strengthening the forest management. Tripura and Assam got the maximum amount of Rs. 16 crores each while the other States of the region received Rs. 5-9 crores for this purpose. Among the eight NE States, including Sikim, the forest cover had increased in Arunachal Pradesh and Tripura.[11]

The expansion of irrigation facilities, operation and maintenance of irrigation system and distribution of water have not received due attention. Irrigation sector is today facing twin issues of sub-optimal sector planning and financial management on the one hand and inadequate water management and maintenance on the other. Involving the farmers in the irrigation system is one obvious remedy for addressing the management problems. In comparison to all-India level only 1.4 per cent of area is under irrigation system in the NER and only 1 per cent in the State of Assam (5,39,000 hectares). However, percentage of total irrigated area in Assam is 65 per cent with respect to total irrigated area in NER. Health is a social goal and considered as an integral component in over all socio-economic development. The majority of health problems are the products of illiteracy, poverty, ignorance, overcrowding, poor environmental conditions and uneven distribution of health manpower and institutions. It is observed that there are only 4.32 per cent of public health centres in the States of NER as compared to India's figure.

There is a need to examine the extent of suicides and levels in different States as a result of different socio-economic conditions. Table 5.4 shows the comparative study of distribution of suicides in different age groups for two years 1996 and 2001. A minute look at

Table 5.4 : Incidence of Suicides by Age Group (1996 & 2001)

States	*By all Groups*		*up to 14*	*15-29*	*30-44*	*45-59*	*60+*
	Male	*Female*					
ANP	38 (76)	13 (35)	1 (4)	15 (47)	29 (47)	6 (12)	— (1)
ASM	1678 (1836)	814 (811)	157 (54)	913 (1003)	804 (976)	501 (537)	117 (77)
MNP	16 (24)	2 (17)	-- (1)	8 (23)	6 (10)	4 (6)	— (1)
MGH	59 (69)	13 (18)	2 (1)	18 (33)	34 (38)	12 (8)	6 (7)
MZM	31 (46)	3 (8)	3 (7)	24 (25)	6 (12)	1 (7)	— (3)
NGN	26 (25)	8 (15)	— (–)	16 (15)	17 (20)	1 (5)	— (–)
TRP	299 (463)	256 (391)	37 (30)	170 (239)	148 (381)	124 (149)	76 (55)
India	51206 (66314)	37503 (42192)	3404 (3007)	33925 (38910)	29138 (36448)	15393 (21579)	6381 (8652)

Note : No. of suicides (By all Groups) in 2001 shown within bracket

the table reveals the fact that in the States of NER, the highest percentage of suicides occur in the age group 15-29 years (35.76 %) followed by 30-44 years (32.06 %) which is also true for the country in 1996 as well as in 2001 while in the percentage of suicides shifted highest in the age group 30-44 years (38.71 %) followed by 15-29 years (36-12 %) in the States of NER. However, percentage of Region's total suicides in comparison to the country decreased from 3.67 per cent in 1996 to 3.53 per cent in 2001. It is striking to note that in both the periods (1996 & 2001) maximum number of suicides occur in the State of Assam (76.54 % & 69.04 %) followed by Tripura (17.05 % & 22.27 p.c.) among the States of NER.

A close look at Table 5.5, it is observed that highest percentage of suicides occur in the State of Assam (75.15 %) followed by Tripura (16.73 %) among the States of NER. It is also striking to note that highest number of suicides occur due to illness (11.64 %) followed by unemployment (4.51 %) and poverty (1.01 %) in 1996 while in 2001, the highest percentage of suicides took place due to

Table 5.5 : Incidence of Suicides in NE States of India (1996 & 2001)

States	*Change in eco-Status (1998)/ Poverty (2001)*		*Illness*		*Dowry*		*Drug Abuse*		*Unemployment*	
	1996	2001	1996	2001	1996	2001	1996	2001	1996	2001
ANP	–	4		3	–	–	–	–	–	–
ASM	11	176	324	160	15	13	24	8	149	336
MNP	–	–	2	–	–	–	2	2	–	–
MGH	–	1	9	18	–	–	–	–	–	–
MZM	–	–	3	–	–	–	5	6	–	2
NGN	–	–	–	1	–	–	4	2	–	–
TRP	–	16	66	71	3	–	5	–	–	–
India	2352	2549	22071	24098	2517	2414	1221	1414	1745	2734

unemployment (12.49 %) followed by poverty (6.65 %) and illness (6.04 %) in the State of Assam. The proportion of suicides due to unemployment, poverty and drug abuse in respect to total suicides in NER is 6.45 per cent in 1996 and 16.68 per cent in 2001 which are observed mainly in the States of Assam and Tripura. In backward areas rapid population growth tends to offset the benefits of development. Rather, it results in family frustration, dependence burden, employment and social tensions leading to a breakdown of an order society.

Dutta (2002, 2003) observed that due to excessive population growth, there are housing shortage, number of unemployment goes up which creates frustration among the younger generation and ultimately affects the society with creation of civil disorder, crime, drug abuse, health hàzards etc. Further, due to illiteracy and poverty, population increases rapidly. Population explosion creates food shortage, unemployment, poverty, crime, illiteracy. Poverty is an important factor in the development of frustration among the young generation as a result of which suicide takes place. Again the food shortage may occur due to over burden of the excess population. All these create social chaos in the society and ultimately the frustrated people raise their ugly faces to create social disturbances through different nasty activities. Thus, terrorism is a multi-causal phenomenon and usually results from multiple causal factors such as economic, political, religious, and sociological factors, among others.

On the other hand, over-population affects the nature of bio-sphere and creates ecological imbalance due to over activities of the people. Over-activities of people, due to population growth, occur by depleting the natural resources like forest land, agricultural land, water etc. and misusing the energy sources. These also create different types of pollution due to modernization which is the effect of industrialization. Direct threats to human life style are the most obvious aspect of environmental deterioration and of these direct threats, the phenomenon commonly lumped under the term pollution has been contributed by over-population and modern industria-lisation. A major factor contributing to environmental degradation in most Indian cities and towns is the inadequate provision of safe drinking water and sanitation.

Conclusion and Suggestion

The objective of development is that all people can enjoy long, healthy and creative lives. It is for all practical purposes a synonym of gender equity and equality. It is important to recognize that discourses on planning have not considered women as part of the complexity called "Development Structures". Considering the indicators used in the present study, it confirms the fact that gender issues are intertwined with the issue of Human Development for which the States of NER are lagging behind and the women of NER are still poorest of the poor despite the favourable social customs and tradition.

The abnormal growth of population in the region may be due to heavy influx of people mainly from the neighbouring countries and also to some extent from other States in search of food, employment and business. As regard sex ratio, NER recorded comparatively a lower sex ratio compared to country's figure. In regard to urbanization it can be concluded that the overall process of urbanization in agro-based NER is very slow basically due to its locational and infrastructural problems. Development of secondary sectors is also not up to the mark in the NER resulting in heavy dependence on agricultural sector.

The social and economic implication of population growth are useful for national planning of any country or of a region. Every development plan contains future estimates of a nation's needs as well as for policy formulation for sectors such as labour force, education, health, urbanization, agriculture etc. The GDP per capita will enable us to understand the economic progress of the country. On education, the projection of school going children, requirement of new schools as well as other infrastructure help us to make the educational planning of the country. The health requirement with respect to health professionals including the family planning situation enables us to formulate the health sector planning. The investment has to be made more and more on health and education of the people of the country in general and NER in particular. For adequate and efficient investment on human resource development, the State governments of the region have to give emphasis on improving the quality and coverage of health and nutritional services as well as educational infrastructure. Creation of sufficient employment and skilled personnel should be the target. More and more importance should be given to meet the needs of old-age dependents in terms of health care, housing facilities, financial as well as social security.

The emphasis should be given more on economic and demographic situation of the region. There is an urgent need for re-examination of pattern of development, particularly of industrialization in the context of balanced regional development in the country. Policy-makers should not ignore the heterogeneous conposition of people of the region while planning development strategies for the States of NER. Through the development of the rural people the process of region's progress can be accelerated. The national spirit should be inculcated in the minds of the people of the States of NER. Efforts should be made to ensure harmonious growth of national and sub-national identities to cure the malady. The root cause of alienation of land and indebtedness among the people is poverty. Thus, to uplift the economic condition of the people of the region, the society of each village and of community must protect the economically weaker sections of the region by improving their economic condition. The developmental schemes for their economic upliftment should be implemented sincerely and expeditiously.

The State Governments of the region and also the Central Government should establish the requisite institutional mechanism and enable environment at all levels of the society to ensure that population factors are appropriately addressed within the decision making and administrative process of all governmental agencies responsible for economic, environment, and social policies and programmas. There is a need for transparency, monitoring and data availability so that equity-related concerns across socio-religious communities including Muslims can be assessed on a continuing basis. For this, regular collection of detailed information by SRCs is essential. An autonomous National Data Bank (NDB) can be a repository of this data which should be publicly available.

Development is the process by which we affect the environment. Environment is what is left after development. Environmental awareness programmes at all levels should be sponsored by governmental and non-governmental agencies engaged in environment development. Environmental awareness should be strengthened through formal and non-formal education. Urban authorities should encourage city dwellers for effective tree plantation nearby their residences. The best agricultural lands with ideal moisture conditions are to be utilized for agricultural purpose only. Industrial and urban activities should not be allowed in such areas. Environmental improvement schemes should be incorporated into the integrated urban development plan.

To achieve sustainable development and a higher quality of life for all people, Governments should reduce and eliminate unsustainable pattern of production and consumption and promote appropriate demographic policies. At the same time the Governments should implement the reforms with extreme caution so that it would not arouse the people's emotion and sentiments by interfering in the social laws, customs, traditions etc. Hence the slogan should be '*Globalisation within limits or reform in a controlled manner*'.

Notes

1. Documents on the Global Science Panel on Population in Sustainable Development, Population Matters to Development and Environment, pp. 367-368, *Population and Development Review*, Vol. 28, Number 2, June 2002.
2. Decument on Environmental Degradation and Human Well-being: The President of Pakistan, *Population and Development Review,* Vol. 31 Number 2, June 2005.
3. Document on Environmental Degradation and Human Well-being: The President of Russia, *Population and Development Review,* Vol. 31 Number 2, June 2005.
4. "China's Local and National Fertility Policies at the end of the Twentieth Century", Gu Bachang, Wang Feng, Guo Zhigang & Zhang Erli in *Population and Development Review,* as Notes and Commentary, pp. 129-147, Vol. 33, Number 1, March 2007.
5. Raina, *Planning Family in India,* 1990, pp. 12-79, Passim.
6. Raina, Population Policy, 1988, pp 5-7; and "Recommendations of the Committee on Population Growth and Family Planning", 14 April 1951, Reprinted as Appendix A2 in Gupta, Sinha and Bardhan, *Evolution of Family Welfare Programme in India,* Vol. 1, 1992.
7. India, Planning Commission, *Third Five Year Plan,* 1961, pp. 25, 72.
8. Page 45 of Vol. 35 No. 1, February. 1998, *Demography.*

9. PRESIDENTIAL ADDRESS: Demography and the Environment, Anne.R. Pebley, *Demography*, Vol. 35(4), November, 1998, pp 377-389.
10. U.R. Rao (1994): 'Space for Sustainable Development,' G.B. Pant Memorial Lecutre, Guwahati.
11. *NE News Letter*, Vol.5, No.4, April 2003.

References

Connelly, Matthew (2006): "Population Control in India: Prologue to the Emergency Period", *Population and Development Review*, pp. 629-668, Vol. 32, No. 4, December 2006.

Croll, Elisabeth J. (1984): "The Single-Child Family: The First-Five Years", in Neville Maxwell and Bruce J. McFarlane (eds.), *China's Changed Road to Development*, New York: Pergamon Press.

Das Gupta, P. C., Folke, and K.G. Maler (1994): "The Environmental Resource Base and Human Welfare." pp 25-40 in *Population, Economic Development, and the Environment*, Ed. K. Lindahl-Kiessling and H. Landberg., Oxford University Press, Oxford.

Dutta, P.C. (1996): "Quality Variation of Some Food Items of Consumption in North-Eastern Region (NER)", *Indian Journal of Regional Science*, Vol. 28 (1).

Dutta, P.C. (2002): "Population Growth and Environmental Crisis in North East India: Problems and Remedies" in *Development Priorities in North East India* (ed), B.J. Deb, Concept Publishing Company, New Delhi.

Dutta, P.C. (2002): *"A Study on the Impacts of Socio-Economic Development in North-East India with Special Reference to the Problems of Population Growth and Urbanisation on Environment"*- UGC sponsored MRP (2000-2002), Report submitted on 18.03.02.

Dutta, P.C. (2003): "Regional Disparity and its consequences in North-Eastern Region of India" in *Economic Liberalization and Regional Disparities in India—Special Focus on the North-Eastern Region* (ed.) A.C. Mohapatyra and Chitta Ranjan Pathak, Star Publishing House, Shillong.

Dutta, P.C. (2005): "Problems of Ethnicity in North East India" in Perspective of *Security and Development in North East India* (ed.) S.K. Agnihotri (IAS) and B. Datta Ray, Concept Publishing Company, New Delhi.

Dutta, P.C. and Y. Deb (2005): "*Problems and Prospects of Peace Process in Assam of North East India*", Paper presented in the National Seminar on Prospects of Peace Process in Assam of North East India, NEICSSR, Shillong, December 9-10.

Foster, A.D., M.R. Resenzweig, and J.R. Behrman (1997): "Population Growth, Income Growth and Deforestation-Management of Village Common Land in India", Unpublished Manuscript, Department of Economics, Brown University.

Hendrik, P. Van Dalen and Kene Henkens (2007): "Longing for the Good Life: Understanding Emigration From a High- Income Country", *Population and Development Review,* pp. 37-66, Vol. 33, No. 1, March, 2007

Livernash, R. and E. Rodenburg (1998): "Population Change, Resources and the Environment", *Population Bullein* 53 (4), 1-40.

Lubcheno, J (1998): "Entering the Century of the Environment: A New Social Contract for Science", *Science* 279 (23), 491-97.

Madhab, Jayanta (1999): "North East, Crisis of Identity, Security and Underdevelopment", *EPW,* Vol. 34, No. 1, Feb. 6-12.

Malthus, T.R (1798): "*An Essay on the Principle of Population as it Affects the Future Improvement of Society*", Reprint, Harmondsworth, Middlesex, England: Perican Books, 1970.

Naik, J.P. (1997): "*The Education Commission and After*" Second Edition New Delhi, (First edtion, 1979, APH Publising Corporation), New Delhi.

Najam, A. (1996): "A Developing Countries Perspective on Population, Environment, and Development." *Population Policy and Policy Review,* 15:1-19.

National Academy of Sciences (1986): "*Population Growth and Economic Development Policy Questions*", Washington DC, National Academy Press.

Nikos Alexandratos (2005): "Countries with Rapid Population Growth and Resource Constraints: Issues of Food, Agriculture, and Development", *Population and Development Review,* pp. 237-258, Vol. 31, No. 2, June 2005.

Ruttan, V.W. (1993): "Population Growth, Environmental Change, and Innovation: Implications for Sustainable Growth in Agriculture", 124-56 in *Population and Land Use in Developing Countries* ed. C.L. Jolly and B.B. Torrey, Washington DC, National Academy Press.

Simon, J. (1981): "*The Ultimate Resource*". Princeton, NJ: Princeton, University Press.

Simon, J. (1997): *The Economics of Population Growth.* Princeton, NJ: Princeton University Press.

United Nations Framework Convention on Climatic Change (UNFCCC) (1998): *Report of the Parties on its Third Session, Held in Kyoto from 1 to 11 December, 1997. Addendum. Part Two: Action Taken by the Conference of the Parties at its Third Session.* New York: United Nations.

Wang, Feng. (2005): "*Can China Afford to Continue its One-Child Policy?*", Asia Pacific Issues 17, Hono-lulu: East-West Centre.

Warrick, J. (1998): "Reassessing Kyoto Agreement, Scientists See Little Environmental Advantage." *Washigton Post*, February 13, p. 14.

6

Demographic Scenario of the States of North Eastern Region of India

An Analysis

A.K. Borah, J. Borbora and *S.V. Borbora*

Introduction

The North East Region of India comprising seven States, namely Arunachal Pradesh, Assam, Manipur, Meghalaya, Nagaland and Tripura covers a total geographical area of 2,55,083 sq. km. (*Source*: Census of India, 2001) and it accounts for 7.5 per cent of the country's total land area. As a region it is consisting of 70 per cent hilly area, undulating hilly terrains and plateaus and only 30 per cent is the plain area which covers mostly two river valleys of Assam, namely Brahmaputra and Barak and certain portions of the State of Tripura. Because of the physiographical nature of this region the habitation of the population is also uneven in the States of the region. However, in a few States the habitation of the population is much more in comparison to other States.

As is well known, the North East Region is a frontier region of India and it is located between 21.57'N-29.30'N latitude and 89.46'E longitude. Being the frontier region of India it is having considerably long international boundaries bordering with China in the North, Bangladesh in the South and South West Bhutan in the North West and Myanmar in the East. The MacMohan line separates the region from Tibet. The region is linked with rest of the country through a narrow corridor commonly known as chicken neck in North Bengal (northern part of the State of West Bengal) and which is approximately 33 kms. wide in the east and 22 kms. in the west.

An Overview of the Demographic Structure of the North-Eastern Region

In the introduction part of this present paper an effort is made to highlight the physiographical settings of the region and also uneven distribution of population as far as their habitations are concerned. While coming to discuss the population distribution in different States of the North East India it is found that there is extremely uneven distribution of population among its constituent States. Table 6.1 shows the uneven distribution of population in the States of the region as per 2001 Census.

Table 6.1: Population Distribution of States of North East India (as per 2001 census)

Sl. No.	*States*	*Area (in sq. kms.)*	*Population (in persons)*
1.	Arunachal Pradesh	83,743	10,91,117
2.	Assam	78,438	2,66,38,407
3.	Manipur	22,327	23,99,634
4.	Meghalaya	22,429	23,06,069
5.	Mizoram	22,081	8,91,058
6.	Nagaland	16,579	19,88,636
7.	Tripura	10,486	31,91,168

Source: Census of India, 2001, Series-1, Paper-I of 2001 (Provisional Report).

As stated in the anterior paragraph that in the States of the region there is uneven distribution of population as it is evident from Table 6.1. Though the State of Arunachal Pradesh covers the largest geographical area in terms of sq. kms. among all other States of the region, it has only 11 lakhs of population. On the other hand, the State of Assam is smaller than the State of Arunachal Pradesh in terms of land area coverage but here the size of population in terms of persons is much more as it contains more than 2.66 crore of persons. The land-man scenario in case of Tripura is also to a large extent similar to Assam. It is the smallest State of North East Region of India in terms of land coverage but it is containing nearly 32 lakhs of person. The other hill States of North East Region of India like Arunachal Pradesh are having less number of population compared to the State of Assam and Tripura. For example, the State of Mizoram which has a land area of 22,081 sq. kms. contains only 8.91 lakh of population. Similarly, in case of male-female distribution of the population of the States of North East India variations are noticed in different States. The following table shows a clear picture in this regard.

Table 6.2 : Male-Female Distribution of the Population of the States of the Region

Sl. No.	*States*	*Persons*	*Males*	*Females*
1.	Arunachal Pradesh	10,91,117	5,73,951	5,17,166
2.	Assam	2,66,38,407	1,37,87,799	1,28,50,608
3.	Manipur	23,88,634	12,07,338	11,81,296
4.	Meghalaya	23,06,069	11,67,840	11,38,229
5.	Mizoram	8,91,058	4,59,783	4,31,275
6.	Nagaland	19,88,636	10,41,686	9,46,950
7.	Tripura	31,91,186	16,36,138	15,55,030

Source: Census of India, 2001, Series-1, Paper-2 of 2001.

The above table shows the state-wise variation of males and females. More importantly in all the States of the region even the ratio of females per thousand males is also different. The Census figures of 2001 in this context gives a clear picture.

Table 6.3 : Sex Ratio of the Population of North-Eastern States of India

Sl. No.	*States*	*Sex Ratio (Female Per, 000 Males)*
1.	Arunachal Pradesh	901
2.	Assam	932
3.	Manipur	978
4.	Meghalaya	975
5.	Mizoram	938
6.	Nagaland	909
7.	Tripura	950

Source: Census of India, 2001, Series-1, Paper-1 of 2001 (Provisional Report).

The above table shows that ratio of females per thousand males is low in case of Arunachal Pradesh and high in Manipur.

The density of population per sq. km in the States of the region is also uneven in nature because the topographical features of the different States are not equally suitable for human habitation. On the other hand the river valleys of Assam, the valley of Tripura and Imphal valley of Manipur shows higher concentration of population as these areas are conducive for human habitation. On the other hand, large areas of the hill States are totally unsuitable for human settlement due to the steep gradients of hills and mountains covered by evergreen rain forest etc. As such due to the physiographic variations the density of population in the States is also not equal. Table 6.4 below shows the density of population per sq. km. in the various States of North East India.

Table 6.4 : Density of population in the States of North East India

Sl. No.	*States*	*Density of Population (in'000 per sq. km.)*
1.	Arunachal Pradesh	13
2.	Assam	340
3.	Manipur	107
4.	Meghalaya	103
5.	Mizoram	42
6.	Nagaland	120
7.	Tripura	304

Source: Census of India, 2001, Series-1, Paper –1 of 2001 (Previsional Report).

From the above table it appears that the State of Assam has recorded highest density of population followed by Tripura. While the State of Arunachal Pradesh has recorded the lowest density of population.

Interestingly, the population trends in different States of the North Eastern Region also over a period of 100 years ranging from 1901 to the present 2001 show a very unusual picture as it is evident from Table 6.5.

Table 6.5 shows that there had been a high rate of growth of population in Assam and Tripura from the period of 1961 onward. However, the variation rate of the increase of population is not same in both the States. On the other hand, Manipur has showed more growth of population from 1971. It may be noted that in case of Arunachal Pradesh no Census data was available till 1961. However within a span of five decades the pc ulation of Arunachal Pradesh has increased more than three times he 1961 Census figure. This

Table 6.5 : Population Trends in North Eastern Region from 1901-2001 (*Thousand Persons*)

Census Year	*States*						
	Arunachal Pradesh	*Assam*	*Manipur*	*Meghalaya*	*Mizoram*	*Nagaland*	*Tripura*
1901	–	3,290	284	341	82	102	173
1911	–	3,849	346	394	91	149	230
1921	–	4,637	384	422	98	159	304
1931	–	5,556	446	481	124	179	382
1941	–	6,695	512	556	153	190	513
1951	–	8,029	578	606	196	213	639
1961	337	10,837	780	769	266	369	1,142
1971	468	14,625	1,073	1,012	332	516	1,556
1981	632	18,041	1,421	1,336	494	775	2,055
1991	865	22,414	1,837	1,775	690	1,210	2,757
2001	1,091	26,638	2,389	2,306	891	1,989	3,191

Source: Census of India, 2001, Series-1, Paper-I of 2001 (Provisional Population Totals).

became possible due to the attainment of the status of Union Territory in 1972 and later the Statehood in 1987. This whole process got a fillip in the infrastructure developmental activities initiated by the State which paved the way for the people of other States of India to participate in the State-building process and thus inflated the population scenario.

Decadal growth rate of population in terms of percentage in the States of North East India is also considered important while discussing the demographic scenario of the North East India as it provides us a very interesting feature if the decadal growth rate of population from 1901-1911 to 1991-2001 is taken into account. Table 6.6 shows the variation in decadal growth of the population of the States of the region.

Table 6.6 shows that decadal variations of population in States like Assam, Tripura, Manipur and Mizoram appear to be very fluctuating particularly after India gained Independence. There was a quantum jump or exponential growth of population in case of Assam from 19.93 per cent to 34.98 per cent in the period between 1941-51 and it continued the same till 1961-71. However, a declining trend was noticed in later periods. Same had happened in case of Manipur as it experienced high population growth between 1951-61 and 1961-71. However, after that decade a gradual declining trend has been noticed with little upward trend in the decade of 1991-2001.

The decadal variation of population in various States of North

Table 6.6 : Decadal Variation of Population of the States of North-East India (In per cent)

States	*1901*	*1911*	*1921*	*1931*	*1941*	*1951*	*1961*	*1971*	*1981*	*1991*
Arunachal Pradesh	–	–	–	–	–		38.91	35.15	36.83	26.21
Assam	16.99	20.48	19.91	20.40	19.93	34.98	34.95	23.26	24.24	18.85
Manipur	21.21	10.92	16.04	14.92	12.80	35.04	37,53	32.46	29.29	30.02
Meghalaya	15.71	7.21	13.83	15.59	8.97	27.03	31.50	32.04	32.86	29.94
Mizoram	10.64	7.90	26.42	22.81	28.42	35.61	24.93	48.55	29.70	29.18
Nagaland	46.76	6.55	12.62	6.04	8.60	14.07	39.88	50.05	56.08	64.41
Tripura	32.48	32.59	25.63	34.14	24.56	78.71	36.28	31.92	34.30	15.74

Source: Census of India, 2001, Series-I Paper-1 of 2001 (Provisonal Population Totals).

East India is generally attributed to inter-state migration of people. High rate of immigration from the neighbouring countries like erstwhile East Pakistan now Bangladesh and also from Nepal causes high rate of population growth in the States like Assam and Tripura. Further, after Independence new political situation has emerged due to the passing of Reorganisation Bill of the State of Assam in the early part of 1970s and concomitantly due to initiation of the process of economic development through developmental plans and programmes bolstering the process of spatial mobility of the people from different regions of India to this region. As stated earlier a large number of people from different parts of the country and also from Bangladesh immigrated to Assam in particular and to other States of the region at large. These are some of the factors of population growth in North East India.

Further the above table shows that population growth rate had become more than double in most of the States of the region from Census Period 1961 and registered comparatively higher growth rate from that period. However, from 1981 Census to 2001 Assam and Tripura have registered a slight decline followed by other States except a marginal increase in case of Manipur and alarming increase of population in case of Nagaland since 1961 onwards. There are many factors which contributed to the high growth rate of population in the region specially in case of Assam and Tripura. Among the factors the most important factor as stated earlier is immigration from the neighbouring countries. Besides inter-state migration for searching new occupation from different parts of India is continuing in this region. As far as immigration from Bangladesh is concerned formerly it was concentrated mostly in Assam and Tripura but gradually it is spreading to other States of the region specially to the foothill areas of Nagaland as these areas showed a continuous growth of population over four decades and also another main factor is the high birth rate in the State of Nagaland. After the Census Papers of 2001 became available many demographers of India attributed high birth rate as the major cause of high population growth in the State of Nagaland.

Table 6.7 below shows the estimated annual birth rate as well as Table 6.8 shows the death-rate over a period of 10 years, i.e. from 1987 to 1997 which confirms the findings of the demographers.

Table 6.7 : Estimated Annual Birth Rate (Per Thousand)

States	*Years*										
	1987	*1988*	*1989*	*1990*	*1991*	*1992*	*1993*	*1994*	*1995*	*1996*	*1997*
Arunachal Pradesh	36.3	40.0	35.6	30.1	30.9	26.6	28.0	23.5	23.8	21.9	21.4
Assam	32.9	29.4	29.7	30.9	30.8	29.5	30.8	29.3	27.6	28.2	-
Manipur	25.9	25.8	22.8	21.1	20.1	19.5	20.5	21.7	20.6	19.6	19.7
Meghalaya	34.9	36.4	31.9	31.8	32.4	29.8	28.5	29.5	29.0	30.4	30.2
Mizoram	-	-	-	-	-	-	-	-	-	15.1	15.1
Nagaland	21.7	22.3	19.7	16.2	18.5	19.2	20.0	20.1	N.A.	N.A.	N.A.
Tripura	28.2	26.6	25.7	24.9	24.4	23.1	23.3	21.9	18.9	18.4	18.3

Table 6.8 : State-wise Estimated Annual Death Rate of the North East India from 1987 to 1997 (Per Thousand)

States	*1987*	*1988*	*1989*	*1990*	*1991*	*1992*	*1993*	*1994*	*1995*	*1996*	*1997*
Arunachal Pradesh	13.2	17.2	14.2	13.2	13.2	9.4	8.9	9.9	6.0	5.5	8.3
Assam	11.8	10.4	10.5	11.5	10.4	10.2	9.2	9.6	9.6	9.9	-
Manipur	5.6	6.8	6.8	5.9	5.4	5.6	4.8	6.7	6.7	5.8	5.9
Meghalaya	9.1	9.1	11.9	7.8	8.8	8.5	6.8	7.1	8.9	8.9	8.8
Mizoram	-	-	-	-	-	-	-	-	-	3.7	4.8
Nagaland	4.9	5.0	4.1	4.1	3.3	3.8	4.7	4.3	N.A.	N.A.	N.A.
Tripura	9.2	8.1	7.7	7.1	7.6	7.6	6.4	5.3	7.7	6.5	6.8

Source: Sample Registrations Bulletins, G.O. I.

From these tables it could be assumed that the birth rates and death rates are neither high nor low except in case of Nagaland which registered a high birth rate during this decade. On the other hand, the death rates in the States of North East India have declined sharply from 1993 onward excepting a slight upward trend in the year 1997.

In general, there is no significant variation among the States regarding birth rates as well as death rates in each of the States of North East India during the decades as mentioned above.

Apart from the birth and death rates mentioned in the above tables it may be pointed out that there are many factors that are involved in the growth of population in the States of the region. Some of the factors may be categorized as biological, social, economic and political. The biological factor refers to birth and death rates difference. If birth rate remains high and death rate declines, population increases in the community or State. Social factor refers to social customs, religious beliefs and practices. In matters of marriage factors like age, type of marriage, monogamy, polygamy, polygyny, widow marriage are taken into consideration. Economic factor is related to occupation, nature of work, availability of economic resources etc. Political factor refers to State policy to control population, improvement of health care service, education etc. The natural and human events are the events like flood, earthquake, war etc. which cause high destruction of life and property. These factors are of course interrelated. Moreover, birth and death ratio is also considered as one contributing factor in this regard.

If we carefully see then we find that since Independence the various State Governments are taking active steps to improve standard of living, public health facilities and also the health care services through the establishment of hospitals, State dispensaries, sub-divisional and village level health centres. As a result of the aforesaid Government efforts the infant mortality rate in various States of the region has declined considerably and the life expectancy has also increased. In other words, the longevity of persons in the States of the region is gradually increasing due to the availability of the network of health care and public health facilities.

Rural-Urban Distribution of Population of North East India

The whole of North East India as a region experienced the process of urbanization chronologically at a posterior period than other parts of

India. During Ahom rule medieval towns like, Guwahati, Nagaon, Jorhat, Rangpur (present Sibsagar), Gargaon were there but these were not the urban centres in modern sense. After the annexation of Assam by the British as a result of the Treaty of Yandaboo and subsequent expansion of business activities including the establishment of plantation, petroleum and coal mining industries, establishment of railway junctions of Assam Bengal Railway line and also with establishment of administrative headquarters first in Assam and later in the hills of North East India the process of urbanization boosted up. After Independence during the early part of the 1970s of the last century there was an exponential growth of urban centres. As a result urban population started growing. Table 6.9 shows the distribution of population as per 2001 Census in the rural and urban region.

Table 6.9 : Rural-Urban Distribution of Population in 2001

States	*Population in 2001 (In persons)*		
	Total	*Rural*	*Urban*
Arunachal Pradesh	10, 91, 117	8, 68,420	2, 22, 697
Assam	2, 66, 38, 407	2, 32, 49, 566	33, 88, 841
Manipur	23, 06, 069	18, 18, 228	5, 70, 406
Megalaya	23, 06, 069	18, 53, 388	4, 52, 681
Mizoram	8, 91, 058	4, 49, 984	4, 41, 074
Nagaland	19, 88, 636	16, 35, 852	3, 52, 784
Tripura	31, 91, 168	26, 48, 031	5, 43, 137

Source: Calculated on the basis of the Census Figure of Urban Population/Total Population from Census, 2001.

The above table reveals some interesting facts regarding the urban distribution of population in different States of North East India. First, the rural population is much more than the urban population in all the States of the region. Secondly, the State of Mizoram contains highest number of urban population in this region as a result of regrouping of villages and putting the same in newly created areas where all urban facilities are available. It is followed by the State of Manipur where also urban population is more in comparison to other States of the region except Mizoram. Percentage-wise over three decades, i.e. from 1991 to 2001 the urban population in certain States have increased considerably as it is evident from Table 6.10 below:

Table 6.10 : Percentage of Urban Population to Total Population During 1981-2001

States	*Year*	
	1991	*2001*
Arunachal Pradesh	12.79	20.41
Assam	11.10	12.72
Manipur	27.52	23.88
Megalaya	18.60	19.63
Mizoram	46.10	49.50
Nagaland	17.21	17.74
Tripura	15.30	17.02

Source: Basic Statistics of N.E.R. of 1995 and 2002.

From the above table it is seen that population in all the States right from 1991 is increasing. In case of Mizoram there was a sharp growth of population in 1991 as it is evident from the above table and also a moderate growth in the decade of 1991-2001. Similarly, the State of Arunachal Pradesh also experienced a continuous growth of urban population since 1991. However, the rate of growth of population in all the States over the decades as shown in the previous table are not at all uniform.

Hills and Plains-wise Distribution of population in North East India

The North Eastern Region of India which covers a geographical area of 2,55,083 sq. kms, physiographically contains almost 70 per cent hill areas and rest 30 per cent are only the plains. As a result, the population distribution in the region is uneven. This has been projected in Table 6.1 of the anterior paragraph followed by the density of population of the various States of the region as projected in the Table 6.4. Now as far as hills-plains distribution of population are concerned it is to be noted that except the State of Assam, Manipur and Tripura the plain areas for human habitation are not suitably available in other States. Even within the State of Assam there are also two hill districts, viz. Karbi Anglong and North Cachar for human habitation. In Tripura except West Tripura, South Tripura and Dholai district the North Tripura is having undulating hilly terrains and hence human habitation is more in those three districts than the North Tripura district. Similarly in case of Manipur except Imphal East and Imphal West districts the other hill areas are sparsely populated.

The following table shows the Hills and Plains-wise distribution of population of the various States of the region as per 2001 Census.

Table 6.11 : *State-wise Hills and Plains Distribution of Population of North Eastern Region (In persons)*

States	*Plains Population*	*Hills Population*
Arunachal Pradesh	–	10, 96, 702
Assam	2, 56, 39, 898	9, 98, 509
Manipur	8, 33, 312	15, 55, 322
Meghalaya	–	23, 06, 069
Mizoram	–	8, 91, 058
Nagaland	–	19, 88, 636
Tripura	15, 30, 531	16, 60, 637

Source: Basic Statistics of N.E.R. of 2002 (calculated separately plains and hills population of the States taking population of the districts).

From the above table it is visible that in the State of Assam, the plains population are much more in comparison to the others viz. Tripura and Manipur. In terms of ranking of the availability of plains population, the State of Manipur occupies the third place. So far as the exclusively hill population is concerned Meghalaya comes first followed by Nagaland as is evident from Table 6.11.

Linguistically also the seven States of the North Eastern Region of India presents a varied panorama of languages which always attracts the attention of the linguists world-wide. In the North-Eastern Region of India various groups of people are living and racially they are identified as Indo-Mongoloids, Austrics, Indo-Aryans and Negritos.

However, linguistically a major chunk of the population speak Tibeto-Burman languages of the great Sino-Tibetan family language group. A small section of the people of the region speak a language of

Monkhemer origin and the rests are mainly speaking languages of Indo-Aryan origin.

Now from the standpoint of languages whose origins are depicted above, various other languages and dialects are spoken by the different ethnic groups. There are almost 319 groups of people belonging to tribes including sub-tribes of the region apart from the caste groups available in Assam plains and Tripura. All these groups speak different languages. In fact, the whole of North East India is a multi-language region where the ethnic groups speak different languages and dialects. Interestingly, in case of dialect speaking groups of the region, one also comes across village-wise variation. But in every state of the region certain major languages are having official recognition of the respective State Government. Moreover to have interaction among the tribal groups certain common spoken languages are used. The State-wise distribution of the principle languages, are given in Table 6.12 below:

Table 6.12 : Languages of Different States of North East India

States	Principle Languages
Arunachal Pradesh	Monpa, Aka, Mijiji, Sherdukpen, Nishi, Apatani, Tagin, Hill Miri-Adi, Khampti, Singpho, Tangsa, Nocte, Wancho, Idu-Mishmi, Miju, Mishimi and Digaru Mishimi,
Assam	Assamese
Manipur	Manipuri
Meghalaya	Khasi, Garo and English
Mizoram	Mizo and English
Nagaland	English, Ao, Konyak, Angami, Chang, Lotha, Sangtam, Sema and Chakhesang
Tripura	Bengali and Kok Borok

Apart from the languages stated above in different States of the region, in the States like Arunachal Pradesh and Nagaland there are no dominant native languages. As much Hindi in Arunachal Pradesh and Nagamese in Nagaland are widely used as lingua-franca among the different tribal groups of the States.

From the point of the adherence of religion by the people of the different States of the North East India it is noticed that the region itself is a multi-religious region. Here one could find numerous groups of people having various types of religious beliefs and practices. However, Hindus, Christians and Muslims are the major religious groups in the region. The distribution of religious groups in different States of North East India as per 1981 Census is given in table below:

Table 6.13 : Distribution of Religious Groups in the States of North East India

States	*Religious Groups*						
	Hindu	*Muslim*	*Christian*	*Sikh*	*Buddhist*	*Jains*	*Others*
Arunachal Pradesh	29.23	4.32	4.32	0.20	16.68	–	51.77
Assam	64.37	31.36	6.37	0.12	0.93	0.12	0.03
Manipur	60.04	6.67	0.06	0.03	0.06	0.06	3.15
Megalaya	18.02	3.10	52.61	0.12	0.20	0.04	25.76
Mizoram	7.14	0.45	83.81	0.08	80.19	–	0.23
Nagaland	14.36	1.52	80.90	–	0.07	0.15	3.68
Tripura	89.38	60.47	1.20	60.01	20.69	0.01	0.01
N.E. (Total)	40.35	7.73	32.75	8.65	3.68	0.35	12.09

From above Table 6.13 it is clear that the Hindus are highly concentrated in Assam, Tripura and Manipur; Christians in Meghalaya, Mizoram and Nagaland and Muslims are more in Assam than in the other States. In other States of the region Muslim religious groups contains a very negligible population. The other religious groups, namely Sikhs, Buddhists and Jains are very few in all the States of the region although Buddhists are comparatively more in Arunachal Pradesh (61.68%) and Sikhs in Tripura (6.01%).

Among the seven States of the region Buddhist population is found to be highest (16.68%) in Arunachal Pradesh. A large majority of Buddhists are concentrated in the districts of Tawang and West Kameng which are close to Tibet. The Buddhists of Changlang district of Eastern Arunachal Pradesh and of Assam originally belonged to the Buddhist communities of Myanmar and its neighbouring areas. Mizoram is also another State of North East India wherein two main pockets of Buddhis concentrations are found. They are situated in Chhimtuipui and Lunglei districts. In Chimtuipui district more than 28 per cent of the district's population consists of Buddhist while in Lunglei district the Buddhists share 16 per cent of the total population.

References

Census Paper 2001, Series-1 and 2.

Basic Statistics of North Eastern Region, 1995 and 2002, G.O.I., NEC Secretariat, *Shillong Sample Resistration Bulletin*, G.O.I.

Manoroma Year Book, 2005, *Malaya Manoroma,* Kottayam.

Ahmed, Aijazuddin, (1999), *Social Geography*, Rawat Publications, Jaipur.

7 Population Growth of North East India

A Geographical Analysis

Subrata Purkayastha

The most striking feature of the demographic characteristic of North East India is its high decadal growth of population, which has always been higher than the national decadal growth rate of population. It is estimated that the population of the region in 1830 was only 1 million. It grew four times to 4 million in 1901. During the last century between 1901-1991 the population of the region grew by about 8 times to 31.4 million as against 3.6 times in India as a whole (Taher *et al.*, 2001). In 2001 Census the region had a population of 38, 4995, 489 persons showing a decadal growth rate of 24.37 per cent as against the national decadal growth rate of 21.38 per cent. The growth rate however varies from State to State, e.g. the highest decadal growth rate is in the State of Nagaland (64.41 %) where it was more than double the growth rate of the nation. This high growth rate which is due to both natural increase as well as migration-induced has a great impact not only on the demographic composition of the region but also socio- economic consequences which are often reflected in political turmoil and consequent conflicts witnessed in the entire region.

This paper is an attempt to study the trend in the growth of population, the factors responsible for the high growth rate and some of the demographic, socio-economic and environmental implication arising out of this. This paper examines the high growth rate of population in the region from 1951 Census onwards in general (as this region experienced a large scale population re-distribution associated with the Partition of India in 1947) and from 1971 Census in particular (as the region once again experienced large scale exodus of population from the erstwhile East Pakistan, majority of whom subsequently went back to the newly created independent nation of Bangladesh).

Regional Setting

North East India lying between 20° N–29.30° North latitude and 89.46° E–97.30° East longitude consists of the seven sister States of Assam, Meghalaya, Nagaland, Mizoram, Manipur, Arunachal Pradesh and Tripura. (In this paper Sikkim has been omitted though otherwise in the recent past Sikkim has been added to North East for policy-matters only). The region has an area of 255037 sq. km (7% of the geographical area of the country) and supports a population size of 38,495,489 (accounting for about 4% of the total population of India) (2001 Census). The region holds a strategic position (hemmed by China in the north, Bhutan in the north-west, Myanmar in the east and Bangladesh in the south and south-east) by having international borders on all sides except the west where it is linked up with the mainland of India by a narrow corridor of about 40 km. width along the Bhutan and Nepal Himalayan Foothill. The region lies where South East Asia ends and South Asia begins, hence the region can be compared to a gateway connecting the subcontinent of India with South East Asia. Here the brown and the yellow races mingle resulting to a highly diversified socio-cultural scenario. There are about 209 indigenous tribes belonging to various racial stocks speaking about 420 languages and dialects which can be traced to diversified linguistic groups and sub-group such as Mon-Khmer speaking Austro Asiatic population represented by the Khasis and Jaintias, the Indo-Aryan linguistic groups of the India mainland, Tibeto-Burman linguistic groups of Mongoloid origin (represented by four distinct branches). These Mongoloid groups probably immigrated to the region from the north and east through the numerous mountain passes. The Indo-Aryans came from the west while the Tai Ahoms entered this region around 1228 A.D. and established their kingdom in the Brahmaputra Valley that lasted till 1826 A.D. Around 17th and 18th centuries came another small groups of Tai people who are now found to be living in Arunachal Pradesh. Around 19th century another significant tribal group of Kukichin, Naga and Kachin immigrated to this region through the present Myanmar to occupy the present Manipur, Mizoram, Nagaland and the eastern districts of Arunachal Pradesh (Taher *et al.*, 2001).

The North East is also characterized by highly diversified physical features. The plains of Brahmaputra, Barak, Imphal Valley and Tripura cover an area of 6878528 sq. km. (accounting for 28% of the region's total area). The Plateau of Meghalaya and Karbi Anglong uplands cover an area of about 32282 sq. km. (approximately 12 per cent of the region's total area) and the rest of the area of about 153970 sq. km. (approximately 60% of the region's total area) are predominantly hilly and mountainous in character having thick vegetation which is intercepted by deep and inaccesible valleys.

Though the region is characterized by socio-economic backwardness and political instability yet it has witnessed a significantly high decadal growth rate of population when compared to the national decadal growth rate in almost all the Census (Table 7.1).

Growth of Population and its Spatial Variation

A cursory glance at the population distribution (Table 7.1) suggests that more than 2/3 of the population are living in the plains. It can be inferred from Table 7.2 that the region had always experienced a higher decadal variation of population when compared to the rest of the

Table 7.1 : Population Distribution among the States of North East India (2001 Census)

States	*Total Population*	*Percentage Share to Total Population of NE*	*Density Persons/sq. km.*
Assam	26638407	69.19	340
Tripura	3191168	8.29	304
Manipur	2388068	6.21	107
Meghalaya	2306069	5.99	103
Nagaland	1988636	5.17	120
Arunachal Pradesh	1096702	2.85	13
Mizoram	891058	2.31	42
North East (Total)	3850018	3.75	151
India	1027015245		312

Source: Census of India (2001), Percentage Share calculated by the Author.

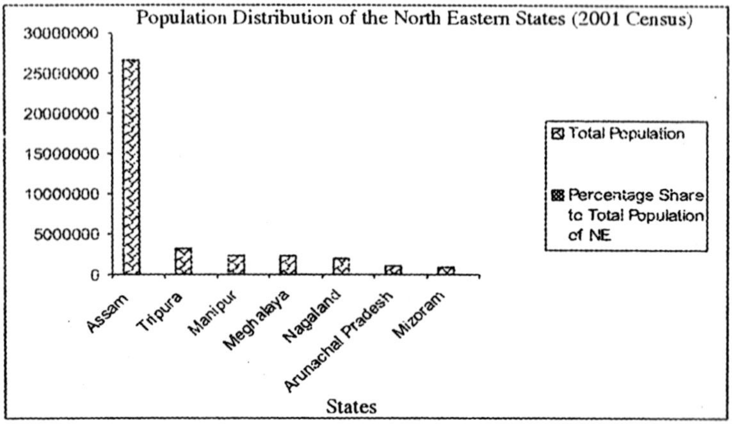

country. It is observed that during the decade of 1951–61, following the Partition the entire region recorded a higher decadal growth (41.32%) rate than the national average (21.51). In fact the states of Assam (34.98%) and Tripura (78.71%) recorded the highest decadal growth rate of the country. The subsequent decades show a fall in the region's growth rate with a slight increase of about 0.72 per cent in the 1981–91 decade. The 1991–2001 decade shows a further fall of about 2.56 per cent from the previous Census, and the difference between the decadal national growth rate and the growth rate of north-east is narrowing down from 19.81 per cent in 1951-61 to about 2.83 per cent in the last Census.

However, this growth rate is not even over space. Certain States in the North East are showing highly explosive growth rate in the last decade. As earlier pointed out, Nagaland had the highest growth rate of above 50 per cent in the last two decades. The present decade indicates that the growth rate of Nagaland has increased by about 12.45 per cent from the previous Census. The 1991–2001 Census suggests that except the States of Assam (18.92%) and Tripura (16.03%) rest of the States have a decadal growth rate which is higher than the national decadal growth rate of 21.54 per cent. (Nagaland 64.53%, Arunachal Pradesh 27.00%, Manipur 24.86%, Meghalaya 30.65%, and Mizoram, 28.32%)

The exponential annual average growth rate of the region in the last decade (1991–2001) works out to be 2.02 per cent as against the national exponential annual average growth rate of 1.95 per cent. This, however, as stated earlier varies from State to State (Table 7.2).

Table 7.2 : Average Annual Exponential Growth Rate of the North Eastern States (1971–2001)

States	*1971–81*	*1981–91*	*1991–2001*
Arunachal Pradesh	3.01	3.14	2.39
Assam	2.10	2.17	1.73
Manipur	2.81	2.57	2.22
Meghalaya	2.78	2.84	2.67
Mizoram	3.96	3.34	2.53
Nagaland	4.06	4.45	4.98
Tripura	2.77	2.95	1.49
India	2.20	2.14	1.93

Source: Basic Statistics of North Eastern Region (NEC).

Taking 1971 Census as the base the growth rate from 1971–2001 of the region has been to the tune of 97.21 per cent as against the country's growth of 87.36 per cent during the same period. This however varies from State to State ranging between 82.14 per cent in Assam to 285.47 per cent in Nagaland followed by Mizoram (168.37%), Meghalaya (127.87%), Arunachal Pradesh (134.18%) and Tripura (105.08%).

A district-level analysis further helps us in understanding the marked variation in population growth among the different States of the region as well as different areas of the State.

At present there are 72 districts in the seven mentioned States of North East. In the last decade (1991–2001) population growth has been as high as 95.16 per cent in Wokha district of Nagaland, though all the districts of Nagaland have shown a very high growth rate of above 45 per cent. In Arunachal Pradesh out of 13 districts, Papum Pare district records the highest decadal growth rate of 67.56 per cent. There were only 4 districts, viz. East Kameng (13.46%), Upper Subansiri (10.50%), Lower Subansiri (15.55%) and Tirap (17.33%) where the decadal growth rate was less than the national average in the last decade. Manipur consisting of 9 districts has only three districts having a decadal growth rate less than the national average while the rest of the 6 districts have seen a higher growth rate than the national average and it ranges between 66.62 per cent in Chandel to 23.87 per cent in Thoubal district. Like-wise all the 7 districts of Meghalaya recorded a higher population growth rate than the national decadal growth rate. In Mizoram all districts except Mamit and Serchipp have a relatively higher growth rate ranging between 38.07 per cent in Aizawl to 23.16 per cent in Lunglei. In the States of Assam and Tripura that recorded a lower growth rate than national average, there are 8 districts (7 districts in Assam and 1 district in Tripura) where the decadal growth rate (1991–2001) was slightly above the national average of 21.54 per cent.

Table 7.3 : District-wise Decadal Growth Rate and Density of Population of the North Eastern States (1991–2001)

Districts	*Growth Rate in % (1991–2001)*	*Density of Population in Persons/sq. km.*
Assam		
Kokrajhar	12	256
Dhubri	23.63	585
Goalpara	23.03	450
Bongaigaon	12.05	420
Barpeta	18.87	508
Kamrup	26.11	580
Nalbari	13.03	509
Darrang	15.82	432
Marigaon	21.35	500
Nagaon	22.26	500
Sonitpur	18.06	316
Lakhimpur	18.30	390
Dhemaji	19.45	176
Tinsukia	19.51	303
Dibrugarh	13.68	350
Sibsagar	15.83	394
Jorhat	14.69	350
Golaghat	14.27	270
Karbi Anglong	22.72	77
North Cachar Hills	24.72	38
Cachar	18.89	382
Karimganj	21.87	557
Hailakandi	20.89	409
Tripura		
West Tripura	18.48	512
South Tripura	6.78	251

(Contd...)

(Contd...)

Dhalai	10.96	128
North Tripura	26.49	290
Nagaland		
Mon	74.12	145
Tuensang	78.11	98
Mokokchong	46.54	144
Zunheboto	60.01	122
Wokha	95.16	99
Dimapur	73.66	333
Kohima	47.92	100
Phek	45.07	73
Manipur		
Senapati	36.09	87
Tamenglong	29.23	25
Churachandpur	29.36	50
Bishnupur	15.27	420
Thoubal	23.87	708
Imphal West	16.70	856
Imphal East	19.49	557
Ukhrul	28.83	31
Arunachal Pradesh		
Tawang	37.60	17.92
West Kameng	32.22	10
East Kameng	13.46	14
Paum Pare	67.56	35
Lower Subansiri	18.13	10
Upper Subansiri	10.50	8
West Siang	15.55	12
East Siang	21.61	24
Upper Siang	20.10	5
Dibang Valley	34.02	4
Lohit	30.83	13
Changlang	31.29	27
Tirap	17.33	42
Meghalaya		
West Garo Hills	28.62	140
East Garo Hills	32.70	96

(Contd...)

(Contd...)

South Garo Hills	31.02	55
West Khasi Hills	33.05	56
Ri Bhoi	51.43	81
East Khasi Hills	23.41	234
Jaintia Hills	35.67	78
Mizoram		
Mamit	– 2.77	20
Kolasib	35.25	48
Aizawl	38.07	91
Champhai	29.88	34
Serchip	17.63	38
Lunglei	23.16	30
Lawnghtlai	35.83	29
Saiha	33.67	44

Source: Basic Statistics of NER, NEC, Shillong. Density of Population calculated by the Author.

Factors Responsible for the High Growth

The high growth rate of population is obviously not only due to natural increase alone but also due to a high rate of migration into the region both from within and outside the country.

Natural Increase

With Independence the region like rest of the country has experienced sharp fall in death rates with slow decline of birth rates and this has contributed significantly to the increased population growth rate. The life expectancy at birth has increased. In Assam (which has more than 68 per cent of the total population of North East) life expectancy has increased from 32.7 years during the time of Independence to about 56 years (2002 World Bank Report) as against nation's life expectancy of 62 years. The IMR of Assam has reduced from 118/1000 in 1978 to about 78/1000 in 2002 as against the country's average of 126/1000 and 63/1000 respectively.

Table 7.4 shows the natural increase of population for the North Eastern States for the year 2001. It is observed that out of the 7 States

Table 7.4 : Estimated Crude Birth Rate and Death Rate/1000 persons (North-Eastern States, 2001)

States	*CBR*	*CDR*	*Natural Increase*
Assam	27.0	9.6	17.4
Tripura	16.1	5.6	10.6
Manipur	18.3	5.2	13.1
Meghalaya	28.3	9.0	19.3
Nagaland	NA	NA	NA
Arunachal Pradesh	22.2	5.7	16.5
Mizoram	15.7	4.4	11.3

Source : Office of the Registrar-General, India.

it is only Meghalaya which is having about 2 per thousand higher natural growth rate of 19.3/1000 against the national average of 17.3/1000 (SRS Data Year 2000). Assam has marginally higher natural growth of 17.4/1000. While the rest of the States Arunachal Pradesh (13.1), Manipur (12.7), Mizoram (11.7) and Tripura (11.1) have a natural growth rate below the national average. Thus the high growth of population is not only due to natural increase that is almost at par with the national trend with slight deviation from year to year. Hence, migration do play a significant role in the higher growth rate of population in the region.

Table 7.5 : Estimated Crude Birth Rate and Crude Death Rate/1000 persons (India, 1991–2001)

Years	*Crude Birth Rate*	*Crude Death Rate*	*Natural Increase*
1991	29.5	9.8	19.7
1992	29.2	10.1	19.1
1993	28.7	9.3	19.4
1994	28.7	9.3	19.4
1995	28.3	9.0	18.5
1996	27.5	9.0	18.3
1997	27.2	8.9	18.3
1998	26.5	9.0	17.5
1999	26.1	8.7	17.4
2000	25.8	8.5	17.3
2001	25.4	8.4	17

Source : Basic Statistics of North Eastern Region, NEC.

Taking 1951 population as the base and the national birth rates and death rates as the norms, it is estimated that within 1951–1991 about 8 million people of the region were migrants (Sharma *et al.*, 1997).

Taking 1991 population as the base and the national decadal natural increase of 20.29/1000 (1991-2001). It is observed that in the last decade about 16.81 per cent (64,71,338 persons) of the total population of North East were migrants (Table 7.6), the share of migrants however varies from State to State. Of the total population (2001 Census) Nagaland had the highest number of migrants (37.63%) followed by Meghalaya (22.10%), Manipur (21.95%), Mizoram (21.43%), Arunachal Pradesh (20.14%), Assam (14.16%), and Tripura (12.17%).

Migration thus turns out to be distinct factor contributing to this high growth of population and it has a long historical background which can be divided into colonial phase and post-independence phase for the convenience of our study.

Table 7.6 : Estimation of Migrant Population in the States of North East India, 2001

States	*Base Year Population (1991)*	*Actual Population (2001)*	*Expected Population (2001)*	*Access Population (Migrants)*	*Percentage of Migrants to Total Population*
Arunachal Pradesh	858392	1096702	875809	220893	20.14
Assam	22294562	26638407	22746919	3891488	14.61
Manipur	1826714	2388068	1863778	524290	21.95
Meghalaya	1760626	2306069	1796349	509720	22.10
Mizoram	686217	891058	700140	190918	21.43
Nagaland	1215573	1988636	1240237	748399	37.63
Tripura	2744827	3188636	2800520	388116	12.17
NE (Total)	31386911	38495089	32023751	6471338	16.81

Source : Calculated by the Author.

Colonial Phase

Before the British annexed Assam and brought under its rule around

1826, immigration was not very high as there was no economic necessity. During the British Rule–labourers, technicians, clerks etc. had to be imported from rest of the country. With the advent of the Tea Industry in last decade of the 19th century and early part of 20th century the British imported tea garden labourers from the Central Indian tribal belt as the local population did not like to work due to low wage and inhospitable jungle terrain (Gopalakrishnan *et al.*, 2002). This group of tribal migrant from Central India later settled here and constituted the various tea tribes of Assam. The next group constituting the East Bengal Muslims were attracted to the virgin alluvial low lying land prone to water logging and converted these wastelands into rich agricultural lands producing jute and vegetables. Assam during the early part of 19th century had low density of population due to high mortality rate and unhealthy climate while adjoining East Bengal (Bangladesh) was densely populated. Hence the surplus agrarian population from these adjoining areas came to settle here. The Nepalese were inducted to the region as soldiers in the British army or to work as chowkidars and other petty services and they later settled here. The literate Bengalees from the adjoining region were brought here by the British as lower officials to man the administration and other ancillary industrial development like communication networks, petroleum industry etc. The Rajasthanis mainly from Marwar region came here during the colonial phase to trade, while the other communities from the country (mainly from plains of Northern India) came to the region with the advent of the British rule to render their services as washerman, barbers, cobblers etc.

Independence Phase

With Indian Independence in 1947 and the partition of the country on communal lines this region experienced an exodus of immigration of the Hindu population from erstwhile East Pakistan. At the time of partition Tripura had sheltered about 1 lakh refugees from the then East Pakistan (Census of India, 1951). In 1947 the estimated refugees were about 1.14 lakh in Assam, out of which majority were settled in Cachar district.

Post-Independence

The decades after Independence marked a new stage of demographic development in the region. The decade 1951–61 witnessed an unprecedented volume of migration when the population growth of the region shot up by 41.32 per cent as against the nation's growth rate of 21.51 per cent, which can be attributed to the consistent flow of migrants from the erstwhile East Pakistan (which was facing communal conflicts targeting the minorities) as well from within the country as a number of Central Government offices were established.

Mass migration of population again affected this region in 1970s when mutual antagonism between Bengali and non-Bengali population over economic and political issues led to the civil war in East Pakistan and ultimately resulted in the Independence of Bangladesh in 1971. It is estimated that about 10 million people left their hearth in East Pakistan for the adjoining areas of India. In the following year with the liberation of Bangladesh most of them returned back but their exact number is however not known (Elahi *et al.,* 1991).

However illegal immigration to this region continues unabated over the decades. The location of the region between South and South East Asia attracts migrants from the neighbouring countries. The boundary of adjoining Bangladesh is more political than natural. There are large numbers of streams flowing from this area to the Bangladesh and the mighty Brahmaputra, which is highly braided in its lower course result in the formation of low lying alluvial deposits locally termed as *chars*. These *chars* are highly fertile and attract the agrarian population from the neighbouring areas. Bangladesh is having environmental ethos similar to that of this region of India. Bangladesh is characterized by higher degree of poverty with lower economic development marked by traditional agrarian economy coupled with environmental problems and high growth of population leading to higher density distribution, thus the surplus population often enters the adjoining region as illegal migrants. Moreover, the earlier immigrants from erstwhile East Bengal who occupy the older char lands often give physical and social shelter to these illegal immigrants. Once inside the region the illegal immigrants get settled and mingle with the earlier comers from the same origin. With high density of population especially in the plains, which support more than 2/3rd population of the region, the surplus population is now moving into the relatively isolated pockets of North East India. This is indicated by the high growth rate of population of States—Nagaland, Arunachal Pradesh etc.

Impact

The excessive nature of population growth both due to natural increase and migration has exerted a great influence on the demographic as well as socio-economic character of the region. In spite of the fact that the percentage of urban population is low here (15.45% as against the country's 27.70%) the urban growth rate is very high suggesting high rate of migration these urban centres. This has resulted in a highly unbalanced sex ratio especially in the urban areas of Arunachal Pradesh (894), Nagaland (909). The declining sex ratio in the context of rapid population growth suggests that there has been a massive male migration, either as sojourners or as permanent residents to this region in the last few decades.

The man-land ratio is increasing in the region. In fact the State of Assam records a higher density (340 persons/sq.km) when compared to the national average (324 persons/sq.km).

The physiological and agricultural density are on the rise, the average size of the land holding has come down from 1.71 hectares in 1970-71 to 1.64 hectares in 1980-81.

Due to higher growth rate of population the forested areas, hill slopes and other marginal areas has been encroached upon resulting in loss of forest cover, land degradation and loss of bio-diversity causing ecological imbalance.

The explosive population growth is halting the pace of socio-economic development of the region. Here about 50 per cent of its main workers are still dependent on traditional agriculture practices and in spite of the high dependency on the agricultural sector there is foodgrain deficiency in the region as the production is not compatible with the rapid population growth (Agarwal, 1987).

References

Gopalakrishnan, R. and Ali, Ahmed, (ed.) (2001) *Essays in Indian Geography: Continuity of Traditions*. Regency Pub., N. Delhi.

Basic Statistics of North-Eastern Region (1980, 1990, 2000 and 2002), Shillong, NEC.

Sharma, H.N. and Dey, P. (1997) Pattern of Population Growth in North East India, *Demographic Transition the third world, scenario ed.* Aizazuddin Ahmed *et al.* Rawat Publications, New Delhi.

Where Do We Stand in 2003 Meghalaya and *NE* and *India* and *the World,* Directorate of Economics and Statistics, Govt. of Meghalaya, Shillong, 2004.

Elahi, K.M. and Sultana, S. (1985) Population Redistribution and Settlement Changes in South Asia: A Historical Evaluation. *Population Redistribution and Development in South Asia*. ed. Leezek A. Kosinsiki *et al.*, 1985, Rawat Pub., Jaipur.

Census of India 2001.

8 Population Growth and Forest Degradation in North East India

Somnath Hazra and *Raj Kumar Sen*

Introduction

In the developing countries, poverty is the main reason for forest degradation, but the north-east region of India gives a different picture, where population growth is the main factor for forest degradation. It is also one of the obstacles to the economic development. In the North East Region of India, the growth rate of population is higher than the country, not because of the increase in fertility rate (infact the fertility rate of hill people is lower than that of the others), but because of migration from the neighbouring States and countries. This is aggravated further as by nature; north-eastern people usually do not move outside the region. The North-East India consists of eight States. These are Arunachal Pradesh, Assam, Meghalaya, Manipur, Tripura, Mizoram, Nagaland and Sikkim. Border of North East India meets the borders of South and South East Asia and near about 98 per cent border of this region meets the international border. Because of this reason legal and illegal migration is easy and natural. Increase in the rate of growth of population means the population density is increasing. To meet the daily necessities and habitation more land is needed, which is the main cause of encroaching the forest land or forest degradation. Our main emphasis is to find out the existence of triangular relationship (migration-population-growth-forest degradation) in the North East India. This paper is divided into four sections. In the first section, we discuss the population dynamics and the relation between migration and population growth of North East India while section 2 deals with the relationship between the population growth and forest degradation. Section 3 addresses the triangular relationship and the last section is for conclusion.

1. Population Dynamics and the Relation between Migration and Population Growth of North East India

The area covered by North Eastern Region of India is near about 2,62, 379 sq. km. and bio-geographically it is divided into two zones, (1) Eastern Himalaya and (2) rest of North East India, which is based on natural composition and climate. The first zone is comprised Arunachal Pradesh and Sikkim, and the second zone is comprised Assam, Nagaland, Manipur, Meghalaya, Mizoram and Tripura. The second zone is most significant zone because it is connected with the India, Indo-Malayan, Indo-Chinese bio-geographic regions as well as a meeting place of Himalayan Mountains. According to the literature, population dynamics of North Eastern Region of India has two basic components. These are (1) dynamics through natural process and (2) dynamics through induced process. If we consider the natural growth rate of population from the First Plan to the last census it is found that the rate of growth of population of North Eastern Region has been higher than the rate of whole country. The increasing trend of growth rate of population is not because of the natural process but mainly due to migration from neighbouring States and countries. From Table 8.1, we have seen the population growth of North Eastern Region in three decades.

Table 8.1: Population of North East India in three Decades

States of North East India	*Population (in '000s)*		
	1981	*1991*	*2001*
Arunachal Pradesh	632	865	1091
Assam	18041	22414	26638
Manipur	1421	1837	2389
Meghalaya	1336	1775	2306
Mizoram	494	690	891
Nagaland	775	1210	1981
Tripura	2053	2757	3191
Sikkim	316	406	541
Total	*25068*	*31945*	39028

Source: TATA Statistical Handbook 2002-2003.

Migration is one of the important factors that has moulded the relationship among the countries and regions of South East Asia. People move both voluntarily and involuntarily for various reasons, like cultural, racial, linguistic, economic and political. No country in the world will say that it has not seen any type of migration. It is a common phenomenon. It may be intra-state or transboundary, transcontinental and may be temporary or continuous. The four countries of South East and East Asia, i.e. China, Myanmar, Bhutan and Bangladesh have links with the region. According to the Census Report we can say that throughout this period immigration continued. It may be proved by the sex ratio of some States of North Eastern Region. In 2002 according to Forehands and Barbora, it is found that the sex ratio of the indigenous population of Arunachal Pradesh is higher than the national average, but it is much lower when the State is taken as a whole. For example, in 2001 according to this study the sex ratio was 955 among the Angami of Nagaland and 1,095 among the Aka of Arunachal Pradesh. However, in 1991 it was 890 in Nagaland as a whole and 861 in Arunachal Pradesh and according to 2001 Census Report it raised marginally i.e. 909 and 901, respectively. Single male migration is one of the reasons for their low overall sex ratio. The marginal increase in 2001 is almost certainly because of the lower rate of migration in 1990s. From Table 8.2 it is found that the average decennial population growth in these States confirms immigration. For example, the Nagaland population rose by 39.88 per cent in the 1960s, 50.05 per cent in the 1970s. 56.08 per cent in the 1980s and 64.41 per cent in 1991-2001, obviously because of migration or induced growth, not natural growth and it may be proved by the data on religion. In 1951 the tribal population of Arunachal Pradesh was 90 per cent and it is found that it declined to 64 per cent in 2001. Most of the population come from the tribal religion, and near about 37.64 per cent of the population was Hindu in 1991, which coincides with the non-tribal population, i.e. 36 per cent. According to the 2001 Census an extensive rise of population in the Muslim majority districts of Assam took place due to influx of Bangladeshi Muslims. Similarly, Hindu Bangladeshis are entering into Tripura and its percentage of tribal population has declined from 58 per cent in 1951 to 30 per cent in 2001.

Table 8.2 : Growth Rate of Population in North East India: 1951–2001

States	*Growth Rate of Population*				
	1951-61	*1961-71*	*1971-81*	*1981-91*	*1991-2001*
Assam	34.98	34.95	23.36**	24.24**	18.85
Arunachal Pradesh*	–	38.91	35.15	36.83	26.21
Manipur	35.04	37.53	32.46	29.29	30.02
Meghalaya	27.03	31.50	32.04	32.86	29.94
Mizoram	35.61	24.93	48.55	39.70	29.18
Nagaland	14.07	39.88	50.05	56.08	64.41
Tripura	78.71	36.28	31.92	34.30	15.74
Sikkim***	17.76	29.38	50.77	28.97	32.98
North-East Total	38.04	35.04	26.40	27.46	22.02
India	21.51	24.80	24.69	23.82	21.34

Notes :

* Census was conducted for the first time in 1961.

** Since Census was not conducted in Assam in 1981, the rates for 1971-1981 and 1981-91 are estimated on the basis of interpolation.

*** The data for Sikkim is incorporated from different Census Reports.

Source: Archana Upadhya (2006).

According to Hazarika (2000) in the early part of the last century migration from Bangladesh became illegal and continuing the flow of population from Bangladesh into India's North Eastern Region was the most important factor of transforming the demographic, cultural and religious profile of this region. It is estimated that the number of illegal migrants in Assam alone varies from 4-5 millions to 10-14 millions. Some researchers have found that the illegal migration from Bangladesh to Assam and other North Eastern States are overestimated in public debates, and they have some doubts regarding the authenticity of the Census data on migration. Since Independence the demographic change and growth rate of population show that in general, the responsibility goes to illegal migration from neighbouring countries to North East India. According to Archana Upadhya (2006), "the high growth rate of population in Tripura during 1951-61 (78.71 per cent), for example, can be explained in terms of migration of Hindu refugees from East Pakistan (Now Bangladesh) in the aftermath of Partition. Secondly, in Assam, the percentage share of Hindus in total population has come down from 72.51 per cent in 1971 to 67.13 per cent in 1991, while those of Muslims and Christians have increased from 24.56 and 2.61 per cent in 1971 to

28.43 and 3.32 per cent in 1991, respectively. While the high growth rate of Christians in the State (95.37 per cent) during 1971-91 might have been contributed, to some extent, by conversion, the high growth rate of (77.42 per cent) Muslims is attributed to migration of Muslim population from Bangladesh. In other States of North East India too, there also has been a rise in the share of Muslim population during the past few decades. Thirdly, in many of the districts of Assam bordering Bangladesh as usually high growth of Muslim population has been noted and their share in total population has increased appreciably, particularly during the post-1971 period."[2]

According to the Census report it is found that the percentage of migrant of Bangladeshi origin and other neighbouring countries is higher in the North Eastern States than the whole country. According to Walter Fernandes (2005) "in 1981, 5.68 per cent of the Arunachal Pradesh population was of foreign origin (including the Chakma) and 14.13 per cent were immigrants from other Indian States outside the north-east. In Assam their proportion was 6.68 per cent and 8.92 per cent, respectively. Only in Tripura the immigrants of foreign (mostly Hindu Bangladeshi) were 22.67 per cent of the population and those from the rest of India were 1.66 per cent."[3] According to 2001 Census report total legal migration from neighbouring countries which are connected with North Eastern Region of India, viz. Bangladesh, Bhutan, China, Mynmar are 3084826, 8337, 23721, 49086 respectively.

2. Relationship between the Population Growth and Forest Degradation

Total forest cover of North Eastern Region of India is 64 per cent of the total geographical area and is called a forest surplus region of India, which comprises 25.7 per cent forest cover of the country. Due to increase in population pressure in that region the forest cover is rapidly decreasing from the entire region. According to Forest Survey of India, near about 1800 sq. km. forest cover got decreased between 1991 and 1999 (Table 8.3). From 1991 to 1999 assessment report, it is found that the maximum loss of forest in North Eastern Region has occurred in the assessment of 1993-1995, i.e. 783 sq.km. Not only the forest cover but also quality of forest is deteriorating and dense forests are becoming open forests or scrub. The area of forest cover recorded during the past 5 assessments in the years 1991 to 1999 by the Forest Survey of India is given in Table 8.3.

Table 8.3 : Scenario of Forest Cover changes in North East India during the past 5 Assessments

N.E. States	*Forest Cover (1999 Assessment)*	*Change during different Assessments*			
		1991-93	*1993-95*	*1995-97*	*1997-99*
Arunachal Pradesh	68,847	-96	-43	-19	+245
Assam	23,688	-243	-447	-237	-136
Manipur	17,384	-64	-63	-140	-34
Meghalaya	15,633	-106	-55	-57	-24
Mizoram	18,338	-156	-121	+199	-437
Nagaland	14,164	+27	-57	-70	-57
Sikkim	3,118	N.A.	N.A.	+2	-11
Tripura	10, 486	+3	0	+8	+199
Total	166917	-635	-783	-314	-289

Source: State of Forest Report 1999, 1997.

Population growth is one of the major factors affecting forest cover throughout the North Eastern Region and the population density is also increasing; therefore, the additional people put pressure on the region's forests to meet the food and habitation. Side by side urbanization has been growing rapidly over the past few decades in this region at a rate of 15 to 20 per cent a year, and the rural population has also been increasing. If we see the population figures the North Eastern Region during 20th century, we find that in most of the North Eastern States population has been increasing eight to ten times. If we consider the Census Statistics during 1991 and 2001, it is seen that in many States the population density increased near about 30 per cent. The increasing population pressure and density of population reflect the per capita availability of forestland. If we consider during 1981-1995, we see that the availability of forestland is decreasing in the North Eastern Region of India; it is found that the rate of decrease of forestland was near about 50 per cent in Nagaland and Meghalaya, and 30 per cent or more in Mizoram, Manipur, and Assam. From this data we can understand the impact of population growth on forest land. Due to increase in population pressure, agricultural activity is also increasing. Jhum or shifting cultivation, a traditional system of agriculture of North Eastern Region, is one of the reasons for the loss of forest cover. For shifting cultivation to meet the food of increased population, more and more land is needed. From Table 8.4

Table 8.4 : Population Change in the North Eastern Region

States	*Population Density 1991 (per km²)*	*Population Density 2001 (per km²)*	*Total Population 1901*	*Total Population 1991*	*Total Population 2001*
Arunachal Pradesh	10	13	–	864,558	1,091,117
Assam	184	320	32,89,680	22,414,322	26,638,407
Manipur	82	107	284,465	1,837,149	2,388,634
Meghalaya	79	103	340,524	1,774,778	2,306,069
Mizoram	–	–	–	689,756	891,058
Nagaland	73	120	101,550	1,209,546	1,988,636
Sikkim	–	–	59,014	406,457	540,493
Tripura	263	304	173,325	2,757,205	3,171,168

Source: Development and Growth in North East India: The Natural Resources, Water and Environment Nexus, Strategy Report, January 2007, World Bank.

we see the incidence of increasing population pressure as well as increasing rate of population density during 1991-2001 and due to this the per capita forest is decreasing in the North Eastern Region and the forest area has been encroached for shifting cultivation. This is clear from Table 8.5 which shows that the per capita availability of

Table 8.5 : Per Capita availability of Forese Land

States	*1981 (ha)*	*1995 (ha)*
Arunachal Pradesh	10.28	6.00
Assam	0.13	0.14
Manipur	1.26	0.83
Meghalaya	1.17	0.54
Mizoram	3.68	2.32
Nagaland	1.85	0.71
Sikkim	–	–
Tripura	0.26	0.23

Source: Development and Growth in North East India: The Natural Resources, Water and Environment Nexus, Strategy Report, January 2007, World Bank.

forest land has gone down in each and every State of this region during 1981-95, the decrease being the highest for Arunachal Pradesh. Table 8.6 also shows that during 1987-97, 12.6 per cent of forest area was under Jhum cultivation on average in this region.

Table 8.6 : Forest Areas and Jhum Cultivation in the North Eastern Region

States	*Total Forest Area (km²)*	*Area Under Jhum 1987-1997 (Km²)*	*% of Forest Area Under Jhum (1987-1997)*
Arunachal Pradesh	51, 500	2, 300	4.5
Assam	27, 000	1, 300	4.8
Manipur	17, 440	3, 600	20.7
Meghalaya	95, 00	1, 800	18.9
Mizoram	15, 900	3, 800	23.9
Nagaland	8, 600	3, 900	45.3
Sikkim	3, 118	–	–
Tripura	7, 000	600	8.6
Total	140, 018	17, 300	12.6

Source: Development and Growth in North East India: The Natural Resources, Water and Environment Nexus, Strategy Report, January 2007, World Bank.

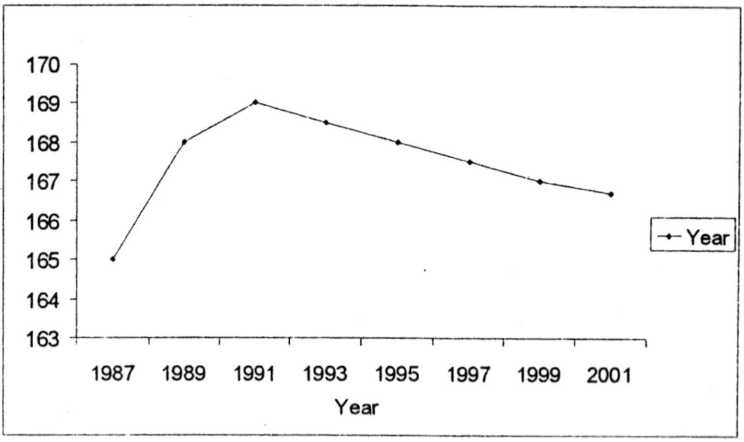

Figure 8.1: Forest cover over time, North Eastern India

Source: Development and Growth in North East India: The Natural Resources, Water and Environment Nexus, Strategy Report, January 2007, World Bank.

Figure 8.1 has given a diagramatic representation of the forest cover for the period 1987-2001 in North East India. This figure shows that it has increased initially during 1987-91 though at a declining rate but after 1991 it has declined continuously. The State specific annual percentage changes in the forest cover shows that barring some isolated fluctuations (ex-Tripura) there has been an uniformity in such changes experienced by the individual States.

3. Triangular Relationship (Migration-Population Growth-Forest Degradation)

From Section 1 it is clear that the population growth in North Eastern India is very much associated with migration. The data of North Eastern Region of India reveal that the migration is the primary reason for increasing the population pressure in this region. As population grows more and more agricultural land will be taken out of production and converted to habitation. To meet the needs of excess population, forests are degraded even though 64 per cent of the total geographical area is covered by forest in North Eastern Region. Since migration to North East India increases the population density of the area, it affects the forest. The degree of forest degradation of this region depends upon population density, as suggested by the theories of Malthus, Boserup and others. In the analysis of the possible impacts of population growth on forests of North Eastern Region, different measures of environmental degradation may be used, but in our paper the focus is on deforestation. In fact it is the most studied impact because deforestation is associated with a significant loss of bio-diversity, soil erosion and global warming. If we consider the global status, according to World Bank Report of 1991, we see that 60 per cent of recent deforestation in the developing world may be for increasing the agricultural activity, 20 per cent for logging operations like mining, petroleum etc. and 20 per cent for houschold use of fuelwood. Migration to the forest frontier followed by large-scale forest degradation has also been documented in other countries, including Guatemala, Panama, Costa Rica, Ecuador, Maxico, Indonesia, Thailand, Nepal, the Philippines, Nigeria, and United Republic of Tanzania and the Sudan. Population growth, migration and deforestation have provided numerous examples in which the migration of farmers to the agricultural sector has resulted in tropical deforestation in dryland areas which is main cause of land slide in north-eastern hill region. These examples also indicate the crucial role of natural resource endowments and their conservation policy, institutions, local and national policy and, in some cases, international markets and cultural factors. Given that many of the areas being settled are characterized by extraordinary bio-diversity and that tropical forests also play crucial roles in determining climate patterns and in preventing global warming, it is important to address the root causes of the migration that leads to deforestation. For this purpose the triangular relationship as noted above needs to be understood properly as this model is of particular application in this area of North East India. The schematic Diagram is as follows.

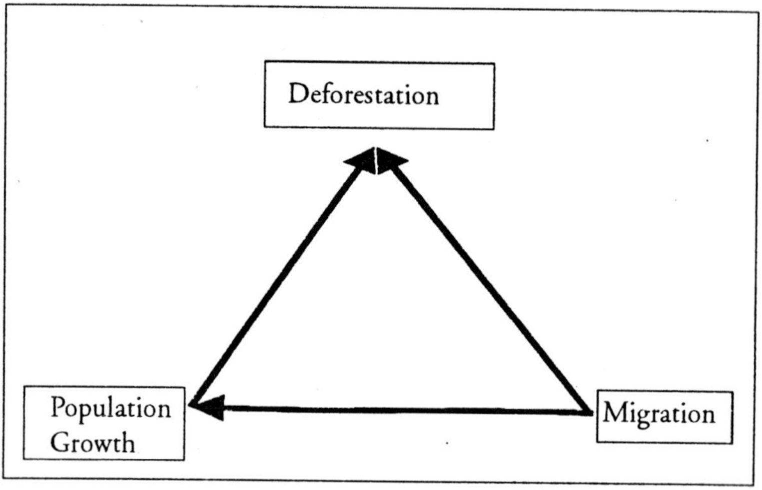

Figure 8.2: Schematic Diagram of Triangular Relationship between Migration, Population Growth and Deforestation in North East India

4. Summary and Conclusions

This paper has examined the relationship between migration, population pressure and forest degradation in the North East Region of India. It also examined the factors that influence encroachment into forest areas and the consequences of population pressure on the forest eco-systems and environment of the North Eastern Region. The paper has also attempted to explain the changing nature of migration and settlement patterns within the North Eastern Region and document the environmental implications of such behaviour. These clarifications provide lessons for future forest protection strategies, as well as new policies for handling with legal and illegal migration from the neighbouring countries to this region. In North East India, changes in population size due to migration significantly affect the structure of settlement and land use patterns. Some of the major activities that are linked to increasing rate of growth of population pressure include deforestation for agricultural expansion, habitation and fuelwood gathering. In this region jhum cultivation is one of the causes of deforestation. It may be suggested that if the cultivators are habituated through training to use the fertilizers then the need for excess land for shifting cultivation would be abolished. At present planned development process cannot adequately benefit the region because of rapid population growth and only a marginal part of the development results contributes towards improving the standard of living of the people. All these points to the urgent need for solution of political problems leading to migration to the North Eastern Region. Unless and until such continuous inflow of migration to this region can be halted, only economic policies will not be able to usher in an environment friendly development of this region leading to a halt in deforestation in the near future.

References

Bhargava, Meena (2002): Forests, People and State: Continuities and Changes, *Economic and Political Weekly*, October.

Census Report (2001): Population Projections of India and States 2001-2026.

Chatterjee, Sudipto et.al (2006). Bio-diversity Significance of North East India, for the study on Natural Resources, Water and Environment Nexus for Development and Growth in North Eastern India, *Forests Conservation Programme.* WWF-India, New Delhi.

Fernandes, Walter (2004): Limits of Law and Order: Approach to the North-East, *Economic and Political Weekly*, October.

Fernandes, Walter (2005): IMDT Act and Immigration in North East India. *Economic and Political Weekly*, July.

Harris, Nigel (2005): Migration and Development, *Economic and Political Weekly*, October.

Hazra, Somnath (2007): Valuing Forests in India and West Bengal: An Overview in *Indian Economy: Economic Ideas, Development and Financial Reforms: Essays in Honor of Prof. Rajkumar Sen.* (ed.) J. Felix Raj. Deep & Deep Publications, New Delhi-110027, India (forthcoming).

Hazra, S. and Sen, R. (2007): Ten Years of WTO and its Impact on India's Environment in *Ten Years of WTO and Towards an Asian Union Vol-1,* (eds.) Rajkumar Sen and J. Felix Raj. Deep & Deep Publications, New Delhi-110027, India (forthcoming).

Hunter, Lori M. (2000): The Environmental Implications of Population Dynamics, *A RAND Programme of Policy–Relevant Research Communication*, RAND.

Katwal, R.P.S et. al (2003): State of Forest Genetic Resources Conservation and Management in India, *Working Paper FGR/65E*, Indian Council of Forestry Research and Education, FAO, Rome, Italy.

Marayama, Mayumi (2006): Borders, Migration and Sub-Reginal Cooperation in East South Asia, *Economic and Political Weekly*, April.

NER Data Bank.

Oinam, Bhagat (2003): Patterns of Ethnic Conflict in the North-East: A Study on Manipur, *Economic and Political Weekly*, May.

Perveen, Sharma (2004): Population Growth and Sustainable Development, *Economic and Political Weekly*, February.

Poffenberger, Mark et.al (2006): Forest Sector Review of North East India, *Draft Discussion Background Paper No-12*, Community Forestry International.

Singh, B. P. (2001): The Eastern Himalaya Wetlands, Forests and Beliefs, *Economic and Political Weekly*, August.

Strategy Report (2007): Development and Growth in North-East India: The Natural Resources, Water and Environment Nexus. Draft, Socially Sustainable Development Department, Environment Unit, South Asia Region.

Updhyay, Archana (2006): Terrorism in the North-East Linkages and Implications. *Economic and Political Weekly*, December 2.

USAID (1998): *Conservation, Population Growth and Migration: Opportunities for Reform of Public and Private Programmes*, The Natural Heritage Institute.

9 The Qualitative and Quantitative Dimensions of Population Dynamics in North East India

Reema Choudhury Chakraborty

Though the North Eastern Region witnesses an inter-state differential in the growth rate of population, the rate is higher in the region as a whole as compared to the all India average. On the other hand, the growth of NSDP in the region is lagging much behind the same for all State average. As a result, the difference of the region's per capita income from all India per capita has been on the increase. This paper seeks to identify the areas of concern to which the region's population dynamics has given rise to.

Adverse Growth Trend of Population

The extent of demographic pressure in a predominantly agricultural society of the kind of North Eastern Region with traditional technology can indeed be an economic threat, unless there is an overhauling of the total agro-economic as well as industrial set up on the one hand and a scientific approach to the population control measures on the other. During the 30 years period between 1971 and 2001, the population of North-Eastern Region has increased almost double from 1.96 crore. to 3.85 crore, the annual growth rate being 2.3 per cent as against all India growth rate of 2.1 per cent.

Within the region, the highest growth rate is recorded by Nagaland, rising from 4.06 per cent to 4.97 per cent during these three decades followed by Manipur and Meghalaya with 2.6 per cent each in 2001 and Mizoram with 2.56 per cent. While Arunachal Pradesh records an annual growth rate of 2.3 per cent in 2001 Census, the lowest growth rate is registered by Tripura with 4.6 per cent,

Table 9.1: Population Growth and Sex Ratio (1971–2001)

States	Population (in lakhs)			Annual Growth Rate (%)			Sex Ratio (No. of females per1000 males)		
	1971	1991	2001	1971	1991	2001	1971	1991	2001
Arunachal Pradesh	4.68 (0.08)	8.6	10.9 (0.10)	3.01	3.14	2.33	861	861	901
Assam	146.3 (2.67)	224.1	266.4 (2.60)	2.10	2.17	1.73	896	925	932
Manipur	10.7 (0.19)	18.4	23.9 (0.23)	2.81	2.57	2.63	980	961	978
Meghalaya	10.1 (0.18)	17.7	23.1 (0.22)	2.78	2.84	2.62	942	924	975
Mizoram	3.3 (0.06)	6.9	8.9 (0.09)	3.96	3.34	2.56	942	921	938
Nagaland	5.2 (0.09)	12.1	19.9 (0.19)	4.06	4.45	4.97	871	890	909
Tripura	15.6 (0.28)	27.6	31.9 (0.31)	2.77	2.95	1.46	943	946	950
All-India	5481 (100.0)	8463.0	10270 (100.0)	2.20	2.15	1.93	930	939	937

N.B: Figures in the bracket indicate % to all-India population.

Source : (1) Basic Statistics of North-Eastern Region 1982, 1995 and 2002.
(2) Economic Survey, 1992–93 and 2006–07.

followed by Assam with 1.73 per cent as against all-India growth rate of 1.93 per cent in 2001. It is important to note here that Nagaland is the only State in the region where annual growth rate has recorded a continuous rise from 4.06 per cent in 1971 to 4.45 per cent in 1991 and onward to 4.97 per cent in 2001, while all other States have registered a decline in the annual growth rate of population. An important finding that emerges from these figures is that the population of all the States of North East as proportion to all-India population has marked an increase during these thirty years except for Assam where the proportion stands out to decline from 2.67 per cent in 1971 to 2.60 per cent in 2001.

Characteristics of Population in North-East

The most important characteristics of population dynamics that the paper has included are birth and death rates, decadal variation, sex ratio and urbanization. The highest birth rate is registered by Meghalaya at 28.5 per thousand, followed by Assam at 27 and the lowest by Mizoram at 16 as against all-India average of 25.8. The death rate per thousand is, however, the highest in Assam at 9.6 per thousand followed by Meghalaya at 9.2 and the lowest in Nagaland (4.3) as against all-India average of 8.5. Nagaland has the distinction of having the region's lowest death rate which declined from 6.3 per thousand in 1981 to 4.3 in 2001. Among the other States with low death rates, mention may be made of Mizoram (5.2), Tripura (5.4), Manipur (5.6) and Arunachal Pradesh (6.0). Only two States of the region, viz. Assam (9.6) and Meghalaya (9.2) registered higher than all-India death rate (8.5) in 2001 though both of them had recorded lower than all-India rate in 1981. What it follows is that these two States have made a poor record of score on their health care and medical efforts on the one hand and population control and family welfare measures on the other.

It is not only because of the largest ratio of birth rate to death rate but also because of the increase in that ratio for decades that Nagaland has recorded the highest decadal population growth from 40 per cent in 1971 to more than 64 per cent in 2001. The other high decadal variation-states of the region are Manipur, Meghalaya and Mizoram in the range between 29 and 30 per cent and Arunachal Pradesh with 26.2 per cent. While Tripura has the distinction of achieving the lowest decadal variation at 15.7 per cent, Assam has also recorded a low of 18.8 per cent as against the all India average of 21.4 per cent in 2001.

With respect to sex ratio, the region presents a mixed picture. While sex ratio is higher than all-India average (937) in Manipur, Meghalaya, Tripura and Mizorarn, it is lower in Arunachal Pradesh, Nagaland and Assam. While the vices of modernity like selection of sex during pregnancy or other illegal measures to get rid of unwanted sex might be assumed to have invaded a section of people, the reason must lie somewhere else for most of the people of these States. This will perhaps require a specialized research to unearth the fact in this area.

Table 9.2 : Birth and Death Rate and Urbanization in NE

States	*Birth Rate (Per 1000)*		*Death Rate (Per 1000)*		*Urbanization (Per cent of Population)*	
	1981	*2001*	*1981*	*2001*	*1991*	*2001*
Arunachal Pradesh	34.2	22.3	16.1	6.0	12.2	20.4
Assam	34.2	26.9	12.4	9.6	11.0	12.7
Manipur	26.6	18.3	6.6	5.6	27.7	23.9
Meghalaya	32.6	28.5	8.2	9.2	18.7	19.6
Mizoram	NA	16.0	NA	5.2	46.2	49.5
Nagaland	23.0	20.1	6.3	4.3	17.3	17.7
Tripura	26.4	16.5	8.0	5.4	15.3	17.0
All States	33.9	25.8	12.5	8.5	25.7	27.8

Sburce: Basic Statistics of NER, 1992 and 2002.

Urbanization in the region is highest in Mizoram at 49.5 per cent and lowest in Assam at 12.7 per cent in 2001, all other States recording in the range 17.24 per cent as against the all States average of 27.8 per cent in the country. Though influence of State income growth on urbanization may be proved as a fact in so far as NE Region is concerned since the per capita income of Assam is the lowest and that of Mizoram is the highest, the presumption does not hold good for the rest of India since the highest urbanized state (44 per cent) in 2001 is Tamil Nadu while the highest per capita income State is Punjab. Thus, the high growth economy may be either rural-centric or urban-centric. And the region's highest per capita income coinciding with highest urbanization should, perhaps, be explained in terms of Mizoram's urban-centric income growth.

Changes in Qualitative Aspects of Population

While dealing with qualitative aspects of the region's population, we have considered mainly three factors, viz., the literacy rate, infant mortality rate and the access to safe drinking water. Literacy rate of the region is not discouraging except for Arunachal Pradesh which accounts for only 54 per cent in 2001 as against all-India average of 64.8 per cent. The achievement in the region is highest in Mizoram at around 89 per cent, followed by Tripura, Manipur and Nagaland with 73.2 per cent, 70.5 per cent and 66.6 per cent respectively, while literacy rate in Assam and Meghalaya marginally falls short of the all India percentage. It follows that these two States and of course Arunachal Pradesh should accord high priority to literacy and education in their development efforts.

The achievement in reduction of infant mortality rate is certainly impressive in the region except for Assam where it is still 68 per 1000 live births against the all-States average of 58 as in 2005. Though infant mortality rate is less than the national average in all other States of the region, the achievement particularly in Manipur, Nagaland and Mizoram is highly appreciable at 13, 18 and 20 respectively. Infant mortality rate has also substantially declined in Tripura and Arunachal Pradesh to 31 and 37 per thousand. Assam requires to gear up its medical facilities particularly in rural areas to prevent large scale infant mortality. The State may draw benefit from study of the success story of Manipur in particular.

However, the region cuts a sorry figure with respect to its access to safe drinking water with all the States remaining below the all India average accessibility of 78 per cent. It is a serious lapse in the region's developmental efforts and the States require a quantum jump to achieve this indispensable social infrastructure.

Table 9.3 : Litaracy, acess to Safe Drinking Water and Infant Mortality in NE

States	*Litaracy Rate (%)*		*Access to Safe Drinking Water (%)*		*Infant Mortality (Per 1000 live births)*	
	1971	*2001*	*1981*	*2001*	*1961*	*2005*
Arunachal Pradesh	13.2	54.3	43.9	77.5	126	37
Assam	33.9	63.2	31.0	58.8	129	68
Manipur	37.8	70.5	19.5	37.0	32	13
Meghalaya	34.6	62.6	25.1	39.0	79	49
Mizoram	72.3	88.8	4.9	36.0	69	20
Nagaland	31.0	66.6	45.6	46.5	68	18
Tripura	35.0	73.2	27.3	52.5	111	31
All-India	34.4	64.8	38.2	77.9	115	58

Source: Economic Survey, 2006–07.

Poverty and Rising Income Gap

The very fact that the north-eastern region shares only 2.7 per cent of national income against 3.8 per cent share in India's population amply clarifies the extent of its economic distance. It is revealed from the population and income data that except for the tiny State of Mizoram with even less than 10 lakh people, the shares in all-India population are substantially higher in all other states than their share in national income in the period between 1990-91 and 2000-01. As for Assam, the largest State of the region, the population share, though declined from 2.67 per cent to 2.57 per cent during the decade, its share in national income has declined from 2.1 per cent to only 1.6 per cent.

The poor level of per capita income in north-eastern region is only obvious. It is not only that the same for all the States of the region has remained below all-India level, but the fact remains that their per capita income difference with national average has been on the increase for all these years. If we argue that larger the State's per capita income difference (with national per capita), the poorer the State is, then it is not only that all the States are poverty-striken but the extent of poverty during the past decades has increased. The most poverty-striken State in the region is, however, Assam with its lowest per capita income and, hence, with highest per capita income difference.

The per capita income at current prices in the region in 2000-01 is highest in Arunachal Pradesh at Rs.14,587 and lowest in Assam at Rs.10,467 as against all-India average of Rs.16,797, while the shortfall below all-India per capita income is highest in Assam with Rs.6,240 and lowest in Mizoram with Rs.1,798 in 2000-01 at current prices. According to the data available in Economic Survey, 2006-07 and Basic Statistics of NER, 2002, the per capita income of the region as a whole fell short of all-India per capita by Rs.1,706 at current prices in 1993-94 and this difference got multiplied by 275 per cent to mark at Rs.6,394 in 2003-04. There was, however, a fourfold increase in the corresponding income difference in Assam from Rs.1,975 to 8,003 in the same period.

Table 9.4 : Work Participation in NER (1991-2001) (%)

States	*Total Workers (Main plus Marginal as % to Total Population) (Per cent)*		*Category of Workers as Proportion to Total Workers*							
			Cultivators (%) Labourers (%)		*Agricultural industry workers (%)*		*Household workers (%)*		*Other workers (%)*	
	1991	*2001*	*1991*	*2001*	*1991*	*2001*	*1991*	*2001*	*1991*	*2001*
Arunachal Pradesh	45.2	44.3	60.4	58.4	5.1	3.8	0.2	1.0	19.5	36.8
Assam	31.2	36.4	50.9	39.5	12.8	14.1	0.1	3.4	11.1	44.1
Manipur	38.5	44.8	61.8	46.0	6.7	11.3	5.8	9.1	15.3	33.5
Meghalaya	40.3	41.4	55.3	47.8	12.5	18.1	0.4	1.9	14.8	32.2
Mizoram	42.1	52.7	61.3	53.9	3.3	5.8	1.0	1.4	22.6	38.8
Nagaland	42.3	42.7	72.6	64.0	1.4	4.1	0.4	2.1	17.2	29.8
Tripura	29.1	36.3	38.1	26.9	23.9	24.0	1.4	2.9	19.1	46.2
All India	37.8	39.1	34.4	32.1	26.4	26.2	3.1	4.1	35.7	37.5

Source : (1) Calculated by the author from work participation figures given in Basic Statistics of NE Region, 2000, 2002.

(2) All India figures for 1991 has been compiled from Basic Statistics Relating to Indian Economy.

Nature of Work Participation in North East

Work participation rate (percentage of total workers to total population) in Assam and Tripura has all-along been lower than the all-India average that moved from 37.8 per cent in 1991 to 39.1 per cent in 2001. In all other States, the rate has been higher than Indian average in the range between 41 and 45 per cent in 2001 as against 36 per cent in both Assam and Tripura. Cultivators form the largest proportion of total workers (including main and marginal workers) ranging between 46 per cent (Manipur) and 64 per cent (Nagaland) in the States other than Tripura and Assam with 27 per cent and 39 per cent respectively. Agricultural labourers form the highest proportion in Tripura with 24 per cent of total workers, while the lowest proportion is marked by Arunachal Pradesh, Nagaland and Mizoram at 3.8 per cent, 4.1 per cent and 5.8 per cent respectively. For other States, the range is between 11 per cent and 18 per cent. The region as a whole, however, accounts for 12 per cent of agricultural labourers as against 26 per cent in the country as a whole.

With respect to household industry workers, Manipur has the largest proportion of total workers at more than 9 per cent as against 4 per cent in the country as a whole. While the lowest proportion is accounted for by Arunachal Pradesh and Mizoram at 1.0 per cent and 1.4 per cent respectively, the proportion in other States ranges between 2 per cent each in Nagaland and Meghalaya and 3.4 per cent in Assam. While the region accounts for huge surplus cultivators in agriculture, they are required to be released in favour of industrial sector including household industries and other small scale units.

Unemployment Problem

According to live register of employment exchanges, the total number of job seekers in North Eastern Region accounted for 23.2 lakh in 2000-01 as against 41.34 million in the country as a whole. It shows

Table 9.5 : Net State Domestic Product in NE and Income Difference with All States Average

NE States	*Net State Domestic Product (Rs. crore)*	*Net State Domestic Product (Rs. crore)*	*Per Capita Net State Domestic Product (Rs. crore)*	*Per Capita Net State Domestic Product (Rs. crore)*	*Increase in the Period*	*Per Capita Income Difference with all-India Average*	*Per Capita Income Difference with all India Average*
	1990–91	2000–01	1990–91	2000–01		1990–91	2000–01
Arunachal Pradesh	460 (0.1)	1591 (0.1)	5397	14587	9190	+32	2120
Assam	9498 (2.1)	27600 (1.6)	4281	10467	6186	1084	6240
Manipur	723 (0.2)	2945 (0.2)	3976	12823	8847	1389	3884
Meghalaya	767 (0.2)	3230 (0.2)	4375	13114	8739	990	3593
Mizoram	306 (0.1)	1288 (0.1)	4474	14909	10435	891	1798
Nagaland	579 (0.1)	2330 (0.15)	4990	12594	7604	375	4113
Tripura	1917 (0.4)	4193 (0.3)	3370	14348	10978	1995	2359
All-India	457690 (100.0)	1719868 (100.0)	5365	16707	11342		

N.B : Figures in the bracket represent percentage to all States total.
Source : Basic Statistics of NER (2000–02), Column No 6–8 has been calculated by the author.

that unemployment in the region is an acute problem as the ratio of its unemployed to all-India total comes to as much as 5.6 per cent against the corresponding population ratio of 3.8 per cent. What is most perturbing is that the job-seekers from technical and vocational background forms just around 1 per cent while 99 per cent are non-vocational aspirants. This is certainly due to the inability of our educational system to prepare students to face the challenges of their future on one hand and lack of employment opportunities on the other.

There is, therefore, a dire necessity of overhauling the educational system with special emphasis on technical and vocational bias. On the other hand, the overburdened agriculture cannot be relieved of its excess labour unless employment opportunities are created in the industrial and infrastructural sectors. Because of the lack of employ-ment in rural areas, there has also been a large scale migration of job seekers to urban areas where, too, the scenario is frustrating.

Summary and Suggestions

Except for Assam and Tripura where annual growth rate of population is less than the all-India average, all other States require to push up their population control measures, while Mizoram with around 5 per cent annual growth rate must make special efforts to bring down the rate to all-India level in order to reap the benefit of development. Assam and Meghalaya which have higher than all-India death rate have to gear up their health care and medical efforts. The sex ratio in the region is found to be lower than all-India ratio in Arunachal Pradesh, Nagaland and Assam. While the vices of modernity like termination of female foetus might have invaded the social tradition of a section of urban people, the reason must lie somewhere else in most cases and will require a research venture to unearth the same. Lack of access to safe drinking water in the whole region, particularly in urban areas, unless remedial measures are taken on war-footing, will soon lead to a serious situation.

The very fact that the North Eastern Region shares only 2.7 per cent of national income against its 3.8 per cent share in population amply explains to the extent of its economic distance and poverty. The most poverty-striken State is, however, Assam with its lowest per capita income in the region. It is not only that per capita income of all the States is below the all-India average, but what is more perturbing is that the per capita income difference is on the rise at an increasing rate.

Work participation needs to be increased in Assam and Tripura where it falls below all-India average. Cultivators as proportion to total workers are larger than all States average except for Tripura, while that of agricultural labourers is less than the national average in all the States of the region. However, the proportion of household industrial workers to total workers in all the States except Manipur is less than at national level. Since agriculture is overburdened, the surplus cultivators cannot be shifted or work participation cannot be raised without a marked development in the small scale and household industrial sectors.

The problem of unemployment in the region is acute and the ratio of its job-seekers to all-India total constitutes 5.6 per cent as against population ratio of 3.8 per cent. The educational system perhaps needs to be job oriented with its bias on skill formation, technical expertise and vocationalisation. Apart from this, entrepreneurial training, industrial incentives including self employment enterprise and development of infrastructure and power generation should be the most urgent tasks. We must not, however, forget that the States of the region are basically agricultural and their economic fate is inseparably linked to the farm sector. Therefore, the region's poverty cannot be removed or prosperity achieved without a revolutionary change in its agro-economic scenerio.

References

Statistical Handbook of Assam, 2001, Government of Assam, Dispur, Guwahati.

Basic Statistics of North-Eastern Region, North-Eastern Council, 1992 and 2002.

Economic Survey, 2006-07, Government of India, New Delhi.

"Growth Trend of Population and its Characteristic Features in N.E. Region", by R.K. Choudhury, appearing in *Population, Poverty and Environment in N.E. India*, edited by B. Datta Ray, H.K. Mazhari, P.M. Passah and M.C. Pandey, Concept Publishing Company, New Delhi, 2000.

10 Population Dynamics and Development Pattern in North Eastern Region

A Case Study of North East's Capital Towns

P.K. Ryngnga

Introduction

Development processes of a country reflect the scenario of demography since population dynamics and development are so closely interlinked. The population distribution, density pattern, migration, employment structure as some features of demography are responsible for development. Population dynamics in the region as in other societies/ regions has two basic components: dynamics through natural process and dynamics through induced process. As regards the natural growth rate of population during three decades (1971–2001), all the States in the region have registered higher growth rate than that of the whole country. As a result, the increasing population pressure in this region has given rise to a strong relationship between regional development and population.

It is against this background, the paper aims to provide explanation to the emerged linkages between the two components. The paper documents a conceptual framework of development, examines the causal explanation about the complexity of population dynamics and development inter-connection; illustrates the impact of population dynamics on quality of life, development and elucidate the constant existence of regional disparities among the capital towns of the region which will be justified on the basis of important choice of indicators and the levels of development is thus represented by delineating the typology of backward/developed region.

The main *Objective* of the present study is as follows —

(i) To comprehend the complex linkages of socio-economic structure and development of the region,

(ii) To analyze the various choices of indicators that is responsible for the persistence of regional disparities, and

(iii) To present the typology of backward or developed region and to delineate them.

Choice of Indicators

The choice of indicators have greatly restricted by the nature of the paucity of appropriate data. In this present work, the indicators that have been selected are:

Index of Socio-Economic Development

- Percentage of literacy rate, female literacy,
- Percentage of ST population,
- Percentage of population to total population.

Index of Infrastructural and Household Amenities Development

- Length of roads per '00 sq. km.
- Percentage of houses with modern facilities; percentages of houses with telephone connectivity.

Index of Quality of Life

Health Facilities

- Number of hospitals and health centre per '000 population,
- Number of beds per '000 population,
- Number of doctors per hundred beds.

Educational Facilities

- Percentage of total literates,

- Number of schools per '000 population,
- Ratio of teachers to students.

Index of Urbanization

- Percentage of Urban Population to Total Population,
- Urban Population Growth (I 991–2001).

In consonance with the above objectives, the paper has been designed into five sections. Section I deals with socio-economic development among the capital towns of North East India followed by the analysis on infrastructural development and amenities in Section II. Section III takes into account the quality of life where it is seen that high growth of population require greater attention for better quality of life and Section IV gives in brief impact of urbanization emphasizing the development level pattern followed by some suggestive measures to improve regional disparities among the capital towns of North-Eastern Region.

Methodology

Once the indicators were made scale free, these have been simply added together to find out the score. The aggregate score for each sector has been divided into four levels by using quartile method. Finally, to find out the overall levels of development, the final scoring of all the sectors have been added together and again using quartile method, levels of development have been calculated.

For this purpose, the method used is—

1. Data obtained from the secondary sources was first altered into variables and subsequently into indicators. To make these comparable with each other normalization by subtracting the mean (x) of indicators and divided by their respective standard deviation (SD), or the simple method is expressed as:

$$\frac{X - \bar{X}}{\eth}$$

where, x is the unit observation, $\bar{X}$ is the mean of variables and $\eth$ is the standard deviation. The normalized data has been added to find the aggregate development score.

2. The level of development is thus shown by representing the score into quartile classes representing different levels of development of the towns,. viz. high, medium, low, very low.

I. Socio-Economic Development

Population dynamics in North Eastern Region is represented by the natural growth rate contributed by factors like low level of development of family planning facility, minority status of tribal communities and other socio-cultural factors. The towns have also received large influx of people due to the development of service, trade, transport and communication. The influx of migrants from the neighbouring countries is also a matter of concern for the region. Both the means, natural and induced have remarkably contributed to alter the demographic characteristics of the towns, which can be observed from Table 10.1 below.

Table 10.1 : Socio-Economic Development Index

NE's Capital Towns	*Total Population*	*ST Population*	*Literacy Rate*	*Female Literacy Rate*	*CS (a+b+c+d)*
Itanagar	-0.290	0.077	-0.006	-0.006	(-)0.225
Guwahati	0.720	-0.149	-0.263	0.072	(+)0.380
Imphal	0.002	-0.197	0.044	0.072	(-)0.079
Shillong	0.085	0.509	0.049	0.096	(+)0.739
Aizawl	0.022	0.070	0.069	-0.078	(+)0.083
Gangtok	-0.270	-0.020	0.008	0.120	(-)0.162
Agartala	-0.043	-0.38	0.074	-0.084	(-)0.443
Kohima	-0.224	0.141	0.023	0.048	(-)0.012

Source: Calculated by the Auth

Category	Values	Towns
High	Above 0.2	Guwahati, Shillong
Medium	0.00–0.02	Aizawl
Low	Below 0.00	Imphal, Kohima, Itanagar, Agartala, Gangtok

As discussed earlier, population dynamics has two basic components—natural and induced. Included among the contributing factors for high growth rate of population are (a) Low levels of development of family planning facility, (b) Status of tribal communities and other socio-cultural factors, and (c) Since time immemorial the capital towns of North-East has also received large influx of people due to the gradual development of services, trade, transport and communication. Both the means—natural and induced—have remarkably contributed to alter the demographic characteristic by taking into account the basic essential demographic figure. Compared to other parts of the country, the North Eastern Region is better placed when it comes to socio-cultural development.

Guwahati and Shillong fall under high category. Shillong accounts for high scheduled tribe population combined with high female literacy rate whereas Guwahati has high total population of over 8 lakhs and high literacy rate which brought these two towns to be placed in high category. Aizawl alone falls under medium level. Although, the overall level of socio-cultural development is noticeable, but the town accounts for low total population which perhaps is responsible for medium level. The low category comprises of Imphal, Kohima, Itanagar, Agartala, Gangtok. The low percentage of total population and scheduled tribe population in these towns explains the low development.

II. Infrastructural and Amenities Development

Roads and household amenities are also vital elements for the requirement for the development of population. In fact transport network are the physical expressions of integration within and between towns.

Table 10.2 : Infrastructure and Household Index

NE's Capital Towns	Length of Roads per '00 sq. km. (a)	Percentage of Houses with Modern Facilities (b)	Percentages of Houses with Telephone Connectivity (c)	CS (a+b+c)
Itanagar	0.09	-0.065	-0.108	-0.263
Guwahati	0.079	0.073	0.137	0.289
Imphal	0.027	0.006	0.027	0.06
Shillong	0.062	0.067	0.159	0.288
Aizawl	0.079	0.010	0.088	0.177
Gangtok	-0.077	-0.01	-0.096	-0.117
Agartala	-0.020	-0.06	-0.037	-0.117
Kohima	-0.059	-0.007	-0.001	-0.067

Source : Calculated by the Author.

Category	Values	Towns
High	Above 0.2	Guwahati, Shillong
Medium	0.00-0.02	Aizawl, Imphal
Low	Below 0.00	Kohima, Itanagar, Agartala, Gangtok

Taking into account the parameters for infrastructure and household amenities, it can be seen that only two towns surface in high category—Shillong, Guwahati, since these two towns have good transport and communication. Although Shillong's topography is not similar to that of Guwahati, yet the road system is somewhat better in comparison to other towns of North East, but the impact of modernization on household amenities and communication in Shillong is responsible for high level of infrastructure and household amenities development. The medium level comprises Imphal and Aizawl towns. Although' the transport and communication services are not so better off, nevertheless expansion and construction of roads and amenities have been going on by leaps and bounds despite inhospitable and rugged topography. The low category comprises Kohima, Itanagar, Agartala, Gangtok. The low level of infrastructure and amenities indicated low or few linkages of roads connecting with other districts. This region of low level infrastructure experiences a poor economic development in regard to tertiary sector. Therefore, there were limited opportunities that compelled them to remain in this category.

III. Quality of Life and Development

When quality of life is concerned, North East capital towns are also far from satisfactory in general. Although life expectancy has gone up in the region along with declining infant mortality and diseases have been effectively brought under control, nevertheless, health situation in North East in general still remains a cause of serious concern. It is deplorable to mention that a sizeable population in all capital towns of North East does not have access to safe drinking water and basic sanitation amenities. A relative comparison revealed that both the indicators of population pressure on hospital beds (1576 persons) and area coverage per hospital (0.66 lakh hec) are higher than that of the country (1324 persons and 0.29 lakh hec).

Table 10.3 : Quality of Life Index

NE's Capital Towns	*Number of Hospitals per '000 Population* (a)	*Number of Beds per '000 Population* (b)	*Number of Doctors per Hundred Beds* (c)	*Percentage of Total Literates* (d)	*Number of Schools per '000 Population* (e)	*CS (a+b+c+d+e)*
Itanagar	-1.84	-0.73	-1.42	-0.006	-1.89	(-) 5886
Guwahati	4.55	1.83	4.98	-0.263	3.30	(+) 14.397
Imphal	0.86	2.06	1.70	0.044	0.85	(+) 5.514
Shillong	-3.69	-0.49	-0.48	0.049	1.08	(-) 3.531
Aizawl	6.15	-0.63	-1.26	0.069	0.83	(+) 5.159
Gangtok	-2.09	-0.89	-1.73	0.008	-1.86	(-) 6.562
Agartala	0.12	-0.49	-0.48	0.074	-1.55	(-) 2.326
Kohima	-6.15	-0.63	-1.26	0.023	-0.76	(-) 8.777

Source: Calculated by the Author.

Category	*Values*	*Towns*
High	Above 5.00	Guwahati, Imphal
Medium	Below 0.00	Aizawl, Shillong, Kohima, Itanagar, Agartala, Gangtok

Two capital towns, i.e. Guwahati and Imphal fall in high category indicating a lesser uneven distribution of health facilities, educational institutions, coupled with the availability of proper equipments and competent manpower. Other capitals like Aizawl, Shillong, Kohima, Itanagar, Agartala, Gangtok have fewer hospitals catering to a small quantity of population. The uneven distribution of hospitals and the non-availability of adequate equipments pulled the level of quality of life.

IV. Index of Urbanization

Urbanization plays a very significant role in determining population dynamics and levels of development. Every urban society experiences gradual changes and the process of urbanization is very much influenced by population dynamics. In this context, this section discusses the positive relation of population and urbanization.

Table 10.4 : Urbanization Index

NE's Capital Towns	*Urban Population to Total Population*	*Urban Population Growth (1991–2001)*	*CS (a+b)*
Itanagar	-0.09	-0.22	(-) 0.31
Guwahati	0.079	0.44	(+) 0.519
Imphal	0.027	-0.29	(-) 0.263
Shillong	0.062	0.24	(+) 0.302
Aizawl	0.079	0.03	(+) 0.109
Gangtok	-0.077	-0.21	(-) 0.287
Agartala	-0.02	-0.02	(-) 0.04
Kohima	-0.059	0.03	(-) 0.029

Source: Calculated by the Author.

Category	*Values*	*Towns*
High	Above 0.20	Guwahati, Shillong
Medium	0.00-0.02	Aizawl
Low	Below 0.00	Itanagar, Imphal, Kohima, Agartala, Gangtok

When we glance at the Index of Urbanization, it can be seen that Guwahati and Shillong fall under high category revealing that the towns experience population flow from rural areas, within and outside the region. However, the overall development of the town itself has attracted processes of urbanization. Aizawl alone falls under medium category, although it is catching up with development yet the nature of topography is still responsible for slower growth. However, other capital towns like Itanagar, Imphal, Kohima, Agartala, Gangtok still have a long way to go in terms of development so as to give a boost to the index of urbanization.

Overall Development

The analysis of the overall level of development is discussed as follows :

Table 10.5 : Overall Development Index

NE's Capital Towns	*Socio-Economic Development Index (a)*	*Infrastructure and Household Index (b)*	*Quality of Life Index (c)*	*Urbanization Index (d)*	*CS (a+b+c+d)*
Itanagar	(-) 0.225	(-) 0.263	(-) 5.886	(-) 0.31	(-) 6.684
Guwahati	(+) 0.380	(+) 0.289	(+)14.397	(+) 0.519	(+) 15.52
Imphal	(-) 0.079	(+) 0.06	(+) 5.514	(-) 0.263	(+) 5.910
Shillong	(+) 0.739	(+) 0.288	(-) 3.531	(+) 0.302	(+) 4.857
Aizawl	(+) 0.083	(+) 0.177	(+) 5.159	(+) 0.109	(+) 5.519
Gangtok	(-) 0.162	(-) 0.117	(-) 6.562	(-) 0.287	(-) 7.126
Agartala	(-) 0.443	(-) 0.117	(-) 2.326	(-) 0.04	(-) 2.920
Kohima	(-) 0.012	(-) 0.067	(-) 8.777	(-) 0.029	(-) 8.878

Source: Calculated by the Author.

Category	*Values*	*Towns*
High	Above 9.00	Guwahati
Medium	0.00-9.00	Shillong, Imphal, Aizawl
Low	Below 0.00	Kohima Itanagar, Agartala, Gangtok

High Level

This comprises the town of Guwahati alone. It is noted that this town stands a better position than any other town in the region in all aspects except the overall socio-economic development.

Medium Level

Imphal, Shillong, Aizawl fall in this category. Except for Imphal, the adverse physical conditions of towns, like Shillong and Aizawl have caused obstacles in carrying out even distribution of development. However, these towns excelled in the recent past as the result of the wearing off of their conservative way of life and broadening their perspective towards their inter-tribal relationship and the outside world.

Low level

This category comprises Kohima, Itanagar, Agartala, Gangtok. These towns still exhibits semi-rural nature and the physical condition do not permit them to have better infrastructural and proper household amenities.

Suggestion and Conclusion

Although the region as a whole suffers from slow and gradual development when compared with mainland of India. Yet in this age of globalization, the region would in fact experience better developmental process in all aspects because of its position (being surrounded by foreign countries) which can intensify foreign direct investment.

In conclusion it can be said that most of the towns in the North East India are located in hilly region except for Guwahati and Imphal. However, it is worth mentioning that the region has experienced important economic growth during the post-Independence period though by no means inadequate. In this process, some have viewed the changes as an effort to break away from the traditional limitations; to others, this interpretation of the capital towns, development inadequacy addresses the perpetuation and continuation of disparities and imbalances within and between various sub-regions resulting in fundamental contradictions in the political and economic relations in the region.

References

Agarwal, A.K. (1987): *Economic Problems and Planning in North East India*, Sterling Publishers Pvt. Ltd., New Delhi.

Bimal, J. Deb (1995): *Regional Development in North East India, Issues and Prospects*, Reliance Publishing House, New Delhi.

Census of India (2001): Provisional Tables, 2004.

Census of India (2001): State District Profile.

Misra, R.P. (1976) (*et al.*): *Regional Development Planning in India: A new Strategy*, Vikas Publishing House Pvt. Ltd, New Delhi.

Rai, R.K., Mohapatra, A.C. *et.al.* (eds.) (1990): *Hill Area Dvelopemnt: Issues and Perspective*, Geographical Society of North Eastern Hill Region, Shillong.

Ryngnga, P.K. (2001) (Unpublished): Levels of Development in the Hills of North Eastern Region, M.Phil. Dissertation.

11 Quality of Life of Women in North East India

Chaiti Sharma Biswas

Introduction

Any study on population dynamics is not merely in exercise of changing size of population, sex ratio, infant mortality etc. but evaluating the dynamics of the quality of life of the enhanced population as well. Any developmental endeavour is meant for enhancing the human well-being and hence quality of life becomes the key issue of studies on population. As quality of life is a multi-dimensional phenomenon so to give proper justice to the measurement of quality of life is necessary to cover all the aspects of life. But it may not be possible due to various constraints to cover each and every aspect of life. As a result, the studies on quality of life are very much guided by the objective of the study as well as the aspects of the life considered. Some consider quality of life as individual satisfaction and others think it as a aggregate satisfaction accrued from various aspects of life like level of economic status, education, health, safety etc. Previously the quality of life is being measured by the growth of GDP or per capita GDP only but it can never be a good measure unless the income distribution is more or less egalitarian. For this reason UNDP has contributed significantly in shifting the development debates from uni-dimensional GDP based measurement to multi-dimensional measurements including non-income variables in the construction of Human Development Index (HDI). However, the HDI development by UNDP can never be an index of the quality of life in real sense of term as various important aspects of life are not considered.

At present Indian economy is passing through the regime of globalization and economic liberalization. The economy has already shown a spectacular GDP growth rate. So it becomes imperative to study how far this enhanced GDP actually contribute to change the quality of life of the people.

Since Independence the States in the North Eastern Region had remained geographically isolated from the rest of India as well as deprived from the mainstream of development endeavour. But after liberalization Government of India has given special attention to bring this region to the mainstream of developmental process. As a result various developmental activities are being launched in this region of which special attention was given for upliftment of the status of women as the vulnerable group of the society. Since no attempts were taken to assess the quality of life in North East India, it becomes important to know the effect of those developmental policies especially on women's quality of life. This study will explore the quality of life of women of the North Eastern Region by State-based NFHS 2 (National Family Health Survey)-1998-99 data. This study will first review the general condition of living of the north-east people and then it will find out the quality of life of women of this region.

Life in North East

Due to mountainous nature modernization of agriculture and development of heavy industry are considerably hampered in the NE region. The NE region is sparsely populated. Assam is the most and Sikkim the least populated State in the NE region (Table 11.1). Sex ratio of the NE region (936 females per 1000 males) is better than that of all-India (933) level. Manipur has the highest sex ratio (978) and Sikkim the lowest (875) in this region. Except Mizoram (19.47 per cent), population below poverty line in the NE States is higher than the all-India figure (26.10 per cent). But literacy scenario of NE India is much impressive (Table 11.1). Except Arunachal Pradesh Assam and Meghalaya, literacy rate in all other NE States are higher than India (65.20 per cent) average.

Per capita net state domestic product (at 1999-2000 price) of all

Table 11.1 : Socio-Demographic Profile of NE Region, 2001

State	*Population (In Millions)*	*Sex Ratio*	*% of Person below Poverty Line*	*% of Literacy*
Arunachal Pradesh	1.09	901	33.47	54.74
Assam	26.64	932	36.09	64.28
Manipur	2.39	978	28.54	68.87
Meghalaya	2.31	975	33.87	63.31
Mizoram	0.89	938	19.47	88.49
Nagaland	1.99	909	32.67	67.11
Sikkim	0.54	875	36.55	69.68
Tripura	3.19	950	34.44	73.66
India	1027.02	933	26.10	65.20

Source: Census of India, 2001, Economic Survey, 1999-2000.

the NE States are less than that of India (Rs. 15,626) (Table 11.2). Surprisingly most of the NE State's per capita consumption expenditure is higher than all-India (Rs. 590.98) average. About 55 per cent of total population belongs to labour force (Table 11.2). Meghalaya has the highest percentage of labour force within this region. Excluding Assam and Meghalaya death rate of rest of the North East States is less than all-India level (8.9 per cent). Death rate is

Table 11.2 : Economic Profile of NE Region, 1999-2000

States	*PC NSDP (Current Price)*	*PC Consumption Expenditure*	*% of Persons of Lab Force*	*Incidence of Unemployment*	*Death Rate (1997)*	*Infant Mortality Rate per Thousand (1991)*
Arunachal Pradesh	13352	672.3	55.3	0.9	5.8	91
Assam	9720	473.4	55.2	4.6	9.9	92
Manipur	12721	596.4	54.4	3.5	5.9	28
Meghalaya	12083	639.1	73.6	0.9	8.8	80
Mizoram	14909	935.5	63.8	2.0	—	53
Nagaland	12594	1005.9	67.6	3.5	—	51
Sikkim	14751	559.9	58.8	3.4	6.5	60
Tripura	13195	589.5	45.1	1.9	6.8	82
India	15626	590.9	61.8	2.3	8.9	77

Source : Economic Survey-2003, 55th Round of NSSO on Levels and Pattern of Consumption Expenditure in India and Employment and Unemployment Situation in India, National Human Development Report, 2002.

lowest in Arunachal Pradesh and highest in Tripura. The per thousand infant mortality rate of Assam, Arunachal Pradesh, Tripura and Meghalaya is more than that of India level (77) among which the infant mortality rate is highest in Assam. In other NE States mortality rates are lower than India level (Table 11.2).

Generally *kutcha* houses are very common in the NE region which may be due to geographic reason or poverty. Around 70 per cent houses are *kutcha* in Tripura, Arunachal Pradesh and Assam but in other NE States less than 53 per cent houses are *kutcha*. Next comes semi-*pucca* houses. About 11.72 to 39 per cent houses are semi-*pucca* in other NE States. As expected percentage of *pucca* houses are smaller relative to *kutcha* and semi-*pucca* houses in the NE Region. Except Sikkim and Arunachal Pradesh the percentage of houses having safe drinking water in this region is much below all-India level (62.30 per cent). Table 11.3 states that except Arunachal Pradesh and Mizoram toilet facilities in other NE States are less relative to India (49.32 per cent) level. Relative to all India average (42.37 per cent) the percentage of house having electricity connection is higher in some states. The percentage of houses with electricity connection in Assam, Meghalaya, Tripura and Arunachal Pradesh is less than the all India level.

Table 11.3 : Distribution of Households with Housing Characteristics in North East India

States	*Type of Houses (1991)*			*Safe Drinking*	*Toilet*	*% of Households*
	Kutcha	*Semi-pucca*	*Pucca*	*Water (1991)*	*Facilities (1997)*	*having Electricity (1991)*
Arunachal Pradesh	73.34	11.72	14.94	70.02	85.84	40.85
Assam	70.22	15.16	14.62	45.86	6.44	18.74
Manipur	53.95	40.65	5.40	38.72	12.41	50.42
Meghalaya	52.98	33.72	13.30	36.16	26.61	29.16
Mizoram	38.38	42.52	19.10	16.21	80.00	59.20
Nagaland	50.91	36.47	12.62	53.37	4.34	53.42
Sikkim	33.94	39.11	26.95	73.19	52.80	60.66
Tripura	73.79	20.71	5.50	37.18	46.72	36.93
India	9.90	3.95	41.61	62.30	49.32	42.37

Source: National Human Development Report, 2001, NSSO 55th Round, Occasional Paper No.1 of 1997, Table 3, pages 112-113, Compendium of India's Fertility and Mortality Indicators, 1999, Census of India, 1991.

Data and Methodology

The data extracted from National Family Health Survey (NFHS-2, 1998-99) are used in this study. The respondents are females aged between 15 to 49 years. All women are married. A number of variables are used to assess the quality of life or well-being. In this analysis some of the variables used are, (1) level of education of women (2) occupation of women, (3) nutrition of women, (4) type of care received during pregnancy and illness, (5) type of toilet facilities they mostly use, (6) whether they watch movies or not, (7) independence of decision making at household level, (8) whether they are beaten since age 15 or not, and (9) frequency of being beaten last twelve months. Some of the above said variables are recoded from the given standard codes of NFHS. These codes are as follows:

> *Occupation of Women:* (1) Not working, (2) Professional, technical and managerial, (3) Clerical, (4) Sales and Manual.
> *Toilet Facilities:* (1) Own flush toilet, (2) Own pit toilet, (3) Shared/public toilet, and (4) No toilet facility/bush/field.
> *Independece of Decision-making:* (1) Financial, (2) Household, and (3) Social Mobility.

Findings

Total 11016 women are covered in NE region of which State-wise distribution of women are 1117 in Arunachal Pradesh, 1441 in Assam, 1435 in Manipur, 945 in Meghalya, 1048 in Mizoram, 818 in Nagaland, 1107 in Sikkim and 1104 in Tripura respectively. In search of women's quality of life this paper will first concentrate on the education variable which is counted as the most important factor of develement because it helps to generate awareness, self-esteem among people, which leads them for further advancement. A handsome number of women in NE Region are illiterate (Table 11.4). About 51.9 per cent women in Arunachal Pradesh have no education followed by Assam and Sikkim. Number of illiterate women in Mizoram is very few (9.1 per cent). Both in Meghalaya and Tripura percentage of

Table 11.4 : Distribution of Women by Level of Education in North East India, 1998-99

States	*No Education Total*	*Primary Total*	*Secondary Total*	*Higher Total*
Arunachal Pradesh	51.9	16.1	27.6	4.4
Assam	46.5	16.8	28.2	8.5
Manipur	31.6	22.5	29.5	16.4
Meghalaya	36.6	33.0	25.4	5.0
Mizoram	9.1	31.7	52.5	6.8
Nagaland	35.1	22.7	36.9	5.1
Sikkim	46.5	22.0	26.1	5.4
Tripura	30.8	30.3	31.4	7.5

Source : NFHS Extracted Data.

primary educated women are more than the women having secondary education. In other NE States the percentage of primary educated women varies from 16.1 to 22.7 per cent. One noticeable feature of this region is that among the literate women majority of them completed secondary education. Mizoram has the highest percentage of women (52.5 per cent) having secondary education. Percentage of women from other States having secondary education varies between 25.4 to 36.9 per cent. It is accepted that as the rate of higher education increases the quality of life becomes better but it is observed that the percentage of women having higher education is marginal in the NE States. In Manipur 16.4 per cent women have higher education, which is the highest among all the NE States. In rest of the NE States 4.4 to 8.5 per cent women have higher education.

Besides education next important factor influencing the quality of life is *job* of women. Screening vividly the job picture, it is observed that in the NE States most of the women do not work (Table 11.5) and this percentage varies from 52.8 per cent to 80.9 per cent. About 78 per cent women in Sikkim and Tripura do not work. Of the total female workforce in NE States a large portion of women are manual workers. In Arunachal Pradesh, Nagaland and Manipur 53.1, 52.5, and 48.8 per cent are manual labourers whereas in Sikkim this type of labour is very low (8.3 per cent). In Meghalaya and Mizoram manual workers consist of 36.7 and 28.6 per cent of total workforce. Next to manual work concentration of women workers are seen in professional,

Table 11.5 : Distribution of Women by Type of Occupation in North East India, 1988-99

States	*Not Working*	*Prof. Tech. Managerial*	*Clerical*	*Sales*	*Manual*
Arunachal Pradesh	41.5	2.4	1.9	1.2	53.1
Assam	80.9	2.5	0.4	1.1	15.0
Manipur	30.1	6.7	2.6	11.8	48.8
Meghalaya	52.8	3.8	1.9	4.8	36.7
Mizoram	50.7	6.9	4.3	9.5	23.6
Nagaland	36.5	4.7	2.9	3.4	52.5
Sikkim	78.4	5.7	2.6	5.0	8.3
Tripura	78.2	3.9	1.0	1.3	15.7

Source : NFHS Extracted Data.

or technical or managerial and clearical jobs. In Mizoram and Manipur around 7 per cent women have professional or technical or managerial jobs followed by Sikkim (5.7 per cent). Women participation in managerial jobs in Assam (2.5 per cent), Arunachal Pradesh (2.4 per cent), Meghalaya (3.8 per cent) and Tripura (3.9 per cent) are scanty. Except Nagaland (4.3 per cent) the share of women in clerical jobs are around 0.4 to 3 per cent. Very little portion of NE women is in sales job. Only in Manipur and Mizoram 10 to 12 per cent women are in sales job, in other States this percentage is negligible.

In Indian society unequal distribution of food among men and women is well known and obviously women get less nutrition than men. In order to know the actual picture of women nutrition in North East India some of the food items used to assess nutrition are (a) *milk* and *curd,* (b) *vegetables* and *fruits.* Vegetables are further divided into green leafy vegetables and other vegetables. Protein includes, pulses, eggs, chicken, meat and fish. Table 11.6 depicts that about 36.8 to 41.8 per cent women in Mizoram, Meghalaya and Arunachal Pradesh never tasted milk and about 34.9 to 69.4 per cent women consume milk occasionally. Except Sikkim and Nagaland very few NE women (10.5 to 32.8 per cent) consume milk daily.

A large portion of women consumes daily green leafy vegetables along with other vegetables (Table 11.7). Now among these two items green leafy vegetables takes the lion's share (58.7 to 91.8 per cent) followed by other vegetables (32.9 to 77.4 per cent) daily, which

Table 11.6 : Distribution of Women having *Milk or Curd* as diet in North East India, 1998-99

States	*Daily*	*Ocasionally*	*Never*	*Total Population*
Arunachal Pradesh	12.3	45.9	41.8	1117
Assam	19.5	69.4	11.1	3441
Manipur	10.5	61.7	27.9	1435
Meghalaya	12.9	46.2	40.8	945
Mizoram	13.3	49.9	36.8	1048
Nagaland	58.8	35.7	5.5	818
Sikkim	60.8	34.9	4.3	1107
Tripura	32.8	52.4	14.8	1104

Source: NFHS Extracted Data.

implies that besides cereals major supporting item for consumption are green leaf vegetables. Most of the NE women consume fruit occasionally (Table 11.7). Still both in Manipur and Meghalaya 15.1 to 13.7 per cent women take fruits daily. In rest of the States a negligible number of women take fruits daily.

A major portion of women in NE India consumes pulses occasionally (Table 11.8). Except Assam, Sikkim and Tripura (45.9 to 47.3 per cent) around 67 to 94 per cent women consume pulses occasionally. Share of women having pulses daily in the NE States ranges from 19.4 to 56.6 per cent. Around 57 per cent Sikkimese women take pulses daily. Though negligible, there are still some percentage of women in NE Region who had never taken pulses. Share of these women ranges from 0.4 to 4.2 per cent.

The picture of protein consumption is miserable in NE. Table 11.8 makes it clear that around 90 per cent women in NE India take egg occasionally. In Sikkim, Assam and Tripura about 56 per cent women get egg as a daily diet. In all other NE States 4.3 to 30.5 per cent women consume eggs daily. Still there are 21 per cent and 14 per cent of women in Sikkim and Manipur who never tasted egg. When one goes through the status of women having taken chicken, meat and fish in NE States similar shocking picture emerges. About 75 to 98 per cent women in this region take chicken, meat or fish occasionally. 10 to 28 per cent women consume chicken in Assam, Manipur, Sikkim, Tripura and Meghalaya. But 1 to 8.7 per cent

Table 11.7 : Distribution of Women having *Vegetables* and Fruits as Diet in North East India

States	*Green Leafy Vegetables*			*Other Vegetables*			*Fruits*			*Total Population*
	Daily	*Occasionally*	*Never*	*Daily*	*Occasionally*	*Never*	*Daily*	*Occasionally*	*Never*	
Arunachal Pradesh	78.2	21.8	0.1	32.9	66.5	0.6	3.0	95.7	1.3	1117
Assam	61.3	38.2	0.4	77.4	22.3	0.3	7.9	87.3	4.8	3441
Manipur	91.8	8.2	–	77.2	22.8	–	15.1	81.3	3.7	1435
Meghalaya	79.9	18.7	1.4	72.5	27.3	0.2	13.7	84.7	1.7	945
Mizoram	89.0	11.0	–	52.9	47.0	0.1	8.2	91.3	0.5	1048
Nagaland	80.8	18.5	0.7	44.7	53.3	2.0	4.2	95.2	0.6	818
Sikkim	77.5	22.5	–	56.8	42.8	0.4	9.7	88.3	2.1	1107
Tripura	58.7	41.2	0.1	76.3	23.1	0.6	9.1	87.6	3.4	1104

Source: NFHS Extracted Data.

Table 11.8 : Distrubution of Women having Protein diet in North East India, 1998-99

States	*Pulses*			*Eggs*			*Chicken/meat/fish*			Total Population
	Daily	*Occasionally*	*Never*	*Daily*	*Occasionally*	*Never*	*Daily*	*Occasionally*	*Never*	
Arunachal Pradesh	23.2	72.6	4.2	2.4	90.0	7.6	8.7	90.1	1.3	1117
Assam	53.3	45.9	0.8	5.1	89.8	5.1	10.4	86.7	2.8	3441
Manipur	4.3	93.9	1.8	2.8	83.1	14.1	19.4	78.9	1.7	1435
Meghalaya	30.5	67.3	2.2	5.5	86.0	8.5	28.5	69.6	1.9	945
Mizoram	22.5	76.3	1.1	3.6	94.2	2.2	1.0	98.3	0.7	1048
Nagaland	19.4	78.6	2.0	2.2	96.5	1.3	8.2	91.7	0.1	818
Sikkim	56.6	43.0	0.4	7.0	71.9	21.0	14.5	75.2	10.4	1107
Tripura	51.4	47.3	1.4	4.0	87.7	8.3	14.0	83.2	2.7	1104

Source: NFHS Extracted Data.

women of Mizoram, Nagaland and Arunachal Pradesh get chicken daily in their dishes.

Another indicator of better life is receiving proper care at the time of illness. As women is the neglected section of the society, it is important to know whether they received care at the time of illness and pregnancy or not. Majority of women (66.7 to 88.7 per cent) in NE States received no disease prevention (Table 11.9). Considering the case of treatment recieved by women at the time of illness, it is found that majority of NE women do not get any tretment (Table 11.9). This share of women not receiving treatment touches the height of 86 to 89.5 per cent in Sikkim and Arunachal Pradesh followed by, Meghalaya (83.3 per cent), and Tripura (80.2 per cent). Except Nagaland (1.1 per cent) majority of NE women has no right to arrange any type of treatment for her sick child. Only 10.5 to 43.8 per cent women have the right to arrange any type of treatment for her sick child. During pregnancy women need some essential care like immunization, antenatal care and delivery care. In all the said three cases majority of women do not get any care. About 66.3 to 92.5 per

Table 11.9 : Distribution of Women received various essential care during Pregnancy and Illness in North East India, 1998-99

States		*Immuni-zation*	*Antental Care*	*Delivery Care*	*Disease Prevention*	*Treatment for Self*	*Treatment for Sick Child*
Arunachal Pradesh	No	89.5	89.5	89.5	78.9	89.5	9.5
	Yes	10.5	10.5	10.5	21.1	10.5	10.5
Assam	No	92.0	87.6	3.3	76.1	63.7	77.0
	Yes	8.0	12.4	–	23.9	36.3	23.0
Manipur	No	92.5	92.5	86.8	88.7	69.8	83.0
	Yes	7.5	7.5	13.2	11.3	30.2	17.0
Meghalaya	No	81.3	89.6	95.8	68.8	83.3	56.3
	Yes	18.8	10.4	4.2	31.3	16.7	43.8
Mizoram	No	91.5	91.5	97.5	67.1	59.5	74.7
	Yes	8.5	8.5	2.5	32.9	40.5	25.3
Nagaland	No	88.9	77.8	88.9	66.7	77.8	1.1
	Yes	11.1	22.2	11.1	33.3	22.2	–
Sikkim	No	78.0	98.0	96.0	88.0	86.0	82.0
	Yes	22.0	2.0	4.0	12.0	14.0	18.0
Tripura	No	66.3	91.1	9.1	88.1	80.2	73.3
	Yes	33.7	8.9	–	11.9	19.8	26.7

Source: NFHS Extracted Data.

cent women do not receive any sort of immunization in NE States. Similarly 77.8 to 98 per cent women do not get any sort of antenatal care, which is very much important for safe delivery; also 86.8 to 97.5 per cent women do not receive any type of delivery care in NE region. Among those few women who received some sort of care, 33.7 per cent in Tripura get immunized followed by Sikkim (22 per cent), Meghalaya (18.8 per cent) Nagaland (11.1 per cent) and Arunachal Pradesh (10.5 per cent). Situation is worst in Assam, Manipur and Nagaland where only 7 per cent women are immunized. Except Nagaland (22.2 per cent) very few NE women (2 to 12.4 per cent) receive antenatal care. The percentage of women geting delivery care in NE States starts from 2.5 and do not exceed 13.2 per cent.

In Nagaland, Arunachal Paradesh, Sikkim, Assam and Meghalaya 25.1 to 45 per cent women has no access to any type of toilet facilities (Table 11.10). In Manipur maximum women (41.9 per cent) use shared toilet. Women of other NE States using shared toilet range from 4 to 17.7 per cent. Only 43 per cent women from Sikkim use flush toilet and 7.4 to 24.3 per cent women of other NE States use flush toilet. Commonly pit toilet is used in most of the houses having own toilet facilities in this region 68.2 per cent women use pit toilet in Tripura followed by Mizoram (55.9 per cent) and Arunachal Pradesh (54.7 per cent). In Assam and Nagaland 43 to 45 per cent women have own pit toilet. In other NE States about 15.3 per cent to 37 per cent women use pit toilet.

Table 11.10 : Distribution of Women having different types of Toilet Facilities in North East India, 1998-99

States	*Own Flush Toilet*	*Own Pit Toilet*	*Shared/Public Toilet*	*No Facility/ Bush/Field*
Arunachal Pradesh	15.9	54.7	4.0	25.3
Assam	19.4	45.2	4.4	30.9
Manipur	13.7	37.0	41.9	7.5
Meghalaya	7.4	34.4	13.2	45.0
Mizoram	24.3	55.9	17.7	2.1
Nagaland	20.2	43.5	11.2	25.1
Tripura	14.0	68.2	8.4	9.3

Source: NFHS Extracted Data.

It is said that better life demands sometimes for recreation. As NFHS data provide only data on watching movie so this variable is used as recreation indicator. 81.8 to 98.9 per cent women do not see movies though there is a variation among States (Table 11.11). Only 18.2 per cent women in Sikkim and 12.9 per cent women in Manipur and 10.1 per cent women in Arunachal Pradesh watch movie at least once a month.

Table 11.11: Distribution of Women who watch Movie at least once a Month in North East India, 1998-99

States	*No*	*Yes*
Arunachal Pradesh	89.9	10.1
Assam	93.9	6.1
Manipur	87.1	12.9
Meghalaya	95.9	4.1
Mizoram	98.9	1.1
Nagaland	98.5	1.5
Sikkim	81.8	18.2
Tripura	94.1	5.9

Source: NFHS Extracted Data.

It is assumed that women who lead better life have some control over decision-making. So it is important to assess how far the NE women have control on decision-making variables at household level. Now these household decisions are divided into three broad categories like *financial, household* and *mobility*. First, the most crucial decision making variable, i.e. the financial decisions are taken into acccount. Table 11.12 confirmed that more than 51 per cent NE women have no right to take financial decisions. Only 47.17 per cent Sikkimese women followed by Arunachal Pradesh (46.65 per cent), Meghalaya (46.11 per cent), and Manipur (45.87 per cent) have financial freedom. In other NE states 16.80 per cent to 33.29 per cent women have control over financial matters. But it is observed that most of the NE women have freedom to take household decisions (72 or 96.3 per cent). In Mizoram, Tripura and Manipur 20.2 to 28 per cent women have no freedom to decide about household matters. Now comes the freedom of social mobility. Like all the Indian States, here also women enjoy less independence regarding social mobility. For the States like

Mizoram, Meghalaya and Arunachal Pradesh only 57.8 to 41.7 per cent women have the freedom of social mobility (Table 11.12). For rest of the NE States this freedom of mibility lies between 13.2 to 31.3 per cent.

Table 11.12 : Distribution of Women by Independence Decision-making in North East India, 1988-99

States	*Financial*		*Household*		*Mobility*	
	No	*Yes*	*No*	*Yes*	*No*	*Yes*
Arunachal Pradesh	53.35	46.65	12.4	87.6	58.3	41.7
Assam	76.37	23.63	16.4	83.6	86.8	13.2
Manipur	54.13	45.87	28.0	72.0	76.7	23.3
Meghalaya	53.89	46.11	14.8	85.2	55.7	44.3
Mizoram	66.95	33.05	20.2	79.8	42.2	57.8
Nagaland	83.20	16.80	3.7	96.3	86.1	13.9
Sikkim	52.83	47.17	9.1	90.9	68.7	31.3
Tripura	66.71	33.29	27.3	72.7	80.2	19.8

Source: NFHS Extracted Data.

Beating women is a very common practice in Indian society. Therefore, it is assumed that with better living this practice will reduce. It is very encouraging to found that a small number of women are being beaten since age 15 in NE (Table 11.13). This percentage varies from 11.1 to 29.8 per cent, among which Maghalaya (29.8 per cent), Arunachal Pradesh (25.9 per cent) and Mizoram (20.1 per cent) women are beaten more relative to Nagaland (18.6 per cent), Manipur

Table 11.13 : Distribution of Women who are beaten & frequency of being beaten within last twelve months in North East India, 1998-99

States	*Beaten since Age 15*		*Number of time between within last 12 months*			
	No	*Yes*	*Once*	*A few times*	*Many times*	*Not beaten*
Arunachal Pradesh	74.1	25.9	18.0	30.8	13.5	37.7
Assam	85.6	14.4	11.1	33.9	10.7	44.4
Manipur	80.2	19.8	13.0	9.2	6.0	71.8
Meghalaya	70.2	29.8	7.4	13.5	9.6	69.5
Mizoram	79.9	20.1	20.9	20.9	5.7	52.6
Nagaland	81.4	18.6	23.0	38.8	17.8	20.4
Sikkim	88.9	11.1	14.6	24.4	27.6	33.3
Tripura	86.2	13.8	17.1	25.0	19.1	38.8

Source : HFHS Extracted Data.

(19.8 per cent), Assam (14.4 per cent) and Sikkim (11.1 per cent) women. In regard to frequency of beating it is found that among the beaten women of NE most of them were beaten few times. This percentage varies from 9.2 per cent (Manipur) to 38.8 per cent (Nagaland). About 6 per cent (Manipur) to 27 per cent (Sikkim) women admit that they were beaten many times within last 12 months.

Conclusion

The above study demonstrates that though the NE region is characterized by sparce population, better sex ratio, handsome literacy rate and lower death rate yet its quality of life is not very much impressive. However it lags behind the India-level with respect to number of persons below poverty line, per capita net State Domestic Product, persons in labour force coupled with higher level of unemployment and higher infant mortality rate. Majority of people have *kutcha* houses in this region. Very little *pacca* houses are available in NE States. Number of houses having safe drinking water, toilet facilities and electricity in this region is not very impressive and the region lags behind all-India-level. In this background the quality of life of NE women is vulnerable. They lack in almost every sphere of life. Only encouraging point is that most of the NE women achieve at least secondary level of education but in higher education the picture becomes reverse. In the NE, most of the women do not work and those who are in workforce are mainly engaged as manual workers. Very few women are in managerial, technical or professional, clerical and sales job. Nutrition figures state that green leafy vegetables and other vegetables are the main diet of the NE women. Occasionally they take milk, pulses, egg, meat, chicken, fish and fruits, which are known as improved diet. Still there exist some women (though in small number) who had never tested milk, pulses, meat, fish etc. A miserable condition is found with regard to medical care at the time of illness, pregnancy and delivery. Very few women are entitled to the above said privileges and even they cannot take decision of treatment about their sick child. As a means of recreation maximum women are not acquainted with watching movies. Though the NE women can take household decisions independently but most of them cannot participate in financial decisions also they have little freedom of mobility. But the point to notice is that the NE women are less prone to domestic violence. Very few women were beaten and the frequency of being beaten is also less. Reviewing the above findings it can be said that all these may be the result of not being in the mainstream development process. It is admitted that job of women helps to enhance the quality of living. As better job needs higher education, so much stress should be given on higher education. Next to education importance must be given to better communication. Better communication will connect the NE Region with rest of India which will encourage inflow of investment, modernization of industry, tourism etc. which may in turn change the quality of life.

References

Bellower, Jeroen, "Quality of Life and Living Conditions in the Netherlands", *Social Indicators Research,* 2002, 58 (1-3), pp. 113-138.

Charlotte Neighbourhood Development Neighbourhood Quality of Life Study *http:/www.ci. Charlotte.nc.us/index.htm.*

Easterly, William, "Life During Growth", *Journal of Economic Growth* Volume 4, Issue 3, September 1999, pp. 239-275.

Economic Survey, 2004-05. Ministry of Finance, Government of India.

Planning Commission, 2002. *National Human Development Report 2001,* Government of India.

Registrar General of India. 1981, 1991, 2001, *General Economic Tables,* Census of India.

Schyns, Peggy and Bellower, Jeroen, "Measuring Quality of Life in Amsterdam from the viewpoint of Participation", The Amsterdam Bureau for Reseach and Statistics/Social and Cultural Planning Office.

Tata Energy Research Insitute 2002, "Impact of Population Growth on Water and Quality of Life", Report No. 1999RD42.

T.K. Majumdar, "Social Indicators—The Social Basis of the Quality of Life in the Metropolies" 1992.

Usava, P. Irina, "Complex Apporoach to the Assessment of Life Quality in Urban Environment: Case Study of Mahiliou in Belaraus", www.prague2003.fsu.edu.

12 Population Dynamics, Quality of Life and the Environment

Arup Kumar Hazarika

The number of people on Earth, where they live, and how they live all affect the demands and pressures placed on the environment. However, the links between demographic change and the environment are more complicated than people once thought. Human population dynamics lead to environmental change and are in turn affected by it. Consumption patterns, development choices, wealth distribution, Government policies and technology can mediate or exacerbate the effects of demographic change on the environment. The precise impact of a given change depends on the interplay among all these factors.

Human population dynamics include phenomena such as population size and rate of change, migration, age structure, household size and gender balance. At a very basic level, the size of the human population determines the total demand for food, water, shelter and other goods and services, which in turn require environmental inputs. Other demographic factors affect the composition of goods and services required, for example, the balance between education and health care in societies with a large proportion of children or elderly people.

Although improved technologies may make it possible to support a larger population, they must be constantly monitored. For example, an improvement in the efficiency of fishing techniques, which makes it possible to feed more people, can lead to overfishing, progressively resulting in less food overall. Improved farming methods may produce more food per acre, and therefore support more people, but the increased population may be too large for the available water or fuel wood, thereby overstraining another set of resources.

What can be done to confront these issues? Over the last decades there has been a flurry of activities. A variety of international agencies, governmental bodies and NGOs have been created for the purpose. Associations of experts, consultants and development workers, each with their own jargon and corporate rules, have been set up. Thousands of books, papers, reports and manuals have been (and are still being) written. Development and environment projects now operate even in the remotest areas of the world. Globally, huge and yet insufficient sums of money are being spent for development aid and environmental initiatives.

High rates of population growth, which are common in the developing world, are largely the result of falling death rates in a context of persistently high fertility. Although infant and child mortality rates are still higher than in the developed world, there has been an overall trend towards a decrease in mortality in the early years of life and an increase in life expectancy. Yet, one may ask: "To what extent is a decrease in mortality associated with improvements in the quality of life for a community as a whole?"

While discussing about the population dynamics, quality of life and the environment, it is important to note that agricultural bio-diversity, food security and that of poverty are very much linked. So, before discussing the issues on the population dynamics it is also important to discuss the impact of these issues on the population dynamics.

Agricultural bio-diversity plays a central role in household food security and income generation, and thus in achieving Millennium Development Goal (MDG) of halving the proportion of hungry and extremely poor people by 2015. However, its wider use to address nutritional deficiencies and other aspects of poverty, all of paramount importance, is yet to be fully realized.

With this in mind, an International Convention was held in Chennai, India, in April 2005, gathering together policy-makers and experts with diverse backgrounds from 25 countries. The aim of the Chennai Convention was to emphasize the unique contribution that agricultural bio-diversity makes to improve livelihoods, through providing a foundation for household food and nutrition security and offering opportunities for income generation. Agriculture is what feeds us but agricultural bio-diversity is what sustains us. The Convention also looked at policies, institutional constraints and other issues that are impeding the full deployment of these natural resources and hence limiting the achievement of the MDGs. Concern was registered at the rapid loss of these resources, which seriously threatens the food and nutrition security of future generations.

Globally, food insecurity and poverty are often found where bio-diversity loss is especially pronounced, as well as in some of the more remote areas of richest remaining biodiversity. In 19 of the 25 bio-diversity-rich "hotspots" for bio-diversity loss defined by Conservation International, population growth rates are higher than the global average, and in the few remaining wilderness areas, twice the global average. Sixteen of the 25 hotspots are in areas where over 20 per cent of the population is malnourished–accounting for a quarter of all the malnourished people in the developing countries. The expansion of agriculture, human settlements and infrastructure has led to massive ecosystem conversion and degradation. Over 83 per cent of the earth's land area is impacted by human activity, as is 98 per cent of the area suitable for producing wheat, rice and maize. Some experts calculate that if present trends of wildlife losses and habitat destruction continue, at least 25 per cent of the world's wild plants and animals could be extinct or vastly reduced in number by the middle of this century. Hydrological functions have deteriorated in watersheds around the world. Present levels of investment to address these challenges are grossly inadequate. Moreover, present investments largely reflect sectoral strategies and ignore the powerful inter-linkages between food insecurity, poverty and bio-diversity loss.

Two—thirds of the rural population—and the rural poor–live in higher risk production environments with variable rainfall, difficult soils and pest complexes. Over 500 million people live in drylands without access to irrigation, and 625 million live in mountainous regions, where considerable natural bio-diversity still remain. It is precisely in such areas that food production must double or triple over the next few decades (often from the low yield levels found today), if nutritional status is to improve. The other third of the rural population live in the "breadbaskets" and "rice bowls" of the world where ecosystems are so heavily modified that ecosystem services have declined.

While international attention is understandably concentrated on the unprecedented rates of urbanization in developing countries, it is often overlooked that rural populations will still be growing in absolute terms in most low-income countries for at least the next 30 years. Despite structural changes in economies, in 2010 atleast half the population in developing countries will likely still be in agriculture. Thus problems of rural food insecurity, poverty and bio-diversity loss will be closely inter-linked.

Historically, policy responses to food insecurity have emphasized increasing the supply of food, through agricultural research and investment, provision of food aid, and development of urban safety nets. Poverty reduction has focused on urban and non-farm development, and to a lesser extent agricultural commercialization by larger-scale farmers. Policy responses to bio-diversity loss have primarily focused on establishment of protected areas and regulation of land and resource use. While all of these approaches can claim some success, sectoral "stove piping" of policies has often exacerbated problems in the other sectors, posing problematic trade-offs.

Efforts to address food security by promoting intensification of production through high agro-chemical input use has resulted in cases of serious pollution of freshwater and coastal biodiversity. Hypoxia due to excessive nutrient loads is especially severe in gulf waters below the Mississippi and Mekong Deltas. Irrigation investments that divert water from critical natural wetlands and failure to provide adequate drainage for irrigation waters both threaten bio-diversity.

While such trade-offs are sometimes unavoidable, there is far greater potential for synergies in achieving food security, poverty reduction and bio-diversity conservation than is generally recognized. A variety of strategies can mobilize and support local people to conserve areas of high bio-diversity, restore bio-diversity in degraded working landscapes, and thereby enhance the natural resource assets of low-income, food-insecure populations. By engaging with local people to conserve aspects of bio-diversity that are critically important to their livelihoods, such strategies can build broader-based, long-term public support for protection of globally threatened bio-diversity.

Investment to increase agricultural productivity is essential in many low-income rural regions. But new "eco-agriculture" approaches can be used that at the same time conserve or enhance natural biodiversity. This is achieved by using the spaces in and around productive areas for habitat networks and by improving the habitat quality of productive areas themselves by reducing agro-chemical pollution, modifying water, soil and vegetation management, or by modifying farming systems to mimic natural ecosystems. For example, scattered trees, woodlots and forest strips cannot only provide woodfuel, vitamin-and calorie rich fruits, and raw materials for locally processed goods, but restore as well habitats for threatened plant and animal species. Dozens of eco-agriculture systems have been documented around the world, from intensive irrigated rice systems to improved fallow system, to shaded coffee and cocoa and other forest garden systems.

Communities can establish, enrich or conserve special bio-diversity reserves. These can be designed and managed to protect wild species that serve as "safety nets" for the poor in times of food scarcity, as well as ecosystem services of local importance. For example, in the drylands of southern Zimbabwe, wild foods, fuels, housing inputs, fertilizer and other products from common woodlands and rangelands provided 24 per cent of average total income for the poorest fifth of households. Farmer groups working through the landcare programme in Australia to rehabilitate degraded crop and grazing lands in Australia have taken land out of production and jointly set up and fenced protected areas for wildlife. These international examples are really very important for undertaking well-organized projects in our region, specifically in the world famous Kaziranga National Park.

Meeting the Millennium Development Goals will require political will, financial commitment and a readiness to attempt innovative solutions. The very fact that five years after the adoption of these goals, most developing countries have been unable to make proportionate progress in the elimination of hunger and poverty indicates the need for an overall change in the manner in which we have addressed this challenge to date. Without such a change we will not achieve the goal of a hunger free world.

Let us keep before our eyes a positive reality: that, given the necessary resources and collaboration, the MDGs can, in fact, be achieved. In a world where 852 million people are hungry, in the words of FAO Director-General, Jacques Diouf, "The question is not whether we can afford to take the urgent and immediate action needed...The question is whether we can afford not to." Can we have a hunger-free world? This is the challenge.

Coming back to the main issue again—the dynamics of population and the management of environmental resources are closely related concerns confronting our contemporary world. Whether we live in rural or urban, developing or developed regions, we need to understand and deal with the linkages between the status of society (e.g., population, socio-economic development, physical health, quality of life) and the condition of the natural environment (e.g., status and future prospects of fresh water, soil, forests, wildlife, biodiversity). This area introduces these linkages and an integrated and participatory approach for addressing them: primary environmental care. The approach is briefly described and illustrated by an example of a real case where it was put into practice.

It is a paradox of our times that in the last decades of the twentieth century, when the world is supporting a population larger than ever before and, on average, healthier and wealthier than ever before, people are increasingly concerned about the future of humankind. The media show images of poverty, hunger, violence, and disease. Recurrent social crises reveal that development efforts do not result in a more equitable distribution of wealth, nor in an overall decrease in the numbers of poor people. Where improvements in national economic indicators have been obtained, it is often at the price of harsh environmental degradation. And population growth—the ultimate sign of the success of the human species—is seen by many as a major cause of environmental stress.

The argument for the latter view is rather straightforward. As population enlarges, there are smaller amounts per person of the relatively stable natural resources, such as water, arable land or timber. More people means more environmental exploitation and/or more poverty. Yet, population growth cannot be separated from patterns of consumption, or from the technology and social systems that people use to produce goods and services. As an illustration of this point, a growing population in a given area means, by definition, a decrease in the amount of water available per person. But the impact of reductions in the per capita availability of water on food production and human health depends very much on the technology used locally for irrigation, water supply and waste disposal.

Under an unchanging technology for water and waste management, a growing population will mean a smaller production of food per capita, and the water available for drinking and hygiene may become less and less healthy due to increasing contamination by human wastes. If, however, the technology is improved to enable more efficient irrigation, water supply and waste treatment, and if the local, political, economic and institutional context is such that these benefits can reach every inhabitant of the area, the overall quality of life may actually improve as the water per capita declines.

Some authors would even maintain that a certain concentration of people is necessary to provide the stimulus and economic conditions needed for technical improvement and development in general. An intriguing argument presented by Esther Boserup in 1981 sees population growth as a main stimulus towards technological progress. According to this perspective, early in human history the growing needs of numbers of people promoted the use of fire, the domestication of animals, the storage of food and the development of agriculture, a productive system supporting much larger populations than hunting and gathering. In the following millennia, population growth stimulated improvements in agricultural productivity *via* both technical innovations and reorganization of societies. More recently, population growth provided the concentrations of labour and the supply of ingenuity to spur the industrial revolution and the development of modern societies, with their high levels of employment in the production of services.

Although improved technologies may make it possible to support a larger population, they must be constantly monitored. For example, an improvement in the efficiency of fishing techniques, which makes it possible to feed more people, can lead to overfishing, progressively resulting in less food overall. Improved farming methods may produce more food per acre, and therefore support more people, but the increased population may be too large for the available water or fuel-wood, thereby overstraining another set of resources. It is not by chance that the progressive exhaustion of renewable resources (e.g., water, soil, fisheries, forested land) is a major concern of both the developing and developed worlds.

What can be done to confront these issues? Over the last decades there has been a flurry of activities. A variety of international agencies, Governmental bodies and NGOs have been created for the purpose. Associations of experts, consultants and development workers, each with their own jargon and corporate rules, have been set up. Thousands of books, papers, reports and manuals have been (and are still being) written. Development and environmental projects now operate even in the remotest areas of the world. Globally, huge and yet insufficient sums of money are being spent for development aid and environmental initiatives.

Have these development efforts been worthwhile? Yes, if we look at improved agricultural yields, increased gross national products, increased literacy and decreased childhood mortality. Not really, however, if we take a closer look at issues of equity and environmental sustainability. In fact, problems of social injustice and environmental degradation are the true Achilles' heel of the 'development' enterprise. How did it happen? Some commonly acknowledged causes of problems include the following:

How does population dynamics fit into the picture? How does it affect not only the environment but also equity, quality of life, and respect for cultural differences? Currently, the human population is growing most rapidly in the poorest regions of the world, where the resources for technological development are most scarce and the institutional structure is weakest. Already today, one person in five cannot get enough food to support an active working life. One quarter of the world's people still are without safe drinking water, and many more are without proper housing and sanitation. Millions of children still die from malnutrition and preventable diseases, and half a million women die each year from pregnancy-related problems. Is it reasonable to expect that vast increases in human numbers will be compatible with improvements in health and quality of life for the multitudes in need? For some it is more reasonable to expect that the weight of human population growth will end up as another burden on the shoulders of the poor and their environment. Thus, a world with many more people is likely to be even less equitable than it is today.

The answer to this question can be controversial, especially for rural areas. At times, increased survival rates due to improved health services and people's behavioural changes are even associated with a poorer quality of life.

High rates of population growth, which are common in the developing world, are largely the result of falling death rates in a context of persistently high fertility. Although infant and child mortality rates are still higher than in the developed world, there has been an overall trend towards a decrease in mortality in the early years of life and an increase in life expectancy. Yet, one may ask: "To what extent is a decrease in mortality associated with improvements in the quality of life for a community as a whole?"

And there is more to 'quality of life' than satisfying material needs. Cultural and biological diversity, for instance, contribute to the resilience of systems, but also make direct and indirect contributions to the quality of life (both present and future).

Thus, some fear that increased numbers of people could be sustained only by technological might and pervasive socio-cultural change, all at the expense of patiently crafted cultural peculiarities. For centuries, local cultures evolved through slow and unique combinations of resistance and adaptation to their environments. Today these cultures are simultaneously facing the dual impacts of pervasive socio-economic change and rapid degradation in ecological conditions. The indicators of 'quantitative' health and welfare, e.g. a decline in mortality rate and an increased in national product per capita tell us little about quality of life, a phenomenon involving culturally relative perceptions of well-being, independence, productivity, social involvement and meaning of existence.

At the global level, population growth in combination with the spreading culture of mass consumption is having major, at times devastating, impacts on the environment and natural resources. But population dynamics also encompasses other forms of population change, including population decline, migration, urbanization (or population distribution) and trends in aging and gender balance. Each of these, in turn, can have significant implications for the environment as well as for equity and the respect of cultural differences. For instance, migration from resource-poor areas to frontier regions has occurred throughout history. While such migration can reduce the environmental pressure in the source areas, the destination areas often suffer from the uncontrolled exploitation of resources, and may also experience cultural conflicts. Furthermore, in a world of six billion people, there simply are not as many frontiers as in the past, and those that remain are often quickly spoiled.

Migration to cities (urbanization) may be beneficial to the environment on some levels, and harmful on others. On the benefits side, the concentration of people means that it is more efficient to provide services such as electricity, sanitation and public transportation. Furthermore, the housing concentration of urban areas, particularly those in the developing world, means that proportionally less land is taken away from agricultural activities. On the problems side, we could count the concentrated production of organic and human waste which, in the absence of modern sanitation systems, is not easily absorbed by the environment. Urban areas are also characterized by higher per capita levels of resource consumption.

At first glance, population aging and gender balance may seem to have less dramatic consequences on the environment. And yet, these too are important. Aging, especially in the developed world, is coming at a tremendous cost to social support mechanisms and the health-care system. As life expectancy climbs into the 1970s in some developing countries, available public sector financial resources may be stretched to meet the growing demands of the health-care and social security systems. This may mean that fewer resources are available to meet other needs, such as environmental management and basic welfare. Gender balance reflects socio-economic processes, such as male outmigration, which can have significant indirect impacts on the environment. Where women are the heads of household, and perhaps the sole providers for a family, they may not have the time and resources available to manage the local environment in a careful and sustainable way.

Affecting demographic phenomena is neither easy nor rapid. Let us consider a reduction in natural increase (this is the portion of population growth that includes births minus deaths, but does not include migration). Today, up to half of the population in poor countries is under 14 years of age. Given this extremely young age distribution, even if the present and next generation only have enough children to replace themselves (approximately two births per woman), the total populatio size of countries will still increase dramatically. This is because the number of people of reproductive age, among whom fertility is highest, greatly outweighs the population in older age groups, among whom mortality is highest. The result is a significant excess of births over deaths, leading to rapid population growth. For instance, it is estimated that the African continent, which contains 12 per cent of the world's population, will contribute about 34 per cent of global population growth between now and the year 2050 (United Nations, 1995).

Given the complex interplay of population, development and environment mentioned above, is there any 'solution' we can pursue? Is there any way to improve the quality of human life while maintaining the quality of the natural environment? Surely there is no one solution applicable to all contexts and societies. The complexity of the issues at stake is such that even initiatives taken with the best intentions and adequate resources can end up in abysmal failures. Yet, there are some lessons from the past that can be brought to bear when searching for the specific solution to fit a specific problem and context.

Primary Environmental Care

Local empowerment can only be based on the concerns of community members and their willingness to be involved. Certainly, it cannot be 'brought in' from outside. From outside, however, it can be impeded.

In this sense, PEC Primary Environmental Care needs to be politically feasible, a condition too often difficult to meet. Other constraints to PEC may be lack of capital, information, expertise, or the capacity of local people to organize, to manage finances or to deal with government officials. Supporting institutions (governmental and non–governmental, national and international, profit-oriented and solidarity-oriented) can help communities to overcome these constraints.

The objectives of PEC are not new, but the approach has the merit of integrating them, affirming that the management of local environments becomes effective and sustainable when linked with the satisfaction of the needs (income, food, health, etc.) of local communities, and when all the concerned people are involved and empowered to participate.

'Meeting local needs' means that people can maintain, produce or gain access to the goods and services (food, shelter, income, health care, education, transportation, etc.) necessary for their life, health and well-being.

'Protecting the local environment' means different activities under different conditions (e.g., eliminating a fire hazard, cleaning and protecting a watershed, preventing flooding, halting an unsustainable extraction of timber from a local forest, improving tilling practices to protect topsoil, restoring a degraded communal building, leaving undisturbed the habitat of wildlife, etc.).

'Empowering local communities' means that communities, groups and individuals obtain greater control over the factors influencing their lives. This usually goes through several stages, in which people discuss and identify their common problems and opportunities and then organize and take action in partnership with others. Securing tenure to the natural resources protected by the work of local people is a most important element of the empowerment process, and essential for sustainability. With security of tenure, in fact, the long-term economic interests of people tend to merge with the long-term 'interests' of the environment.

If a community engages in primary environmental care, many

sensitive issues are bound to be encountered, and many conflicts between local and non-local interests and opinions are likely to emerge. Such conflicts can arise in the planning stages (e.g., when trade-offs must be set among environmental, economic and social goals, and priorities for action must be agreed upon) or during implementation of activities, when some can try to take advantage of others, or problems and mistakes become apparent.

The 'community' may also be united and well defined only in theory. Community members may not feel a sense of common identity, may not be equally aware or concerned about problems and ready to commit resources or may not manage to achieve any suitable agreement about what to do. A lengthy process of conflict management and negotiation may be necessary before PEC activities can take off. In fact, major differences, contrasts and power imbalances are common among community members and sub-groups. Women, ethnic minorities or religious minorities may not be allowed to participate in decision-making or in common endeavours on the same conditions as others. In such cases, PEC requires a significant change in local habits and departure from cultural norms.

'Primary environmental care' is an approach to community-based sustainable development matured on the basis of field experience. Many people and organizations—from both developing and industrialized countries—contributed to the development of this approach. Most of them worked in participatory projects in poor urban and rural areas. Others were involved in Primary Health Care, and Water and Sanitation Programmes. Others were employed in large and small-scale integrated rural development schemes. Still others were simply concerned about improving their own quality of life and the quality of life of their communities—by making optimal use of scarce resources. The knowledge and skills these people acquired from their practice with methods and tools, their tribulations with conflicts and failures and their excitement as they solved problems and helped people, all contributed to a consensus on goals to strive for, and ways to approach them. To give visibility, legitimacy, incentive and impetus to such a consensus, a name package was found: Primary Environmental Care (PEC).

Whatever it may be, the world population continues to increase, with the most rapid growth forecast to occur in developing countries. According to estimates by the United Nations, the population of developing regions is projected to increase from about 4.9 billion in 2000 to 8.1 billion by 2050, while that of industrialized regions, currently 1.2 billion, is expected to change little over the next 50 years. Areas experiencing rapid population growth are also those where the majority of the earth's remaining bio-diversity can be found. However, bio-diversity conservation is generally considered a low priority compared with meeting the needs of a rapidly growing population for jobs, food, housing, health and education. This in turn reflects widespread misunderstanding of the important role of healthy ecosystems in sustaining a growing population.

Continuing population growth is difficult to reconcile with any practical vision of sustainable development. Among other changes, the shift to sustainability requires a demographic transition leading to stabilization of human population. Fortunately, we are seeing this trend taking place steadily around the world. The fertility rate has dramatically fallen in most countries, and globally it is now at half the rate of the 1960s. It is expected to drop below replacement level in the next few decades–a goal that has been already met in more than one-third of the countries of the world. Given the complexity of demographic phenomena, effective action on population issues from a sustainability perspective requires a sophisticated understanding of how changes in the size, composition and location of human populations affect the use of natural resources and environmental quality.

IUCN has expressed its concern on population and environment through a number of Resolutions. For instance, Resolution GA 15.03 of 1981 on "People, resources and environment" called for Governments to develop strategies that inter-relate population control, production and consumption policies and sustainable use to conservation of the environment.

References

Buck, L.E., C.C. Geisler, J. Schelhas, E. Wollenberg, eds. 2001. *Biological Diversity: Balancing Interests through Adaptive Collaborative Management.* CRC Publishers: Chelsea, Michigan.

Chung, B.R. 1999. *Community-Based Land use Planning in Conservation Areas: Lessons from Local Participatory Processes that seek to Balance Economic uses with Ecosystem Protection.* Training Manual, America Verde No.3. The Nature Conservancy: Arlington, Virginia.

Cincotta, R.P. and R. Engelman. 2000. *Nature's Place: Human Population and the Future of Biological Diversity.* Population Action International, Washington, D.C.

Current, D. 1995. "Economic and institutional analysis of projects promoting on-farm tree planting in Costa Rica." In D. Current, E. Lutz and S.J. Scherr, eds. *Costs, Benefits and Farmer Adoption of Agroforestry: Project Experience in Central America and the Caribbean.* A CATIEIFPRI–World Bank Project. World Bank Environment Paper No. 14. The World Bank: Washington, D.C., pp. 45-80.

DeWalt, B., F. Olivera and J. Betancourt Correa. 2000. Mid-term evaluation of the Mexico community forestry project. World Bank: Washington, D.C. FAO. 2002. *The State of Food Insecurity in the World:* 2002. Food and Agriculture Organization of the United Nations: Rome.

Frazier, S. 1999. 'Ramsar sites overview: a synopsis of the world's wetlands of internationalimportance'. Wet lands International, Wageningen, The Netherland.

Garrity, D. 2003. *The Role of Agroforestry in Sustaining Livelihoods and Protecting Bio-diversity.* Paper presented to the CIFOR International Conference on "Rural Livelihoods, Forests and Bio-diversity", Bonn, Germany, May 19–23. IFAD (International Fund for Agricultural Development), 2001. *Rural Poverty Report 2001: The Challenge of Ending Rural Poverty.* Oxford University Press: Oxford, U.K.

IUCN. 2000. *IUCN Red List of Threatened Species.* World Conservation Union: Gland, Switzerland.

Kaimowitz, D. 2003. *Forest Law Enforcement and Rural Livelihoods.* Center for International Forestry Research: Bogor, Indonesia.

Lacher, T., R. Slack, L. Coburn and M. Goldstein. The role of agro-eco-systems in wild bio-diversity. In W.W. Collins and C.O. Qualset, eds. *Bio-diversity in Agro-eco-systems.* CRC Press: New York.

Landell-Mills, N. and I. Porras. 2002. *Silver Bullet or Fool's Gold? A Global Review of Markets for Forest Environmental Services*. International Institute for Environment and Development: London.

Leakey, R.R.B. 1999. 'Agroforestry for biodiversity in farming systems'. In W.W. Collins and C.O. Qualset, eds. *Bio-diversity in Agro-eco-systems*. CRC Press: New York.

Lee, David and Chris Barrett, eds. 2000. *Trade-offs and Synergies: Agricultural Intensification, Economic Development and the Environment*. Commonwealth Agricultural Bureau International, London.

McNeely, J.A. and S.J. Scherr. 2002. *Eco-agriculture: Strategies to Feed the World and Save Wild Bio-diversity*. Island Press, Washington, D.C.

Molnar, A. 2003. *Alternative Conservation Strategies: Conserve What and for Whom?* Forest Trends: Washington, D.C. Draft.

Pagiola, S., J. Bishop and N. Landell-Mills, eds. 2002. *Selling Forest Environmental Services: Market-based Mechanisms for Conservation and Development*. Earthscan Publications Limited:London.

Population Dynamics Environment and Quality of Life in North East India, B. Misra, Department of Economics, North Eastern Hill University.

Revenga, C., J. Brunner, N. Henninger, K. Kassem and R. Payne. 2000. *Pilot Analysis of Global Ecosystems: Freshwater Systems*. World Resources Institute: Washington, D.C.

Sanderson, E.W., M. Jaiteh, M.A. Levy, K.H. Redford, A.V. Wannebo and G. Woolmer. 2002. The human footprint and the last of the wild. *Bio-Science* 52 (10): 891–904.

Scherr, S.J. 1999. *Soil Degradation: A Threat to Developing Country Food Security by 2020?* Food, Agriculture and the Environment Discussion Paper 27. International Food Policy Research Institute, Washington, D.C.

Scherr, S.J. and the Hunger Task Force. 2003. *Halving Global Hunger*. Background Report of the Millennium Project Hunger Task Force. Earth Institute, Columbia University: New York.

Scherr, S.J., A. White and D. Kaimowitz. 2003. *A New Agenda for Forest Conservation and Poverty Alleviation: Making Markets Work for Low-Income Producers*. Forest Trends and the Center for International Forestry Research: Washington, D.C.

Smith, J. and S.J. Scherr. 2002. *Forest Carbon and Local Livelihoods: Assessment of Opportunities and Policy Recommendations*. CIFOR Occasional Paper No. 37. Center for International Forestry Research and Forest Trends: Bogor, Indonesia.

Sutherland, M. and B. Scarsbrick. 2001. Conservation of Bio-diversity through Landcare.

United Nations. 2002. *The United Nations and the MDG's: a Core Strategy*. United Nations: New York.

White, A. and A. Martin. 2002. *Who Owns the World's Forests?* Forest Trends: Washington, D.C.

Wood, S., K. Sebastian and S.J. Scherr. 2000. *Pilot Analysis of Global Ecosystems: Agro-eco-systems*. International Food Policy Research Institute and World Resources Institute, Washington, D.C.

World Bank. 2002. *World Development Report 2002*. The World Bank: Washington, D.C.

13 Population Dynamics and the Demographic Dividend in Meghalaya

Utpal Kumar Dey

Introduction

It is a long standing debate whether the continuous growth of population is pro - or anti-development of economics. There is no doubt that the size and composition of population always play an important role behind the development of an economy. On the one hand, it is the source of labour force for the production and other socio-economic activities in the economy. Hence rising population increases the supply of labourer and thus (if properly utilised) raise the scope of production in an economy. But that is possible if there is shortage of labour in the economy and production activities are on a sub-optimal level. On the other hand, if the population size crosses the carrying capacity of the system then it instead of adding to the growth, create several impediments due to rising needs for food, shelter etc. and management of waste materials that it generates beyond the assimilating capacity of the environment. Also if the increased labourers do not find any gainful employment, it generates the problem of unemployment and other related issues.

Malthus (1798) was very much concerned about the growth of population to outrun the availability of food supply. The increasing pressure of the human population on the nature and diminishing marginal productivity of resources leading to Malthusian catastrophe was underlined in his book, *An Essay on the Principles of Population.* The pessimistic views have also been found in Ehrlich (1968), Meadows *et al.* (1972), Ehrlich and Ehrlich (1990) etc. who were of the opinion that if the population continues to grow the world would be falling short of resources especially the critical natural resources after some years. However, labourers in the production units to a certain extent can be substituted by machineries through the improvement of technology that would certainly compound the problem of unemployment. However, the rising waste materials and other environmental problems can also be better managed through the innovation of improved technology, which is possible when an economy grows and that is associated with the rise in human qualities and not the size of population only. Hence Johnson (2000), Simon (1981, 1996) pointed out that rising population is not a problem but it enhances the utility of resources through improved and judicious management. In their opinion, if there is freedom and markets are free and fair that would solve many of the problems.

However, one can safely argue that if technological improvement does not match with the rising requirements of the growing population, rapid growth of population may act as a retarding factor for the growth and development of the economy. That is, if income does not grow at vleast at the identical rate of population growth, per capita income will necessarily fall and also reduce access to the per capita availability of other resources needed to maintain a particular standard of living. Then there will be a rise in pressure on natural, especially common resources as they will be increasingly dependent on such resources for their livelihood. Therefore, rapid growth of population in many cases leads to environmental and natural resource degradation. Mikesell (1995) also pointed out that crowding is one of the consequences of population growth that reduces the quality of life.

Moreover, rising population means rising requirement of land for agricultural purposes to produce more (unless technology helps rise in productivity in the same way) and hence it expedites cutting and felling of trees by the people for extension of cultivation, settlement purposes, etc. leading to depletion of forest resources and thus severe environmental change. That is why many environmentalists think population growth is the greatest threat to sustainable development, and perhaps to the survival of the human species itself. Even though the application of modern seed, fertiliser, irrigation, technology yields better result in the short-run, the long-run productivity of soil is adversely affected as already observed in several parts of India.

Trend of Population in Meghalaya and Other North Eastern States of India

Trend of population during 1951 to 2001 in Meghalaya and other North Eastern States is shown in Table13.1. Since 1951 a tremendous growth of population has been observed in the North Eastern Region of the country. The population in the region has registered an increase from under 1.03 crores in 1951 to over 3.83 crores in 2001. That is population has increased to more than three times during these five decades as against 2.8 times in the country as a whole.

Table 13.1: Trend of Population in North Eastern Region of India, 1951 to 2001

	Population (In Thousand)						*Annual Exponential Growth Rate (in percentage)*		
States	*1951*	*1961*	*1971*	*1981*	*1991*	*2001*	*1951–71*	*1971–2001*	*1951–2001*
Arunachal Pradesh	N. A	337	468	632	865	1097	3.28*	2.84	2.95*
Assam	8029	10837	14625	18041	22414	26655	3.00	2.00	2.40
Manipur	578	780	1073	1421	1837	2166	3.09	2.34	2.64
Meghalaya	606	769	1012	1336	1775	2318	2.56	2.76	2.68
Mizoram	196	266	332	494	690	888	2.64	3.28	3.02
Nagaland	213	369	516	775	1210	1990	4.42	4.50	4.47
Tripura	639	1142	1556	2053	2757	3199	4.45	2.40	3.22
NER	10261	14500	19582	24750	31548	38316	3.23	2.24	2.64
All-India	361088	439235	548160	683329	846303	1028737	2.09	2.10	2.09

Note: * indicates that the base year for Arunachal Pradesh is 1961 instead of 1951.
Source: Census of India, 2001

During 1951–1971, the highest annual exponential growth rate of population among the North-Eastern States was recorded by Tripura (4.45 per cent), which was followed by Nagaland with 4.42 per cent (Table 13.1). The annual exponential growth rate of population in Meghalaya during that period was 2.56 per cent only, which was the lowest among all the North Eastern States. However, the overall annual exponential rate of growth during 1951 to 2001 in Meghalaya was 2.68 per cent. During the same period, Nagaland recorded the highest annual exponential rate of growth of population, which was 4.47 per

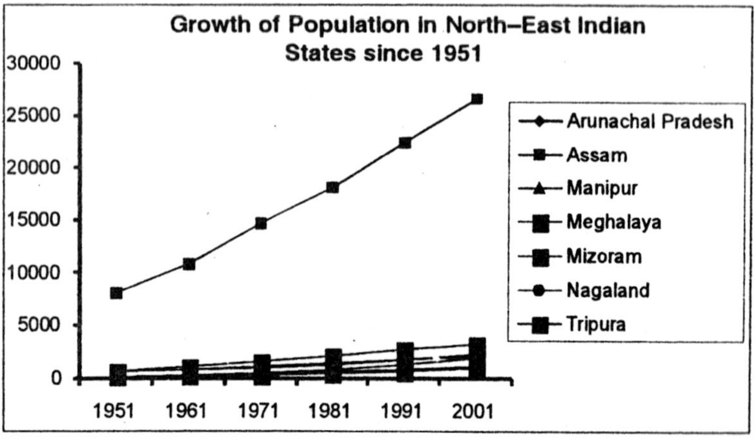

cent. Annual exponential growth rate during 1951 to 2001 was the lowest in Assam and highest in Nagaland. Also, during 1971 to 2001, annual exponential growth rate was highest in Nagaland and lowest in Assam. Annual exponential growth rate has increased during the later sub-period in the State of Meghalaya, Nagaland and Mizoram, while in the other North Eastern States it has declined. Though growth rate of population in Meghalaya was the lowest during 1951 to 1971 sub-periods, it became higher than the States of Assam, Manipur and Tripura in the later sub-periods. The growth rate significantly declined in Tripura, Arunachal Pradesh, Assam and Manipur, which together more than offset the rising annual exponential growth rate of other North Eastern States and led to decline in overall growth rate in post 1971 period. Here, population growth has been not only due to the natural growth but also due to the net in migration from the neighbouring countries especially Bangladesh. These States, mainly Tripura and Assam were highly affected due to partition (at the time of Independence) and even at the time of Bangladesh War, we had observed huge influx of people. But during 1980s and 1990s the net in migration has come down significantly and the population growth that was observed during that time was mainly due to the natural growth. Moreover, the population controlling measures have been successfully implemented in those States and not in Meghalaya, Nagaland and Mizoram. Though the overall annual exponential growth rate has declined in 1980s and 1990s, it was still higher than the all-India average. Composition of Population in Meghalaya, Nagaland and Mizoram. Though the overall annual exponential growth rate has declined in 1980s and 1990s, it was still higher than the all-India average.

Composition of Population in Meghalaya

The majority of the population in Meghalaya are tribals. The main tribes of the State are the Khasis, Jaintias and Garos. These groups are also divided into different sub-groups such as Khynriam, Pnar, Bhoi, War, etc. in case of Khasis and Jainitias. These people belong to a number of clans and are essentially differentiated from each other by their locations and functions they perform (Gopalakrishnan, 2001). The Khasis and Jaintias are mainly settled in four districts of the State, viz. East Khasi Hills, West Khasi Hills, Jaintia Hills and Ri Bhoi districts, whereas the Garos are primarily living in the three districts of the western part of the State, known as East Garo Hills, West Garo Hills and South Garo Hills districts. Besides these, there are other groups of minor tribes Mikir, Lalung, Biate, Dimasa, Hajong, Hmar, Kuki, Lakhar, Koch, Rabha, etc. who are settled in the State.

District-wise Trend of Population in Meghalaya

Population in Meghalaya has been increasing at a steady rate since 1951, which has been higher than the national average. Yet now the density of population (103 per sq. km) is much lower than the national average (313 per sq. km, according to 2001 Census Report), that is less than one-third of the national average. Though the State is endowed with huge forest, mineral resources, it is unable to absorb the rising population because of the lack of enterprises and technological development. Therefore, even with very low population density the State failed to create sufficient employment opportunities and hence the growing population became more and more dependent on their surrounding natural resources for the sustenance and the dependence is intense among the poorer section. The district-wise variation in population over time has been displayed in Table 13.2.

Table 13.2 : District-wise Variation of Population in Meghalaya 1971–2001

State/Districts	Persons				Males				Females			
	1971	1981	1991	2001	1971	1981	1991	2001	1971	1981	1991	2001
Jaintia Hills	113562	156402	220473	299108	56810	79052	111753	149891	56752	77350	108720	149217
	(11.22)	(11.71)	(12.42)	(12.89)	(50.03)	(50.54)	(50.69)	(50.11)	(49.97)	49.46)	(49.31)	(49.89)
East Khasi Hills	327922	411489	537914	660923	198972	262952	341670	333553	181678	248462	323548	327370
	(32.41)	(30.80)	(30.31)	(28.50)	(52.27)	(51.42)	(51.26)	(50.47)	(47.73)	(48.58)	(48.64)	(49.53)
West Khasi Hills	110872	161576	220157	296049	56687	82906	112860	150419	54185	78670	107297	145630
	(10.96)	(12.09)	(12.40)	(12.77)	(51.13)	(51.31)	(51.26)	(50.81)	(48.87)	(48.69)	(48.74)	(49.19)
East Garo Hills	102698	136550	188830	250582	53218	70365	96444	127474	49480	66185	92386	123108
	(10.15)	(10.22)	(10.64)	(10.81)	(51.82)	(51.53)	(51.07)	(50.87)	(48.18)	(48.47)	(48.93)	(49.13)
West Garo Hills	248913	306347	401571	518390	155280	188435	244960	263424	148637	181442	235140	254966
	(24.61)	(22.94)	(22.63)	(22.35)	(51.09)	(50.95)	(51.02)	(50.82)	(48.91)	(49.05)	(48.98)	(49.18)
Ri Bhoi	52728*	99925*	127304*	192790	N.A.	N.A.	N.A.	99319	N.A.	N.A.	N.A.	93471
	(5.21)	(7.48)	(7.17)	(8.31)	51.52	N.A.	N.A.	N.A.				(48.48)
South Garo Hills	55004*	63530*	78529*	100980	N.A.	N.A.	N.A.	52007	N.A.	N.A.	N.A.	48973
	(5.43)	(4.75)	(4.42)	(4.35)	(51.50)							(48.50)
Meghalaya	1011699	1335819	1774778	2318822	520967	683710	907687	1176087	490732	652109	867091	1142735
	(100.00)	(100.00)	(100.00)	(100.00)	(51.49)	(51.18)	(51.14)	(50.72)	(48.51)	(48.82)	(48.86)	(49.28)

Notes: (1) Population for Ri Bhoi and South Garo Hills are not available for the years 1971, 1981 and 1991 since these two districts are newly created on June 4, and June 18, 1992 respectively. Here, value is approximated by assuming growth rate figures available in Basic Statistics of North Eastern Region.

(2) Figures in the brackets of males and females indicate the percentage to Total Population of each district.

(3) Figures in the brackets of persons indicate the percentage of Total Population of the State.

(4) * Population of East Khasi Hills and West Garo Hills in 1971,1981 and 1991 have been estimated by the scholar by assuming estimated population of Ri Bhoi and South Garo Hills districts. So for those years the male and female figures may not be added up to total population of those districts.

(5). N. A. indicates not available and earlier Ri Bhoi was part of East Khasi Hills and South Garo Hills was part of West Garo Hills.

Sources: (1) Census of India, 1981, Series-14, Part A & B: General Population Totals and Primary Census Abstract.

(2) Census of India, 1991, Series-1; Paper–2 of 1992.

(3) Census of India, 2001, Primary Census Abstract, Meghalaya, Series-18.

(4) Basic Statistics of North-Eastern Region, 2002.

During the past three decades, the growth of population in the State was nearly 130 per cent over the total population of 1971. In absolute terms, the population of the State increased by 1307123 persons during 1971 to 2001. In all the districts population growth followed more or less the similar trend.

Table 13.3 represents the inter-district variation in decadal growth rate and annual exponential growth rate of population in Meghalaya and in India as a whole since 1971.

Table 13.3 reveals that the decadal growth rate of population in the State was increasing from 1971–1981 to 1981–1991 and we observe a deceleration in the growth rate during 1991–2001. Whereas the decadal growth rate of population in India as a whole from 1971 onwards indicated a declining trend. In other words, we have seen that the decadal growth rate of population in the State since 1971 has always been much higher in comparison to that of India as a whole.

Table 13.3 : Changes in Decadal Growth Rate, Decadal Variation and Average Exponential Growth Rate of Population in Meghalaya (in Percentage)

State	*Decadal Variation in Population*				*Average Annual Exponential Growth Rate*			
Period	*1971–1981*	*1981–1991*	*1991–2001*	*1971–2001*	*1971–1981*	*1981–1991*	*1991–2001*	*1971–2001*
Jaintia Hills	37.72	40.97	35.67	163.39	3.20	3.43	3.05	3.23
East Khasi Hills	25.48	30.72	22.86	101.55	2.27	2.68	2.06	2.34
West Khasi Hills	45.73	36.26	34.47	167.02	3.77	3.09	2.96	3.27
East Garo Hills	32.96	38.29	32.70	144.00	2.85	3.24	2.83	2.97
West Garo Hills	23.07	31.08	29.09	108.26	2.08	2.71	2.55	2.45
Ri Bhoi	89.51	27.40	51.44	265.63	6.39	2.42	4.15	4.32
South Garo Hills	15.50	23.61	28.69	83.50	1.44	2.12	2.51	2.03
Meghalaya	32.04	32.86	30.65	129.20	2.78	2.84	2.67	2.76
India	24.66	23.86	21.56	87.67	2.20	2.15		1.95

Sources: Census of India, 2001; Basic Statistics of North-Eastern Region, 1995, 2000 and 2002.

Among the districts during 1971–1981, West Garo Hills and South Garo Hills districts recorded much lower rates of growth of population than the State while all other districts experienced higher rates of growth than the State average. In 1981–1991, Jaintia Hills recorded the highest rate of growth of population with 40.97 per cent and South Garo Hills experienced the lowest growth rate of 23.61 per cent. During 1991–2001, the decadal growth rate in Ri Bhoi district was the highest (51.44%) and in the East Khasi Hills district the growth rate was the lowest (22.86%). During the period from 1971 to 2001, the growth rate was the highest in West Khasi Hills (167.02%) and lowest in South Garo Hills (83.59%). Here one point to be noted is that during all the sub-periods all the districts have higher growth rates than the national average except during 1971–1981 and 1981–1991, when the growth rates in South Garo Hills were lower than national average and during 1971–1981 the figure of West Garo Hills was also lower than the national average. Moreover, during 1991–2001 growth rate was increasing in Ri Bhoi and South Garo Hills, while in other districts it was declining.

Average annual exponential growth rate of population for the State it has been found that it always remained above 2 per cent since 1971 onwards, and declined marginally during 1991 to 2001. All-India average annual exponential growth rate declined at a faster rate and reached 1.95 per cent per annum during 1991 to 2001 as compared to 2.67 per cent of the State of Meghalaya. Thus, both in absolute terms as well as in terms of the growth rate, the State had continued to witness (though the density is still low, considering the poor technology and economic growth) what we may think whether it can be designated as Population Explosion or not.

Density and Sex Ratio of Population in Meghalaya

Over time variation in density of population in the State of Meghalaya is very unevenly distributed. An inter-district comparison shows that East Khasi Hills and West Garo Hills have been more densely populated districts; while Jaintia Hills, West Khasi Hills and South Garo Hills districts on the other hand, have low density of population (Table 13.4). From merely 27 persons per square kilometre in 1951, the density of population rose to 45 persons per square kilometre in 1971 and then to 103 per square kilometre in 2001. However, still now the density of population in the State is much lower than the national average of 313 per square kilometre, according to 2001 Census Report.

Table 13.4 : District-wise Variation in Density of Population in Meghalaya (1951–2001)

State/Districts	*1951*	*1961*	*1971*	*1981*	*1991*	*2001*
Jaintia Hills	17	21	30	41	58	78
East Khasi Hills	81	103	119	149	191	241
West Khasi Hills	13	1?	21	31	42	56
East Garo Hills	24	30	39	52	73	96
West Garo Hills	48	62	67	82	108	140
Ri Bhoi	N.A	N.A	22*	48*	54	79
South Garo Hills	N.A	N.A	27*	34*	42	55
Meghalaya	27	45	45	60	79	103
All-India	117	134	177	216	267	313

Note: * Values are estimated by the Scholar.
Source: Census of India, 2001; Basic Statistics of North-Eastern Region, 1981 and 2002.

Since 1951, there is a sharp increase in the density of population in all the districts of Meghalaya. In Jaintia Hills, the density of population was only 17 persons per square kilometre in 1951 but has increased to 78 persons per square kilometre in 2001. In East Khasi Hills, we observed rapid increase in population especially due to urbanisation. Here the density of population in 1951 was 81 persons per square kilometre and increased to 241 persons per square kilometre in 2001. In West Khasi Hills, the density increased from 13 persons per square kilometre in 1951 and rose to 56 persons per square kilometre in 2001. In East Garo Hills and West Garo Hills districts, in 1951, the density of population was only 24 and 48 persons per square kilometre and rose to 96 and 140 persons per square kilometre respectively in 2001. Even in the newly districts like Ri Bhoi and South Garo Hills also, the density of population has increased sharply from 54 and 42 persons per square kilometre in 1991 to 79 and 55 persons per square kilometre in 2001. Only East Khasi Hills and West Garo Hills districts stand above the state average in terms of density of population. The density of population thus varies significantly across different districts of the State. However, the coefficient of variation in density of population decreased from 69.13 per cent in 1951 to 57.37 per cent in 2001. But the range of variation increased from 68 to 186 during 1951 to 2001. The density in East

Khasi Hills has always been the highest because of the availability of socio-economic activity, educational scope and better infrastructure.

Table 13.5 shows the district-wise variation in sex ratio of population in Meghalaya since 1951. The sex ratio in Meghalaya has always been higher than that of all-India average since 1951, except in 1961 when it was marginally lower. It has been observed from the Table 13.5 that sex ratio has increased in the State since 1961, whereas it has continuously declined at all-India level till 1991, after which, we observe a marginal increase. This is in consonance with the existing notion of the matrilineal society of Meghalaya at all-India level, the much-hyped campaign against gender discrimination, sex determination, etc. failed to increase the sex ratio to the desired level.

The percentage decadal variation of sex ratio in the State since 1951 has been varying significantly. During 1951–1961, the variation in sex ratio in the State was negative (-1.26 per cent) and during 1971–1981 it rose by 1.27 per cent. In the period, 1981–1991, it increased marginally by 0.10 per cent and during 1991 to 2001 it increased by 1.78 per cent. By taking into account the two sub-periods (1951–1971 and 1971–2001), the percentage decadal growth rate of sex ratio in the country was 1.70 per cent in 1951-1971 and 0.32 per cent in 1971–2001, whereas the figures in the State were -0.74 and 3.18 per cent respectively during 1951–1971 and 1971–2001.

More or less similar variation in sex ratio is observed in the different districts of Meghalaya. In 1971, sex ratio in Jaintia Hills (999), West Khasi Hills (956), and West Garo Hills (968) were above the State average sex ratio (942). In the other districts, the sex ratios were below the State average. Almost in all the districts we observe rising sex ratio, except in Ri Bhoi district where it has remained constant at 941 during 1991–2001.

According to 2001 Census, the Jaintia Hills district had the highest sex ratio of 996 and Ri Bhoi district recorded the lowest sex ratio of 941 among all the districts of Meghalaya. However, all the districts recorded comparatively higher sex ratio than the national average of 933 in 2001. The rise in sex ratio is due to: (i) the improvement in medical facilities that resulted in improvement in females life expectancy, (ii) fall in high death rate of women during the pre-

Table 13.5 : District-wise Sex Ratio and its Dicadal Growth in Meghalaya (1951–2001)

Districts/State	*1951*	*1961*	*1971*	*1981*	*1991*	*2001*	*Percentage a Decadal Variation*						
							1951–1961	*1961–1971*	*1971–1981*	*1981–1991*	*1991–2001*	*1951–1971*	*1971–2001*
Jaintia Hills	954	1015	999	978	973	996	6.39	-1.58	-2.10	-0.51	2.36	4.72	-0.30
East Khasi Hills	950	898	916	951	948	981	-5.47	2.00	3.82	-0.32	3.48	-3.58	7.10
West Khasi Hills	948	927	956	949	951	968	-2.22	3.13	-0.73	0.21	1.79	0.84	1.26
East Garo Hills	958	976	930	941	958	966	1.88	-4.71	1.18	1.81	0.84	-2.92	3.87
West Garo Hills	945	951	968	1096	959	968	0.63	1.79	13.22	-12.50	0.94	2.43	0.00
Ri Bhoi	921	870	893	921	941	941	-5.54	2.64	3.14	2.17	0.00	-3.04	5.38
South Garo Hills	965	971	909	967	963	942	0.62	-6.39	6.38	-0.41	-2.18	-5.80	3.63
Meghalaya	949	937	942	954	955	972	-1.26	0.53	1.27	0.10	1.78	-0.74	3.18
All-India	946	941	930	934	927	933	-0.53	-1.17	0.43	-0.75	0.65	-1.69	0.32

Sources : (i) Census of India, 2001, Primary Census Abstract, Meghalaya, Series -18.
(ii) Basic Statistics of North-Eastern Region, 2002.

pregnancy and post-pregnancy periods, (iii) out-migration of male workers and (iv) non-discrimination among sex in case of birth because of matrilineal society.

Literacy of Population in Meghalaya

Literacy is considered to be an index of socio-cultural and economic advancement and is recognized as a basic need for the development of human resource in an area. Education is an instrument of social change and economic development as it imbibes knowledge and enhances skill of the people. The quality of population can be judged from the level of literacy and the level of technical training attained by the people in the country. It is experienced that the more a country is developed, the more are the people of it educated and the less they are victimised and exploited. Not only this, it is education that has the supremacy to promote gender quality and empowering of women.

The literacy rate of Meghalaya is increasing progressively from only 29.49 per cent in 1971 to 62.56 per cent in 2001 (Table 13.6). In spite of a rapid increase, the literacy rate in the State is still lower than the national average. Looking at the sex-wise growth of literacy since 1971, it is noticed that for the males it has gone up to 65.43 per cent from 34.12 per cent in 1971 and in case of females it has gone up to 54.61 per cent from 24.56 per cent. It may, however, be mentioned that literacy rate relates to the persons for the age group of five and above up to 1971 Census. From 1981 onwards, the literacy rate shown in the table relates to the person of the age group seven years and above.

Table 13.6 : Percentage of Literacy in Meghalaya and India (1971–2001)

Years	*Meghalaya*			*All-India*		
	Persons	*Males*	*Females*	*Persons*	*Males*	*Females*
1971	29.49	34.12	24.56	29.48	39.52	18.70
1981	34.08	37.89	30.08	36.23	46.89	24.82
1991	49.10	53.12	44.85	52.21	64.13	39.29
2001	62.56	65.43	54.61	64.84	75.26	53.67

Source: Census of India, 1971, 1981, 1991 and 2001.

From Table 13.7, it is observed that in all the districts of Meghalaya, the rural literacy rate have been increasing rapidly since 1971 except in West Khasi Hills, where it declined during 1981 to 1991. Moreover the difference between male and female literacy rates has been declining over time in both the rural and urban areas. But the gap between the rural and urban literacy rates has been widened though both have been increasing over time. This is particularly because of the better educational facilities available in the urban areas, less poverty and better utilisation of educational awareness campaign in the urban areas, that is, total literacy campaign, etc.

Table 13.7 : District-wise Percentage of Literacy in Rural and Urban Areas to Total Population in Meghalaya (1971-2001)

Districts/State		*Rural*				*Urban*			
		1971	*1981*	*1991*	*2001*	*1971*	*1981*	*1991*	*2001*
Jaintia Hills	P	17.20	19.98	24.15	37.06	51.58	65.84	64.83	74.28
	M	18.72	19.51	48.71	35.54	55.91	70.15	51.89	75.23
	F	15.69	20.46	51.28	38.59	47.05	62.00	48.10	73.37
East Khasi Hills	P	26.59	31.87	36.91	53.02	66.11	63.63	70.49	76.33
	M	29.97	33.07	51.98	52.94	70.80	67.73	55.90	78.80
	F	23.20	30.10	48.01	53.10	60.52	59.10	44.09	73.85
West Khasi Hills	P	27.21	30.43	25.45	47.99	51.78	53.25	50.52	63.93
	M	30.43	32.42	52.92	49.25	55.97	53.66	*	64.13
	F	23.84	28.32	47.07	46.69	46.50	46.33	*	63.72
East Garo Hills	P	30.13	31.92	35.98	45.19	43.43	52.68	*	66.46
	M	35.21	37.26	57.96	49.92	42.13	59.29	*	69.02
	F	24.66	26.26	42.03	40.30	32.16	40.70	*	63.73
West Garo Hills	P	28.20	*	*	36.60	63.78	*	*	73.52
	M	60.42	*	*	41.88	48.47	*	*	76.66
	F	39.58	*	*	31.15	51.52	*	*	70.23
Ri Bhoi	P	*	*	*	50.66	*	*	*	58.87
	M	*	*	*	53.37	*	*	*	60.58
	F	*	*	*	47.78	*	*	*	57.07
South Garo Hills	P	*	*	*	40.98	*	*	*	69.17
	M	*	*	*	46.50	*	*	*	71.61
	F	*	*	*	35.16	*	*	*	66.37
Meghalaya	P	23.40	26.98	32.60	44.20	65.22	62.30	67.68	73.48
	M	27.68	30.20	54.79	46.54	69.93	66.72	54.58	75.74
	F	18.94	23.64	45.20	41.78	*	58.82	45.41	71.19

Note: P=Persons, M=Males and F=Females and * indicates that data are not available.

Source: Census of India, 1981, 1991 and 2001.

Spatio-Temporal Variation in Growth of Urban Population in Meghalaya

The process of urbanisation has some positive as well as negative implications. Of the adverse implications of urbanisation, especially when it results in the growth of cities and towns, the most serious is its impact on the environment. The expansion of urban areas depletes productive agricultural land. Moreover, raising income levels of the people results in increased consumption and utilisation of resources that contributes to the deterioration of the environment. Water, which is becoming a scarce resource, is increasingly polluted with urban and industrial waste, unless those are properly managed. Moreover at the time of urban expansion, destruction of forest areas takes place. Alóng with that, the management of urban sewage has become an important issue in many countries. Again, when rural-urban migration takes place, initially the low income families stay at the outskrits and slum areas without basic civic facilities and they put more pressure on local environment including the forest for their survival and development. As far as the State of Meghalaya is concerned, it is still underdeveloped and large number of the people is still live in the rural areas (80.42 per cent, according to 2001 Census). That means the process of urbanisation has been very slow in the State.

Table 13.8 : District-wise Distribution of Rural-Urban Population in Meghalaya (1971 to 2001)

Districts/State	*Rural in (Per cent)*				*Urban (in Percentage)*			
	1971	1981	1991	2001	1971	1981	1991	2001
Jaintia Hills	92.14	91.74	90.66	91.62	7.86	8.26	9.34	8.38
East Khasi Hills	67.75	64.65	65.25	57.98	32.25	35.35	34.75	42.02
West Khasi Hills	*	97.60	93.49	88.31	*	2.40	6.51	11.69
East Garo Hills	*	96.86	93.64	85.67	*	3.14	6.36	14.33
West Garo Hills	94.90	89.34	89.88	88.62	5.10	10.66	10.18	11.38
Ri Bhoi	*	*	*	93.16	*	*	*	6.84
South Garo Hills	*	*	*	91.44	*	*	*	8.56
Meghalaya	85.46	81.93	81.40	80.42	14.54	18.07	18.60	19.58

Note : * indicates that data are not available.

Source : Census of India, 1971, 1981, 1991 Series-1 Paper–2; Census of India, 2001.

District-wise distribution of rural-urban population in Meghalaya since 1971 is shown in Table 13.8. Though population has been increasing significantly in some urban centres, the pace of urbanisation in Meghalaya is rather slow. At present, there are in total 16 urban centres in Meghalaya, of which seven are the district headquarters and the rest are the sub-divisional headquarters/towns. Of these urban centres/towns, Shillong Urban Agglomeration is the biggest and is classified as the Class–I Town with a population of 267662 (2001 Census). Other towns in the State fell within Class-III and Class-IV category.

Before 1971, Shillong Urban Agglomeration was the capital of the then undivided Assam. During 1971, urban population in the State was concentrated mainly in Shillong Municipal, Shillong Cantonment, Mawlai, Nongthymmai, Jowai and Tura. But, between, 1971 and 2001, with changes in the number of districts (from two in 1971 to seven in 1992) new urban centres have emerged. In 1981, there were 12 towns in the State (5 Statutory and 7 Census Towns) and increased to 16 (10 Statutory Towns and 6 Census Towns) in 2001.

In 1971, total number of urban population in the State was 1.47 lakhs. In 1981, it was almost doubled to 2.41 lakhs (a rise of 63.98 per cent), which further increased to 3.30 lakhs in 1991 (an increase of 36.76 per cent). In 2001, the urban population figure reached to 4.54 lakhs that is an increase of 37.59 per cent over 1991. The growth rate of urban population has been declining over time. Shillong Urban Agglomeration, itself has recorded significant decrease in growth rate from 42.32 per cent in 1971–1981 to 15.80 per cent in 1991–2001. However, in the towns like Jowai, Mawlai and Shillong Cantonment, the growth rate increased during the period 1971–1981 to 1981–1991 and declined thereafter. Nongthymmai, Pynthorumkhrah and Madanriting observed a substantial growth since 1981–1991 onwards. Sohra has shown only a marginal increase, from 28.47 per cent in 1981–1991 to 28.76 per cent in 1991-2001 and all other towns show a decline in growth rate during this period as is observed from Table 13.9. The deceleration in growth of urban population, especially of the large town in Meghalaya may be due to the saturation of opportunities available in the urban area and non-expansion of activities. Also because of growing opportunities and activities coupled with the rising infrastructure in rural areas, migration of population from rural areas has been declining.

Table 13.9 : Population and Growth Rate of Urban Areas in Meghalaya, 1981–2001

Districts	*Urban Areas/Towns/Cities*	*Urban Population*			*Growth Rate*	
		1981	*1991*	*2001*	*1981 –1991*	*1991 –2001*
Jaintia Hills	Jowai (M)	12923	20601	25057	59.41	21.63
East Khasi Hills	Shillong (UA) (1–7)	174703	231143	267662	32.31	15.80
	1. Shillong (M)	109244	131728	132867	20.58	0.86
	2. Shillong Cantt. (CB)	6620	11075	12396	67.30	1193
	3. Nongthytnmai (CT)	21558	26816	34292	24.39	27,88
	4. Mawlai (CT)	20405	30442	38303	49.19	25.82
	5. Pynthorumkhrah (CT)	10711	14322	22115	33.71	54.41
	6. Madanriting (CT)	6165	8927	16318	44.80	82.79
	7. Nongmynsong (CT)	NA	NA	11371	NA	NA
	Sohra (CT)	6097	7833	10086	28.47	28,76
West Khasi Hills	Nongstoin (TC)	3880	14339	23106	269.56	61.14
	Mairang (TC)	NA	NA	11492	NA	NA
East Garo Hills	Williamnagar (MB)	4290	12004	18247	179.81	52.01
	Resubelpara (MB)	NA	NA	17660	NA	NA
West Garo Hills	Tuna (M)	35257	45740	58978	29.73	28.94
Ri Bhoi	Nongpoh (TC)	NA	NA	13180	NA	NA
South Garo Hills	Baghmara (MB)	4183	6220	8643	48.70	38.95
Total	All-Towns	241333	330047	454111	36.76	37.59

Note: NA. means not available, M means Municipality, UA means Urban Agglomeration, CB means Cantonment Board, CT means Census Town, TC means Town Committee and MB means Municipal Board.

Source : Census of India, 1981, 1991 and 2001.

Age-Sex Structure of Population in Meghalaya

Population differs greatly in the way members are distributed in the various age groups and sex categories, as the age and sex composition of population are important factors both biologically and socially (Banerjee, 1994, p. 47). The age structure of the people is legally the outcome of the regime of fertility and mortality that prevailed in the past. One of the implications of population growth is ageing. In developed countries, the proportion of the population in the older age groups is very high and increasing (because of slower fertility rate); while in the developing countries it is still lower and increasing at a moderate rate. The rise in dependency ratio in the age structure of the population has been observed in those countries where declines in fertility and mortality occurred much earlier and at a faster rate. The spatial distribution of population of Meghalaya according to age and sex structure is given in Table 13.10. It is observed that the percentage of females is higher in Meghalaya in the age group of 0–14 years than that of their male counterparts from 1971 to 2001. The higher percentage of females in the 0–14 age group indicates the rising percentage of newborn females than that of males. Though the percentage of both male and female in 0–14 year's age group to total population has been declining up to 1991, it again increased in 2001. The percentage of total population in the age group 0–14 years has decreased from 43.55 per cent in 1971 to 42.43 per cent in 1981 and further to 26.40 per cent in 1991. However, it again increased to 42.30 per cent in 2001. The decline of population in the age group 0–14 years is an indication of fall in the fertility during 1971 to 1991. The proportion of female in the reproductive age group 15–49 years has increased marginally from 46.39 per cent in 1971 to 48.65 per cent in 2001 period. The percentage of 60+ of the age group in both male and female section remained more or less same throughout the whole period of discussion. Thus, the age structure from 1971 to 2001 period suggests a trend of progressive type of growth of population. There is no discrimination among sexes at the time of birth and the proportion of people in working age group has also increased.

Dependency Ratio of Population in Meghalaya

The growth of population growth is largely associated with the variation in dependency ratio. Normally population is divided into three broad age groups, that is, dependent children (0–14 years), the economically active adult (15-59 years) and dependent old (above 60 years). A high dependency ratio leads to an increase in the demand

Table 13.10 : Age Distribution of Population in Meghalaya by Sex, 1971 to 2001 (in percentage)

Age	1971			1981			1991			2001		
Group	Persons	Males	Females	Persons	Males	Females	Persons	Males	Females	Persons	Males	Females
00–14	43.55	42.45	44.74	42.43	41.81	43.08	26.40	25.99	26.84	42.30	42.23	42.37
15–19	9.06	8.87	9.27	10.53	10.40	10.66	9.71	9.68	9.75	10.77	10.79	10.76
20–24	8.13	7.64	8.65	8.48	7.80	9.17	8.52	7.99	9.08	8.42	8.03	8.82
25–29	8.44	7.88	9.02	8.36	7.75	8.99	8.66	8.07	9.28	7.94	7.42	8.48
30–34	6.39	6.48	6.28	6.30	6.51	6.07	6.39	6.50	6.28	6.37	6.35	6.39
35–39	6.08	6.73	5.38	6.09	6.51	5.65	6.06	6.42	5.68	6.52	6.71	6.32
40–49	8.61	9.37	7.79	8.40	9.07	7.73	8.27	8.98	7.53	8.38	8.86	7.88
50–59	5.08	5.60	4.54	4.10	5.35	4.45	4.68	5.01	4.34	4.61	4.87	4.34
60+	4.63	4.95	4.30	4.46	4.78	4.13	4.44	4.78	4.08	4.56	4.59	4.53

Sources: (1) Census of India, 1981 Series-14 Meghalaya, Part-III General Economic Tables and Social and Cultural Tables.
(2) Census of India, 1991 Series-16 Meghalaya, Part-III-B Series, Economic Tables.
(3) Census of India, 2001, Primary Census Abstract.

for food for consumption, housing and shelter and many other necessities, while it reduces potential savings and investments. Whereas the increase of population in the age group of 15–59 years, may aggravate unemployment problem if sufficient opportunities are not created to match the increase. Here, we observe no significant change in dependency ratio in Meghalaya. Though percentage of dependant children declined during 1971 to 1991, it again increased during 1991 to 2001.

Changes in Birth and Death Rates of Population in Meghalaya

It is also necessary to have a look at the birth rate and death rate while analysing the growth of population. In Meghalaya, the birth and death rates have been fluctuating throughout the years, while they have shown a downward trend at the all-India level. Based on the data of the Sample Registration System issued by the Registrar General Office, the birth rate in Meghalaya stood at 18.0 per cent in 1976 and continuously increased to 39.1 per cent in 1985 and thereafter continuously followed a declining trend and reached a level of 29.0 per cent in 1995. However, in 1996, it was 30.4 per cent and thereafter it declined again to 24.7 per cent in 2003. Though the birth rate ultimately showed a declining trend over the years, it was higher than that of the national average. The death rate, on the other hand, was 15.5 per cent in 1976 and declined rapidly to 8.3 per cent in 1983 and again increased to 12.7 per cent in 1985. From 1985 the death rate fell through the years and after some fluctuations it finally reached to a level of 6.8 per cent in 1993. Thereafter, it recorded a continuous fluctuation and finally reached to 7.4 per cent in 2003. In 2003, both birth rate and death rate in the State was lower than that of all-India average. Comparing the natural growth rate of the State with that of the country, it is observed that in almost all the years the natural growth rate of the State was higher than that of the country. The natural growth rate of the State indicates a similar trend to that of the decadal growth rate of population in the State. The rate was always above 20 per cent except a few years and natural rate of growth has been higher than the all-India natural rate of growth. Comparing with the total growth of population in the State we can safely argue that the growth of population in Meghalaya has been largely due to natural rate of growth and not migration.

Table 13.11 : Birth and Death Rates in Meghalaya during 1976 to 2003 (in percentage)

Years	*Mehalaya*			*All-India*		
	Birth Rate	*Death Rate*	*Natural Growth Rate*	*Birth Rate*	*Death Rate*	*Natural Growth Rate*
1976	33.5	15.5	18.0	34.4	15.0	19.4
1977	32.5	14.1	18.4	33.0	14.7	18.3
1978	32.0	10.2	21.8	33.3	14.2	19.1
1979	33.2	12.1	21.1	33.1	13.0	20.1
1980	31.2	11.1	20.1	33.3	12.5	20.8
1981	32.6	8.2	24.4	33.9	12.5	21.4
1982	31.1	8.9	22.2	33.8	11.9	21.9
1983	30.0	8.3	21.7	33.7	11.9	21.8
1984	38.3	11.8	26.5	33.9	12.6	21.3
1985	39.1	12.7	26.4	32.9	11.8	21.1
1986	33.4	10.1	23.3	32.6	11.1	21.5
1987	39.9	9.1	30.8	32.2	10.9	21.3
1988	36.4	9.1	27.3	31.5	10.9	20.6
1989	31.9	11.9	20.0	30.6	10.3	20.3
1990	31.8	7.8	24.0	30.2	9.7	20.5
1991	32.4	8.8	23.6	29.5	9.8	19.7
1992	29.8	8.5	21.3	29.2	10.1	19.1
1993	28.5	6.8	21.7	28.7	9.3	19.4
1994	29.5	7.1	22.4	28.7	9.3	19.4
1995	29.0	8.9	20.1	28.3	9.0	19.3
1996	30.4	8.9	21.5	27.5	9.0	18.5
1997	30.2	8.8	21.4	27.2	8.9	18.3
1998	29.2	9.0	20.2	26.5	9.0	17.5
1999	28.7	9.1	19.6	26.1	8.7	17.4
2000	28.5	9.2	19.3	25.8	8.5	17.3
2001	28.3	9.0	19.3	25.4	8.4	17.0
2002	25.8	7.7	18.1	25.0	8.1	16.9
2003	24. 7	7.4	17.3	24.8	8.0	16.8

Source : Basic Statistics of North-Eastern Region, 2002; Statistical Hand Book of Meghalaya, 2005.

Spatio-Temporal Variation in Labour Force and their Composition in Meghalaya

The spatial pattern of the distribution of working population in the State of Meghalaya is presented in Table 13.12. Table 13.12 shows that the majority of the total workers (Main and marginal) in Meghalaya were cultivators (48.14 per cent), followed by those engaged in the tertiary sector (31.98 per cent). Agricultural labourers are accounted for 17.70 per cent of the total workers while the secondary sector accounted for only 2.19 per cent. The trend is observed to be similar for both male and female workers. Interestingly female cultivators accounted for the bulk of female total workers in Meghalaya (52.78 per cent). While at the all-India level, the majority of female workers were the agricultural labourers, followed by the cultivators. The tertiary sector in Meghalaya is also accounted for a greater proportion of female workers than at the all-India level. During last few decades, we observe a significant growth of the tertiary sector and thus a shift of workers from primary to the tertiary sector, whereas the growth of secondary sector remained at a very low level.

Broadly speaking, the proportion of total workers in the population is higher in the rural areas than in the urban areas. In general, total work participation rate in the State showed a decreasing trend from 1981 onwards. This decrease is more perceptible in the rural areas than in the urban areas where the work participation rate has almost remained at around 30 per cent. In case of male workers, there has been a slight decline in the rate over the years. The work participation rate in the State was 45.92 per cent in 1981 and declined to 41.84 per cent in 2001. The male work participation rate, on the other hand, was 48.34 per cent and that of female was 35.15 per cent in 2001 as compared to 53.96 per cent and 37.49 per cent respectively in 1981 (Table 13.13). The percentage of total workers in the rural areas of the State was 48.85 per cent in 1981, which also declined to 44.11 per cent in 2001. Correspondingly, the male work participation declined by around 5.99 per cent (from 55.42 per cent to 49.43 per cent) and the female work participation rate also declined by 3.43 per cent (from 42.05 per cent to 38.62 per cent) during 1981 to 2001 period.

Table 13.12 : Percentage Distribution of Total Main Workers (Main and Marginal) by Activity, Meghalaya and All-India, 2001

State/Country	T/R/U	Cultivators			Agriculture Labourers			Household Industry			Others		
		P	M	F	P	M	F	P	M	F	P	M	F
Meghalaya	T	48.14	44.86	52.78	17.70	15.99	20.12	2.19	1.65	2.95	31.98	37.51	24.15
	R	55.99	53.75	58.94	20.01	18.62	21.85	2.28	1.67	3.08	21.72	25.96	16.13
	U	4.39	3.39	6.51	4.79	3.70	7.12	1.69	1.55	2.01	89.12	91.36	84.36
All-India	T	31.71	31.34	32.51	26.69	20.82	39.43	4.07	3.02	6.36	37.52	44.82	21.70
	R	40.14	42.19	36.46	33.20	27.48	43.40	3.77	2.83	5.44	22.90	27.49	14.70
	U	3.21	2.99	4.26	4.71	3.42	11.03	5.10	3.50	12.93	86.98	90.09	71.78

Note: P=Persons, M=Males, F=Females, T=Total, R=Rural and U=Urban.
Source: Census of India, 2001.

Table 13.13 : Percentage Distribution of Workers in Meghalaya during 1981 to 2001

T/R/U	Sex	Total Workers			Main Workers			Marginal Workers			Non-Workers		
		1981	1991	2001	1981	1991	2001	1981	1991	2001	1981	1991	2001
Total	Persons	45.92	42.67	41.84	43.43	40.32	32.65	2.49	2.35	9.19	54.08	57.33	58.16
	Males	53.96	50.07	48.34	53.11	49.54	41.30	0.85	0.53	7.04	46.04	49.93	51.66
	Females	37.49	34.93	35.15	33.29	30.67	23.74	4.20	4.26	11.41	62.51	65.07	64.85
Rural	Persons	48.85	45.04	44.11	45.90	42.30	33.60	2.95	2.74	10.51	51.15	54.96	55.89
	Males		55.42	51.02	49.43	54.43	50.42	41.54	0.99	0.60	7.89	44.58	48.98
50.57													
	Females	42.05	38.85	38.62	37.06	33.90	25.41	4.99	4.95	13.21	57.97	61.15	61.38
Urban	Persons	32.63	32.30	32.51	32.27	31.64	28.73	0.36	0.66	3.77	67.37	67.70	67.49
	Males	47.55	46.01	42.82	47.33	45.78	40.30	0.22	0.23	3.52	52.45	53.99	56.18
	Females	16.12	17.23	20.98	15.61	16.10	16.95	0.51	1.13	4.03	83.88	82.77	79.02

Source : Census of India 1981, 1991 and 2001.

On the other hand, in the urban areas of the State, the work participation rate declined marginally from 32.63 per cent in 1981 to 32.51 per cent in 2001. In case of male workers, there was a decline in participation rate from 47.55 per cent to 42.82 per cent and for female workers there was an increase from 16.12 per cent to 20.98 per cent during the same period. Main and marginal workers have been declining during the same period. In this case also the same trend is observed for both male and female workers in rural and urban areas. In the case of non-workers, there has been an increase since 1981, except in 2001 for urban non-workers. On the other hand, female non-workers have declined marginally from 83.88 per cent in 1981 to 79.02 per cent in 2001.

Socio-Economic Dimensions

If we look at the performance of the State economy, it is observed that per capita NSDP at 1980-81 prices has increased from Rs. 1361 in 1980-81 to Rs. 2020 in 1990-91 and the ranking among all the major 25 States in India improved slightly from 17 to 14. Annual average compound growth rate during that period was 4.03 per cent and the rank in terms of growth however was 8. However, the annual compound growth rate (at 1993-94 prices) declined to 2.62 per cent during 1993-94 to 1999-2000. There is virtually no change in contribution of secondary sector to NSDP, which was 11.92 per cent in 1993-94 and still pegged at 11.45 per cent in 1999-2000. Agricultural productivity also has not improved much while per capita availability of land has declined from 2.22 hectares in 1971 to 0.97 hectare in 2001 Though incidence of poverty declined by 12.73 per cent during 1983 to 1999-2000, the rate of decline has been slower than the other North-Eastern States except Assam and still now about one–third of its population is living below poverty line (*North-Eastern Council 1981, 1985, 1992, 1995, 2000 and 2002*). In terms of human development index the ranking of the State among major 25 States on India declined from 15 in 1981 to 1991 and the index increased marginally from 0.317 to 0.365 during that period. Whereas, despite having higher population growth, lower economic growth States like

Nagaland, Mizoram have improved their human development significantly and ranked within top five States (GOI, 2002).

Conclusion

It is observed that during 1971 to 2001, there has been a tremendous growth of population in Meghalaya. The decadal growth rate of population in the State was always higher than the average national growth rate. The annual exponential growth rate was also above 2 per cent since 1971. The density has also increased but still much below the national average. The sex ratio has been higher than that of the country as a whole since 1971. The proportion of female in the children age group has increased over time leading to an increase in overall sex ratio. This is in conformity with the matrilineal society (as noted earlier) in Meghalaya. Also percentage of people in the working age group has increased over time. But there has been no significant development in industrial sector. Hence there has been a rise in pressure on primary and tertiary sector. Also work participation rate for that group has declined due to lack of rise in opportunities. However, the literacy rate of the State was much lower than that of the national average. This is perhaps due to non-availability of educational facilities to most the people in the State especially those who are settled in the rural areas (more than 80 per cent). Still now most of the people are cultivators and agricultural labourers. Among the cultivators especially in rural areas, percentage of female has increased over time and also in urban other informal activities percentage of female is very high. So there has been increase in pressure on natural resources, especially mineral and forest. As minerals are mostly under private ownership (and hence not accessible to many common people) and there is open access to forest in many cases, stress on forest has also increased. Whatever little development is observed is primarily due to the extraction of natural resources. Looking at the overall socio-economic performance of the State it is clear that though population growth has not created much negative externality in the way of economic development, due to lack of proper population planning (settlement, human resource development etc.) the State has failed to capitalise dividend from the observed demographic changes over the years. Increasingly available manpower should be properly managed to increase their efficiency which could be utilised competitively to accelerate the growth process for the welfare of the people.

References

Banerjee, M. (1994): "Demographic Profile of Meghalaya," in Sanu Mukherjee *et al.* (eds.), *Demographic Profile of North-East India*, Omsons Publications, New Delhi, pp. 45–51.

Choudhury, R. K. (2000): "Growth Trend of Population and its Characteristic Features in North-East Region," in B. Datta, Ray, *et al.* (eds.), *Population, Poverty and Environment in North-East India*, Concept Publishing Company, New Delhi, pp. 23–36.

Ehrlich, P. (1968): *The Population Bomb*, Ballantine Books, New York.

Ehrlich, A. R and P. R. Ehrlich (1990): *The Population Explosion*, New York, Simor and Schuster.

North-Eastern Council: *Basic Statistics of North-Eastern Region, 1981, 1985, 1992, 1995, 2000 and 2002.*

Government of India, Directorate of Census Operations: *Census of India*, 1981, Series–14, Meghalaya, Part–III.

Government of India, Directorate of Census Operations: *Census of India*, 1991, Series-16, Meghalaya, Part–III–B Series.

Government of India, Directorate of Census Operations: *Census of India*, 2001, Series–18, Meghalaya, Provisional Population Totals.

Government of India, Directorate of Census Operations: *Census of India*, 2001, Series–18, Meghalaya, Primary Census Abstract.

Government of India (2002), *National Human Development Report 2001.*

Government of Meghalaya, Directorate of Economics and Statistics: *Statistical Hand Book Meghalaya*, 2005, Meghalaya, Shillong.

Johnson, Gale D. (2000): "Population, Food and Knowledge," in *The American Economic Review*, Vol. 90, No. 1, pp. 1–14.

Malthus, T. R (1798): *An Essay on the Principles of Population*, Cambridge, Cambridge Press.

Meadows *et al.* (1972): *The Limits to Growth*, Universe Books, New York.

Mikesell, Raymond F. (1995): *Economic Development and the Environment: A Comparison of Sustainable Development with Conventional Development Economics*, Mansell Publishing, London.

Simon, J.L.(1981): *The Ultimate Resource,* Princeton University Press, Princeton, USA.

Simon, J. L. (1996): *The Ultimate Resource, 22*[nd] Edition, Princeton University Press, Princeton, USA.

14 Polemics of Migration in Population Dynamics of Assam

K. Alam

Introduction and History of Migration

Migration has been an important factor in the population growth of Assam since the beginning of twentieth century. There is no doubt that migration from other parts of India and subsequently from foreign countries like East Pakistan/Bangladesh and Nepal has been responsible to a great extent for the consistently high population growth rate and also for the changing population composition of Assam over the years. However, immigration is a historical phenomenon in Assam. Various ethnic groups who now from part of the indigenous people of the State once came to Assam from different lands to settle in Assam from the hoary past. The earlier migrants came from the East, such as Khamptis, Phakials, Turungs and Shyam tribes and also Mishing (*Miri*), Tiwa (*Lalung*), Karbi (*Mikir*), Dimasa, Chutiyas, Bodos (*Kacharis*), Koches, Rabhas, Meches, and also Morans, Barahis and Deuris etc. In the historical period, Ahoms or Shans came to Assam as invaders in 1228 and ruled Assam for long 600 years till the coming of the Britishers. The Aryan Hindus began to come from the West during the reign of the rulers of Pragjyotishpur, Bhaskar Barman being the most prominent one. When the Ahoms adopted Hinduism as their religion, they brought a large number of Brahmins and other high caste Hindus to Assam for the purpose of religious and other functions. Because of their racial, educational and intellectual superiority, they now form the most important component of the mainstream Assamese society, although they do not have the advantage of number. There was also earlier Muslim settlement in Assam starting from 1206 with the aggression of Baktiar Khilji and later on Mughal invasion under Mirjumla. Thus Muslims came to Assam as invaders and also administrators. Besides, a number of Muslim preachers and saints also came to Assam, and under their influence a sizeable number of low caste Hindus and tribals were converted to Islam. Moreover, a number of Muslim artisans and other specialists came to Assam on invitation of the Ahom kings and they settled in Assam permanently. The Ahoms and the earlier Muslims are now completely assimilated with the mainstream Assamese society.

When the British rule was established in Assam in 1826, a series of migration of outside people of various categories took place in Assam. The first group of such migrants were the literate Bengali Hindus who came to Assam in sizeable number to man the various subordinate posts of the newly established British administration in Assam, under the patronage of the Government. They were felt to be essential, as there was dearth of English knowing educated people in the State to do the jobs of clerks and subordinate officers.

The second stream of migrants was the tea garden workforce for the fast developing tea plantation in Assam. When the tea plantation was being developed in the State from 1836, there was acute shortage of labour force to work on the tea gardens. Therefore, a large number of labour force had to be imported from the labour surplus regions of India— Chotanagpur and Santhal Parganas of the present day Jharkhand, Chhattisgarh, Bihar, Orissa States etc. Such migration, which started in 1853, reached its peak in 1935, and continued till 1937 under the patronage and control of the British Government. The approximate number of such tea garden workers was 23 lakhs according to 2001 Census that is about 8.2 per cent of the State population. They are legal migrants who returned themselves as Assamese speakers and thus form part of the Assamese population.

The next group of migrants were the poor, landless Muslim cultivators from erstwhile East Bengal, particularly from its Mymensing district. A brief description of the State of Assam's economy, its population and condition of agriculture at the start of the British rule in the State would explain the circumstances which favoured the large scale migration of such people to Assam. When the British rule started in Assam, the economy of the State was in a deplorable condition. Thanks to internal conflicts within the Ahom ruling family, leading to the Burmese invasion and occupation of Assam, unprecedented atrocities were perpetrated by the rampaging Burmese army on the hapless local people. As a result, many people were killed, many had to flee to distant places from where very few could return, besides, many people perished due to attack of epidemic diseases like cholera, black fever, dysentry, small pox etc. Consequently, the number of population of Assam fell very sharply and the few that survived, lost their enterprising and hardworking character because of the pernicious habit of opium taking among the people of Assam. In consequence, the area of cultivation fell very sharply. Again, because of the old fashioned traditional methods of cultivation practised by the indigenous farmers, the agricultural production, particularly foodgrains production decreased very sharply resulting in food shortage to meet the increasing demand for food. Under these circumstances and also because of the availability of vast tracks of cultivable fallow and wastelands, particularly in the vast riverine and forest areas in Assam, the migration of land hungry poor cultivators from the East Bengal districts started from the beginning of 20th century. They first came to Goalpara district mostly at the invitation of the zamindars. Their number increased from 49.1 thousand in 1901 to 118.2 thousand in 1911. In the next two decades, the Muslim migrants from Bengal occupied various islets and riverine areas of Barpeta subdivision of the then Kamrup district and Darrang. By 1931 the Muslim settlers captured most of the wastelands of Brahmaputra Valley. By 1941 they entered Lakhimpur district. Again, when Sir Sadullah became Prime Minister of Assam second time in August 1942, he invited the Muslim peasants from East Bengal for settlement in Assam under the pretext of raising Assam's food production under the 'Grow More Food' campaign. According to the 2001 Census, the number of these Bengali Muslim settlers became as many as 40 lakhs. All these people migrated to Assam well before the Independence. They are now undisputed citizens of the country. As they returned as Assamese speakers in the Censuses, they helped the Assamese to maintain its status of majority language. They are treated as 'Na Asamiya', that is 'neo Assamese'. They have proved to be an asset in the economy of Assam for boosting up agricultural production. It is these Bengali Muslims who introduced jute cultivation in the State. They also provided cheap labour for the various development and construction works. As they are educationally backward, they did not pose any problem for the indigenous people for the Government and other white colour jobs.

The third stream of migrants was the Nepalese who came from their native land and settled in Assam in mostly forest areas and hill slopes in the pre-Independence period. They are legal migrants whose number was 4 lakh according to 2001 Census. They are mostly engaged in army, particularly Assam Rifles, watch and ward jobs in various Government and private establishments, dairying, woodcutting etc. These Nepali migrants who are parmanently settled in Assam have adopted Assamese langauage and are getting assimilated with the local people of the State.

Besides, during the pre-Independence period, a sizeable number of Marwari and Bihari people also came over to Assam and settled here. The former were engaged in trade, commerce and industry and the latter in all sorts of manual jobs. Their combined number was 26 lakh in 2001.

Immigration to Assam did not stop with the attainment of Independence on 15th August 1947. In the immediate post-Independence period, a new stream of migrants, mostly Bengali Hindu Refugees came to Assam from East Pakistan as a result of partition and subsequent communal riots. The number of such Bengali Hindu refugees increased from 2.67 lakh in 1951 to 6 lakh in 1961. According to the policy of the Government of India, they were given citizenship of the country. Again, at the time of Bangladesh War of Independence in 1971, large number of the then East Pakistani nationals both Hindus and Muslims had to take shelter in border areas of Assam and West Bengal. At the end of the war, many of the Hindu refugees wanted to settle in India because of atmosphere of insecurity prevailing in Bangladesh. In subsequent period also because of occasional eruption of communal conflicts in Bangladesh, Bengali Hindus continued to come to Assam as migrants. To put a stop on such relentless migration from Bangladesh, Special Citizenship Act was passed in 1985 in terms of the Assam Accord. According to this Act, the migrants to Assam from East Pakistan/Bangladesh were divided into three categories—First, the migrants who came to Assam before 1-1-1966 and settled here permanently shall be citizens of India without any dispute. Secondly, those who came to Assam during the period from 1-1-66 to 24-3-71 shall be citizens of India without voting right for ten years from their registration as migrants. Thirdly, those who came to India on or after 25-3-71 would be considered as illegal migrants. They are to be detected and deported by following legal procedure.

Estimates of Migration

It is commonly believed that a large number of illegal migrants have come over to Assam mainly from Bangladesh since 25th March, 1971, the cut-off year of the citizenship. Many of these illegal migrants got themselves enumerated in the Census as genuine citizens. Under these circumstances, a hue and cry was raised by the indigenous people about their growing number, which would disturb the socio-political balance in the State and threaten the ethnic identity of the Assamese people. No rational estimates of the post-1971 migrants to Assam have however been made and "this has led to wild guesses made by different interest groups to suit their convenience," (Saikia *et al.*, 2003).

An objective study was made under the Omiya Kumar Das Institute of Social Change and Development (Guwahati) in 2003 to estimate the various categories of migrants to Assam from 1951 to 1991, based strictly on Census data by using relevant statistical methods (Saikia *et al*, 2003). There are broadly two methods of estimating migrants in the population—Direct Method using Census Place of Birth Statistics and Indirect Method using Residual or Vital Statistics Method and Survival Method.

There are mainly two types of migration to Assam–Interstate, that is, who came from other States of India and International, that is, who came from other countries. International migrants may be again classified as Legal and Illegal. Legal foreign migrants are those who have reported their place of birth in a foreign country, others are regarded as illegal foreign migrants.

Estimates of Migration on Place of Birth Statistics

The following Table 14.1 gives the extent of migration to Assam during 1951 to 1991 arrived at by the method of place of birth statistics.

Table 14.1 : Migration to Assam: 1951-1991 (based on Place of Birth Data)

Years	Inter-state Migrants (Lakh)	%	International Migrants (Lakh)	%	Total Migrants (Lakh)	%
1951	4.50	–	8.66	–	13.16	–
1961	4.68	+4.09	8.13	+6.11	12.81	-2.63
1971	5.05	+7.98	9.60	+18.01	14.65	+14.35
1991	5.37	+6.16	3.40	-64.62	8.76	-40.21
Total	19.60		29.79		49.38	

Source: OKDI Study (2003).

The estimates based on place of birth data show that there was a decrease in the number of total migrants by 2.63 per cent between 1951-1961, however, the number of migrants increased by 14.35 per cent during 1961-1971. It is significant that during the 20-year period of 1971-1991, there was a sharp fall in the number of total migrants and particularly International migrants by (64.62%). However, inter-state migrants show a steady rise during this period. It has been alleged that census place of birth statistics suffer from some gross inaccuracies. Because the respondents may not give the correct place of birth for various reasons. Therefore, the migration estimates based on this method may not be reliable.

As mentioned earlier, one of the indirect methods of estimating migration is the Residual or Vital Statistical Method. According to this method migration is calculated in the Census year as the difference between the population of the Census year and the sum of the population of the preceding Census year and the difference of births and deaths between the two Census years. Using this method, the migration figures over the successive decades are found to be as follows:

Table 14.2 : Estimates of Migration to Assam by Vital Statistics Method

Years	*Migrants (Lakh)*
1951-1961	10.63
1961-9171	6.69
1971-1981	4.50
1981-1991	3.92
Total	25.74

Source: Ibid.

The extent of migration to Assam arrived at by Vital Statistics Method also shows a declining trend over the decades. Vital Statistics Method also is not a foolproof method to estimate migration of a State. Because, the data of births and deaths within a Census decade are seldom accurate or comprehensive.

Estimates of Migration by Survival Method

The Survival Method is more reliable for estimating migration. It is more accurate than the Vital Statistics Method. Because in the Survival Method, the total population is split into different age-group and their corresponding survival ratios are used instead of the single birth and death figures for the entire population as in the Vital Statistics Method. Moreover, by applying Assam's natural growth as in the migrant population, the OKDI Study has estimated the number of net migration to Assam over the decades, which are given in the following Table.

Table 14.3 : Net Migration to Assam (in lakh) based on Survival Method

Period	*Number of Migrants (Lakh)*
1951-61	10.68
1961-71	8.02
1971-19	9.76
Total	28.46

Source: Ibid.

The estimates made by Survival Method also show a declining

trend in the net migration to Assam. Let us now discuss the trend of inter-state and international migration to Assam as estimated by the Survival Method.

Table 14.4 : Inter-state and International Migration (in Lakh) (by Survival Method)

Period	Inter-state	International	Total
1951-61	2.61	8.07	10.681961-71
3.40	4.61	8.01	
1971-91	2.90	6.86	9.76

Source: Ibid.

The above Table 14.4 shows that the estimated figures of international migrants are more than that of the inter-state migrants over the decades, but the trend of international migration has registered a decline over the years. The international or foreign migants may be divided into legal and illegal. OKDI study defined legal foreign migrants as those who have reported their place of birth in a foreign country, and others as illegal foreign migrants. According to their estimates on the basis of Survival Method, the number of these two categories of foreign migrants is as follows:

Table 14.5 : Number of Legal and Illegal Migrants (lakh) (by Survival Method)

Period	Total Foreign Migrants	Legal Foreign *Migrants*	Illegal Foreign Migrants
1951-1961	8.07	3.14	4.93
1961-1971	4.95	3.30	1.65
1971-1991	6.86	4.08	6.56
Total	19.89	6.85	13.04

Source: *Ibid.*

According to the estimates based on Survival Method made by the OKDI study, the number of illegal foreign migrants exceeded that of legal migrants over the decades. However, illegal foreign migration showed a declining trend. In total during the period from 1951 to 1991, the total number of illegal foreign migrants to Assam was 13.04 lakh.

Issue of Illegal Migration

It is notable that the definition of illegal foreign migrants as given above is quite restrictive and vague. The status of the foreign migrants was made clear by the Citizenship (Amendment) Act, 1985, which was passed in terms of the Assam Accord of 1985. According to this special Citizenship Act, those foreign nationals who entered India on or before 1-1-66 and settled here permanently, shall be citizens of India and their nationality cannot be questioned, and those who came to Assam between 1-1-66 and 24-3-71 shall be citizens of India for all practical purposes, but without having right to vote for ten years from the date of resistration. Illegal migrants are those persons who entered India on or after 25th March, 1971 without valid passport or other travel documents and also those foreigners who have entered India under a valid passport or travel document continued to stay even after the expiry of the authorised period. As has already been pointed out that legal migrants are mostly Bengali Hindu Refugees who came to India in large numbers from East Pakistan (Bangladesh) as a result of Partition which caused communal riots over there. Later on also there were flows of Hindu refugees from Bangladesh from time to time as a result of eruption of communal riots creating an atmosphere of insecurity for the Hindu citizens. These people were settled throughout Assam, but mostly in the districts of Barak Valley, Dhubri, Goalpara, Kamrup and Nagaon.

The illegal migrants or infiltrators are mostly from Bangladesh and some also from Nepal. In the category of illegal migrants, there are both Hindus and Muslims. Although they are not citizens, they somehow managed to get enumerated in the various Censuses. Their existence in Assam's population cannot be denied, but there is controversy regarding their number. Most of the figures of illegal migrants as given by various organisations and responsible persons seem to be highly exaggerated. These estimates are not based on any scientific analysis of Census data. Some such estimates are given below:

First Prafulla Kr. Mahanta, the then President of AASU gave an estimate of 70 lakh of foreigners in the population of Assam in the AASU Memorandum to the Prime Minister, February 2, 1980.

Secondly, at the start of the Anti-Foreigners Movement in 1978, the Gauhati University Teacher's Co-ordination Committee estimated the number at 40 lakhs.

Thirdly, Kuldip Nayar, the renowned journalist, in an article in the *Sentinel* of 15-11-95 pointed out that illegal migrants constituted 40 per cent of the State's population.

Fourthly, no less a person than the Governor of Assam S.K. Sinha, in his report to the Government of India gave a figure of 90 lakh foreigners in Assam.

On closer analysis it would be found that all these estimates are far from reality. These estimates are not based on any scientific analysis. All these are emotional exaggeration. Thus if we take the case of the Governor's estimates of 90 lakhs foreigners in Assam, then around 30 per cent of the population would be foreigners, that is, one in every three people in Assam would be a foreigner. That is obviously an absurd idea. Further, according to 1971 Census, the proportion of immigrant Muslims, Bengali Hindus and Nepalis in the population of Assam are respectively 18, 19.70 and 2.40 that is around 40 per cent in total. Thus according to Mr. Nayar's view, the entire population of immigrant Muslims, Bengali Hindus and Nepalis would come under the label of foreigners.

Now let us scrutinise the basis of AASU's estimates of infiltrators in Assam. The basis of AASU's estimate is the difference in the population growth rates between India and Assam during the two decades after Independence. The following Table 14.6 will give the necessary input for their argument.

Table 14.6 : Population Growth Rate—India and Assam (in per cent)

	1951-61	1961-71
India	21.64	24.80
Assam	34.97	34.95

Source: Census Report of 1961 and 1971.

The AASU's argument is that the higher growth rate of Assam's population in comparison with India indicates the existence of large number of foregners in Assam's population. Their exact number can be obtained if we estimate the population of Assam at India's growth rate. Calculated in this way, Assam's population in 1971 would have been 118.25 lakhs, but in reality it was 146.25 lakhs. Therefore, these excess 28 lakhs are the infiltrators. However, this argument seems to be simplistic and facetious. Dr. Susanta Dass, a noted population researcher remarked, "This simple Euclidean inference does not fit to a complicated non-Euclidean Science like Demography". He pointed out that, there was a spectacular hike in population growth in both Assam and India during 1941 to 1961, net decadal increase being 75.38 per cent for Assam and 62.58 per cent for India, more or less the same. This was caused in both the cases due to reaching the second stage of demographic transition as a result of the start of development planning in which mortality rate fell sharply, while birth rate remaining the same. Secondly, during the period 1951 to 1971 there was inflow of large number of Hindu refugees from East Pakistan. Their number would be around 14.7 lakhs. Thirdly, immigration of Indian nationals from other States particularly Marwaris and Biharis increased sharply with the opening of the railway link *via* North Bengal after Independence to take advantage of the expanding secondary and tertiary sector in Assam and to meet the increasing demand for labour force in the State. Therefore, the number of Hindi speakers increased from 3.07 lakhs (3.82% of Assam's population) to 7.92 lakhs (5.42% of Assam's population) during this period. Fourthly, a large number of people from other States came to Assam after Independence to serve as employees in Government, semi-Government and private organisations and enterprises in the State and this inter state migration also boosted the population growth of the State. It is notable that in 1971, there were 1.85 lakhs of such inter-state migrants, constituting 1.26 per cent of the State's population.

It is significant that although during the earlier decades prior to 1971, population growth rate of Assam had been consistently above that of all-India, yet from 1971 to 1991, population growth rate of Assam for the first time has fallen below that of all-India, although marginally and in 2001, Assam's population growth rate of 18.85 per cent is significantly lower than India's growth rate of 21.38 per cent.

One of the reasons for this phenomenon might be, according to Dass due to the effective implementation of the Indira-Mujib Pact of 1972, which stopped the inflow of Bengali Hindus from Bangladesh with effect from 25th March, 1971. If there had been any infiltration after this date, it must have been negligible or so little that it is not reflected in the Census data.

Issue to Muslim Infiltration into Assam

It is widely believed in Assam that the Partition of country on the basis of religion did not deter the inflow of Muslims from East Pakistan (Bangladesh) into Assam. Even after 1947 there has been unabated inflow of Muslim migrants. This is reflected in the rising rate of growth of Muslim population in the State. The rate of increase of the Muslims in Assam has been 27.5 per cent during 1951-61, as against the natural increase of 22.4 per cent. At the former rate, the number of Muslims in Assam on March 1, 1961 should have been 25,44,818 and so the passport holders numbering 6952, the number of illegal Muslim migrants stood at 2,13,739 (Barpujari, 1998).

Again, it is argued that the proportion of Muslims in Assam's population was 25 per cent in 1971, but it became 28 per cent in 1991, showing an increase of 3 per cent during the 20-year period. This increase must have happened as a result of large scale Muslim infiltrators from Bangladesh. But the current argument as an explanation for this 3 per cent increase in Muslim proportion is that after 1971, a large chunk of Assam was taken away for creating the hill States of Meghalaya, Mizoram and Nagaland. As a result, the total population of Assam was proportionately reduced, but it did not reduce the Muslim population of Assam as there were very few Muslim population in these hill States, therefore, Muslim population of Assam has remained unaffected, but number of total population of other communities got reduced. This explains the increase of Muslim population by 3 per cent, although their absolute number showed a growth at the normal rate.

Again, as per 1991 Census, the general population growth rate in Assam was 52.26 per cent while that of Muslim population was

77.42 per cent. Thus, is argued that this higher growth of Muslim population must be due to the entry of illegal infiltrants. However, it is argued to the contrary that since comparatively Muslims are in general socio-economically very backward, they suffer from extreme poverty, illiteracy and orthodoxy. They lack the idea of birth control and hence we find the higher population growth rate of Muslim population in Assam. It is to be noted that higher growth rate of Muslim population is an all-India phenomenon. Thus the 1991 Census reveals that while the growth rate of Muslim population in Assam was 77.42 per cent, it was 88.36 per cent in Haryana, 80.76 per cent in Madhya Pradesh and 110.30 per cent in Punjab. In the case of these States, there is no problem of Muslim infiltration. Moreover higher growth rate of population was not found only in the case of Muslims, but also in other minority communities. Thus as against 77.42 per cent growth of Muslim population, the growth rate of Christian population was 98.77 per cent and that of Scheduled Tribe population was as high as 153.34 per cent. Lastly as mentioned earlier, since 1971 population growth rate of Assam started to lag behind that of India as a whole, it nullifies the existence of large scale Bangladeshi Muslim infiltrants entering Assam since 1971.

Conclusion

It is true that Assam might have illegal migrants, both Hindus and Muslims in her population, but it cannot be so large as has been fancifully estimated. The Government with its vast administrative and police network has enough power to detect and deport the illegal migrants living in the State. That the number of such illegal migrants is far below the fancied figure will be evident from the following example. According to one Government report, during the period from 1-1-86 to 31-7-93, mostly under the AGP rule, as many as 2,87,625 enquiries regarding suspected foreigners were made by the police and out of which 2,84,647 cases were sent to the Screening Committees, which after varifying the cases, referred 25,051 cases to the Tribunals. The Tribunals, after adjudication, could detect only 8,694 number of persons as deportable Bangladeshi nationals.

References

1. H.K. Barpujari, *North-East India—Problems, Policies and Prospects,* Guwahati, 1998.
2. S.K. Dass, Immigration and Demographic Transformation of Assam, *EPW,* Vol. XV No. 19, May 10, 1980. *Infiltration into Assam: A Fact or a Fiction,* Karimaganj, 2003.
3. Saikia, Goswami and Goswami, *Populution Growth in Assam (1951-1991) with focus on Migration,* New Delhi, 2003.
4. S.U. Ahmed, *Muslims in Assam (1200-2000),* Nagaon, 1999.
5. J.B. Bhattacharjee, *Social Tension in North-East India,* Shillong, 1995.
6, Myron Weiner, *Sons of the Soil,* 1978.
7. The AASU Memorandum to the Prime Minister, 2 February, 1980.
8. M. Kar, *Muslims in Assam Politics,* New Delhi, 1997.
9. Census Reports, 1951, 1961, 1971, 1991, and 2001.
10. Sanjoy Hazarika, *Strangers of the Mist,* New Delhi, 1994.

15 Dynamics of Population Growth in Assam and its Socio-Economic Implications

Lakhyahira Datta

Introduction

Assam located between 24.3°N and 28°N latitudes and 89°E and 96.1°E longitudes is the most populous State in North East India. The State has an area of 78,488 km^2 representing 2.39 per cent of the country's area and shelters 26,655,528 persons accounting for 2.59 per cent of the total population according to 2001 Census.

At the beginning of the twentieth century (1901), the total population of Assam was 3.29 million which rose to 8.02 million in the mid of the century (1951) showing an increase of 2.44 times. During 1951 to 2001, the population of Assam got increased by 3.31 times. This clearly indicates that the growth of population in Assam was comparatively more in the latter half of the twentieth century than that of the early half. The annual growth rate of population during the period from 1901 to 1951 was 1.79 per cent while it increased to 2.43 per cent during 1951 to 2001. The prodigious growth of population leads to various socio-economic and environmental problems like problems of unemployment, housing, health, problem of shortage of agricultural land, environmental degradation etc. Moreover, in the last thirty years food production in the State could not cope with the demand of the increasing population. As there has not been significant development in the secondary and tertiary sectors of economy in Assam, along with high increase of population the pressure on agricultural land resource has been increasing in the State.

Trend of Population Growth in Assam during the Twentieth Century

In the first decade (1901-11) of the twentieth century the decadal growth of population was 16.99 per cent, which was about three times than that of the country as a whole (5.75 per cent). While in the second decade (1911-1921), the growth rate of population in Assam rose to 20.48 per cent when the country witnessed a negative growth rate (-0.31 per cent). It is observed that in the demographic history of Assam the growth rate of population in Assam were always higher than the country's average except two decades, i.e. 1971-81 and 1991-2001. Assam recorded the highest decadal growth rate of population during the period 1951-1961 recording as high as 34.98 per cent followed by 34.95 per cent in 1961-1971 as against the country's average 21.51 per cent and 24.80 per cent respectively (Table 15.1).

In the pre-Independence period, the growth of population in Assam was significantly high mainly because of migration of people from erstwhile East Bengal. Various colonization schemes were implemented in Assam during the early part of the century. Under these schemes land in the active floodplain zone of the Brahmaputra Valley was allotted to the land hungry immigrant peasants who came from the then East Bengal. They occupied mainly the *char* lands of lower and central Assam. The total Bengal born immigrant population in Assam in 1911 was enumerated as 194,000 persons which rose to 376, 000 persons and 576, 000 persons in 1921 and 1931 respectively.

The probable impact of such immigration was felt seriously by C.S. Mullan, the then Superintendent of Census Operation, 1931 and he made remarks regarding the future implications of such unabated immigration to Assam. He commented "probably the most important event in the province during the last twenty five years — an event, moreover, which seems likely to alter permanently the whole future of Assam .... the whole structure of Assamese culture and civilization" (Bhuyan, 2002).

In addition to these immigrant peasants from East Bengal, there was another stream of migration from Nepal during 1911–1931. Though they were mostly graziers, some of them were agricultural labourers, porters and ex-servicemen. In 1901, their total population was 21,347 which increased to 88,300 in 1931.

Assam also received a sizeable number of tea garden labourers. Though transportation of tea garden labourers by England based companies from Bihar, Madhya Pradesh, Andhra Pradesh and Orissa was started as early as 1835, it gained its momentum in the later half of the 19th century and early part of the 20th century. They were mostly Munda, Santhal, Ho, Oraon and Gond people. According to Census reports, their total numbers were 6.54 lakh in 1901 which increased to 14 lakh in 1931 and 22.5 lakh in 1971 constituting 15.32 per cent of total population of Assam in 1971.

Table 15.1: Trend of Population Growth in Assam and India 1901–2001

Years	Decadal Growth in Percentage					
	Assam			India		
	Total	Rural	Urban	Total	Rural	Urban
1901–1911	16.99	17.91	20.55	5.75	6.45	0.35
1911–1921	20.48	20.08	36.80	0.31	-1.29	8.27
1921–1931	19.91	19.70	27.58	11.00	9.98	19.12
1931–1941	20.40	20.16	28.30	14.22	11.81	31.97
1941–1951	19.93	18.46	65.73	13.31	8.79	41.43
1951–1961	34.98	30.87	127.57	21.51	20.49	26.41
1961–1971	34.95	32.62	65.01	24.80	21.86	38.23
1971–1981	23.36	21.92	38.25	24.66	19.37	46.17
1981–1991	24.24	22.56	39.58	23.86	20.00	36.46
1991–2001	18.85	16.5	38.24	21.54	18.10	31.48

Source : Census of India I971, 1991 and 2001, Primary Census Abstract.

In the period between 1931–1941, Assam recorded a high growth rate of population (20.40 per cent) especially due to the influx of large number of land hungry people. According to the Report of the Line System Committee (1938), a major section of them were Muslim immigrant peasants from Sylhet, Rangpur and Maymensingh districts of East Bengal and they occupied vast tract of culturable waste land of the Brahmaputra and Barak Valleys of Assam. In order to restrict their settlement in some indigenous people dominated areas of Assam particularly in the Brahmaputra Valley, some lines were created and reserved some land for old settlers of Assam, viz., tribals.

After the Second World War, grow more food campaign was launched in Assam and as a part of the programme again land was allotted to some immigrant peasants from the then East Bengal who came and settled in the Brahmaputra and Barak Valleys of Assam in order to produce foodgrains.

The difference in growth rates of population between Assam and India as a whole during the period from 1901 to 1941 was very significant. During that forty years period the population of Assam grows at the rate of 103.51 per cent while country's growth rate was only 33.67 per cent. This clearly indicates that this alarming growth of population in Assam was mainly due to immigration.

Just after Independence, i.e. 1941–51 and 1951–61, the State recorded a significantly high growth of population. Though major section of people who entered Assam during the above mentioned periods were Muslim immigrant peasants, a section of them were Hindus who registered their names as refugees. According to 1951 Census, there were 2,74,445 refugees in Assam recording 3.41 per cent of total population of Assam. Within Assam Cachar district received the highest (93,177 persons) refugee population (Bhuyan, 2002).

It is mentioned earlier that in the demographic history of Assam, the highest growth rate of population was recorded by the State during 1951–1961 (34.98 per cent) period. After liberation of Bangladesh, there was large scale migration of refugee population to Assam during the seventies. The growth rate further indicates that in addition to refugee population, a sizable number of population were also added to the population of Assam. These people can be considered as illegal immigrants in Assam. As a result in 1979, Assam movement was started for detection and deportation of foreign nationals from Assam. The situation was turmoil and 1981 Census could not be held in Assam. However, considering the estimated figure, the growth of population during 1971–81 was calculated as 23.36 per cent which was slightly lower than the country as a whole. In the last decade, i.e. 1991–2001, the growth rate of population in Assam was comparatively lower than the preceding decades.

So far population growth in urban areas is concerned the highest growth rate was recorded during 1951–1961 recording as high as 127.57 per cent, followed by 1941–51 (65.73 per cent) and 1961–1971 (65.01 per cent) periods. It may be mentioned here that a section of

Hindu refugees were literates and they generally settled in the urban areas. In addition to this after Independence new administrative headquarters were declared as towns. Moreover, there was also migration of people to the urban centres from the neighbouring rural area in search of better economic opportunities. Therefore, these were the contributing factor of high rate of population growth in the urban areas.

In case of rural population growth rate except 1991–2001 period, Assam recorded comparatively higher rural population growth than the nation as a whole. That was mainly migration of immigrant peasants to the rural areas and high birth rate in rural areas.

Growth Pattern of Scheduled Castes and Scheduled Tribes Population

Scheduled Castes and Scheduled Tribes people are socio-economically backward communities in the Indian society. The decadal growth rate of scheduled caste and scheduled tribe population from 1961 in Assam are presented in Table 15.2 to clearly understand the temporal pattern of growth.

Table 15.2 reveals that growth rate of scheduled caste population was significantly high during 1961–1971 and 1971-1991. This was probably due to migration of refugee population from East Bengal especially after liberation of Bangladesh. A major section of the refugee population was constituted by Namasudra, a scheduled caste group. In case of scheduled tribes also highest growth was recorded during 1971–1991 period. Both S.C. and S.T. population recorded comparatively low growth rates during 1991–2001.

Table 15.2: Decadal Growth Pattern of Scheduled Caste (S.C.) and Scheduled Tribe (S.T.) Population in Assam, 1961–2001

Years	*Total S.C. Population*	*Decadal Growth Rate (in p.c.)*	*Total S.T. Population*	*Decadal Growth Rate (in p.c.)*
1961	731490	–	1164641	–
1971	912557	24.75	1606648	37.95
1991	1669412	81.84	2874441	78.91
2001	1825949	10.03	3308570	15.10

Source: Census of India, 1961, 1971, 1991 and 2001.

Growth Rate of Population of Major Religious Groups

Analysis of variations of growth rates of major religious groups gives an insight about the causes of growth of population in the State.

Table 15.3 : Growth of Population of Two Major Religious Communities

Religious Communities	*Population*			*Percentage to Total Population*			*Growth Rate*	
	1951	*1971*	*1991*	*1951*	*1971*	*1991*	*1951–1971*	*1971–1991*
Hindu	5886063	10604618	15047293	66.65	72.51	67.13	80.16	41.89
Muslim	1981859	3592124	6373204	24.68	24.56	28.43	81.25	77.42

Source: Census of India, 1951, 1971 and 1991.

It is observed that during 1951–71 period the growth rates of population of both Hindus and Muslims were almost same recording more than 80 per cent, while during 1971–1991 period the growth rates of Hindu population was 41.89 per cent as against 77.42 per cent for the Muslim population. This clearly indicates that such type of high growth rate of Muslim population cannot be possible by natural growth alone but a part of that increase might be due to migration from Bangladesh. In support of this above analysis the comment put forward by Jogesh Ch. Bhuyan, Retired Deputy Director, Census of India is quoted here: "The natural growth rate of Assam in 1991 for all the religious groups combined is estimated as 19.4 per thousand. If the natural growth for the non-Muslims is slightly lower than 19.4, say 19 per thousand, then the excess of about four lakh non-Muslims may be due to migration for the entire twenty. years period from 1971 to 1991. If the decadal natural growth rate for the Muslims during this period is considered to be 20.5 per cent, then the growth rate for this period is calculated at 45.2 per cent. In that case, the excess of about 11.5 lakhs may be considered as illegal Immigrants of Muslims, mostly from Bangladesh" (*Dialogue*, 2002).

Spatio-Temporal Pattern of Population Growth

Across the State there has been spatio-temporal variation in the population growth. The variation in the physical framework, degree of transport accessibility, availability of plain land for agriculture, degree of urbanization, government plan programmes and schemes for allotment of land to immigrant peasants and degree of immigration are mainly responsible for variation of population growth.

Among the districts of Assam Barpeta, Sonitpur, Dhemaji, Nagaon and Morigaon districts recorded very high increase of population (more than 2 per cent annual growth rate) during the early half of the century (1901–1951), while all the districts of Assam except Jorhat, Sibsagar, Dibrugarh, Karimganj and Cachar recorded very high increase of population (more than 2 per cent annual growth rate), during the later half of the century (1951–2001).

Table 15.4 reveals that during the different decades from 1901 to 1991, comparatively high growth rates were recorded by the districts of lower and central Assam than the upper Assam districts except Dhemaji. It is worthwhile to mention that Dhemaji recorded stupendous growth rates during post-Independence period. In addition to this, other two districts of upper Assam, viz. Lakhimpur and Tinsukia also exhibited comparatively high growth rates in the four decades of the post-Independence period. The two hill districts, viz. Karbi Anglong and North Cachar hills also recorded high growth rates of population in the post-Independence period. During. 1991–2001 period all the districts of Assam recorded slightly declining tendency in the growth rate of population than the previous decades except Kamrup (26.11 per cent), N.C. Hills (24.72 per cent), Goalpara (23.03 per cent) and Dhubri (22.88 per cent).

Causes of High Growth of Population

The foregoing analysis clearly indicates that migration is the main determining factor of high population growth in Assam. However, in addition to this, prevalence of high birth rate and slightly declining death rate of population in the post-Independence period is also

Table 15.4 : District level Decadal Variation in Population Growth in Assam (in per cent) during 1901–2001

Districts/State	*1901–1911*	*1911–1921*	*1921–1931*	*1931–1941*	*1941–1951*	*1951–1961*	*1961–1971*	*1971–1991*	*1991–2001*
Dhubri	33.76	11.42	6.05	10.57	15.21	27.62	40.51	56.57	22.88
Kokrajhar	16.7	90.75	39.68	26.59	0.5	46.34	54.3	76.78	13.13
Bongaigaon	29.94	26.94	15.94	20.85	4	60.51	40.29	64.64	12.05
Goalpara	27.41	37.07	20.5	7.73	11.33	37.22	45.88	54.12	23.03
Barpeta	20.02	34.04	69.02	44.06	18.77	32.62	35.81	43.02	18.87
Nalbari	13.33	14.2	27.92	39.31	9.48	49.62	42.02	49.27	13.02
Kamrup	11.16	7.06	9.32	14.6	21.87	37.73	38.8	65.72	26.11
Darrang	-0.25	11.78	26	35.3	24.13	44.75	43.24	55.63	15.82
Sonitpur	24.33	40.69	20.5	19.73	24.26	35.82	27.62	57.14	18.06
Lakhimpur	17.3	22 82	25.99	36.98	21.62	50.46	43.39	56.29	18.29
Dhemaji	45.3	63.3	16.9	8.41	3.35	68.56	103.42	107.5	19.45
Morigaon	15.5	31.99	41.66	30.87	24.32	37:87	37.51	50.9	21.35
Nagaon	15.84	31.94	41.35	10.34	41.41	35.91	38.99	51.26	22.26
Golaghat	16.25	20.14	18.29	1.48	19.52	26.04	30.85	59.12	14.27
Jorhat	16.62	17.54	8.88	15.12	15.03	24.17	17.47	33.1	14.69
Sibsagar	13.41	20.46	14.44	15.64	15.98	23.36	19.47	38.76	15.83
Dibrugarh	27.1	38.4	22.34	10.87	26.23	31.35	22.93	37.78	13.68
Tinsukia	27.1	28.32	27	34.77	11.09	35.92	31.02	47.03	19.51
Karbi Anglong	NA	NA	NA	NA	30.96	79.21	68.28	74.72	22.72
N.C.Hills	-33.12	5.92	13.6	13.75	6.16	36.95	40	98.3	24.72
Karimganj	12.94	3.19	5.91	9.52	29.87	22.96	25.13	42.08	21.87
Hailakandi	16.09	7.59	7.08	10.29	17.48	27.23	23.61	45.94	20.68
Cachar	12.33	5.98	7.6	13.08	23.92	22.6	23.96	47.59	18.89
Assam	16.99	20.48	19.91	20.4	19.93	34.98	34.95	53.26	18.92
India	5.75	-0.31	11	14.22	13.35	21.51	24.8	54.38	21.25

NA=Not Available.

Source: Aspect of Population Profiles of Assam, Census of India, Series 4, Assam, 1991, Census of India,1991,Series, 1, Paper 1 of 1992, Vol.II, Final Population Tables, Census of India, 2001, Primary Census Abstract, Series 19. Assam.

another contributing factor. In the post-Independence period due to extension of medical facilities, the death rates have been declining rapidly in comparison to birth rates. The birth rate is high among the peasant communities due to early marriage, low level of literacy of females, religious beliefs etc. As a result natural growth remains high even in the beginning of the present millennium, Moreover, a major section of the household of Assam live below poverty line who are mostly agricultural people. They consider their children as the potential source of augmenting their family income and they have no restriction in the family size and therefore it is obvious to have high fertility among them.

Socio-Economic Implications

The staggering growth of population in Assam has manifold implication which impedes the development of the State.

There has been imbalance sex ratio due to sex selective migration. In 1951 sex ratio in Assam was 868 females per thousand males which, however, rose to 869, 896, 923 and 935 in 1961, 1971, 1991 and 2001 respectively. The presence of large number of sojourners coupled with growing imbalance in sex ratio has serious social implications for the quality of life of Assam. A large number of male population from outside Assam especially the people related to trade and commerce and labour class without social mooring also added consequential social problems in the State. Moreover, a sizable amount of income generated in the State also invested outside the State and not ploughed back for the development of the State.

The high population growth resulting from high fertility rate leads to more population in the young age group (0–14 years). Undoubtedly they would soon enter into the reproductive age group and add more population to the State. The dependency ratio also is very high in Assam reflecting a very discoursing situation because it is considered as one of the main constraints of economic development of a region. According 1971 Census Assam had 46.95 per cent of population below 15 years of age which showed a slight decline in 1991 (40.22 per cent).

With the increasing population, the main agricultural land ratio has been increasing. Agriculture of the State of Assam is subsistence and development in this sector is very meagre when compared to agriculturally developed States of India like Punjab and Haryana. The agricultural density of Assam was 542 persons per square km. in1971, which rose to 844 persons per km^2 in 2001. This high agricultural density of population exerts tremendous pressure on agricultural land of the State.

Per capita cultivated land also has been declining from 0.167 hectare in 1960-61 to only 0.10 hectare in 2000-01. Moreover, average size of operational holding is very small indicating a discouraging agricultural economy of Assam. It has also been declining from

1.5 hectare in 1960-61 to 1.09 hectare in 2000–01 (Table 15.5). At present more than two-thirds of the holdings are economically non viable which create problem in the mechanization of agriculture as well as in the development of agriculture.

Table 15.5 : Average Size of Operational Holding and Per Capita Cultivated Land in Assam

(Area in hectares)

Year	*Average size of operational holding*	*Per capita cultivated land*
1960–61	1.5	0.167
1970–71	1.37	0.15
1980–81	1.31	0.14
1990–91	1.27	0.125
2000–01	1.09	0.10

Source : World Agricultural Census, Assam, 1970–71.
Economic Survey Assam, 2000-01, 2004-05, Directorate of Economics and Statistics, Govt. of Assam.

Because of high growth rate of population, a section of poor people even have no shelter. In Assam shortage of houses was estimated at 3109000 numbers in 1971, which increased to 3977000 in 1991 However, in 2001 this figure decreased to 2100000 (Basic Statistics of North-Eastern Region, 1995 and 2001). In urban areas the houses in the slum areas are in dilapidated condition.

The most important problem that has been gaining ground in the State is the problem of unemployment. Not only a large proportion of total population is non-workers, among the workers also, a sizable section is underemployed. According to the live Register of Employment Exchange in 1984 the total numbers of population recorded as job seeker in Assam was 4,79,300. Unfortunately that figure rose to about three times recording as high as 14,90,300 in 1999. The high growth of population in Assam is mainly responsible for increasing pattern of unemployment in the State. At present it takes a serious turn especially in Assam and a section of youth takes the path of violence. Situation is turmoil in some areas. At present insurgency problem is a burning problem in the State resulting mainly from high rate of population growth especially from migration, unemployment and inequality in the mobilization of resource as well as low level of economic development.

In addition to this, with the large scale increase of population, some areas originally agricultural land, forest land and waste land are now used for settlement. Moreover there has been large scale deforestation due to extension of settlement, extension of agricultural land and use of land for other purposes. Unplanned human settlement especially in the hilly and foothill areas resulted in soil erosion and flood which affect the economy of the State. In addition to this, industrialization and urbanization lead to pollution and environmental degradation.

Lastly, it may be mentioned here that though there has been development in the agricultural front, in the last thirty years the food production cannot cope with the increasing demand of the growing population. The analysis of last thirty years data reveals that in 1970-71, there was deficit of 11,705.9 tonnes of foodgrains which rose to 66,240 tonnes in 2000-01. Thus the above analysis indicates that unless the rampant growth of population is checked, the economic development of the State is very difficult.

Conclusion

Assam recorded a significantly high growth of population during the twentieth century mainly due to large scale migration and high fertility rate. The rapid growth of population may be considered as the main obstacle in the development of the State. Therefore, necessary steps should be taken to check the immigration on the one hand and educate the people about family planning on the other. At the same time, necessary steps should be taken to develop infrastructure for proper resource management and development through proper planning. In small size of operation holdings intensive cultivation of crops along with the development of piggeries, fisheries, poultry farmings etc. can be done to get maximum benefit. Proper scientific crop rotation with high intensity of cropping also helps to reduce the shortage of production of food crops. It also helps to enhance fertility of the soil. As the economy of the State is primarily agriculture, proper crop calendar considering the physiographic framework, climate and edaphic condition should be prepared for micro-level agricultural planning in the State. This help in the sustainable agricultural development in the State. In addition to this proper training and education should be imparted especially to the rural masses. It is expected that this will help in reducing population growth, poverty, social disturbance and other problems in the State of Assam. Especially education of female is highly essential as it is instrumental in reducing fertility.

As development can be considered as the best contraceptive, human resource development is the need of the hour to minimize all the problems related to high population growth.

References

Allen, B.C. (1905): *Assam District Gazetteers*, Government. of Assam.

'Aspects of Population Profile of Assam', *Census of India*, Series 4, 1991.

Basic Agricultural Statistics, Assam (1971-72, 1975-76, 1980-81, 1991-92, 1998-99, 2003-04), Directorate of Agriculture, Government of Assam.

Bora, H.N. (2001): 'Immigration' in Bhagabati, A.K. *et al.* (eds.) *Geography of Assam*, Rajesh Publications, New Delhi.

Bhuyan, J.C. (2002): *Dialogue.*

Census of India (1901, 1931, 1951, 1961, 1971, 1991, 2001).

Economic Survey, Assam (2000-2001), Directorate of Economics and Statistics, Government. of Assam.

Kar, B.K. (1998) 'Population Pressure and Problems of Development in Assam', Proceeding Volume of *National Association of Geographers, India* (Eastern Region), Deportment. of Geography, Cotton College, Assam.

Report of the Line System Committee (1938): Assam Government Press, Shillong.

World Agricultural Census, (1970–71): Directorate of Economics and Statistics, Government. of Assam.

16 Victims of 'Suspicious' Identity
The *Char* Dwellers of Assam

Gorky Chakraborty

> "*If you want your country's well-being*
> *Don't look upon any compatriot as a stranger*"[1]

Introduction

The above epithet may not always reverberate the existential reality of North East India since the compatriots, in the region are often viewed through the exclusivist prism of 'indigenous' and 'foreigner' identities. Discourses on demography get weird to the axiomatic spectrum of 'indigenous-foreigner-minority' notions. Viewed through this spectacle, the much hyped issues such as, 'influx of foreigners', 'loss of culture', 'identity-crisis', 'demographic invasion', 'loss of economic livelihood', 'politics of appeasement' etc. hide the dialectic of dominance and resistance and the hiatus created due to the politics of privilege and deprivation in the region, while highlighting only the notions of 'cultural exclusivism'. This adversely affects the politico-economic stability and influences the socio-cultural psyche of the people in the region. Inadequate macro-level analysis and non-availability of micro-level data related to the dynamics of demographic discourses not only increases information gap but also generates several 'hysterical-myths', which worsens the situation further.

The term indigenous, foreigners and minority can be interpreted in virious ways. Leaving aside the value judgement associated with these terms, if we analyze them in the phenomenological and/or non-coercive sense, we may arrive at a broad-based, if not ideal conclusion. 'Indigenous' in this sense means "close to earth, being non-alienated from the surroundings, its constituents being bound together primarily by ontologically and historically crystallized moral bindings instead of the coercive power of the State, minimum presence of a crystallized elite sector usurping the role of the community as a whole in the matter of perception, interpretation, elaboration, legitimization of essential elements of culture etc."[2] If one analyzes the term 'indigenous' in this manner, it is irrelevent whether an indigenous people is autochthonous or not in the chronological sense.

Similarly, the question of 'foreigner' can be considered keeping in view several parameters, e.g. "a time-frame of migration, time-frame of recognition of citizen with reference to State institution, historical context of migration, demographic structure of the host area and the migrants, role of migrants in the political-economic and socio-cultural processes of the host area, nature of development activities, nature of link that the migrants are having with the area of origion, geo-cultural area with deeper structural mutuality cutting across State political boundaries, wider geo-political context and short, medium and long term process".[3] But it must be admitted that in terms of all these paramenters the situation is not identical in all the north-eastem States. However, it is also true that there has hardly been an integrated study covering all these aspects, as a result of which, all attempts to resolve the issue of 'foreigner' has been partial in North East India.

The United Nations describes the term 'minority' as "only those non-dominant groups in a population, which possess and preserve stable ethnic, religious or linguistic traditions or characteristics which are different from those of the rest of the population".[4] If this interpretation is accepted then Assam along with various other places of North East India, as far as population pattern is concerned, seems more likely to be a State/region made up of minorities.

In the light of the above framework, an attempt will be made to deal with the much neglected, if not forgotten *char* area of Assam, who are the worst victims of a ubiquitous 'indigenous-foreigner-minority' syndrome. The demographic characteristics and the socio-economic profile of the *char* dwellers along with their changes over the years have been discussed in this paper. But severe dearth of data concerning the *char* areas of Assam has been an impediment in analyzing these areas.

The *Char* Areas of Assam

The mid-channel bars (locally and henceforth referred as *char*) are an integral part of the fluvial process of the river Brahmaputra and its tributaries in Assam. The extremely braided channels of the river along with its suspended particles and bed load combine together during floods giving rise to 'almond' shaped alluvial formations known as *chars*. Since these formations are built under flood environment, the height of the *char* is never greater than the height of the highest food. They are extremely unstable and can be wiped out by erosion during the next flood. Above all, these *char* follows a peculiar patten of migration. They are subjected to erosion on their upstream and deposition on the downstream, due to which they migrate downstream. This affects the geometry and location of the *chars* during almost every year.[5]

These natural habitates of the river-plane were converted into areas of human habitation during the colonial period, when the British administrators induced large number of peasants from the densely populated districts of erstwhile East Bengal to migrate and settle in the wastelands of Assam as a part of their land settlement schemes to increase the area under cultivation in general and cash crops in particular and ultimately augment the revenue generation process in this otherwise revenue meagre State of colonial India. This migration and settlement of immigrants, which gathered momentum after the Partition of Bengal in 1905 thereafter had wide ranging impact upon the economy of Assam. The immigrants not only brought huge tracts of uncultured wastes under the plough but also introduced wide variety of crops at a commercial scale in the State. Today, jute, tobacco, sugarcane along with wide varieties of spices, oilseeds and vegetables cultivated in the State are the living example of their historic effort.[6] But the overwhelming number of immigrants in their spree to cultivate more land intruded into those natural habitates including *char*, forest, wetlands and other virgin tracts, which were outside the domain of permanent human activities. This undoubtedly raised the agricultural production, but in the long-run generated environmental strains too.

Even today, habitation in the *chars*, which are always in a state of continuous flux due to flood and erosion, necessitates the movement of the *char* dwellers to other safer places, including the mainland areas. Moreover, they being the residents of such areas, which are naturally secluded from the mainland, the attire, activities and traits of the *char* dwellers along with the information gap concerning these area, more than often, gives rise to suspicion among the inhabitants of mainland. Thus, the *char* dwellers become stangers to their compatriots in the very state into which their forefathers have settled to improve agriculture, over a century ago.

The Present Scenario in the *Char* Areas of Assam

The geomorphology of the *chars* is such that nothing seems to be enduringly settled here—neither land or people. According to the Socio-economic Survey Reports (the only source of data concerning the *char* of Assam), during 1992-93 to 2002-03, the number of *char* villages of the Brahmaputra has risen from 2,089 to 2,251 (See Tables 16.1 and 16.2). There have been 162 new *chars*, which were formed during this time period. But this increase has not been uniform among the Brahmaputra Valley zone of Assam. As per the Report, overall number of *char* villages has decreased in Nalbari, Barpeta, Goalpara, Bongaigaon, Morigaon, Lakhimpur and Tinsukia districts whereas it has increased in Kamrup, Dhubri, Darrang, Nagaon, Jorhat, Sonitpur and Dhemaji districts respectively. Similarly, during 1992-93, Barpeta district had the highest number of *char* villages (351) followed by Dhubri (313) and Jorhat (210). Whereas during 2003-04, Dhubri district has the highest number of *char* villages (480) followed by Jorhat (293) and Barpeta (277).

The total population of the *char* villages in Assam increased from 16, 00,244 in 1992-93 to 24,90,397 in 2003-04. Barpeta had the largest population (2,75,525) followed by Dhubri (2,33,206) and Jorhat (1,41,901) during 1992-93. Presently Dhubri district has the largest *char* population (6,89,909) followed by Barpeta (2,68,344) and Jorhat (2,15,095). It is observed that other than Barpeta district there has been a rise in *char* population in all the districts of Assam.

The total *char* area in the Brahmaputra has increased from 23900 ha to 36092 ha during the period 1992-93 and 2003-04. Similarly, the cultivable land has also increased from 167300 ha to 24277 ha during the same period. But if we juxtapose this data with the population figures, it becomes evident that both in terms of per capita land availability and per capita availability of cultivable land there has been a fall during 1992-93 and 2003-04. Moreover, cultivable land as a percentage of total land has declined from 70 per cent to 67.13 per cent during the same time period.

Table 16.1: Selected Statistics of the *Char* Areas in Assam, 1992-93 (Land in ha)

District	*Char Villages*	*Total Population*	*Total Land*	*Cultivable Land*	*Literacy (%)*	*B.P.L. Population (%)*
Kamrup	148	105687	5401.72	3781.20	16.85	53.0
Nalbari	58	62892	8558.97	5500.58	7.90	54.2
Barpeta	351	275525	2788.136	19516.95	12.90	55.0
Goalpara	187	130007	11623.45	8136.41	8.38	53.2
Bongaigaon	150	110215	11357.00	7956.90	12.85	54.0
Dhubri	313	233206	86952.22	60847.65	19.06	54.02
Darrang	121	125876	6661.36	4662.95	10.12	55.0
Morigaon	41	55581	6804.66	4763.26	8.02	52.5
Nagaon	29	45161	3265.25	22885.67	9.44	55.0
Jorhat	210	141901	5576.38	3903.46	31.90	25.0
Sonitpur	118	92061	24014.06	20309.84	12.63	43.0
Lakhimpur	182	110200	12069.51	8455.65	14.01	49.0
Dhemaji	95	68998	13517.00	9461.90	14.44	46.8
Tinsukia	86	33034	10324.00	7226.80	14.20	34.5
Total	2089	1600244	239000.00	167300.00	15.45	48.90

Table 16.2 : Selected Statistics of the *Char* Areas in Assam, 2003-04

Districts	*Char Villages*	*Total Population*	*Total Land*	*Cultivable Land*	*Literacy (%)*	*B.P.L. Population (%)*
Kamrup	175	154508	17162	11654	15.16	68.00
Nalbari	32	83602	13432	8996	16.24	68.36
Barpeta	277	268344	36655	24736	17.63	66.78
Goalpara	179	186826	19860	13728	13.65	68.57
Bongaigaon	117	135809	14266	9520	12.48	67.50
Dhubri	480	689909	99898	67124	14.60	69.00
Darrang	134	142405	16756	11239	12.34	66.94
Morigaon	39	91324	11932	7954	18.50	67.00
Nagaon	43	89803	12036	8056	17.59	66.79
Jorhat	293	215095	42174	28016	60.55	64.00
Sonitpur	145	145729	24168	16410	16.93	68.00
Lakhimpur	109	143235	21523	14451	18.50	69.02
Dhemaji	149	91203	19676	11347	15.69	70.93
Tinsukia	79	52605	14094	9496	14.00	68.90
Total	2251	2490397	360927	242277	19.31	67.90

Source: Socio-Economic Survey Report, 1993-94 and 2003, *Char* Area Development Authority, Government of Assam, Dispur, Assam.

The *char* villages are one of the largest repositories of illiterate population in the State. They are perhaps one of the most illiterate population groups in the entire region. Between 1992-93 and 2002-03, their literacy level has risen from 15.45 to 19.31 per cent. But during the same period there has been a fall in literacy rates among the *Char* villages of Bongaigaon, Kamrup, Dhubri and Tinsukia districts. Again, if we calculate the literacy rate of the *char* areas excluding Jorhat district, where Majuli (the culturally rich largest river island in the world) is located, the rate falls further to 15.64 per cent only. In fact, this lower rate of literacy in the *char* areas excluding Majuli seems to be related (other than historic and cultural factors) to the wide disparity in terms of availability of educational infrastructure in these two areas. It is also evident in terms of the availability of health infrastructure. Table 16.3 compares the difference between these two areas.

Table 16.3 : Comparative Analysis of the Population served by the Educational and Health Institutions in Majuli and other *Char areas* of Assam

Educational Facilities	*Majuli*	*Other Char Areas*
L.P. School	508	1592
M.E. School	1558	5218
High School	2389	17775
Higher Secondary	53773	268825
Colleges	26886	227530
P.H.C	26886	51711
Sub-Center	11949	19958

Source: http://assamgovt.nic.in/aare/interim_report5.doc

Agriculture is the main source of livelihood of these people. Till date, they have continued solely with farm activities, the same occupation for which they were encouraged by the British to migrate from East Bengal to Assam. But now, a higher rate of population growth, fall in the availabilitity of cultivable land, continuous menace of land erosion and lack of occupational diversification in the *char* areas along with host of other related problems, act together to create extraordinary pressure upon their livelihood pattern. It seems that due to these deterrents, the number of people living below the poverty line has increased dramatically in the *char* of Assam. Tables 16.1 and 16.2 indicate that the BPL population increased substantially from 48.90 per cent to 67.90 per cent during 1992-93 to 2003-04.

Changing Pattern in the *Char* Areas

The *char* area is home to 9.37 per cent of the population in Assam but has only 4 per cent of the States's agricultural land. On the other hand, whereas the density of population for the State is 340 persons per sq. km. it is 690 persons per sq. km for the *char* areas. As a result of which there is tremendous pressure upon land in these areas. On the other hand, agriculture, over the years is becoming less remunerative due to the interplay of several factors such as land erosion, lack of better inputs, erratic use of chemical fertilizer, improper marketing linkages along with a skewed pattern of land ownership in the *char* areas. Above all, lack of occupational diversification and absence of non-farm activities does not help in the process of transfer of population from agriculture to non-agricultural activities. An analysis of the data available (Tables 16.1 & 16.2) for the *char* areas shows this trend. Table 16.3 exhibits the decadal change in various aspects concerned with the *char* areas of Assam.

It is observed from Table 16.4 that the overall decadal growth rate (55.63 per cent) of population in the *char* areas of Assam has been far higher than the State average (18.85 per cent during 1991-2001), which must have added further pressure to the limited resource base in these areas. Increase in overall density of population by 0.21 per cent during the same period has also increased the pressure upon land in the *char* areas. Along with it, if we consider that there has been a fall in the per capita availability of cultivable land (the only source of livelihood) in these areas, the situation becomes even worse. Under these circumstances, migration from the *char* areas to the mainland in search of better living condition seems nothing unusual.

Table 16.4 : Decadal Variation in the *Char* Areas of Assam 1992-93 to 2003-04

Districts	*Villages (%)*	*Population (%)*	*Density of Pop. (%)*	*Per capita Availability of Cltv. Land (ha)*	*Literacy (%)*	*BPL Pop. (%)*
Kamrup	18.24	46.19	-10.56	0.04	-1.69	15.00
Nalbari	-44.83	32.93	-1.13	0.01	8.34	14.16
Barpeta	-21.08	-2.60	-2.56	0.02	4.73	11.78
Goalpara	-4.28	43.70	-1.77	0.01	5.27	15.37
Bongaigaon	-28.20	23.22	-0.18	0.00	-0.39	13.50
Dhubri	53.35	195	4.32	-0.16	-4.46	14.80
Darrang	10.74	4.80	-11.9	0.05	2.22	11.94
Morigaon	-4.88	64.31	-0.52	0.01	10.48	14.50
Nagaon	48.27	98.95	-6.37	0.04	8.15	11.79
Jorhat	39.52	51.58	-20.35	0.10	28.65	39.00
Sonitpur	22.88	58.29	2.20	-0.11	4.30	25.00
Lakhimpur	-39.78	29.28	-2.48	0.02	4.49	20.02
Dhemaji	56.84	32.18	0.27	-0.02	1.25	24.13
Tinsukia	-8.14	59.24	0.53	-0.04	-0.20	34.40
Total	7.75	55.63	0.21	-0.01	3.86	19.00

It is also observed from Table 16.4 that there has been a fall in the density of population among the 10 out of the 14 districts where the *char* villages are located in Assam. Although, this fall in population density is partly related to the increase in the total land area of the *chars* in these districts during the period, yet in the overall analysis, it is not unnatural that out-migration of the *char* dwellers from these villages of the concerned districts have played a role in reducing the density of population. Among these districts, where the density of population has decreased, other than Jorhat and Lakhimpur (where also the presence of Muslim *char* dwellers are in no way negligible), in all the other areas, *chars* are totally inhabited by the Muslim population. As a result, when they move out of the *chars* to the mainland areas, the *char* dwellers become a victim of the notion of 'suspicious' population, in the eyes of the mainlanders in Assam.

Lieu of Conclusion

It is often argued that migration is the oldest action against poverty. It is beneficial to both the regions: one, into which the migrants move, gets benefited economically and on the other, it helps to break the equilibrium of poverty from which they come. But ironically, the existential reality in the North East India is such that when the helpless *char* dwellers migrate from the *chars*, they become the victims of 'suspicious' identity. Their attire, nature, behaviour, language and religion on one hand and the lack of knowledge on the part of the people of the mainland about the *chars* on the other, ultimately leads to a scenario, where these *char* dwellers are straightaway labelled as *Bangladeshis* or illegal immigrants from across the international border. It is unfortunate that while the mainstream media as well as organizations from the mainland dump them as illegal immigrants, the same institutions never care to trace of root cause of their migration from the *char* areas. The net result is the generation of mistrust, suspicion and discord among the two population groups, where the mainland Hindus population falls prey to the age-old-bogey of 'invading immigrants' reducing them to minority, while the *char* dwellers suffer from the 'constructed' propaganda of 'suspicious' identity. Under such a situation, the identity-based politics of the region remains entrapped within the contours of 'cultural', where the notions of 'indigenous-foreigner-minority' become the only rallying points and all other issues of deprivation, dominance and discord affecting the life and livelihood of the masses are swept aside the carpet. In such a milieu, the compatriots become strangers and the well-being of the region gets hampered.

Notes & References

1. These lines of the Urdu Poet Altaf Hussain Hali (1937-1914), which capture the dilemma of Muslim identity has been quoted from Jalal, Ayesha, 'Exploding Communalism: The Politics of Muslim Identity in South Asia', Bose, Sugata, & Jalal, Ayesha, *Nationalism, Democracy and Development: State and Politics in India* (New Delhi: Oxford University Press, 1998).
2. As quoted in 'An Interview with Prof. B.K. Roy Burman', in Datta, P.S., *North East As I See It* (New Delhi: Omsons Publications, 1994).
3. *Ibid.*
4. As quoted by Choudhury, Rabijit, 'Minority Movements: Emergence of The United Minorities Front', in Datta, P.S. (ed.), *Ethnic Movements in Poly-Cultural Assam* (New Delhi: Vikas Publishing House, 1990).

5. Bhagabati, Abani Kumar, 'Bio-diversity and Associated Problems in the Islands of the Brahmaputra, Assam', in *Geographical Review of India*, Vol. 63, No. 4, 2001.
6. In fact, area under jute increased substantially from a meagre of 5 thousand acres during 1901-02 to 277 thousand acres by 1941-42. It was similar for various other crops also that were cultivated by the immigrant cultivators from East Bengal. For detailed analysis regarding the contribution made by the immigrant farm-settlers from East Bengal towards the agricultural economy of Assam, see Doullah, Sujaud M., *Immigration of East Bengal Settlers and Agriculture Development of the Assam Valley* (New Delhi: Institute of Objective Studies, 2003).

17 Urbanization in Assam

Growth of Slums and Related Problems

Jayasree Borah

During the 20th century, most of the Indian cities have experienced rapid growth in association with the development of transport and communication system and industrialization. As a result of this, not only are the cities changing markedly both in area and population, but their problems are also becoming more and more complex and varied. Rapid urbanization and unplanned growth of the cities has resulted in growth of slums, sprawls, urban blight, bastees and squatter settlements. Such types of growth is mainly responsible for environmental pollution, encroachment of open land, green belt and wetland, degradation of urban infrastructure and increasing number of different socio-economic problems like crime, violence, child labour, beggary, drug addiction, prostitution, etc.

Assam, one of the lowly urbanized States of the country, is also responding to this new trend of urbanization and its consequences. It is being more so due to the high rate of flow of migration from the rural areas in search of employment opportunities. This is bringing a marked change in the physical as well as the socio-economic landscape of different urban centres of the State in general and Guwahati in particular. The present work is concerned with trend of urbanization, characteristics of process of urbanization and distribution pattern of different types of urban centres in Assam. It will also attempt to study the causes of growth of slums and associated problems particularly in Guwahati City.

Methodology

The study is based on secondary data collected from Census of India

2001, and Statistical Handbook of Assam 2002. Data pertaining to rural urban population and urban centres are standardized, ordered and grouped. Then relationship between geographical aspects and distribution pattern are analysed to draw conclusion. Certain quantitative techniques like ratio of urban population, urban density and nearest neighbour statistics are used for this purpose. Besides these, a field study was conducted in Guwahati City during 2005-06 period to study the slum areas and related problems.

Geographical Background of the Study Region (2001):

- Area–78,438 sq.km.
- Total Population–26,638,407.
- Population Density–340 per sq.km.
- Urban Population–3,389,413.
- Rural Population–23,248,994.
- Percentage of Urban Population–12.72%.
- Percentage of Rural Population–87.28%.
- Growth of Urban Population–12.72%.
- Growth of Rural Population–16.97%.
- No. of Urban Centres–125.

Trend of Urbanization

Among the States and Union Territories of the country, urban population in Himachal Pradesh is lowest (9.8%) followed by Bihar (10.5%) and Assam (12.7%). However, the decadal growth rate of urban population in Assam is higher than the national average. The decadal growth rate of the urban population of Assam during 1981-91 was 39.6 per cent against National growth rate of 36.5 per cent and during 1991–2001 it is 36.24 per cent against that of the national growth rate of 31.13 per cent. Thus the difference in growth rate between the States and the Nation increased from 3.1 per cent to 5.11 per cent. In contrast to the growth of 36.24 per cent of urban population, the percentage increase of rural population was only 16.67 per cent in the State.

Another important characteristic process of urbanization in Assam is that the growth rate is higher in class V towns with a decadal percentage growth of +154.53. This is mainly because of inclusion of new towns in this class. However, the decadal growth rate in respect of class I town is 60.31 and class II town is 68.76 per cent while in class III town it is only 1.46, class IV –0.31 and class VI it is lowest with 57.87 per cent. Such type of spatial variations in the growth of urban population is due to limited infrastructure facilities in the small and medium sized towns. For this the flow of unskilled agricultural labourer and also educated unemployed persons to the large towns and mainly to Guwahati Metropolis is very high. In Assam, in terms of concentration of urban population, Kamrup District occupies first position with 35.81 per cent where Guwahati City is located. In contrast to this, almost 50 per cent of the districts of the State have urbanization level significantly below the State level (less than 10%) with Nalbari at the lowest position (2.4%). The main causes of low rate of urbanisation are less development of industrial sector, limited trade and commerce and traditional leaning towards agriculture.

Guwahati, the capital city of Assam with a population of ten lakh, is the largest urban centre of entire North East India and also the leading administrative, commercial, industrial and socio-cultural node of the region. During the last decade, the city has experienced tremendous population growth and socio-economic development along with noticeable increase in density, spatial expansion and transformation of socio-economic setting. At present Guwahati alone constitutes almost 25 per cent of the State's total urban population. Such type of uneven distribution of urban population disturbs both the rural and urban environment. Overcrowding of cities, de-population of rural areas, high pressure of population on limited civic amenities and facilities, problem of transport and communication, unbalanced utilization of land, etc., are some of the ill-effects of such distribution pattern.

Growth of Slums and other related Problems

Although the pace of urbanization is considered as a sign of economic development, the un-scientific growth of urban centres will lead to a number of socio-econUrbanization in Assam Urbanization in Assam Urbanization in Assam Urbanization in Assam omic and environment related problems. In Assam the large gap of rural and urban areas in respect of service, facilities, accessibility, etc., the concentration of industries, trade and commerce and other services of the urban centres attract large number of unskilled labour group and unemployed youth. Such types of growth creates immense problem of air, water and land pollution, destruction of green belt and hill sides, disturbance of eco-system of wetland and grassland, waste disposal at open land and drains, etc. Especially in Guwahati City, the increasing population pressure has created the problem of housing, water supply, health services, transport facility, pollution, etc. and finally the growth of bastees, slums or blighted areas. The urban infrastructure, which is already very weak, crumbles under the population pressure and the quality of urban services further deteriorates. Increasing numbers of the poor people continue to live in sub-standard housing in such settlements without any service. As a result, poverty, pollution, congestion and some other social problems continue to rise at an alarming rate.

There are 7 cities/towns of Assam with reported growth of slum and they are Guwahati, Dhubri, Tezpur, Dibrugarh, Jorhat, Tinsukia and Silchar. Here all total 82,289 slum population is recorded. The main causes of development of slums in these areas are absence of employment opportunities in the rural areas outside the agricultural sector, high rate of rural urban migration, inadequate civic amenities in the urban centres, unplanned growth of factories without any housing facilities for the labourers and unscientific land use planning. At present there are 740,206 urban poor in Assam most of which are slum dwellers. Among these the highest number is found in Kamrup district accounting for 20.5 per cent of total urban poor in the State (Government. of Assam, 2004). Again during the last decade the growth of slum population is highest in the six class I towns where the percentage share of urban population is significantly high (41.9). As these towns provide more economic opportunities, most of the unemployed rural people migrate to these urban centres. Such heavy concentration of population in these class I towns ultimately leads to formation of bastees, slums and squatter colonies with very little basic amenities.

Table 17.1 : Towns of Assam Reporting Slum Areas in 2001

Towns/Cities	*Total Urban Copulation*	*Total Slum Copulation*
1. Guwahati	809,895	8,457
2. Dhubri	64,168	18,927
3. Tezpur	80,575	483
4. Tinsukia	85,563	4,225
5. Dibrugarh	121,893	9,211
6. Jorhat	67,588	10,808
7. Silchar	142,199	30,088

In Assam among the slum population, sex ratio is relatively low, i.e. 893 while it is highest in Kerela (1073) followed by Meghalaya (1003). In Assam the low sex ratio shows the high rate of male selective migration to the slum areas. Some other important characteristics of slum population of the State are medium literary rate (76.4%), low percentage of child population (12.6%) and medium size of workers among total slum population (32.0%).

In Guwahati City at present there are 15 slums with a total population of 56,000 (Table 17.2). In addition to this, the office of Municipal Administration has identified 39 slums in the greater

Table 17. 2 : List of Slums in Guwahati City (According to the GMC)

Sl. No.	*Name of Slum Pocket*	*Approximate Population*
1.	Sarania Harijan Colony	3500
2.	Morasali Harijan Colony	3500
3.	Rajabari Uzanbazar Harijan Colony	1500
4.	Fatasil Harijan Colony	8500
5.	I Bijoynagar No.2	3000
6.	Sijubari Hatigaon	5000
7.	Manipuri Basti	4000
8.	Ulubari Kachari Basti	5000
9.	Chatribari Kachari Basti	2500
10.	Namoni Luitpar Kharghuli	3000
11.	Bhutnath Durgasarobar	5000
12.	Dhirenpara	5000
13.	Bishnupur	5000
14.	Marowary Harijan Colony	1500
15.	Krishnanagar Japarigog	–
Total Population		56,000

Total Nos. of Household Population in Slum Pockets within Guwahati Municipal Corporation

Sl. No.	*Name of Slum Pocket*	*Total no. of Households*	*Male*	*Female*	*Population Total*
1.	Rajabari (Uzanbazar)	520	1888	1456	3344
2.	Athgaon	1275	4811	4104	8915
3.	Manipuri Basti	1255	4630	3835	8465
4.	Fatasil Harizan Colony	1379	5819	4800	10619
5.	Bishnupur	1487	5958	4886	10844
6.	Tokobari	1324	4628	3921	8549
7.	Solapara Harizan Basti	924	3395	2804	6199
8.	Islampur Hedayathpur Harizan Colony	1896	5865	4363	10228
9.	Lakhtokia	835	3103	2665	5768
10.	Kacharibasti	1129	4880	3852	1129
11.	Sontipur (east)	995	3580	3271	6851
12.	Paltanbazar Harizan Basti	807	2462	2670	5132
13.	Gandhi Basti	659	2274	2181	4455
14.	Bimalanagar	910	3277	2186	5463
15.	Kumarpara	1111	4080	3607	7687
16.	Dhirenpara	1360	3960	3377	7337
17.	Barnachal Madhuban	354	1273	894	2122
18.	Hatigaon Sizubari	3492	8288	7404	15692
19.	Birubari	250	729	710	1439
20.	Guwahati University Harizan Colony	822	2959	2637	5596
21.	Krishna Nagar (Japorigog)	469	1903	1377	3280
22.	Bijoynagar (Noonmati)	245	50	520	1070
23.	Namani Luitpar Kharpuli	330	1535	1520	3055
24.	Ambikagiri Nagar	325	1249	1210	2459
25.	Madhabpur Mahendranagar	450	1785	1745	3530
26.	Lechubagan Hengrabari	440	1780	1760	3540

Guwahati with a population of 113, 064 (Table 17.3). All these slums can be broadly divided into two categories, viz. the temporary one and the permanent type. The temporary slums are growing up by encroaching the river-side, hill sides, marshy land and road-sides while the permanent and semi-permanent types are found by the Railway. line, near the industrial sites, market place and at old residential areas. During field survey, the following salient features were observed in the slum areas of Guwahati City.

Table 17.3 : List of Slums in Greater Guwahati (According to the Office of the Municipal Administration, MAD)

Sl. No.	*Name of the Slum Areas*	*No. of Population*	*No. of Family*
1.	Ambari Satgaon	3500	300
2.	Tony Police Basti, Krishnagar	1900	200
3.	Sharaswati Basti Bikash Mandal	3000	430
4.	Pandu Nath Slum Areas	2670	445
5.	Gosala Harijon Colony	3400	486
6.	Maligaon (Central Gotanagar)	2800	421
7.	Ramsing Bill	3750	536
8.	Balaji Harijon Colony	–	–
9.	Chitrasal	2000	307
10.	Jaypur	3580	512
11.	Bishnupur	2000	339
12.	Bhaskar Nagar	2500	268
13.	Arkatipur Basti	2802	295
14.	Akashi Nagar	1900	210
15.	Balaji Nagar	2200	230
16.	Salbari	3500	380
17.	Pitani Nagar	3000	315
18.	Panikal, Rajbhawan Road	3000	310
19.	Pukhuripar	5000	718
20.	Fakirtola	6000	857
21.	Ambedkar	3000	428
22.	Tokobari Kalimandir	4000	571
23.	Lichubagan	2100	360
24.	Hafiznagar	5500	2760
25.	Natunbasti Uria Basti	2500	500
26.	Sabipul Balmiki Harijan Colony	2100	300
27.	Bimala Nagar	3000	500
28.	Pital Karkhana	3300	660
29.	Barsasara	3100	620
30.	Borsojai	3600	720
31.	Ulubari Kachari Basti	3000	600
32.	Uranggiri	2000	600
33.	Vetapara	2000	400
34.	Sijubari	4500	900
35.	Bongaon	2750	550
36.	Basistha Telegu Harijon Colony	2000	400
37.	Punjabi Colony	2000	400
38.	Marakhali	3000	600
39.	Vaskargiri Nagar	1052	210
40.	Prativa BBM	–	–
	Total	113064	19558

With the increasing flow of the poor and unskilled people mainly from the rural areas to the city, the slum areas are increasing in size and number, from 15 in 1998 to 40 in 2001 (population=113,064)

- The two important factors that determine their distribution pattern are topography and land use. In Guwahati city the slums are mainly found in physically disadvantageous places and near the market places and industrial sites.
- The slum areas are almost equally distributed in different parts of the city right from the core areas to the outer peripheries and from riversides to the hill slopes.
- Almost all the old slums are found to be concentrated by the side of the river Brahmaputra, Railway lines and wholesale market places of Fancy Bazar and Paltan Bazar at the core area.
- The newly developed slums are located at the hill slides, by the side of the National Highway towards south and near the Industrial Estates towards the east.
- Most of the slums are overcrowded with worst housing and sanitation conditions where even proper toilet facilities are not available.
- The surrounding areas of all the slums are full of filth and dirt with clogged drains, water logging, and absence of proper sewage system.
- These people usually earn very meagre income which is also not regular except the Harijon colonies. These families are engaged in different Government Organizations with a fixed salary.
- The unemployment rate among the slum dwellers is 40 per cent (Census of India, 2001) of the total workforce. Of these, 95 per cent are engaged in informal sector.
- The problem of child labour is very common among these people. During field survey it has been found that the riverside areas have highest illiteracy rate, poorest quality of living and highest number of child labour.
- The lack of basic amenities like toilet facilities, water supply,

electricity, free education for the children, supply of food products and fuel at Government controlled rate, free health services, proper means of sanitation, etc. is another serious problem for these group of people under study.

- The absence of these facilities is leading to a number of social problems like illiteracy, ill health, high rate of child mortality, poverty, child labour, beggary, crime, gambling, drug addiction, black marketing, juvenile delinquency, prostitution etc.

Recommendations

Most of the important urban centres of Assam can be described as excessively grown with the problems of shortage of housing, congested streets and pavements, shortage of public utilities, lack of open space, degraded residential environment and increasing air, water, and land pollution. To meet these problems, some development strategies and schemes are to be adopted at the micro-level. Undoubtedly the growth of cities and large towns, which are already overcrowded, depends upon how well we are able to plan for the unplanned. Since 1970s, attempts have been made to guide the urban development process in our country. In Assam also development authorities and Department of Town and Country Planning were established to prepare Master Plan and Regional Plans. In Guwahati, under the City Development Plan, Government has undertaken a programme which will provide shelter and other important infrastructure at an affordable price. The State Government has kept Rs. 110 crore for this purpose. From 2009, the Guwahati Municipal Corporation has agreed to spend 15 per cent of its revenue expenditure on delivery of services to these underprivileged groups of people.

It is needless to say that the growing slum areas and increasing number of urban poor have aggravated the socio-economic and environmental problems in the important urban centres of the State. A scientific land use plan is required to enable better planning for these areas. There should be proper demarcation of green belt, residential areas, open space, market place, Government land and the areas encroached and degraded by the slum dwellers. The planning and development of a few satellite towns at the outskirts of the overgrown cities will help in checking the increasing rate of migration. Moreover, provision should be there for low cost housing, income generating employment opportunities and proper drainage and sanitation system to improve the living conditions of these people. This will also help in developing the urban environment and changing the quality of life in the city.

References

1. Borah, Jayshree, "Social Problems of Slum Dwellers of Guwahati City", an unpublished project report, sponsored by ICSSR, 2006.
2. *Census of India, 2001,* Slum Population of India, Vol. I, Series I, New Delhi–2005, pp. 133–134.
3. *East India Human Development Report,* National Council of Applied Economic Research, 2004, Oxford University. Press.

18 Migration and its Role in the Growth of Population in Guwahati City

Aditya Ch. Deka and *L. Datta*

Introduction

Population of Guwahati City, the nerve centre of N.E. India has been increasing at a tremendous rate during the last century more particularly in the later half. Migration to the city from the neighbouring areas as well as from the other parts of India can be considered as the most important contributing factor of this growth.

Migration takes place due to several reasons and especially for males, employment and other economic opportunities available in the area of destination are the major reasons of migration. On the other hand for females, social causes such as marriage and shifting of families of working male population are important causes of migration. However, in urban area like Guwahati City a section of the female population has migrated to the City for economic causes. The study of migration pattern in any area gets special attention due to its impact on the demographic, political and socio-economic conditions in the place of destination as well as in the place of origin. In North East India specially in the context of Assam the study of migration is very relevant because major cause of population explosion is migration. Study of migration pattern in Guwahati merits special attention not only for the study of the growth of urban population in the city but also due to its environmental implication. During the last 100 years (1901-2001) city's population has increased from 11.7 thousand to 818.8 thousand showing an increase by about 8.3 times as compared to 8.1 times increase for the State as a whole. Though the total area under the urban jurisdiction also has showed an increase during the period, it is not at par with the growing population. Consequently, the fast increase in the urban population has been creating slum settlement, putting pressure on civic amenities such as education, health, water supply, rising urban crimes, increase of the vehicular traffic, population in the city environment etc. This especially leads to environmental degradation in the city. Moreover, unplanned settlement in the hill areas resulting from unauthorised occupation by poorer sections of people who have been migrating from other areas to the Guwahati city also create problem like deforestation on the hill sides which resulted in erosion in the hill slope, foothills and artificial flood in the down plain areas of the city. As these multi-dimensional changes in the physical and socio-economic environment of the city are directly related to the high increase of population, an attempt has been made in this paper to analyse the magration to the Guwahati city, which is the main contributing factor of the population growth.

Data and Methodology

This study is based primarily on secondary data collected from Census of India, 1991, General Population Table and Migration Tables, Census of India, 1971-2001. Rural-urban, urban-urban migration rates are also analysed considering the last place of residence and pattern of migration from other areas. The reason behind the migration streams have been studied in greater details taking data from different Government. reports. Field survey is also conducted in different factories to find out the actual pattern of migration, causes of gender variation in migration. Using simple statistical method the variation in migration and disparity in migration are also analysed for clear understanding for the problem.

Growth of Population

Guwahati is the most populous city of Assam and also the whole of North East India and is called as the gateway of North East India. It is registered as a class I town. It has also become the administrative, commercial, educational and political hub of entire region.

According to 2001 Census, the population of the city was 8,18,809 of which 4,46,311 (54.50 per cent) were males and 3,72,498 (45.50 per cent) were females. Considering the size of population the municipal corporation area has been divided into 60 wards. This variation is mainly due to the variation of physical features, historical development and socio-economic activities. During the last 100 years (1901-2001) city's population has increased from 11.7 thousand to 818.8 thousand showing an increase by about 8.3 times as compared to 8.1 times increase for the State as a whole. The average decadal variation of population growth between 1901 and 1951 was around 30 per cent. Even that was more higher than of Assam. Subsequently, during the period 1951 to 2001, the average decadal variation growth was around 112 per cent as against 27 per cent for State as a whole. (Table 18.1).

The city is characterized by a very high rate of population growth, which is even higher than the State's average growth throughout the last century. At the beginning of the twentieth century, the city's population was 11.6 thousand. It increased to 43.61 thousand in 1951 and 818.8 thousand in 2001 (Table 18.1) witnessing an average annual exponential growth rate of 3.12 per cent during 1901-1951 and 4.98 per cent during 1951-2001 as against State's corresponding growth rates of 1.79 per cent and 2.43 per cent. As a consequence the city's popualtion to the state's total increased from 0.35 per cent in 1901 to 0.54 per cent in 1951 and 3.07 per cent in 2001.

During the last few years of the Ahom Rule and first few years of the British occupation the population of Guwahati was a little over 10,000. The actual Census was taken in the years 1872 when the total population recorded in Guwahati was 11,492. The total population of the city declined by 275 in the year 1891. This decrease in population of -2.35 per cent may be attributed to the high mortality caused by 'Kalazar' (an epidemic type fever) that broke out in 1888 in Guwahati and some other parts of the Kamrup district.

Table 18.1 shows the decadal variation of population with variation as well as in sex ratio. Since 1991 the population of Guwahati began to increase, first steadily and gradually, and then at a higher

Table 18.1 : Trend of Growth of Population in Guwahati during 1901–2001

Years	*Population*	*Male*	*Female*	*Sex-ratio*	*Decadal Growth in Percentage*			*Decadal Variation*	*Annual Exponential Growth Rate in Per cent*		*Percentage City's Share of Population to Assam's*
Total					*Years*	*Guwahati*	*Assam*	*Guwahati*	*Guwahati*	*Assam*	
1901	11661	7772	3889	500	–	–	–	–	–	–	0.35
1911	12481	8138	4343	534	1901-1911	7.03	16.99	820	0.68	1.58	0.32
1921	16480	10786	5684	528	1911-1921	32.04	20.48	3999	2.82	1.88	0.36
1931	21797	14506	7291	503	1921-1931	32.26	19.9	5317	2.84	1.83	0.39
1941	29598	18883	10715	567	1931-1941	35.79	20.4	7801	3.16	1.87	0.44
1951	43615	27990	15625	558	1941-1951	47.36	19.93	14017	6.12	1.83	0.54
1961	136239	88882	47357	532	1951-1961	212.37	34.98	92624	12.06	3.04	1.26
1971	200377	119740	80637	673	1261-1971	47.08	34.95	64138	3.93	3.04	1.37
1981	NA	NA	NA	NA	1971-1981	NA	23.36	NA	NA	2.12	NA
1991	584342	327725	256617	783	1981-1991	191.62	24.24	383965	5.5	2.19	2.61
2001	818809	446311	371448	834	1991-2001	40.13	18.85	234467	3.43	1.73	1.07

Source: Census of India, 1991, Part II-A. General Population Table, Dicectrorate census Operations, Assam.
Data for 2001 colleeted from Census of India, Series 19, Primary, Census Abstract, Dicectrorate of Census Operations, Assam.

rate with influx of the immigrants both from inside and outside Assam. In the first decade the increase was 7.03 per cent. This increase was partly because of natural growth and partly due to migration from other localities. A significant increase in number was observed in between 1911-1931. This increase may be attributed to the migration of population from Bengal to the towns of Assam for Government services and also due to migration from rural areas. In the next decade (1931-1941) Guwahati recorded an increase of 35.79 per cent in its population. The population had further increased in between 1941 and 1951 mainly due to migration of refugee population from East Bengal and Sylhet when the rate of increase was 47.36 per cent. The unprecedented growth of 212.37 per cent was recorded in the decade 1951-1961. This increase was partly due to natural increase, immigration, enumeration and partly because of inclusion of some additional areas within the municipality area before 1961. During 1971-1991, the population growth rate was very high (191.62 per cent) mainly due to shifting of capital of Assam from Shillong to Guwahati (Dispur) during the early seventies of the last century and also partly due to migration from the neighbouring rural areas of Kamrup and other districts of Assam. The rate of population growth during 1991-2001, was 40.13 per cent. This increase was also partly due to natural increase of population and partly due to migration from rural to urban which was more in 1991 (Table 18.1). The major attractions for which the population from other parts has been migrating to the city are economic opportunities, development of industrial and administrative activities and availability of medical and educational facilities.

The increasing pressure of population has changed the urban landscape. The slums have been increasing in number and size at a very faster rate. New colonies have developed and the buildup areas have increased day by day. The influence of the city on the neighbouring areas is reflected not only by the population density but by other demographic characteristics as well. The growth of population is one such variable, which reflects the city's influence on the periphery of the city. Majority of the migrants are earning their livelihood through services and pretty business. A major section of them are engaged as daily labourers. However, a section of them belongs to the student category. Again it reveals from the field study that the illiterate landless agricultural labourers constitute the highest number of total migrants who are mostly concentrated in the slum areas.

Young adults constitute the major part among the migrants to the city. It is observed that 64 per cent of the total migrants from the neighbouring areas fall in the age group of 15-25.

Density of Population

Density of population indicates man and land ratio and gives a measure of population concentration in urban areas. Pre-Independence (1901-1941) population density in Guwahati city was 2143 per sq. km. In the post-Independence period, density of population in Guwahati increased to 2632 in 1951, 3154 in 1961, 3525 in 1971, 5120 in 1981, 5550 in 1991 and 6481 in 2001 (Table 18.2).

Tabel 18.2 : Density of population in Guwahati

Year	*Area of Guwahati in km*	*No. of Persons/sq.km.*
1941	14	2160
1951	16.6	2632
1961	32.0	3154
1971	84.0	3525
1991	216.79	5550
2001	264 (approx)	6481

Source: Guwahati Municipal Corporation (2001).

It is clear that the city is growing with an unplanned urban sprawling because of higher density of population. The maximum congregation could be seen at Fancy Bazar, Athgan, Paltan Bazar, Pandu Miligaon, Gopinath Nagar, Ulubari, Sarania, Bhangagarh, Japorigog, Ganeshguri, Noonmati, Bamunimaidan, Silpukhuri, etc. The density of population in the trade and business centres is found to be high in comparison to the adjacent habitational areas. The commerical landuse gradually displaced the residential concentration towards the peripheral areas. Variation of density within the city is another important feature. Core area of the city exhibits highest concentration of population. Commercial areas like Fancy Bazar, Paltan Bazar, Ganeshguri, Garhpandu, Athgaon etc. shows spatial variation in population density. The density of population is comparatively less in the wards of the peripheral zones.

According to 2001 Census, the more populated ward numbers are 41 (20,360), 60 (20,456 persons), 14 (21,125 persons), 21 (21,572 persons), 58 (22,741 persons), 46 (23,455 persons), 51 (25,989 persons), 49 (26,314 persons) and 12 (33,846 persons). On the other hand, the least populated ward numbers are 40 (3420 persons), 43 (5400 persons), 31 (5616 persons) and 52 (6490 persons).

Age Composition

The city has a imbalanced sex-ratio. The sex-ratio of population of Guwahati was found to be uniform 1901 to 1951 varying from 503-567. But during 1951-1961 it increased to 597 and rose 834 females per thousand male population. This indicates a highly imbalanced sex-ratio in the city population. One of the important characteristics is that the city's population is constituted by active population. About 63 per cent population belongs to the age group of 15-55 years. This condition is due to the recent development of the city in the field of industry, commerce and trade. In addition to this, opening of new offices and institutions have given employment opportunities for the young active population.

Trends of Migration in Guwahati City from 1971-2001

In the present study, trend and pattern of migration are analysed for the last three decades of the twentieth century due to paucity of data. Guwahati city received 117,805 persons as migrants constituting as high as 58.79 per cent of the total population of the city enumerated from their place of birth according to 1971 Census. This figure, however, rose to 276,835 persons in 1991 constituting 47.37 per cent of the total population of the city. In 2001, the total migrants in the Guwahati city was recorded as 378,657 persons which is about three times than that of 1971 accounting for 46.48 per cent of total population as against 25.50 per cent for the State of Assam as a whole.

Table 18.3 clearly indicates that proportions of migrants in Guwahati are always more than the proportions of migrants for the State as a whole during 1971-2001. The study reveals that a major section of migrants of Guwahati city is constituted by the local people of Assam. According to 1991 and 2001 Census people who had migrated from various parts of Assam to Guwahati city contributed as high as 66.30 per cent and 78.86 per cent of total migrants in 1991 and 2001 respectively. The decadal increase of migrant population was 135 per cent during the period 1971-1991 while it was 36.78 per cent in 1991-2001 (Table 18.3). The population of Guwahati city claimed 3.07 per cent of the total population of Assam in 2001, while proportion of migrants was 54.65 per cent of total migrants of Assam. The above analysis clearly indicates that migration to Guwahati city was very high which exerts tremendous pressure on its economy and it also affects the physico-social environment.

The temporal analysis further reveals that there has been rapid decadal growth of migrants during the last three decades of the twentieth century. The growth rate of migrant population during 1971-1991 (134.99%) was higher than the period 1991-2001 (36.78%) because of migration of population especially from Shillong to Guwahati due to shifting of capital of Assam from Shillong to Dispur (Guwahati) during the early seventies of the last century.

Patterns of Migration

Every city receives two types of migration one from rural areas and the other from urban areas and these movements of population are known as rural-urban and urban-rural migration streams.

According to 1991 Census rural-urban migrants consituted 57.46 per cent while urban-urban migrants constituted 41.92 per cent of the total migrants. After a decade, i.e. in 2001 (Table 18.2) there was increase in rural-urban migration (21.78 per cent). Regarding rural-urban migration it has been observed in all the towns and cities, it is an important and dominating stream in the initial period of the urban development of any city because an urban centre needs unskilled and semi-skilled labourers or workers for construction works and for other physical works (non-technical works). So, initially urban-urban

Table18.3 : Growth of Total Population and Migrants in Guwahati 1901-2001 and Proportion of Migrants to Total Population of Guwahati and Assam

Years	*Population of Guwahati city*						*Migrants of Guwahati city*					*% of Migrants*	*P.C. of*
	Persons	*Male (in p.c.)*	*Female (in p.c.)*		*Decadal Growth (in p.c.)*	*Net Increase*	*Total*	*Male (in p.c.)*	*Female (in p.c.)*	*Decadal Growth (in p.c.)*	*Net Increase*	*to Total Population of Guwahati and Assam*	*Migrants to Total Population*
1971	200,377	59.76	40.24	1961-1971	47.08	641,38	117,805	64.50	35.50	–	N.A.	58.79	34.56
1991	584,342	56.08	43.92	1971-1991	372.07	383,965	276,835	57.04	42.96	134.99	159, 030	47.37	24.13
2001	814575	54.71	45.29	1991-2001	39.40	234,467	378, 657	56.43	43.57	36.78	101, 822	46.24	25.50

Source: Cenus of India, Migration Tables, 1971, 1991, 2001.

migrants are lesser in number. According to 2001 Census, rural-urban migration was a dominating stream is Guwahati city which indicated the social and economic development of the city which is related to the second stage of Zelinsky's Mobility Transition Model (Zelinsky, 1971).

Table 18.4 : Guwahati City : Proportion of Migrants in Different Streams 1991-2001

Stream	*% of Migrants in Different Streams*		*Males*		*Females*	
	1991	*2001*	*1991*	*2001*	*1991*	*2001*
Rural-Urban	57.76	59.18	34.03	34.98	23.43	24.19
Urban-Urban	41.92	20.14	22.64	10.47	19.28	9.66

Source: Census of India, Migration Tables, 1991 & 2001.

It is further observed that migration to Guwahati city is sex selective like any other parts of the world. In 1991 population of male was more than the female in rural-urban stream (Table 18.4). Both the proportions of male and female were sharply decreasing in case of urban-urban migration while proportions of females and males were slightly increasing in respect of rural-urban migration.

Sex and Migration

It is observed that migration is mostly sex selective. Generally among the migrants proportion of male is more than the proportion of female. According to 2001 Census 1,01,822 migrants entered the city after 1991 (Table 18.5). Among these migrants 56.43 per cent were males and 43.57 per cent were females. The following important facts have emerged from this data. Firstly, the proportion of male migrants had declined from 57.04 per cent in 1991 to 56.43 per cent in 2001 whereas proportion of female migrants had increased from 42.96 per cent to 43.57 per cent.

The increase of proportion of female migration might be primarily due to migration of families, i.e. social cause like marriage. Though generally female migration is not induced by economic reason such

Table 18.5 : Number and Percentage of Migrants in Guwahati City

Migrants	*1991*		*2001*		*1991-2001*
	Migrants	*% to Total Population*	*Migrants*	*% to Total Population*	*Increase of Migrants*
Total migrants	276,835	47.93	378,657	46.48	101,822
Male migrants	157,918	57.04	213,669	56.43	55,751
Female migrants	115,917	42.96	164,988	43.57	46,071

Source: Census of India, Migration Tables, 1991 and 2001.

as employment and business etc. it is largely dependent on the social reasons such as associational reasons and marriage migration. In Guwahati city, however, unlike the rual areas, the working women now have been residing independently or in the working women hostels. Females have been partipating in different economic activities and especially in the city the opportunities are available not only in services but also in construction, workshops, tea stalls etc. As a result the size of female migrants presently has been increasing. In the field survey it is observed that in some industries of Amingaon and Khanapara of Guwahati like Enami, Uzala etc. and wine factory of Boragaon area, the proportions of female labourers are quite more. They are representing more than two-thirds of the total fourth-grade employees mainly because of low wage and high efficiency (Field Survey, 2006).

Causes of Migration

The major cause of voluntary migration to the city are economic. According to the Census report, 36.87 per cent (1991) and 33.80 per cent (2001) of the total migrants moved due to economic causes. The Guwahati city has 462 number of factories. These factories are providing jobs to a large number of persons especially to the labourers both skilled as well as semi-skilled. Obviously a major section of migrants are employed in these factories. Generally majority of the un-skilled migrants are, however, engaged in other economic activities like construction, daily labour etc. (Table 18.6).

Table 18.6 : Guwahati City: Reasons of Migration, 1991 and 2001

Reasons	*Proportion of Migrants to Total Migrants*		*Male*	*Female*	*Male*	*Female*
	1991	*2001*	*1991*		*2001*	
Employment	21.99	20.75	20.00	1.98	32.86	5.15
Economic Opportunity Other than Employment	14.88	13.05	12.87	2.00	17.04	1.02
Marriage	17.31	14.03	9.83	12.71	7.66	10.28
Family Moved	22.55	17.94	0.42	16.91	0.22	13.84
Natural Calamities	00.35	N.A.	0.22	0.13	N.A.	N.A.
Others	22.92	34.23	13.70	9.22	18.22	16.02

N.A.=Not Available.
Source: Census of India, Migration Tables, 1991 and 2001.

According to Census 1991 and 2001, out of the total migrants about 17 per cent and 14 per cent migrants respectively in 1991 and 2001 changed their residence due to marriage. However, the proportion of female were always more than male in both the Census periods (Table 18.6). A major section of females also migrated to the city constituting 16.19 per cent and 13.84 per cent in 1991 and 2001 respectively because of transfer of residence of family. The above analysis indicates that the male migration was associated mainly with economic reasons wheras female migration was due to social reasons. The reasons of migration of 22.92 per cent in 1991 and 34.23 per cent in 2001 are however not analysed in the census reports.

The total number of registered factories in Assam was 2691 in 2002 (Statistical Handbook of Assam). Most of the factories are located in Kamrup district (21.44 per cent), followed by Dibrugarh (10.63 per cent) and Cachar (5.39 per cent). It is mentioned earlier that Guwahati city has 462 numbers of factories which claim about 17 per cent of total factories of Assam. Guwahati is the gateway of North East India. As a result in the post-Independence period there has not only been development of transport and communication, but also development of trade and commerce, tourism industry etc. Due to this economic advantage and industrial development, migrants are attracted to Guwahati city. All these factors allured a large number of migrants from other districts of the State and the other parts of the country.

Distance and Migratrion

Distance plays an important role in the flow of migrants. The number of migrants to a place desreases as the distance increases. According 1991 Census 66.30 per cent of the total migrant population in the Guwahati city was constituted by the migrants whose place of birth were within Assam (Table 18.7). However, place of birth of a section of them (14.60 per cent) was mentioned as within Kamrup District. Proportion of migrants from other States of India to Guwahati city was 29.08 per cent in 1991 which declined to 19.62 per cent in 2001. This may be due to disturbances in Assam since 1979. The proportion of migrants within the district of Kamrup, however, increased from 14.60 per cent to 35.91 per cent within the above mentioned period, i.e. 1991 to 2001.

Table 18.7 : Distance and Migration Proportion of Migrants to Total Migrants in Percentage

	1991	2001
Within Kamrup District	14.60	35.91
Other Districts of Assam	51.70	42.96
Other States of India	29.08	19.62

Source : Census of India, Migration Table, 1991 and 2001.

Analysis of distance and types of migration to Guwahati city again throws light on the fact that the proportion of rural-urban migration are always higher than the urban-urban migration except the migrants from outside Assam in 1991 (Table 18.8).

Table 18.8 : Distance and Streams of Migration in per cent

	Rural-Urban Migration		*Urban-Urban Migration*	
	1991	2001	1991	2001
From different places of Kamrup District fo Guwahati	12.77	20.33	2.40	0.10
From different Districts of Assam	29.07	27.76	22.40	12.59
From outside of Assam	13.57	11.06	15.18	7.55

Source : Cenus of India, Migration Tables, 1991 and 2001.

It further reveals from the study that the migrants from different districts of Assam are decreasing in the context of rural-urban as well as urban-urban from 29.07 per cent to 27.76 per cent and 22.40 per cent to 12.59 per cent respectively during 1991 to 2001 (Table 18.8). Migrants from outside Assam are also decreasing from rural to urban and urban to urban (Table 18.8).

The increase of rural and urban-urban migration from different neighbouring areas of Guwahati within Kamrup district from 12.77 per cent in 1991 to 20.33 per cent in 2001 was the result of pull factor in the city. The poor people of the city fringe areas generally have come and settled in the slum areas and have worked as *Thela* puller, rickshaw puller, vegetable sellers, daily workers etc. Some service holders have also permanently shifted their residence with their families due to attraction of facilities available in the city. Some, however, want to return to their residence after performing their duties, if their permanent residences are not far away from the city. These are daily commuters in the city who generally belong to the categories of vegetable sellers, fish traders etc.

The above analysis reveals that from rural areas of the different districts of Assam as well as with Kamrup district people are attracted to Guwahati for better economic opportunities, educational facilities etc. On the other hand, in case of urban-urban migration within Kamrup district involving Hazo, Rangia and Suwalkuchi the proportion of migrants are descreasing from 2.40 per cent to 0.10 per cent in 1991 and 2001 respectively. This decrease in the proportion is due to the fact that the inhabitants of the small neighouring towns have enjoyed similar facility in their own towns. Moreover, because of limited distance, the people can daily come and go back to their respective place of residence after performing their duties in the town. Therefore, a major section of people of neighbouring towns prefer to settle permanently in their own place and avoid congested life of the city.

The migrants from the other States of India are the people mostly from Punjab, Rajasthan, Uttar Pradesh, Bihar, West Bengal, Nagaland, Tripura, Manipur, Meghalaya and Mizoram. Guwahati city received migrants from all the States and Union territories except Daman and

Table 18.9 : Total, Rural and Urban Migrants from different States and Union Territories of India into Guwahati City, 2001

States and Union Territories	*Total Migrants*	*In percentage to Total Migrant Population*	*Total Rural Migrants*	*Total Urban Migrants*
Jammu and Kashmir	125	0.17	33	82
Himachal Pradesh	112	0.15	51	42
Punjab	1407	1.89	742	564
Chandigarh	109	0.15	39	63
Uttarakhand	156	0.21	58	79
Haryana	902	1.21	428	404
Delhi	731	0.98	96	5796
Rajasthan	6175	8.31	2810	2987
Uttar Pradesh	4974	6.69	3003	1632
Bihar	28080	37.79	22157	4175
Sikkim	77	0.1	26	42
Arunachal Pradesh	639	0.86	240	337
Nagaland	839	1.13	196	569
Manipur	982	1.32	470	422
Mizoram	187	0.25	67	102
Tripura	2847	3.83	1549	113
Meghalaya	7499	10.92	1567	5433
Assam				
West Bengal	13646	18.36	5505	7327
Jharkhand	618	0.83	297	290
Chhattisgarh	48	0.06	23	22
Madhya Pradesh	318	0.42	114	170
Gujarat	292	0.39	101	170
Daman and Diu	0	0	0	0
Dadra and Nagar Haveli	7	0.01	0	7
Maharashtra	417	0.56	55	325
Andhra Pradesh	1555	2.09	1093	383
Karnataka	140	0.2	29	100
Goa	10	0.01	0	10
Lakshadweep	0	0	0	0
Kerala	445	0.6	216	198
Tamil Nadu	311	0.42	52	224
Pondicherry	4	0.01	0	2
Andaman & Nicobar Islands	7	0.01	2	5
Orissa	639	0.86	322	288

Source: Census of Inda, 2001.

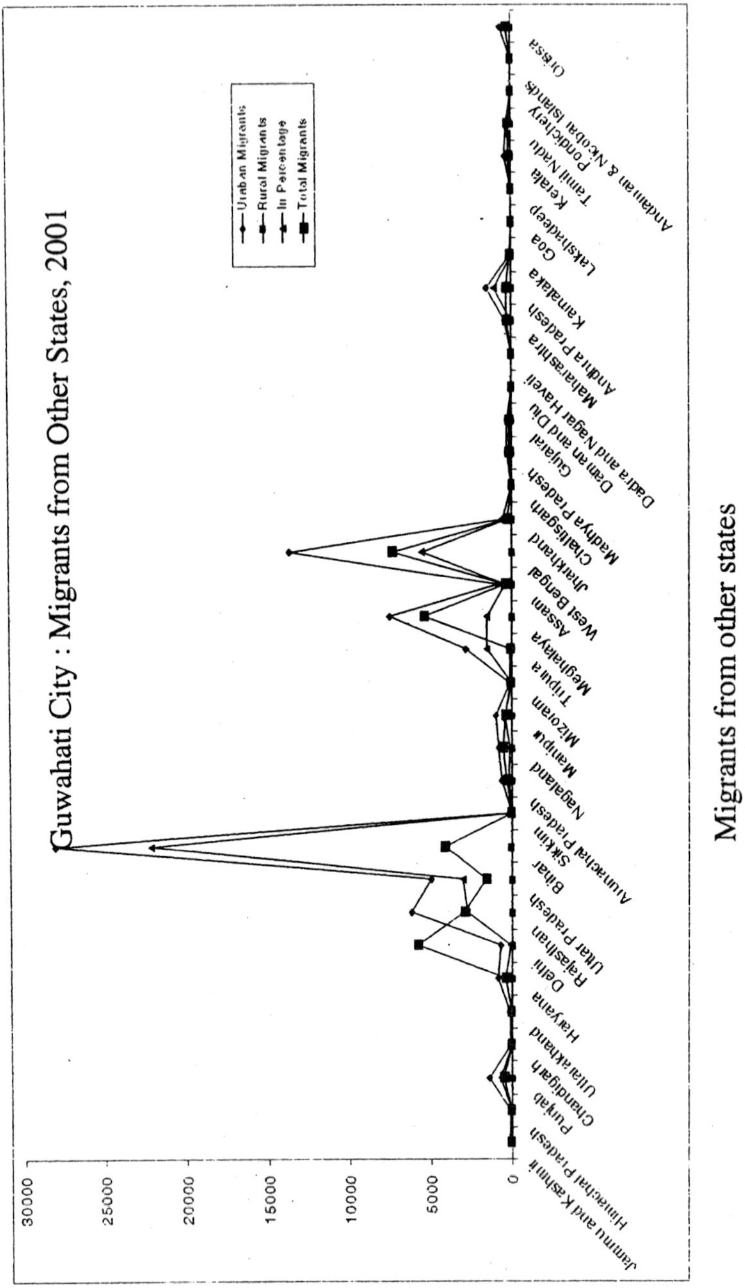
Guwahati City : Migrants from Other States, 2001
Urban Migrants
Rural Migrants
In Percentage
Total Migrants
30000
25000
20000
15000
10000
5000
0
Jammu and Kashmir
Himachal Pradesh
Punjab
Chandigarh
Uttarakhand
Haryana
Delhi
Rajasthan
Uttar Pradesh
Bihar
Sikkim
Arunachal Pradesh
Nagaland
Manipur
Mizoram
Tripura
Meghalaya
Assam
West Bengal
Jharkhand
Chattisgarh
Madhya Pradesh
Gujarat
Daman and Diu
Dadra and Nagar Haveli
Maharashtra
Andhra Pradesh
Karnataka
Goa
Lakshadeep
Kerala
Tamil Nadu
Pondichery
Andaman & Nicobar Islands
Orissa
Migrants from other states

Diu and Lakshadweep. Absolute number of migrants from other States ranged between 28,028 persons from Bihar, only 4 persons from Pondichery 2001.

According to 2001 Census Guwahati city received maximum number of migrants from Bihar (37.79 per cent) that followed by West Bengal (18.36 per cent), Meghalaya (10.92 per cent), Rajasthan (1.63 per cent) and Uttar Pradesh (1.31 per cent). From States like Bihar, Uttar Pradesh, Punjab, Tripura and Andhra Pradesh the size of rural migrants to Guwahati city are higher than the urban migrants (Table 18.9).

These migrants have provided Guwahati city with much needed workers in industries, construction work and shops. They also have been working as rickshaw pullers, thela pullers, cooli, washerman, barber, cobbler etc.

Conclusion

The study has considered six important aspects of composition of migrant population in Guwahati, namely trend of migration, sex and migration, distance and migration, rural-urban stream of migration, causes of migration and migration from other districts and States into Guwahati city. Data for 1991 and 2001 are considered in the present study for comparative analysis of the changes in migration pattern and composition.

Guwahati city recorded highest growth in total population between 1971 to 1991 (about 91%). According to 2001 Census and the total migrants in Guwahati city was recorded as 378,657 persons accounting for 46.48 per cent of the total population as against 25.50 per cent for the State as a whole. This figure was more than three times than that of 1971. The migration is mostly sex selective. Male migrants consituted 64.50 per cent of total migrants in 1971 which, however decreased to 56.43 per cent in 2001. The proportion of female migrants was 35.50 per cent in 1971 which increased to 43.57 per cent in 2001. The study further reveals that female migration in Guwahati during that period was largely due to the social reasons whereas male migration was mainly due to economic reasons. Between the two major types of migration proportion of rural-urban migration was always more than the urban-urban migration. However, the percentage of rural-urban migrants increased with the economic and social development of the city. Proportion of rural-urban migrants increased in short distance migration but urban-urban migrants decreased in both long and short distance migration.

All the States and Union Territories contributed to their share of migrants. Highest migrants was recorded from Bihar (37.79 per cent) followed by West Bengal (18.36 per cent), Meghalaya (10.92 per cent) in the city.

It reveals from the above analysis that high growth of population in Guwahati city is mainly due to migration. The study further shows that because of high rate of migration of population, there has been unplanned growth of settlement, development of unhealthy slum areas, increase in crime and increase in environmental pollution both social and natural. Therefore it is high time to check the unauthorised occupation in the hilly and foothill areas of the city, stop deforestation and increase awareness as regards afforestation etc. Steps should be taken for infrastructural facilities like drainage, water supply and sanitation.

References

Hassan Mohanmmad Izhar, (2005), *Population Geography,* Rawat Publications, Jaipur-302004 (India).

Chandna, R.C. (1986). *A Geography of Population*, Kalyani Publishers, Daryaganj, New Delhi-110002.

Census of India, *Migration Table, 1971.*

Census of India, *Migration Table, Vol. I, 1991.*

Census of India, 2001, *Series 19, Primary Census Abstract,* Directorate of Census Operations, Assam.

Census of India, 1991, *Part II-A. General Population Table.* Directorate of Census Operations, Assam.

19 Women in Urban Informal Sector in Guwahati

Zona Bhuyan

Introduction

The meaning of the term "informal sector" has remained somewhat ambiguous despite a large number of research studies in recent times. The International Labour Organization (ILO), in its classic Kenya Mission Report, introduced the concept of the 'informal sector', into international usage in 1972. ILO defines 'informal' as a "...way of doing things characterized by— ease of entry and exit; reliance of indigenous resources; family ownership; small scale operations; labour intensive and adaptive technology; skills acquired outside of the formal sector; and unregulated and competitive markets" (ILO, 1972). Since that time, different authors have introduced many other definitions to the concept of "informal sector". A recent ILO report used the term "informal sector" to describe a "...range of economic units in urban areas which are largely owned and operated by single individuals with little capital and labour, and which produce and distribute goods and services with a view to generating income and employment" (Charmes, 2000). The Fifteenth International Conference of Labour Statisticians states informal sector as consisting of production units that "...typically operate at a low level of organization, with little or no division of labour and capital..., and on a small scale... labour relations—where they exist—are based mostly on casual employment, kinship or personal and social relations rather than contractual arrangements with formal guarantees" (ICLS, January 1993).

The significance of informal employment in the Developing World is that when workers cannot find opportunities in traditional wage employment, the need for subsistence demands that they find work somewhere else—much of what accounts for "informal" employment. Women's share of informal employment has remained high, estimated at typically 60/80 per cent, although in a few countries, men dominate urban informal sector activities. However, women perhaps number much more than that reflected in available statistics. They comprise mostly of underpaid family helpers and home-based workers. A United Nation's Report issued during that International Agency's Decade for Women (1976 to 1985) observed: "Women comprise about half the world's population, perform about two-thirds of its work, receive only one-tenth of its income and own less than one hundredth of world assets" (Boyden, 1993). Nearly, a decade later, a UNDP, Human Development Report concluded that it still is the case and "...no country treats its women as well as it treats its men" (UNDP, 1993).

The Informal Sector (IS) has grown over the last 3 decades or so in the developing countries particularly in Asia, due to (a) sharp rise in levels of urbanization, (b) upturn in Asian economies (particularly the SE Asian economies like Indonesia, Philippines and Thailand etc., (c) work opportunities for women in these economies, and (d) Structural Adjustment Programmes (SAP). Though the economies have grown, formal sector employments have not kept pace with, thus creating pressure on the informal sector employments. Even before the crisis, official statistics indicated that the informal sector accounted for over half of total non-agricultural employment in Latin America and the Caribbeans, nearly half in East Asia, and as much as 80 per cent in other parts of Asia and in Africa (Chen, 2001).

This literature review includes theoretical and conceptual writings, empirical studies and discussion papers on women and their participation in urban informal sectors. Hart (1973) put forwarded the concept of "informal sector" that first appeared in the early. 1970s with the launch of the World Employment Programme by the International Labour Organization (ILO) and its classic Kenya report. Studies on the importance of the informal sector in providing job opportunities for the lower income groups (and migrants) in general have been undertaken by Todaro (1969), Quijano-Obregon (1974), Mazumdar (1976), Sethuraman (1981), Tony (2004). Bivens and

Sarah (2004) made a study on the workforce development in five selected countries to explore the feasibility of a multi-country study examining various issues regarding employment standards and changes in formal and informal employment. Armstrong and McGee (1987), Nelson (1988), Mathew (1989) and Perera (1994) have opined that lack of suitable premises (physical accommodation) is a major reason why informal sector entrepreneurs appropriate their houses as the working space and the operational base.

Momsen *et al.* (1987) discussed the fact that women have been invisible to geography for a long time which has of late begun to take into account 'half the human in human geography'. More women are involved in undocumented or "disguised" wage work than in the formal labour force (Dunlop and Velkoff, 1999). Florez (2003) has stated that rural to urban migrations impact the probability of being employed in the informal sector—under any definition used. Greig (2005) has observed that some gender issues in employment are a direct consequence of economic integration—the process of globalization has increased the persistent gender gaps. Though women are still spending more time working, there is a low value attached to women's work and the divisions of labour being gender-based in both private and public spheres there is limited access in employment for women. Mitra (2005) examines whether women in India are able to participate fully in the labour market and states that the tendency for specialized activities concentrated in different geographic locations of a city further restricts the possibility of women workers being engaged in diverse jobs thus, aggravating the situation of a excess supply of labour in a particular activity and thereby, depressing the wage rates in the sector to the detriment of women workers further.

The Problem

The informal sector is an integral part of global production and marketing chains. What is particular to the informal sector is the absence of rights and social protection of the workers involved in it. In every other respect, and particularly from the economic point of view, the formal and informal sectors form an integral whole. The plethora of established institutions and programmes include WIEGO (Women in Informal Employment Globalizing and Organizing) an international coalition established to support organizing of women workers in the informal sector at international level. It includes already existing women worker's organization, some of which are themselves international networks, such as Home Net (Home workers) and Street Net (street vendors), or national unions, such as the Self-employed Women's Association (India) and the Self-Employed Women's Union (South Africa).

This paper attempts to discuss the participation of women in the urban informal sector in the city of Guwahati. The city with a population close to one million (8 lakhs+in 2001 Census) covers an area of 217 sq. km. It is ethnically diverse, though the largest segment of population are Assamese speaking. Its importance lies in the fact that Guwahati is the only city that connects all the seven states of the region and serves as the financial hub of the region.

Background to the City of Guwahati

The city of Guwahati, the largest city in the entire North Eastern Region, and also the capital complex of the State of Assam, with the municipal corporation area of more than 313 sq. km. have witnessed a rapid growth in population particularly during the last one and a half decades. Of all the (state) capital cities in the country, Guwahati presents a host of interesting but complex characteristics peculiar to its geographical location. The city has become the hub of business, transportation, industrial and commercial activities not only for Assam but also for the entire North Eastern part of India. Apart from its size (being the largest urban centre of the region) and location, it spawns demand on a wide range of goods and services both for consumption within the city as well as in the region, that allows the IS to grow.

Informal sectors are much diversified in the larger cities and Guwahati city is no exception. Due to its diversified nature, the informal sector provides a host of job opportunities for migrants from rural areas of the state as well as from the region. One usually may find fairly high participation of women in these diversified urban informal sectors as compared to those of men. The increased economic burden placed on the families, forces the women to work in the urban informal sectors thereby generating surplus money to their families. In addition, they prefer to get into the informal sector because of the flexibility it offers to women in terms of time of work, location, and the variety of work opportunities.

Methodology

A survey was conducted during February to April, 2007 of a total of 51 respondents on random sampling basis, consisting primarily of women engaged in the various urban informal activities. Although inferences are drawn based on very small sample size of 51 respondents, the inferences surprisingly conform with intuitive observations based on other's personal experiences of living in the city.

The questionaire was designed to collect a selected range of information on individuals covering the following areas:

- Demographic Characteristics (age, marital status, educational level, religious background, type of house, holding status and status of migration);
- Economic Characteristics (employment status, working period, reason for work, nature of work, net monthly income, place/location of work, activities engaged in);

Analysis

The analysis of the data is based on percentages and simple cross tabulations to explore the relationships between the demographic attributes and economic characteristics.

Demographic Characteristics of the Respondents

Data presented in Table 19.1 reveals that of the total women in informal sector sampled for the study in Greater Guwahati (city), participation percentage (47.06 per cent) of women with respect to their marital status is fairly high within the age-group of 26-35 years followed by women participation rate of about 29.41 per cent that falls within the age group of 36-45 years and the least (1.96 and 7.84) percentages of women engaged in the various informal sector activities belongs to the age group of less than 15 years and more than 46 years, respectively.

Table 19.1 : Percentage of Women belonging to Different Age Groups and their Marital Status

Marital Status	*Age Structure*					
	<15	*16-25*	*26-35*	*36-45*	*46+*	*Total*
Married	2.94	2.94	47.06	38.24	8.82	100.00
Single	0.00	42.86	50.00	7.14	0.00	100.00
Widow	0.00	0.00	33.33	33.33	33.33	100.00
Total	1.96	13.73	47.06	29.41	7.84	100.00

Source : Fieldwork by Author, 2007.

From Table 19.2, it can be observed that the highest rate of participation (66.67 per cent) of women engaged in the occupations mentioned above is mostly confined to married women. About 27.45 per cent of women are single and the remaining 5.88 per cent are widows. We can also observe that women (both married and single) are engaged in almost all the sub-group occupations, except women who are single as we do not find them engaged in the sales and trade occupations. Within the textiles and garments traders, about 53 per cent of women are married, 30 per cent of women single and 15.38 per cent of women are widows. Again, in the caring and personal services, 60 per cent of women are singles and 40 per cent of women are married. In the sales occupation, 80 per cent of women are married and 20 per cent of women are widowed. In the elementary trades covering construction occupation nearly 100 per cent of women are married, largely because the wageworker families work together as migrant workers.

Table 19.2 : Percentage of Women by Occupational Sub-groups and Marital Status

Marital Status	*Occupational Structure (Sub-groups)*						
	Textiles, Printing and other Skilled Trades (54)	*Caring Personal Service Occupations (61)*	*Leisure and other Personal Service Occupations (62)*	*Sales Occupations (71)*	*Elementary trades, plant and storage related occupations (91)*	*Elementary Administration and Service Occupations (92)*	*Total*
Married	53.85	40.00	50.00	80.00	100.00	70.59	66.67
Single	30.77	60.00	50.00	0.00	20.00	29.41	27.45
Widow	15.38	0.00	0.00	20.00	0.00	0.00	5.88
Total	100.00	100.00	100.00	100.00	100.00	100.00	100.00

Source : Fieldwork by Author, 2007.

Table 19.3 gives us the idea of the relationship between the participation of women engaged in the various informal sector occupations (minor groups as classified by ILO) and their marital status. Table 19.3 shows us that the highest (31.37) percentage of women are engaged in the cleaning occupations, followed by fairly high (25.49) percentage women in the textiles and garments trades and about 13.73 per cent in the elementary occupations (construction). A relatively low percentage (5.88, 3.92 and 1.96) of women are enagaged in the childcare and personal services, hairdressers, sales assistants and retail cashiers; healthcare services, sales; housekeeping and personal service, respectively. About 20.59 per cent of married women and 28.57 per cent of single women are working in the textiles and garment trades. Again in the cleaning occupations, 35.29 per cent and 28.57 per cent of women are married and single, respectively. Even in the hairdressing occupation, we find both married (5.88 per cent) and single (7.14 per cent) women, there is no marital status requirements. We find only 66.67 per cent and 33.33 per cent of widowed women engaged in the textiles and garment trades (occupation) and in sales assistants and retail cashiers occupation, respectively.

From Table 19.4, it can be seen that within the illiterate category the highest (51.43) percentage of women seem to be within the group of 26-35 years followed by 34.29 per cent of women that falls under the age group of 36-45 years and only small (8.57, 2.86

Table19.3 : Percentage of Women by Occupation (Minor Groups) and Marital Status

Marital Status	*Occupational Structure (Minor Groups)*										
	Textiles and Garment Traders (54)	*Healthcare Personal Services (611)*	*Childcare Personal Services (612)*	*Hairdressers (622)*	*House-keeping (623)*	*Sales Assistant Retail Cashiers (711)*	*Sales (712)*	*Construc-tion (912)*	*Personal Service (922)*	*Cleaning (923)*	*Total*
Married	20.59	5.88	0.00	5.88	0.00	5.88	5.88	20.59	0.00	35.29	100.00
Single	28.57	0.00	21.43	7.14	7.14	0.00	0.00	0.00	7.14	28.57	100.00
Widow	66.67	0.00	0.00	0.00	0.00	33.33	0.00	0.00	0.00	0.00	100.00
Total	25.49	3.92	5.88	5.88	1.96	5.88	3.92	13.73	1.96	31.37	100.00

Source: Fieldwork by Author, 2007.

and 2.86) percentages of illiterate women falls within the age group of 16-25 years, less than 15 and more than 46 years. We could find that nearly 66.67per cent and 33.33 per cent of literate women falls under the age group of 16-25 years and 36-45 years, respectively.

Table 19.4 : Percentage of Women by Age Groups and Educational Qualification

Educational Qualification	*Age Structure*					
	<15	*16-25*	*26-35*	*36-45*	*46+*	*Total*
Illiterate	2.86	8.57	51.43	34.29	2.86	100.00
Literate	0.00	66.67	0.00	33.33	0.00	100.00
Primary	0.00	0.00	0.00	0.00	100.00	100.00
Middle	0.00	0.00	0.00	100.00	0.00	100.00
Matric	0.00	33.33	66.67	0.00	0.00	100.00
Higher Secondary	0.00	25.00	50.00	0.00	25.00	100.00
Tertiary	0.00	0.00	100.00	0.00	0.00	100.00
Total	1.96	13.73	47.06	29.41	7.84	100.00

Source: Fieldwork by Author, 2007.

Table 19.5, explains the relationship between the participation percentage of women engaged in these occupations (minor groups) as classified by the ILO and their educational qualification. It further exhibits that the highest (68.63) percentage of women working in the above mentioned occupations (minor groups) are illiterate. Merely, 5.88 per cent of women engaged in these various informal sector activities are literate and/or matric passed and relatively very low per cent (3.92 each) of women have been qualified in the primary, middle and tertiary educational levels. Only, 7.84 per cent of women have completed their higher secondary qualification.

Economic Characteristics of the Respondents

Table 19.6, indicates the relationship between the different age groups of women and their income distribution. From Table 19.6, it clearly exhibits that the highest (47.06 per cent) percentage of income earned is found between the age-group of 26-35 years followed by women

Table19.5: Percentage of Women by Occupations (Minor Groups) and Educational Qualification

Educational Qualification	Occupational Structure (Minor Groups)										
	Textiles and Garments Traders (54)	*Health-care Personal Services*	*Childcare Personal Services*	*Hairdressers (622)*	*House-keeping (623)*	*Sales Assistant Retail Cashiers*	*Sales (712)*	*Construction (912)*	*Personal Service (922)*	*Cleaning (923)*	*Total*
Illiterate	23.08	100.00	33.33	100.00	100.00	100.00	100.00	100.00	0.00	81.25	68.63
Literate	7.69	0.00	66.67	0.00	0.00	0.00	0.00	0.00	0.00	0.00	5.88
Primary	7.69	0.00	0.00	0.00	0.00	0.00	0.00	0.00	0.00	6.25	3.92
Middle	15.38	0.00	0.00	0.00	0.00	0.00	0.00	0.00	0.00	6.00	3.92
Matric	7.69	0.00	0.00	0.00	0.00	0.00	0.00	0.00	0.00	6.25	5.88
Higher Secondary	23.08	0.00	0.00	0.00	0.00	0.00	0.00	0.00	0.00	6.25	7.84
Tertiary	15.38	0.00	0.00	0.00	0.00	0.00	0.00	0.00	0.00	0.00	3.92
Total	100.00	100.00	100.00	100.00	100.00	100.00	100.00	100.00	100.00	100.00	100.00

Source: Fieldwork by Author, 2007.

Table 19.6 : Percentage of Women by Age Groups and Income Earned

Income Distribution	*Age Structure (in yrs.)*					
	<15	16-25	26-35	36-45	46+	Total
<1000	10.00	30.00	40.00	20.00	0.00	100.00
1001-2000	0.00	13.33	43.33	33.33	10.00	100.00
2001-3000	0.00	0.00	55.56	33.33	11.11	100.00
3001-4000	0.00	0.00	100.00	0.00	0.00	100.00
4000+	0.00	0.00	100.00	0.00	0.00	100.00
Total	1.96	13.73	47.06	29.41	7.84	100.00

Source: Fieldwork by Author, 2007.

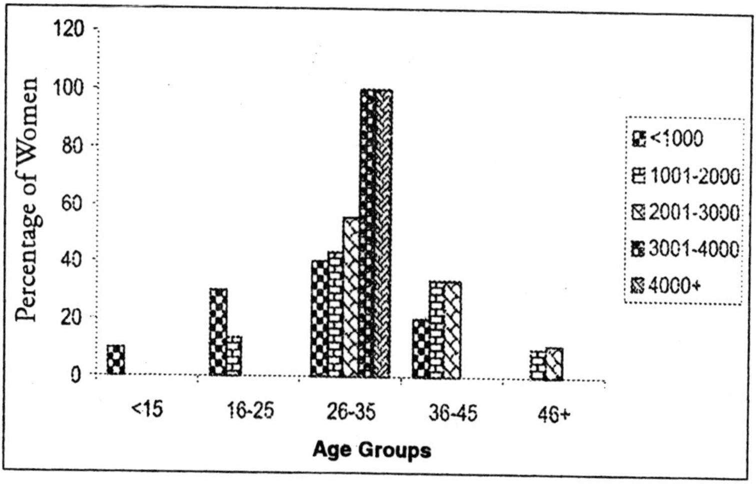

Fig. 19.1 : Income Categories and % of Women in Age Groups

between the age group of 36 to 45 years (29.41per cent); whereas the least (10 per cent) percentage is observed in the case of age-group below 15 years that largely constitutes of children.

Table 19.7, provides the relationship between the participation of women engaged in the various informal sector occupations (minor groups as classified by ILO) and their income distribution. From Table 19.7, it can be inferred that the highest (58.82) percentage of women earn within Rs. 1001-2000/ month, followed by 19.61 per cent of women earning below Rs. 10000/ month and another 17.65 per cent of women earning between Rs. 2001 and 3000/ month, nearly 85 per cent earn below Rs. 3000 a month, which keep them on the fringes of poverty but could make it meaningful earning by supplementing any regular income of husband or any other family members. Only 1.96 per cent of women seem to earn between Rs. 3001 to 4000 and/or 4000/ month, respectively. Within the textile and other related services, around 46 per cent women earn very low monthly income Rs.1001-2000 and around 28 per cent, Rs. 2001-3000/ month. Again in the

Table 19.7 : Percentage of Women by Occupation (Sub-groups) and Income distribution

Income Distribution (in Rs.)	*Occupational Structure (Sub-groups)*						
	Textiles, Printing and other Skilled Trades (54)	*Caring Personal Service Occupations (61)*	*Leisure and other personal service occupations (62)*	*Sales Occupations (71)*	*Elementary Trades, Plant and Storage related Occupations (91)*	*Elementary Administration and Service Occupations (92)*	*Total*
<1000	15.38	40.00	0.00	60.00	0.00	17.65	19.61
1001-2000	46.15	40.00	100.00	20.00	85.71	64.71	58.82
2001-3000	23.08	20.00	0.00	20.00	14.29	17.65	17.65
4000+	7.69	0.00	0.00	0.00	0.00	0.00	1.96
Total	100.00	100.00	100.00	100.00	100.00	100.00	100.00

Source: Fieldwork by Author, 2007.

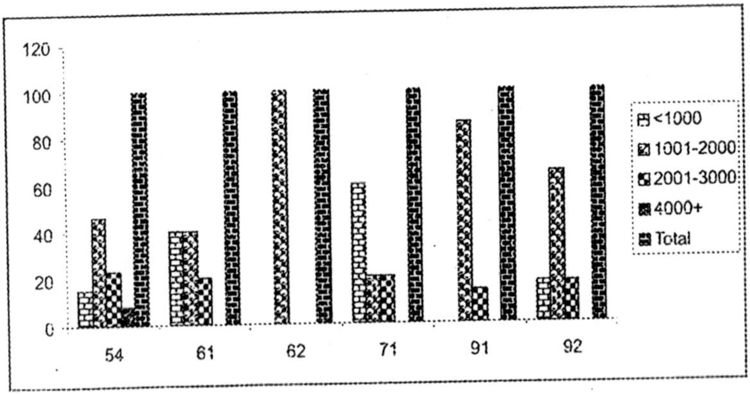

Fig. 19.2 : Occupation (Sub-groups) and % of Women by Income Distribution

Occupation Sub-groups:

54: Textiles, Printing and other skilled trades; 61: Leisure and other personal service; 71: Sales; 91: Elementary trades, plant and storage; 92: Elementary administration and service occupation.

caring and personal services, 40 per cent of women earn below Rs. 1000 and 40 per cent between Rs. 1001 and Rs. 2000/month. In the leisure and other personal services, nearly 100 per cent earn between Rs. 1001 and Rs. 2000/ month.

5. Findings

Therefore, women who are engaged in IS can be broadly grouped as under three categories:

1. Services

(i) *Healthcare, childcare and personal services*: The women engaged in these particular occupations are predominantly illiterate. Most of these women are either single or married. They are also low income earners (below Rs. 1000 to 2001-3000) and have no job security and do not have any written contract.

(ii) *Hairdressers:* Most of these women too are either married or single and are aged between the age of 36 to 45 years. Women in this occupation are illiterate and lack of job security, for they do not have any written contract on their job conditions. Their monthly incomes vary between Rs. 1001 and Rs. 2000.

(iii) *Housekeeping*: Women engaged in this occupation are generally, single and illiterate, and are mostly aged between 36 and 45 years. Their monthly income ranges between Rs. 1001 and Rs. 2000.

(iv) *Personal Service:* Women engaged in this occupation (Domestic helpers/cook) are single and fall within the age group of 26-35 years. Their monthly income varies between less than Rs. 1000 and Rs. 2001-3000.

(v) *Cleaning Occupation:* About 31.37per cent of both married and single women engaged in this particular occupation include domestic helpers and cleaners. Most of these women are illiterate (81.25 per cent) and few have either done their primary education or higher secondary education (6.25 per cent each). They do not have any job security as they do not have any written contract or agreement. Their monthly income varies between the range below Rs. 1000 and Rs. 2001-3000 but most of them earn between Rs. 1001 and Rs. 2000/-month.

2. Trades

(i) *Textiles and Garment related Services:* Women engaged in this occupation include tailors and dressmakers, weavers and knitters, curtain makers and alteration hand. They are mostly widowed women comprising about 66.67 per cent, married (20.59 per cent) and single 28.57 per cent. Many of the women workforces are illiterates (23.08 per cent), some have had their above primary level education and others have even had their higher secondary education. They earn between a wide ranges of below Rs. 1001 and Rs. 4000 monthly. They too do not have any written contract; therefore, they lack their job security.

(ii) *Sales Assistants and Retail Cashiers:* Women engaged in this occupation include women who own Pan shops and that they do not have any fixed location. Their monthly income varies between below Rs. 1000 and Rs. 2001-3000. These women are illiterates and they too do not have any social security protection.

3. Construction

Elementary Construction and related Occupation: Women engaged in this particular occupation comprise about 13.73 per cent that work at the construction sites as wage-worker. All the women involved in this occupation are illiterates and are mostly daily wage labourers earning between the range of Rs. 1001 and Rs. 2001-3000 monthly.

6. Conclusion

One may conclude from the above study that women commonly engaged in the IS in Guwahati are in textiles, printing and other skilled trades, caring/personal care occupations, leisure and other personal services, sales elementary trades and related areas and elementary service occupations. Further analysis shows that 31.37 per cent of women are engaged in the cleaning occupations (domestic helpers and cleaners), that constitute highest percentage, followed by 25.49 per cent of women in the textiles and garments trade occupation (tailors and dressmakers, weavers and knitters, curtain makers and alteration hand) and about 13.73 per cent in the elementary construction occupations. One the other hand, a few women are engaged in the childcare and personal services (5.88 per cent). hairdressers, sales assistants and retail cashiers (3.92 per cent); helthcare services (1.96 per cent), sales (5.88 per cent); housekeeping and personal services (1.96 per cent). Invariably the women in IS work beyond eight hours in order to supplement the family incomes. Their contributions to the family income range between Rs. 1001 and Rs. 2000 per month. The survey reveals that within each income category, the distribution is normal with the modal frequency in the age 26-45 years.

The results from this survey, therefore, provide a glimpse into the urban informal sectors in the city of Guwahati, and the principal sectors that the women are primarily engaged in. Moreover, the empirical analysis provides us with a perception of the extent of participation of the women in the UIS, and the problems they are faced with, such as lack of job security and low income and long hours of work. They do not figure in the calculus of the GDP of the city, though, often their contributions are indispensable. It needs, further detailed study to understand the extent, the biases the women workers in IS face and the sufferings they undergo on a daily basis in a growing urban environment.

References

Armstrong, A. and McGee, T.G. (1985) *Theatres of Accumulation: Studies in Asian and Latin American Urbanization,* London: Methuen.

Avirgan Tony, Bivens Josh L. and Gammage Sarah (eds.) (2004) *Online: Good Jobs, Bad Jobs and No Jobs: Labour Markets and Informal Work in Egypt, El Salvador, India, Russia and South Africa.* Acquired from http://*www.gpn.org* (downloaded 18 July 2006).

Bivens Josh L. and Gammage Sarah (2004) Will better workers lead to better jobs in the developing work? In Avirgan Tony, Bivens Josh L. and Grammage Sarah (eds.) *Good Jobs, Bad Jobs, No Jobs: Labour Markets and Informal Work in Egypt, El Salvador, India, Russia and South Africa.*

Boyden (2000) Online: After the Carnage: Women in Post Conflict Combodia. Aquired from pdf.doc.org/pdf_docs/PNA CN501.pdf (downloaded 18 April, 2007).

Charmes, J. (2000) Online: *Skills development for the informal economy:* Acquired from http://*www.ilo.org* (downloaded 18 July 2006).

Chen Alter M. (2001) Online: Women in the Informal Sector: A Global Picture, A Global Movement. Aquired from *htt://www.worldbank.org* (downloaded 12 March 2007).

Dunlop, E.J. and Velkoff, A.V. (1999) Online: Informal Source of Work for Women, In *Women of the World,* United States. Acquired from http// *www.census.gov/ipc/prod/wid-9802.pdf* (downloaded 17 September 2006).

Florez, E. C. (2003) Online: *Migration and the Urban Informal Sector in Colombia.* Acquired from http://*www.pum.princeton.edu* (downloaded 26 September 2006).

Greig, F. (2005) Online: *Gender at Work: Increased Participation Requires Institutional Charge.* Acquired from http:// *www.un.org/womenwatch/daw/ egm/enabling-environment2005* (downloaded 26 September 2006).

Hart, K (1973) 'Informal Income Opportunities and Urban Employment in Ghana', *Modern African Studies,* 11 (1): pp. 113-17.

International Conference on Labour Statistics (1993) Online: *Current International Recommendations on Labour Statistics: ILO 2000,* Geneva. Acquired from http://*www.ilo.org* (downloaded 18 July 2006).

International Labour Office (1972) Online: Employability in the Global Economy: How training matters, *World Employment Report,* Geneva. Acquired from http://*www.ilo.org* (downloaded 18 July 2006).

Mathew, P.M. (1989). 'Urban Informal Sector: How it should be understood? Nagarlok', *Urban Affairs Quarterly,* XX (4): pp. 57-65.

Mazumdar, D. (1976) 'The Urban Informal Sector', *World Development,* 4 (8): pp. 54-57.

Mitra, A. (2005) 'Women in the Urban Informal Sector: Perpetuation of Meagre Earnings', *In the Hague,* 36 (2): pp. 291-316.

Momsen, H. Janet and Townsend, G. Janet (1987) *Geography of Gender in the Third World,* New York: State Unviersity of New York Press.

Nelson, N. (1988) 'How Women and Men Get by: The Sexual Division of Labour in the Informal Sector of a Nairobi Squatter Settlement', in J. Gugler (ed.), *The Urbanization of the Third World,* New York: Oxford Unviersity Press, pp. 183-203.

Perera Ranjith L.A.S. (1994) *Accommodating Informal Sector Enterprises in the Urban Built-Environment: Introduction*, Bangkok: Asian Institute of Technology, pp. 1-14.

Quijano-Obregon, A. (1974) 'The Marginal Pole of the Economy and the Marginalized Labour Force', *Economy and Society*, 6 (1): pp. 393-428.

Sethuraman, S.V. (1981) *The Urban Informal Sector in Developing Countries: Employment, Poverty and Environment*, Geneva: ILO, p. 173.

Todaro, M (1969) *A Model of Labour Migration and Urban Employment in Less Developed Countries*, New York: Plenum.

UNDP (1993). *Human Development Report 1993*, New York: Oxford Unviversity Press.

20 Between the Border and the Fence
The Border Fencing Affected Population of Tripura

Malabika Das Gupta

introduction

India's longest international border is with Bangladesh. Bangladesh shares its border with five Indian States, namely West Bengal, Tripura, Assam, Mizoram and Meghalaya. The Indo-Bangladesh border is extremely porous and difficult to police as it runs through jungles, hills, villages and paddy and jute fields. It also has a small riverine portion. Since it is virtually impossible to distinguish a Bangladeshi national from his Indian counterpart, it is easy for illegal immigrants to cross the porous border and enter India. Smuggling, arms and drug trafficking and trafficking in women and children are some of the problems associated with the porous border. Militants who have bases in Bangladesh use the border route to cross over into India to commit subversive acts and then return to their safe haven across the border, taking advantage of its porosity.

India had suggested joint patrolling of the border to tackle some of the crass-border problems it faces but Bangladesh did not agree to the Indian proposal. However, Bangladesh did agree to coordinated patrolling, but this exercise was incapable of solving a problem of this magnitude. As a result, India has been forced to take its own steps to solve its border-related problems with Bangladesh like illegal immigration and arms trafficking. As it has seen a positive impact of border fencing in its north-western frontier, India has decided to erect an eight foot high double fence of rolled barbed wire stretched between concrete pillars along the Indo-Bangladesh border with a road for patrolling running parallel to the fence. The project has already been implemented in many places along India's border with Bangladesh and work is in progress in other areas. The work of fencing off the Indo-Bangladesh border is scheduled to be completed by the end of 2007. In keeping with the terms of the Indira-Mujib Pact with Bangladesh which prohibits the construction of any structure with a defence potential within 150 yards on either side of the boundary, the fence is being built 150 yards inside the Indo-Bangladesh border.

There are thousands of people living in or cultivating land within 150 yards of the zero line all along the Indo-Bangladesh border in all the five states of India that share a common boundary with Bangladesh. Therefore, even if border fencing takes care of the cross-border problems it is supposed to address, it will create serious problems for the Indian citizens who live in and/or earn a living from the area lying between the fence and the Indo-Bangladesh border as they will now face a life full of danger, uncertainty and economic loss.[1]

The Objective of the Study

The objective of the study is (1) to examine in what ways and to what extent the section of the population of Tripura caught between the border and the fence has been affected by the attempt to secure the border by building a fence along it. (2) Another objective of the study is to suggest measures for mitigating the problems of this section of the population of Tripura.

Why has Tripura been Selected for Study?

Tripura has been selected for study because the state has an 865 km-long porous border with Bangladesh through which illegal immigrants and smuggled goods have an easy entry into the state. Cross-border crimes like dacoity and cattle lifting are common in Tripura and goods are also smuggled from India into Bangladesh through the state. Most importantly, insurgents freely cross over into Bangladesh after launching an operation in Tripura, making it virtually impossible for the state to curb extremist activities. Militants often launch attacks on Tripura from their base camps in Bangladesh, taking advantage of the porous border and the inadequate surveillance. Another problem that the state has to contend with is arms smuggling from across the border by various insurgent groups. The state has also been selected for study because border fencing has already started in Tripura in a bid to check these problems. Barbed wire fences have been erected or are in the process of being erected inside the Indian Territory in Tripura 150 yards away from the zero line on the Indo-Bangladesh border. The Union Home Ministry has earmarked Rs.11.19 million for constructing a 736 km-long border fence, 815 km. of roads and 2339 metres of bridges along Tripura's border with Bangladesh to guard the border effectively. By March 2007, 653 km. of the State's border with Bangladesh had been fenced off and work was going on in the remaining 83 km. stretch that is ultimately going to be fenced off. Tripura has been selected for study because the available data on people caught between the border and the fence are not capable of capturing the full extent of their plight. Though some quantitative data are available to indicate the magnitude of the problems facing the people of the state who are trapped between the border and the fence, they are incapable of capturing the wide variety of problems that the border fence will create for these people. According to a survey by the Tripura Government, at least 7,123 families or about 40,000 people of the state will be adversely affected because their properties are located between the fence and the border. Again, when the border fencing is completed, it is estimated that nearly 120 square km. of farmland of the state well fall outside the border fence. These statistics capture only a minor part of the problems that the people of Tripura caught between the border and the fence will encounter once the work of fencing off the border is completed.

The Methodology Adopted and the Areas Selected for Study

In order to gauge the full extent of the travails of the people of Tripura who have already been or are going to be caught between the border and the fence, survey-based findings are essential. So, in order to get more detailed information on the different ways in which the border fence will affect their lives, the field survey method was adopted for the study.[2] Field-work was done in the selected areas in December 2005 and January 2006. Representative areas in West Tripura and Dhalai districts where the typical impact of border fencing on people living in and/or earning a living from the area lying between the fence and the zero line could be observed were purposively selected after holding discussions with Government officials and people's representatives. The areas selected included both rural and urban areas. Areas where the border fence is already in position or areas where it is under construction or where plans are afoot to erect it were included in the purposively selected sample. Care was also taken to ensure that the selected areas lying between the border and the fence had inhabitants with different occupations. The affected households living in the purposively selected areas were identified with the help of the local municipal councillors or Panchayat members as the case may be. The members of these households were interviewed. Discussions were held with the women of the affected households to find out their special problems due to border fencing. By and large, the data collected from the field visits were impressionistic and not of a quantitative nature.

Two border-adjoining areas within the jurisdiction of Agartala Municipal Council Ramnagar and Jaypur were selected. South Ramnagar and Jaypur, that are situated in Ward No. 10 of the Agartala Municipal Corporation in West Tripura District and about the Indo-Bangladesh border were selected for study because though both these localities are situated within the municipal limits of Agartala, they are quite different from each other. South Ramnagar is an urbanised area where very few people depend on agriculture whereas the residents of Jaypur depend mainly on cultivation. It was felt that survey work in these two areas of Agartala Municipal Council would capture the travails of both agriculturists and wage workers caught between the border and the fence. At the time of our visit to these two places in December 2005 and January 2006, it was found that the site where the border fence is going to come up had only been demarcated in South Ramnagar but trenches had already been dug for putting up the posts for the border fence in Jaypur. In South Ramnagar, none of the 41 families that will be caught between the border and the fence when the border fence is ready have any agricultural land. The area of this locality that has fallen within the Indian territorial limits but outside the barbed wire fence comprises about 100 *kanis*[3] of land consisting of homestead plots although some water bodies and cultivated plots on khas lands are also situated there. The inhabitants of this area are mostly Muslim day labourers who have lived there for generations. Jaypur is a border area situated within the municipal limits of Agartala where most of the people are agriculturists. This area also has a predominantly Muslim population. In Jaypur, large tracts of agricultural land will fall outside the barbed wire fence once it comes up. Data were also collected from Ganganagar village in Dhalai District that about Bangladesh where the border has already been fenced off.

Findings of the Survey among a Section of the People of Tripura who are caught between the Border and the Fence

The field survey revealed that the people caught between the border and the fence are exposed to a wide variety of problems that can be classified under several heads. The problems of the women who are trapped between the border and the fence are, important enough to deserve a special mention.

(a) Problems of Farmers whose Land will fall between the Border and the Fence

As Jaypur is a predominantly agricultural area, the field survey revealed that there are quite a few families there who will lose their effective control over all or a part of their agricultural land as it will fall outside the border fence. 46 families with agricultural land will be affected in Jaypur when the border fence comes up. Cultivating their land when the border fence comes up will be fraught with diffculties and the outcome of the effort will be uncertain. Gates will be situated at intervals along the barbed wire fence and will be manned by the Border

Security Force but for security reasons, they will be opened at fixed times during the day and kept locked during the night. This will restrict the access of the farmers to their farmlands situated outside the fence, making it difficult for them to tend their plots. When the crops are ready for harvesting, it will be difficult for them to guard their crops against Bangladeshi miscreants who can make off with the harvest as surveillance by the Indian Security Forces will not extend beyond the border fence.

(b) Problem of Homestead Lands and Homes Falling Outside the Fence

It was found during the discussions with the people who will find themselves caught between the border and the fence in South Ramnagar that their homestead plots, homes and sometimes parts of their homes will fall outside the barbed wire fencing once it comes up. Moving out of their homes and buying homestead plots elsewhere to solve the problems created by the border fence are obviously not a viable proposition for the families that will be adversely affected by the border fencing in South Ramnagar. They quite rightly feel that nobody will be interested in buying their ancestral plots now that they will fall wholly or partly outside the fence. Even if anybody shows an interest in buying their property, a pittance will be offered for it though the market rate of property in the South Ramnagar area of Agartala has sky rocketed with urban development taking place in and around the area. If they cannot sell their plots and make a capital gain from the sale, they will be unable to buy alternative lands nearby. They will be priced out of the land market near their old homes, as land prices are very high in the area. They were not at all hopeful of getting compensation from the government for their ancestral property that would fall outside the fence. They were extremely doubtful whether compensation would be paid for the homesteads, the trees growing on the homestead land and the standing crops in the kitchen gardens to the *bonafide* owners of homestead plots in the area lying between the border and the fence. The victims were almost certain that only those 'lucky' enough to own land on the 35 feet stretch falling within the border fence and the adjoining road would be compensated for their loss of land but at a rate that would be considerably lower than the going market rate.

(c) Loss of User Rights over Land Falling between the Fence and the Border

A few of the men we talked to in South Ramnagar used a water body that will now be located outside the border fence as a fishery. They had cleaned up the water body through collective effort and strengthened its banks with bamboo poles. At present, they buy fingerlings and rear them in the pond. When the fish become big they sell them in the market after retaining a part of the catch for their household consumption. Once the fence comes up, their apprehension is that the fishery will not yield any income to them as the Bangladeshis will have an easier access to the water body that will become unprotected because of its location outside the fence. They feel that they will lose their income from fishing and their families will be deprived of an important source of protein from their diet because the men will lose their user rights over the water body due to the construction of the border fence. The people interviewed were absolutely sure that the families that enjoyed user rights over land lying beyond the fence were not going to get any compensation for their loss of user rights over land.

(d) Loss of Livelihood

However, the border fencing will not deprive the inhabitants of South Ramnagar of their ownership and user rights over land located outside the fence only. Most of the men folk of the affected families are apprehensive that once the border fence comes up; their entire livelihood will be threatened. As the men of these families are day labourers, they leave their homes early in the morning in search of jobs and return home late at night after their day's work is done They fear that the gates in the border fence will not be opened early enough and will be locked for the night at sundown so that they will not be able to leave for work in time or return home at night.

Though the area outside the border fence has very little agricultural land, some of the men of South Ramnagar work as casual labourers in the fields on the khas lands that are located outside the border fence. They are afraid that the agricultural land of the locality that will fall outside the border fence will no longer be cultivated by the occupiers of these khas lands as Bangladeshis will be able to harvest the crops when they are ready, given the unprotected nature of the fields after the border fence comes up. These agricultural lands will therefore turn into wastelands. If that happens, the victims of border fencing felt that they will lose their supplementary source of income from agricultural labour.

The threat of losing a livelihood as a result of the construction of the border fence has become a reality for Ajir Mian, a resident of the Muslim village of Ganganagar in Salema Block of Dhalai District. As has already been mentioned, Ganganagar village is contiguous to the Bangladesh border and the border has already been fenced off there. Mian reported that he had taken 5 *kanis* of land on barga. He used his barga land for growing paddy and used to earn an annual income of about Rs. 6000 from the sale of the paddy he grew on this piece of land. Unfortunately, all his barga land had fallen outside the border fence. He felt there was a security risk involved in cultivating his unprotected barga land as it had become easily accessible from Bangladesh and stopped cultivating it. He thought it was not worth his while to cultivate his barga land because the Bangladeshis could easily harvest the standing crop on his land. His barga land has become a wasteland now and he and his wife and children have become poorer as he does not earn any income from it.[4]

(e)Special Problems of Women caught between the Border and the Fence

While talking to the women of South Ramnagar, we found that in some ways their plight will probably be even worse than that of their men folk. Where homestead plots fall outside the border fence, the women are apprehensive that once the border fence comes up, they will not be able to use the lands and vegetables they grow in their kitchen gardens at present to supplement the food intake of their families because people from across the border will steal them as their homestead lands will become unprotected and vulnerable because of their location.

Quite a few of the women of South Ramnagar work in the fields situated on the Indian side of the border that will fall outside the border fence or collect rice stems from the fields once the harvesting is over. They also collect fuelwood from trees growing on khas lands in the affected area, as they cannot afford to buy any other source of fuel. Their apprehension is that they will not be able to work in the fields or collect fuel from the areas that fall outside the fence as they will face a security threat from across the border since these areas will lie outside the barbed wire fencing.

The women are not going to lose only their ownership and user land rights over land as a result of border fencing. Like the men of the affected households, the womenfolk of South Ramnagar are daily wage earners or they work as maidservants in their neighbourhood in the city. Like the men of the locality, they too fear that the border fence will jeopardise their earnings as they will not be able to cross the border fence as and when they need to do so to earn their living. The South Ramnagar women we talked were worried that sending their children to school in town or seeking medical help at night will pose problems once the border fence comes up. The women whose homes and homestead plots will fall outside the fence are also extremely apprehensive about their personal safety and security in their own homes as they feel that they will be more exposed to the risk of attacks from across the border since their houses will be located outside the barbed wire fence. We found during the course of our visit to Jaypur that the women of the locality were mentally very disturbed because the border fence was coming up in their locality. Not only were they upset at the prospect of losing their ownership and user right over land, they were extremely concerned about their personal safety as a consequence of border fencing. They perceived a threat to their safety and 'honour' not only from across the border but also from the Indian security personnel whose presence will become much more visible once the border fence comes up.

So, border fencing will open up issues that are wider and more serious than the mere loss of land rights for women. Even as far as the impact of border fencing on the land rights of women is concerned, women seem to be more adversely affected than the men of the locality. Even though women are less likely to lose ownership rights over land due to border fencing because to start with, their ownership rights were more limited than those of the males, they enjoyed a wider range of user rights over land which they will lose as a result of border fencing. This curtailment of their user rights over land outside the border fence could seriously endanger the nutritional status of their entire family, including that of their children. However, as the above discussion shows, irrespective of their gender, people who are caught between the border and the fence are extremely vulnerable and their problems cannot be overlooked even if border fencing seems to be unavoidable under the given circumstances.[5]

What is to be done ?

Border fencing may be a necessary evil to check the problems emanating from the porous Indo-Bangladesh border but the plight of the people of Tripura who are caught on the other side of the fence should not be forgotten. Ideally, they should be rehabilitated inside the fence where their homes, farm lands and livelihoods will be secure and they will not be exposed to a constant threat of attacks from Bangladesh. Rehabilitating them elsewhere will become an absolute necessity if the proposal of the BSF for the creation of a 'no habitation zone of 150 yards along the Indo-Bangladesh border is accepted by the Central Government on the plea that a similar arrangement along the Indo-Pak border in Punjab and Rajasthan where no houses are allowed to be constructed within 150 yards of the border has helped to improve surveillance. However, finding suitable house sites and farm lands to relocate these families will pose a problem for the State Government because there is acute pressure on land in Tripura. Issuing identity cards to the citizens of India who are caught between the border and the fence so that they can freely cross the fence without any harassment from the security personnel is a second best solution but it will not take care of their security concerns. Their problems will be solved permanently if the fence can be moved right up to the border but this solution can become a reality only if Bangladesh agrees to it. As of today, any chance deviation from the 150 yards restriction in constructing the fence leads to firing from the Bangladesh security forces and border skirmishes. So, the problem of the people left on the other side of the fence seems to evade a solution not only in Tripura but in all the states of India bordering Bangladesh.

Notes

1. Another set of people living close to the Indo-Bangladesh border whose homes, homestead plots, agricultural lands or means of livelihood like shops and other establishments fall within the area occupied by the border fence and the road running parallel to it face the problem of displacement due to the construction of the border fence. Their problem will not be addressed directly in this paper.
2. The field study formed a part of a project on Land Rights of Women in Tripura sponsored by the National Commission for Women that was undertaken by the author on behalf of the Tripura State Commission for Women.
3. 1 *kani* equals to 0. 25 acres.
4. Ajir Mian used to take decisions regarding the use of the barga land and the sale of its produce jointly with his wife. So, she also has lost the right to take decisions regarding the use to which her husband's barga land should be put and the disposal of its produce as a result of border fencing.
5. For example, the people of Ganganagar, which is an extremist-affected area, felt the incidence of extremist activities mounted from across the Bangladesh border has come down dramatically after the border fence has come up in the area. The people of Ganganagar were frequent victims of cattle thefts from across the border. Bangladeshi thieves had decamped with thirty cows from the cowshed of one of the residents of Ganganagar under the cover of night before the border fence had come up. Such incidents are unheard of now that the border fence has come up in the area.

21 Demographic Disequilibrium and the Trend of Multi-culturalism in Tripura

Suchintya Bhattacharya

Introduction

A cursory glance at a map of India and Bangladesh will show why the State of Tripura had to receive a large proportion of refugees. It appears that Tripura being surrounded on three sides by Bangladesh and having a common border with the districts of Chittagong, Noakhali, Comilla and Sylhet, it was the easiest harbourage of minority community of Bangladesh to migrate due to political or communal troubles. In fact, the influx of migrants in Tripura began since 1942 when a great commual riot took place in Rongpur district of Bangladesh. Again, communal riots broke out on a large scale in the district of Noakhali and Chandpur sub-division of the district of Comilla in response to the 'Direct Action Day' declared by the Muslim League in Calcutta on 16th August of 1946. And within the span of four years early in 1950 a large scale communal riot was directed against the minorities. As a result, the influx of displaced persons upto 1958 rose to 3.74 lakhs. Another wave of migration traffic started from the middle of 1963 consequent on the great communal riot in Khulna, Jessore and other districts of Bangladesh.[1]

Population Dynamics

In terms of population, Tripura ranks second highest among the North Eastern States of India after Assam with the average annual exponential growth rate of 1.46 per cent as revealed from the data of Census 2001. The state ranks seventeenth position in terms of density of population, although, it is the second most smallest state in the entire country after Goa.[2]

The total population of Tripura as per Census, 2001 was 31,99,203 comprising 16,42,225 male and remaining 15,56,978 females. The decadal growth rate during 1991-2001 was registered as the sharpest. It declined from 34.30 per cent for 1981-1991 to 16.03 per cent for the period of 1991-2001, that means a decrease of 18.27 per cent. The average exponential growth rate has declined from 2.95 per cent per annum during 1981-1991 to 1.46 per cent per annum during 1991-2001. The data of Census, 2001 also reveals that a decline of more than five percentange points in decadel growth rate during 1991-2001 from the previous Census decade was recorded in Mizoram, Arunachal Pradesh and Tripura among the North Eastern States.[3] The estimated mid year population of Tripura in 2004 was 33,55,000 comprising 17,21,000 males and reamaining 16,34,000 females whereas Census 2001 reveals that the population of India at 0.00 hrs. of 1st March 2001 stood at 1,02, 88,30,774 with average exponential growth rate of 1.93 per cent per annum during 1991-2001. The demographic features of the N.E. States in 2001 are as follows :[4]

Table 21.I

States	*Population (in lakhs)*	*Annual Exponential Growth Rate*	*Density*	*Sex-ratio Females per '000 Males*
Arunachal Pradesh	10.98	2.33	13	901
Assam	266.56	1.73	340	932
Manipur	23.89	2.63	107	978
Meghalaya	23.19	2.62	103	975
Mizoram	8.89	2.56	42	938
Nagaland	19.89	4.97	120	909
Tripura	31.99	1.46	305	948

Mention may be made in this context that in 1998 revision, by Population Division, the decadal growth rate has declined at all-India level from 23.86 per cent for 1981-1991 to 21.56 per cent for the period of 1991-2001, a decrease of 2.30 per cent. The percentage decadal growth has declined during the Census decade 1991-2001 as, compared to the previous Census decade in all the states / Union Territories except Haryana,

Uttar Pradesh, Bihar, Sikkim, Nagaland, Manipur, Gujraat, Daman and Diu and Dadra and Nagar Haveli. The following Table 21.2 shows the key demographic features in 1991 and 2001 for Tripura and all-India.[5]

Table 21.2

Sl. No.	*Items*	*Unit*	*1991 Ceusus*		*2001 Ceusus*	
			Tripura	*India*	*Tripura*	*India*
1.	Population	In lakhs	27.57	8463	31.99	10288
2.	Decadal Growth Rate	Per cent	34.3	23.9	16.03	21.56
3.	Density	Per sq. km.	263	273	305	313
4.	Sex-rate Female	Per '000 Males	945	927	948	933
5.	Literacy Rate	Per cent	60.44	52,21	73,20	65.38
6.	ST Population	Per cent	30.95	7.95	31.05	8.20
7.	SC Population	Per cent	16.36	16.73	17.37	16.20

Source : Census RGI.

From the above Table 21.2 it is evident that Tripura is now the second highest populated state after Assam and as regards density of population it is 305 per sq.km whereas in India it is 313. It also indicates 42 more people live in a sq.km in the state than they lived a decade ago. The ST population of the state is 31.05 whereas at all-India level the percentage is 8.20.[6]

Demographic Disequilibrium caused by Immigration

It will be evident from the fact that according to 1941 Census Report the total population of Tripura was 5.13 lakhs and out of this the number of tribal people was 2.56 lakhs i.e. 50.09 per cent of the total population.[7] A comparative study of the population figures as enumerated in the Census Report from 1931 to 2001 is given in Table 21.3 :

Table 21.3 shows progressive decline in ratio of tribal population and rapid increase of the non-tribals. It is significant to note that the non-tribal population of Tripura increased by 71.05 per cent during the period from 1961 to 1971 whereas, India records a growth rate of only 24.5 per cent during the same period. On the other hand, the ratio of tribal population to total population of the state gradually decreased from 50.25 per cent in 1931 to 28.44 per cent in 1981 in

Table 20.1 : Population of Tripura, 1931-2001

Year of Census	*Total Population*	*Tribal Population*	*Percentage %*
1931	382450	192249	50.25
1941	513010	256991	50.09
1951	645707	237953	36.85
1961	1142005	360070	31.53
1971	1556142	450544	28.95
1981	2053058	583920	28.44
1991	2757205	853345	30.95
2001	3199203	993426	31.05

Source : Census Report from 1931 to 2001.

spite of upward growth of population.[8] This demographic disequilibrium in respect of tribal and non-tribal people of this state has been primarily caused by influx of refugees from Chakla Roshnabad and the neighbouring region of Bengal. The demographic changes in the state during the said period as shown below :

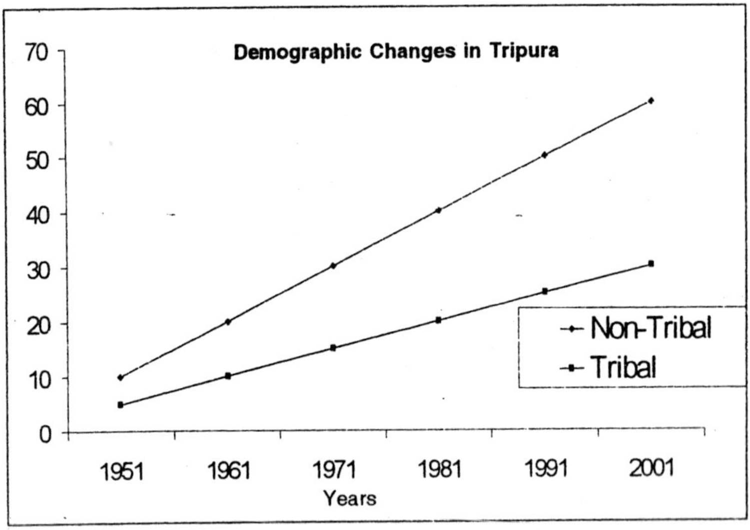

According to the Ceusus Report of 2001 the rural mixed population forms 82.94 per cent whereas 17.06 per cent of the mixed population live in urban areas as against 27.78 per cent at all-India level. Their main occupations are related to agriculture, horticulture, forestry and allied productive activities. Naturally, due to growing landlessness there is a bitter scramble for land for survival. Now in the competition for acquiring land in this race the tribal had been losing ground to the non-tribals until the Autonomous District Council was constituted in the eighties with an area of 7132.56 sq. kms, i.e. 68 per cent of total area of the state.[9] Yet, due to inadequacies of safeguards growing landlessness among the poorer sections of both tribal and non-tribal population groups has been very acute.

Multi-cultural Heritage

Tripura reasonably claims a prominent place in the Union for a hoary cultural heritage of her people. From the distant past, the Royal Palace had been the centre of all literary and other cultural activities of the state. Most of the modern members of the royal family of Tripura were great patrons of art and literature and had high regard for the eminent scholars of the country. Mention may be made that the first great king of the Tripura was Dharmamanikya (1431-1462) who was a patron of learning specially in Bengali and Sanskrit, although he himself was a Bodo speaker.[10] He is said to have inaugurated the *Rajmala,* a verse chronicle of the royal house. The next king Dhanyamanikya (1490-1515) is said to have encouraged translation into Bengali of Sanskrit text, viz. *Jyotish Ratnakar* and *Utkal Khanda Panchali.* Apart from Rajmala, *Champakvijyaya* was composed by a Muslim poet at the instance of Mirkhan, a powerful army personnel who helped Champak Roy, the Dewan of Ratnamanikya II (1685-1712), the ruler of Tripura himself to get reinstated to the throne. The modern period in the literary history of Tripura dates back to the time of Maharaja Birchandra Manikya during which a spiritual contact with Bengal was made and this contact became all the more significant due to poet Rabindranath Tagore's continued association with the ruler and by his benign influence over them.[11]

The 'religion' figure for Census -2001 reveals that 85.60 per cent of the population was the Hindu population. The Muslims, Christians and Buddhists population were 8 per cent, 3.2 per cent and 3.1 per cent respectively in 2001. The following Table 21.4 shows the religious communities of the state in 2001.[12]

Table 21.4: Religious Communities of state

Sl. No.	*Religious Community*	*Population*	*Proportion*	*Literacy Rate*	*Female Literacy Rate*	*Proportion of Child Population*
1.	Hindus	27,39,310	85.60	75.30	67.30	13.00
2.	Muslims	2,54,442	8.00	60.90	51.40	18.60
3.	Christians	1,02,489	3,20	67.90	57.30	15.70
4.	Buddhists	98,922	3.10	49.20	37.40	17.90
5.	Sikhs	1,182	0.04	98.40	89.50	4.50
6	Jains	477	0.01	82.90	78.40	4.90
7.	Others	1,277	0.04	75.40	65.30	12.10
8.	Religion not stated	1,104	0.03	73.10	65.90	14.00

It appears from the above Table 21.4 that there are four predominant communities in Tripura professing different religious beliefs, viz. Hindus, Muslims, Buddhits and Christians. Most of the tribal people have their own tribal customs and beliefs but in the broader sense of religion they are believed to be the followers of Hindusim. Only the Lushai, Kuki and some people of the Garo community have retained themselves as Christians. The Mog and Chakma communities and a few people of other tribes were declared as scheduled tribes but they profess Buddhism.[13] The number of people professing Jainism and Sikhism is very negligible.

During the period of Muslim rule in Bengal, Tripura was subjected to Muslim invasion on a number of occasions. It was during this period that Muslims in some numbers entered into Tripura from the Western side and settled in Udaipur and Sonamura along with the ruling class.[14] This accounts for the majority of Muslim population in Sonamura and Udaipur areas which lay either across the route of the invading armies or happened to be the principal seat of administration. The Mog and Chakma communities profess Buddhism and they are to be found mainly in Sabroom, Belonia, Amarpur and Kailashar Sub-Division of the State.[15] The rate of increase among the Christians was very small upto 1911 but from 1920 their number began to increase rapidly when the Lushais and Kukis embraced Christanity in large numbers. The number of Sikhs, Jains and Parsees residing in the state is very few. They are not permanent settlers but they come over here for purposes of service and trade. It is interesting to note that although the religion of the majority of tribal people is termed as Hinduism, it is in fact, a curious mixture of Hinduism and Animism. The old gods have not yet been ousted and they are worshipped side by side with those of the Hindus by priests. They worship forces such as the god of water, the god of fire, the god of forests, the god of earth etc. A trace of their old faith is to be found in their present practice of striking a bamboo in the ground during religious festival and worshipping it. Sacrifice forms an important part of their religion.

Process of Acculturation

Acculturation is the process through which the tribal cultures are usually transformed or modified. It involves acceptance and adoption. A tribe in contact with other cultures may accept some of the traits of their neighbour such as the employment of Hindu priest in indigenous ceremonies and festivals by some of the tribes in Tripura which is an example of simple acceptance. They have been subjected to the influence of the plains which presented a higher culture with a more effective productive organisation. Bengali Hindu culture is not antagonistic and the economic and political superiority of the plains set an ideal before them and they eagerly began to imitate or assimilate those elements of culture which attracted their attention most. We shall now try to show these influences categorically in the various spheres of life.

In the field of agriculture some tribals are still in the stage of primitive method of cultivation. They practice temporary hill cultivation *(Jhum)* as the most important source of food supply and this has become the foremost productive system among them. But the example of the plain dwellers has deeply influenced them in this respect. Like other neighbouring tribes, they have also turned to some modernisation of their agricultural practices and therefore practising settled wet rice cultivation now. It has been considered by the majority of them that shifting cultivation is no longer profitable. *Jhum* cultivation is being replaced by plough cultivation. The plough, the harrow and the bullocks are taking the place of *dama, tisim* and *yagul khitariya.*[16]

It may be recollected that Late Maharaja Bir Bikram Kishore Manikya Bahadur (1923–47) in order to induce his tribal subjects viz., Puran Tipra, Noatias, Jamatias, Riangs and Halams to plough cultivation instead of *Jhum* cultivation, reserved a large fertile ploughable area by an order dated 20th Bhadra, 1341 T.E.(1931) and by a subsequent order dated lst Aswin 1353 T.E. (1943). The area was extended later. Again in order to develop the vast tracts of wild land and populate them, he opened a new Department called the Immigration and Reclamation Department.[17] Soon after the opening of this department vigorus attempts were made for the study of material conditions of various tracts of land awaiting development. Reclamation work had commenced in Kulai Haor, Dhalai Valley of Kaishahar Sub-division and various other places and nearly 400 sq. miles of land were distributed amongst the immigrants.[18] The Agriculture department which was re-organised at the instance of His Highness took up the work of introducing superior quality of cotton, paddy, jute, tobacco, sugarcane and potato in the high lands and in the plains. As a further step the department opened an enquiry office in a specially constructed shed in the heart of Agartala Bazar to furnish people with all information regarding agricultural operation, seeds, appliance, plants and cattle diseases.

As a result of this contact initiated by the kings considerable changes took place in the environment, economy and socio-religious life-patterns of the tribals and non-tribals of Tripura.

Reference may be made in this context that of the many festivals that we have in Tripura the worship of the fourteen gods popularly known as *kharchi puja* occupies the pride of place. This is celebrated with enthusiasm in July every year. Though originally a tribal festival devotees, both tribals and non-tribals, from every corner of Tripura come in thousands to the holy place thus setting a good example of communal harmony and cultural understanding.

Planning and Strategy for Development

Keeping in mind the spirit of the Constitution which recognises both cultural differences and the values of equal citizenship and equal rights the administrative authority applies the concept of multiculturalism and socio-economic and political justice in promoting the process of integration of the tribals into the national mainstream.

The State Government rightly feels that strategy for development has taken into account the need of the people and state, its strengths, resources and weaknesses. The aim of the developmental planning is to provide a direction to the development policies and programmes make the people aware of these programmes and to involve them in the process of development of the State. Accordingly the State Planning Board was reconstituted in the year of 2003 with a view to giving a new direction to developmental policies and programmes and providing the people an opportunity to involve themselves in the process of development.

The State Planning Board carried out a detailed evaluation of the sectoral achievements and drew up a road map for future development in the respective sectors. The recommendations for the development of under-privileged sections, viz. ST, SC, OBC, have been worked out sector-wise. For example alternative technology and training may be imported so that cash crop cultivation can be taken up gradually in place of traditional *jhum* cultivation in the *tilla* land. A tleast 50 ST families per year may be taken up for raising rubber, areca nut and horticultural plantations with wage subsidy in the gestation period. *Jhumia* settlers are to be encouraged to create market facilities by themselves and marketing infrastrcture is to be created in different interior areas. Besides agriculture, ST people in the re-grouped villages may be allowed for rubber, bamboo and areca nut plantation in forest area. As has been done in Mizoram, the State Government may formulate a policy under which the *jhumia* and tribal people living in the forest should have the rights in procurement, selling, and management of bamboos.

It is also encouraging to note that in perspective of the objectives of 'Approach to People's Plan in Tripura' five long-term plans have been prepared and approved by the State Government for implementation within fixed timeframe. These five long-term perspective plans are as follows :

1. Perspective Plan for achieving self-sufficiency in food production (2000-01 to 2009-10).

2. Perspective Plan for development of horticulture in Tripura (2002-12).
3. Perspective Plan for development of Animal Resources (2002-12).
4. Perspective Plan for attaining self-sufficiency in fish production (2002-12).
5. Perspective Plan for development of forestry sector (2002-03 to 2011-12).

In 2005, the Government of Tripura through Tripura Forest Department submitted a project proposal of Tripura Forest Environmental Improvement and poverty alleviation to Japan Bank for International Cooperation for financial assistance and both the sides agreed to conduct surveys under JBIC's special assistance facility.[19] The basic thrust of the aforesaid project to put in a nutshell is Formation of a comprehensive project for forest resource development and conservation that will alleviate poverty keeping in view unique socio-economic and sensitive socio-political situations of Tripura during the project formation.

Conclusion

A policy of complete assimilation or absorption of the tribal people within the fold of the non-tribals is considered by some scholars as incompatible with cultural patterns of India. It has been pointed out that the Indian society is composed of heterogenous cultures prevailing in different parts of the country. Despite the apparent diversity, there is, however, a keynote of cultural unity pervading the country. Naturally, it has been urged that there is hardly any need of complete assimilation of the tribal peoples and their cultures. On the other hand, the tribal culture as such in its various forms may thrive as one of the many segments of the totality of the Indian culture.

Accordingly, it has been upheld by most scholars in the field that the integration of the tribal people within the larger Indian socio-economic fabric is the crying need of the day. This integration does not necessarily mean or presuppose any assimilation. The integration is to be made compatible with the heterogeneity of the Indian culture. Even the various tribal communities with their respective cultural patterns may be allowed to maintain their identity or distinctiveness within the larger Indian Society. If this policy is followed in State of Tripura, it would imply that the different tribal communities of the State shall be allowed to preserve their respective cultural distinctiveness as integral part of the larger society of the State. This view has been most seriously considered by all experts on the perspectives of Indian cultural patterns.

In a vast country like India numerous cultural groups are quite likely to persist, and it is only through a very slow and steady process of integration that these may be made part and parcel of the Indian society as a whole. Different component cultural elements/complexes within their respective cultural individuality may acquire some common denominators of the national culture and thereby develop a keen sense of national unity. This kind of integration of various component elements within a particular nation is quite possible, and this has already been experimented in different parts of the world. The most classic example has been set by Russia. Russia is also composed of diverse ethnic and cultural groups ranging from the most primitive tribal stage of Siberia to the most sophisticated and industrialised white Russians. In Russia all peoples with their respective cultural patterns have been integrated into a wholesome nation. At the same time, each segment or integrant of the Union has been given complete freedom to nourish, retain and develop its own culture, and the Union Government as well encourages and renders all possible assistance towards that end. This has been made possible because all different peoples with varied cultures have been brought within the framework of a single economic system which has been working with tremendous success. Accordingly, in spite of diverse cultural and ethnic groups the national integration has been more successfully achieved than in any other parts of the world. In America, Switzerland and in other countries as well diverse ethnic and cultural groups have been also integrated into nationhood. But in these countries all peoples have not been brought within the framework of a single economic system as in Russia. Accordingly, discriminations and differentiations prevail amongst different segments of all those nations.

In the perspective of all these approaches, the tribal people of India are to be dealt with. It is again in the perspective of the works done by the Government and people of other countries of the world that the tribal problems of India are to be examined and solved for making them part and parcel of the Indian nation. What is needed most is to carry out all round development works in all walks of the tribal life, not certainly by destroying their cultural values and distinctiveness.

This approach is to be made with regard to the tribal people of Tripura as well whose cultural patterns have variations from one community to another. There is, of course, a fundamental note of unity in cultural patterns prevailing amongst all sections of the tribal people of Tripura. In such a case the problem of integrating the diverse tribal communities within the bigger framework of Indian nation would be more easier. Originally, the whole State of Tripura was peopled and dominated by different tribal communities and the State was also ruled over by a tribal Chieftain for a long time. The enlightened monarchs of the State for carrying out effective administration recruited talents and persons of ability. In this respect, Tripura monarchs encouraged the Bengali Hindus to settle down in Tripura and appointed them in various positions. This ensured a flow of the Bengali Hindus into the State of Tripura, and a large number of them became permanently settled in different parts of the State. Not only that, these alien settlers even started flourishing at the cost of the tribal people. This proved disastrous in the sense that the tribals were gradually reduced to abject poverty and economic ruination. Bengalees as has been outlined in the foregoing pages has at the same time yielded good results as well. This establishment of a close contact has proved to be most beneficial in the sense that there has been taken place marked changes or transformation in the tribal life-patterns. In other words, this close contact with alien culture has smoothened the path of modernisation of the tribal communities of Tripura.

Task Ahead

What is thus needed most is the preparation of a Master Plan with long-term and short-term programmes of work to be carried out for the welfare and benefits of the tribal people of the State. Such programmes are again to be implemented phase-wise in accordance with the available resources. The following suggestions may accordingly be made :

1. The tribal communities of Tripura are economically very backward. What is needed most is the economic upliftment which can be effectively done only by making a scientific study of the problems faced by these people. It has been already stated that the shifting cultivation has found to be most uneconomical and less productive. So, *jhuming* is to be replaced by plough-cultivation or permanent agricultural operation. It may be borne in mind that the tribal people are now quite conscious of the benefits of the plough-cultivation. But unfortunately, they have neither the means nor the available land for the same. Naturally so, immediate provisions are to be made for the distribution of available irrigated land, offering financial assistance for the purchase of bullocks, agricultural tools, crop-seeds and to do everything possible for safeguarding their interests by prohibiting money lending and also by not permitting the traders and merchants to carry on activities for the exploitation of the tribal people.
2. It may be, noted that the available land for agricultural operation is quite insufficient to meet the demand of the tribal people. So, wastelands or unwanted forest lands are to be converted into agricultural holdings. Before sufficient agricultural land is available, shifting cultivation cannot be ignored or stopped altogther. It is noteworthy that the landscape of Tripura State does not also permit agricultural operations everywhere. In many areas, land is suitable for *jhuming* only. Accordingly, *jhuming* or shifting cultivation may be encouraged on a more scientific basis.
3. A good number of the tribal people live primarily in forest areas but the The Forest Conservation Act, 1980, does not permit anybody to stay in the forest land and, in view of the

apex court's direction, the state forest department has already served notices to vacate the forest. According to estimates, there are some 215,000 tribal people living in about 14,000 hectares of forest land for decades. Tribal people account for about 30 per cent of Tripura's 3.1 million people. The government's decision to evict the settlers from the forest land has triggered a blazing row with the main opposition Congress Party and the Indigenous Nationalist Party of Tripura (INPT), a tribal-based political front. The Left Front Governement finds itself in a spot and has demanded immediate passing of the Scheduled Tribes (Recognition of Forest Right) Bill, 2005 by the Parliament.

4. Tripura may be chosen as a potential gateway for the port of Chittagong of Bangladesh from the entire North East Region. Parliamentary Standing Committee under the Ministry of Commerce has already earmarked 28 items, which can be profitably traded with Bangladesh through the State. The list includes such items of national interest like tea from Assam and Tripura, Coal from Meghalaya and Bamboo products from Tripura, Assam and Mizoram.[20]

Now, if the national planners and policy-makers take up the matter as a comprehensive deal, comprising rapid extension of infrastuctural facilities on the one hand and talks with Bangladesh on the other, it is believed that not only the future of Tripura would brighten up, but also the entire region would find its easy outlet to the global market taking the advantage of the possible Agartala-Chittagong route so coming up and if this really goes on the burden-state of one day may usher into an economically reckonable state in a very near future.

Notes

1. Menon, K.D. : *Tripura District Gazetteers*, 1975, Calcutta.
2. *Economic Review of Tripura 2004-05*; Directorate of Economics and Statistics Government, of Tripura, Agartala.
3. *Economic Review* 2004-05.
4. *Census - 2001*, RGI

5. *Economic Review 2004-05.*
6. *Ibid.*
7. *Census Report from 1931–2001.*
8. Bhattacharya, S. : *Genesis of Tribal Extremism in Tripura*, New Delhi, 1991.
9. *Tripura* : Director of Public Relations and Tourism, Government. of Tripura.
10. *Ibid.*
11. *Ibid.*
12. *Economic Review.*
13. *Ibid.*
14. *Tripura,* Government. of Tripura.
15. Menon, K.D. *Tripura District Gazetteers - 1975.*
16. *Ibid.*
17. *Ibid.*
18. *Ibid.*
19. Japan Bank for International Cooperation Agreement, 2005.
20. Gauguly, J.B. : *Tripura Tribes in Transition,* New Delhi, 1998.

22 Factors Affecting Changing Ratio in Nagaland

Mithilesh Kumar Sinha

Prologue

Consumerist culture oriented economic development, commercialization of medical profession and sexist biases in our society, combined together have created a sad scenario of 'missing girls'. Global comparison of sex ratios shows that sex ratios in Europe, North America, Caribbean, Central Asia, the poorest regions of Sub-Saharan Africa are favourable to women as these countries neither kill/neglect girls nor do they use NRTs for production of sons. The lowest sex ratio is found in some parts of India. Deficit of women in India since 1901 arising out of violence against women over life cycle, from womb to tomb—female infanticide, neglect of girl child in terms of health and nutrition, child marriage and repeated pregnancy taking heavy toll of girls' lives in addition to selective elimination of female foetuses and selection of male at a pre-conception stage, has taken new turn with widespread use of New Reproductive Technologies (NRTs) in India. NRTs are based on principle of selection of desirable and rejection of the unwanted. In India, the desirable is the baby boy and the unwanted is the baby girl. The result is obvious. The Census results of 2001 have revealed that with sex ratio of 927 girls for 1000 boys. India had deficit of lakh girls in the age group of 0.6 years.

Nagaland is a State that does not conform to the general perception of women's status in India. Apart from traditional practices that have generally cared for women and the girl child, the positive achievements are improving sex ratios, absence of female foeticides and low material mortality rate (Human Development Report: 2004).

In Nagaland, Child Sex Ratio as per 1991 Census of India was 993 girls for 1000 boys but in 2001 Census and CSR (0-6 years age groups) has declined and it became 975 girls for 1000 boys. Nagaland has deficit of approximately 1.82 lakh women and 1.5 lakh girls in age-group of 0-6 years.

Sex Ratio—A Global Scenario

Data published by United Nations give a dismal scene of declining sex ratio in the world. The average Child Sex Ratio (CSR in the 50) (0-4 age group) in the developed region comprising Europe, North America, Australia, New Zealand and Japan showed a steady decline in the 50-year period, from 957 female children (per 1000 male children) in 1950 to 949 in 2000. In contrast, the CSR for this age group in the least developed countries (49 in all 34 in Africa, nine in Asia, one in Latin America and the Caribbean and five in Oceania) stood at 998 in 1950, much higher than in the developed bloc, and in 2000 it was 976.

Similarly, the CSR of the 5-9 age group was 1002 girl children in 1950 and 977 in 2000. Though the decline is shrap, the figure remains much higher than the corresponding figure for this group in the more developed regions. Even in South-East Asia, where in 1950 the CSR

Table 22.1: Global Child Sex Ratio

Country	*0-4 Age Group*		*5-9 Age Group*	
	1950	*2000*	*1950*	*2000*
North America	977	951	957	952
Latin America and Caribbean	977	962	982	964
Northern Europe	953	949	960	952
Iraq	945	964	954	965
Saudi Arabia	968	955	968	955
Iran	986	951	980	949
Afghanistan	948	947	933	939
Pakistan	968	944	999	939
Asia	944	936	956	932
China	892	898	903	897
Nepal	992	943	979	934
Bangladesh	1014	954	1003	950
Sri Lanka	758	966	868	970
India	976	941	982	934
South-East India	1003	963	1013	967

Source: World Population Prospects: The 2002 Revision, Vol. II Sex and Age Distribution of Population, United Nations.

stood at 1,003, the figure came down to 963 in 2000, and reasons for the decline were not entirely cultural. If they were so, then in the absence of sex-selection technology, female children would still have been eliminated by mass foeticide. As in Africa, the CSR decline in Islamic countries between 1950 and 2000 was not prominent. In fact, Afghanistan showed a marginal improvment. And Iraq, reeling under the weight of UN sanctions, showed a dramatic improvement in the survival of the girl child in the 0-4 age group. In 2000, its CSR stood at 964, higher than the world average of 948 (Table 22.1).

Golbal Male-Female Sex Ratio

In the Western hemisphere, the trend has been in favour of feminine population, whereas in Asia, in general and in India, in particular, the trend has been congenial to a masculine population (Table 22.2).

Table 22.2: Male-Female Sex Ratio of Selected Countries (Number of Females per thousand males)

Country	Sex Ratio
China	944
India	933
Sri Lanka	948*
Bangladesh	953
Japan	1041
USA	1029
Indonesia	1004
Brazil	1025
Russian Federation	1140
U.K	1160
Canada	991*
Egypt	982*
Nigeria	1016

Note: Figures of the year of 1919.
Source: Census 2001, Government of India.

Perspective of Sex Ratio in India

There is an official admission to the fact that "it is increasingly becoming a common practice across the country to determine the sex of the unborn child or foetus and eliminate it if the foetus is found to be a female". This practice is referred to as Pre-Birth Elimination of Female (PBEF).PBEF involves two stages: determination of the sex of the foetus and induced termination if the foetus is not of the desired sex. It is believed that one of the significant contributors to the adverse child sex ratio in India is the practice of female foetuses (Ministry of Health and Family Welfare, India: 2003).

India witnessed continued decline in sex ratio since 1901 from 972 to 930 women per thousand men in 1971. In 1991, it became the lowest in the history of Census, i.e. 927. Again, in 2001 the sex ratio of total population was 933 (Table 22.3). Social sterotyping and violence at the domestic and societal level are some other manifestations. Discrimination against the girl children, adolescent girl and women persists in parts of the country (Nongbri: 2005). The number of female children is dwindling fast and female foeticide is one of the primary reasons for this decline (Table 22.3). Despite a legal ban in India on sex selection of babies, a study indicates that the practice is still widely prevalent and it is estimated that at least 10 million female births may have been aborted in the past 20 years. The study, based on a national survey of 1.1 million Indian households and published in *Lancet* journal on January 9, 2006, claims that nearly 500,000 female babies are lost in India every year because of selective abortion (Surroor: 2006). The researchers discovered that the "girl deficit" was more common among educated families, especially in homes where the first-born was a girl.

Table 22.3 : Female-Male Ratio and Child Sex Ratio in India

Year	*1901*	*1911*	*1921*	*1931*	*1941*	*1951*	*1961*	*1971*	*1981*	*1991*	*2001*
Sex Ratio (FMR)	972	964	955	950	945	946	941	930	934	927	933
CSR (0-6 Age Group)	–	–	–	–	–	–	–	–	962	945	927

Source: Census 2001, GoI.

Methodology

The study is based on district-wise secondary data obtained from published report, Directorate of Census Operations, Controller of Publications, Civil Lines, New Delhi. Districts of Nagaland have been categorised in three groups on the basis of sex ratio and Juvanile sex ratio that is 870-900, 901-925 and 925 and above as unfavourable sex ratio, intermediate sex ratio and favourable sex ratio respectively. Population literacy (Male+Female+Rural Male and Female+Urban Male and Female) has been considered for detailed investigation.

Dynamics of Declining Women in North-East India

There are variations in Female-Male Ratio (FMR) between different states of North Eastern Region. The FMR tends to be substantially below unity in all the states of this region. The FMR is observed to be lowest in Arunachal Pradesh in 1991 (0.859) but in 2001 it has improved (0.901). In 2001, Sikkim has the lowest FMR (0.875) (Table 22.4).

Table 22.4 : FMR in Different States of North Eastern Region

States	1991	2001
Assam	0.923	0.932
Arunachal Pradesh	0.859	0.901
Manipur	0.958	0.978
Meghalaya	0.955	0.975
Mizoram	0.921	0.938
Nagaland	0.886	0.909
Sikkim	0.878	0.875
Tripura	0.945	0.950

Source: GoI (2004), Census of India: Website: Sex Ratio.

Dynamics of Declining Women in India and Nagaland

Legacy of continuing declining sex ratio in India in the history of Census of India has taken new turn with widespread use of New Reproductive Techologies (NRTs) in urban India. The result is obvious. The Census result of 2001 have revealed that with sex ratio of 933 women for 1000 men. India had deficit of 3.5 crores women when it entered in the new millennium.

Nagaland socio-cultural practices, which value the girl child, have contributed to the success of reversing the sex ratio, besides government and civil society interventions. Moreover, the use of NRTs Nagaland is not state-wide. That is why the sex ratio in Nagaland which had steadily declined from 933 in 1961 to 863 in 1981, showed a positive reverse trend during the last two decades. From 863 in 1981, it rose to 886 in 1991 and finally, to 909 in 2001. Though Nagaland witnessed positive reverse trend during the two decades, but sex ratio here is not favourable (955 and above). In Nagaland intermediate sex ratio (901-955) is prevailing. Still with the ratio of 909 women for 1000 men, Nagaland had deficit of 1.62 lakh women (Tabel 22.5).

Table 22.5 : Demographic Profile of India and Nagaland

	India	*Nagaland*
Population	102.7 crores	19.89 lakhs
Males	53.1 crores	10.89 lakhs
Females	49.6 crores	9.47 lakhs
Deficit of Women in 2001	3.5 crores	0.95 lakhs
Sex Ratio (no. of women per 1000 men)	933	909

Source : Census of India, 2001.

District-wise Sex Ratio in Nagaland

It is a welcome feature that all the districts of Nagaland have registered an increase in female-male ratio in 2001 in comparison to 1991. But no district has shown favourable sex ratio. Two districts (Dimapur and Mon) have registered unfavourable sex ratio (854 and 881 respectively.

It is the most distressing factor that in urban areas of Nagaland in all districts sex ratio is unfavourable i.e., below 900 in both the Censuses of 1991 and 2001. Dimapur district reflects low premium accorded to a girl child (746) (Table 22.6).

Political Economy of Missing Girls in India and Nagaland

The declining juvenile sex ratio is the most distressing factor reflecting low premium accorded to a girl child in India (Patel: 2003). As per the Census of India, juvenile sex ratio were 971, 945 and 927 for

Table 22.6 : District-wise Sex Ratio

Districts	*1991*			*2001*		
	Total	*Urban*	*Rural*	*Total*	*Urban*	*Rural*
Dimapur	830	765	830	854	746	920
Kohima	859	745	909	944	870	970
Mokokchung	912	798	935	919	821	935
Mon	872	695	887	881	838	884
Phek	880	663	902	923	760	940
Tuensang	889	702	910	913	784	923
Wokha	946	793	917	927	848	952
Zunheboto	964	844	982	945	823	968

Source: State Human Development Report, 2004, Government of Nagaland.

1981, 1991 and 2001 respectively. In 2001, India had 158 million nfants and children of which 82 million were males and 76 million vere females. There was a deficit of 6 million female infants and girls. This is a result of the widespread use of sex determination and sex re-selection tests throughout the country (including in Kerala), along vith high rates of female infanticide in the Bimaru States, rural Tamil Nadu and Gujarat. Millions of girls have been missing in the post-ndependence period. According to UNFPA (2003), 70 districts in 6 States and Union Territories recorded more than a 50 point decline in the child sex ratio in the last one decade.

In Nagaland, as per Censuses of 1991 and 2001 juvenile sex ratio (0-6 age group) were 993 and 975 respectively. This shows that it has witnessed declining child sex ratio. If we go through district-wise juveline sex ratio we find that in urban areas juvenile sex ratio has been declining and getting intermediate juvenile sex ratio. Two districts (Mon and Zunheboto) have witnessed unfavourable juvenile sex ratio (852 and 889 respectively in 2001).

As a whole Nagaland had deficit of 1.5 lakh girls in age-group of 0.6 years (Table 22.7).

Findings and Discussion

Literacy, population growth, extent of proverty, medical facility and urbanisation have considered for detailed analysis. At first stage,

Table 22.7 : District-wise Juvenile Sex Ratio

Districts	*1991*			*2001*		
	Total	*Urban*	*Rural*	*Total*	*Urban*	*Rural*
Dimapur	973	986	950	981	1004	940
Kohima	1013	1031	957	979	990	941
Mokokchung	1010	1028	929	1004	1019	916
Mon	995	990	1059	975	985	852
Phek	969	972	939	934	936	919
Tuensang	975	982	921	978	979	970
Wokha	1001	993	1036	999	1004	980
Zunheboto	1030	1039	976	949	958	889
Nagaland	993	–	–	975	–	–

Source: State Human Development Report 2004, Government of Nagaland.

urbanisation has been rejected since it has no relation with the change in sex ratio.

Literacy has been considered for detailed analysis. Male and female literacy level have been considered. It is a common belief that the female literacy has some relationship with the number of females in the society but it does not hold true in case of Nagaland. Dimapur district has most unfavourable sex ratio but its female literacy is 73.43 per cent which is much higher than state average. Female literacy (61.9%) as per 2001 Census. The district of Tuensang has the lower rate of female literacy (46.12%) but had sex ratio of 913, higher to state average of 909 in 2001.

If we go through district-wise urban sex ratio we find that in all the districts male-female sex disparity is very high. All the districts have registered most unfavourable sex ratio below 900 female per 1000 male while in all the districts urban female literacies (more than 75%) which are much higher than state average urban female literacy.

Literacy rate of all the districts have shown an increase from 1991 to 2001 but juvenile disparity has increased during the same period. For example Juvenile sex ratios in Mokokchung, Kohima, Wokha and Junheboto are positive (1010, 1013, 1001 and 1030 respectively) in 1991 but they have declined in 2001 and become below 1000 except Mokokchung (1004, 979, 999 and 949 respectively) while these districts have registered an increase of female literacy rate from 1991 (74.88%, 61.41%, 65.99% and 57.63% respectively) to 2001 (82.20%, 66.64%, 76.46% and 65.80% repectively) (Table 22.8).

Table 22.8 : District-wise Literacy Rate in Per cent

Districts	1991							2001						
	TL	ML	FL	RML	RFL	UML	UFL	TL	ML	FL	RML	RFL	UML	UFL
Dimapur	–	–	–	–	–	–	–	78.15	82.16	73.34	79.74	71.15	85.34	76.86
Kohima	69.16	75.58	61.41	69.99	54.43	87.01	79.33	74.28	81.44	66.64	77.96	62.02	91.18	81.19
Mokokchung	77.85	80.52	74.88	79.00	72.89	88.26	86.86	84.27	86.14	82.20	84.93	80.48	93.32	93.88
Mon	36.22	41.90	29.10	39.12	26.79	73.94	66.17	42.25	46.70	37.12	43.90	34.48	89.33	79.08
Phek	62.59	72.28	51.34	70.57	50.08	89.07	69.33	71.35	78.97	63.08	77.34	61.48	94.52	83.35
Tuensang	48.39	53.98	41.98	51.28	39.58	78.93	72.74	51.30	55.97	46.12	53.56	43.84	84.61	78.81
Wokha	73.92	81.06	65.99	78.97	62.40	90.03	85.40	81.28	85.69	76.46	83.53	72.92	92.25	88.68
Zunheboto	64.36	70.76	57.63	68.46	55.19	87.03	78.29	69.73	73.43	65.80	69.50	61.86	93.41	90.06

Source: State Human Development Report, 2004, Government of Nagaland.

Decadal population growth rates (1991-2001) has relationship with sex ratio. We find that decadal population growth is higher in the group of districts with unfavourable sex ratio. For example, Dimapur, Mon and Tuensang districts have higher decadal population growth rates (73.3%, 73.42% and 78.1% respectively) with unfavourable sex ratio.

Economic, social and health deprivation seems to have some influence on sex ratio of human population. The extent of economic, social and health deprivation is the highest in Mon and Tuensang with eighth and seventh rank (Table 22.9). These two districts have unfavourable sex ratio. Zunheboto has 2nd rank in Human Poverty Index and it has intermediate sex ratio, indicating an association between HPI and sex ratio in Nagaland.

Table 22.9 : Human Poverty Index

	Dimapur	*Mokokchung*	*Wokha*	*Kohima*	*Phek*	*Zunheboto*	*Tuensang*	*Mon*
HPI Rank	29.25 (4)	19.90 (1)	27.05 (3)	33.08 (5)	40.88 (6)	24.72 (2)	48.98 (7)	49.09 (8)

Source : State Human Development Report, 2004, Government of India.

Availability of medical facilities seems to have some influence on sex ratio since mortality in girl child has direct bearing on sex ratio. It has been observed that the girl baby does not get attention of health care similar to boy baby. It has been observed that in Dimapur and Mon districts Rural Population Serviced per PHC is 46122 and 40581 and the male female sex disparity is high in these disricts (Table 20.10).

Table 20.10: Rural Population Serviced per PHC

	DMR	*MKG*	*WKH*	*KHM*	*PHEK*	*ZHBOO*	*TNSG*	*MON*
Rural Population Serviced per PHC	3303	20567	35013	13538	40581	17820	16842	46122

Source: As on Table 22.9.

Conclusion

It is emanted from above discussion that the sex ratio in Nagaland has improved in 2001 as compared to 1991 but this state is still having intermediate sex ratio. In urban area male-female sex ratio is the most unfavourable which shows that killing girl foetus is in practice. So we need to counter those who believe that it is better to kill a female foetus than to give birth to an unwanted female child. There may be also various socio-economic factors which are responsible for disparity between male and female sex. Population growth rate and poverty emerged as two most important factors, which seem to have exerted influence on sex-ratio in Nagaland. Education level and medical facilities also have positive infuence on sex-ratio, that is higher the literacy and medical facility, the more favourable will be the sex-ratio. Hence, our slogans are :

> *"Eliminate Inequality, not Women", "Destroy Dowry, not Daughters", Say "No" to Sex Discrimination, Say "Yes" to Gender Justice.*

To stop a gender imbalanced society we will have to convince doctors and clients, states and civil society that "Daughters are not for slaughter".

References

Human Development Report, Government of Nagaland (2004): "Overview" p. 7.

"Missing...Mapping the Adverse Child Sex-Ratio in India", Office of the Registrar General and Census Commissioner, India, Ministry of Health and Family Welfare and United Nations Population Fund.

Nongbri, C. (2005): "Role of Universities in the Empowerment of Women: A look into the Induction Programmes", *University News*, Vol. 43, No 47, November 21-27, p. 141.

Patel, Vibhuti (2003): "The Girl Child: Health Status in the Post Independence Period", *The National Medical Journal of India*, AIIMS-Delhi, Vol. 16, Supplement 2, pp. 42-45.

Surroor Hasan (2006): 10 Million Female Births Aborted in India: Study", *The Hindu*, January, p. 13.

23 Population Growth and Trend in Nagaland

Manoj Kumar Singh

Introduction

The total population of Nagaland as per 2001 Census is 19.88 lakh of which males form 10.42 lakh and females 9.47 lakh. Among various districts, Tuensang has largest population (4.14 lakh), followed by Kohima (3.14 lakh). The least populated district is Phek (1.48 lakh). Nagaland witnessed the highest growth rate in population over the last decade. This unprecendented growth rate of population is a cause of serious concern to the demographers and policy-planners in the state. A Total Fertility Rate (TFR) of 2.1 is considered to be the replacement level of fertility, which needs to be achieved in all states for population stabilization. As per the national family health survey, Nagaland had a TFR of 3.77 during 1998, amongst the largest in the country. There is thus a need for policy intervention to tackle this spiralling population growth, which can seriously hamper the planning process and development aspirations of the state. The density of population is another factor of concern in Nagaland because of the alarming increase in the population. The density, which was 47 per sq. km. in 1981, increased to 73 in 1991 and 120 per sq. km. in 2001. This will have serious implications on the ability of the state to meet the infrastructure requirements of its people, especially in the fledgling urban areas.

1. Decadal Growth

Nagaland has recorded progressively high decadal growth in population, increasing from 39.9 per cent in 1979 to 64.4 per cent in 2001. This decadal growth rate has been one of the highest in the country. The population grew by 5.0 per cent per annum during 1981-91, which again increased to 6.4 per cent per annum during 1991-2001 (Table 23.1).

Table 23.1 : Demographic Profile of Nagaland

Sl. No.	*Particulars*	*1961*	*1971*	*1981*	*1991*	*2001*
1.	Total Population ('000)	369	516	775	1210	1989
2.	Decennial Growth of Population (in per cent)	28.68	39.88	50.05	56.08	64.41

Source : Census of India ; National Family Health Survey, 1998-99.

District-wise Population Growth Trend

If we observe district-wise growth trend, we find that decadal growth rate of population in the districts is uneven. During the decade 1991-2001, Wokha district registered maximum growth rate of 95 per cent, followed by Tuensang (78%). The district of Mokokchung registered the lowest growth rate of 43 per cent during the period, followed by Kohima district (49.96%).

But it is very interesting to note that during the decade 1981-1991 Wokha district which registered a maximum growth rate during the decade 1991-2001, registered the lowest growth rate of 41.96 per cent. During the decade 1971-1981 Kohima district registered a maximum growth rate of 91.49 per cent whereas the district of Mon registered the lowest growth rate of 23.07 per cent (Table 23.2).

Literacy Rate : The district of Mokokchung, Kohima, Phek establish the principle " higher the literacy lower the growth rate of population". These three districts have registered higher literacy (84.27%, 74.28% and 71.35% respectively) and they have witnessed low decadal growth of population (43.48%, 49.96%, 45.12% respectively as per Census of 2001) but the district of Wokha does not show any relationship between literacy and the growth of population. Though it has registered highest literacy rate (81.28%), it has also witnessed the highest growth rate of population (95.01%). Female literacy affects the growth rate of population. The district of

Table 23.2 : Distribution of Population

Districts	*Total Population (in lakh)*			*Decadal growth rate (in percent)*			*Literacy rate (in percent)*		
	1981	*1991*	*2001*	*1971-81*	*1981-91*	*1991-2001*	*2001*		
							Males	*Females*	*Person*
Dimapur	N.A	NA	3.08	N.A	N.A	73.30	82.16	73.34	78.15
Mokokchung	1.42	1.58	2.27	25.88	50.58	43.48	86.14	82.2	84.27
Wokha	0.58	0.83	1.61	49.92	41.96	95.01	85.69	76.46	81.2
Kohima	2.50	3.87	3.14	91.49	65.10	49.96	81.44	66.64	74.28
Phek	0.71	1.02	1.48	58.36	44.19	45.12	78.97	63.08	71.35
Zunheboto	0.61	0.96	1.54	29.87	35.04	61.00	73.43	65.8	69.73
Tuensang	1.52	2.32	4.14	39.93	69.92	78.10	55.97	46.12	51.3
Mon	0.79	1.49	2.59	23.07	59.37	73.42	46.7	37.12	42.25
Nagaland	7.75	12.09	19.88	50.05	50.86	64.41	71.77	61.92	67.11

Note : Districts arranged according to rank of Human Development Index.
Source : Census of India 2001.

Tuensang and Mon registered lower female literacy (46.12% and 37.12% respectively) and growth rate of population is also higher in these two districts (71.10% and 73.42% respectively), whereas Mokokchung district has the lowest growth rate of population. We can say that except Wokha district all the districts have shown that if literacy rate is high, population will show declining trend (Table 23.2)

2. Sex-Ratio

The sex-ratio of the state has been favourable to females till 1961. After 1961 however the sex-ratio has remained unfavourable to the females and the general trends during this period, over the decades, is that of decreasing sex-ratio. The sex-ratio in Nagaland, which has steadily declined from 933 in 1961 to 863 in 1981, showed a positive, reverse trend during the last two decades. From 863 in 1981, it rose to 886 in 1991 and finally to 909 in 2001. This is a welcome feature as far as the demographic pattern is concerned.

Among the various districts, Zunheboto and Kohima had the highest sex-ratio of 945 and 944 respectively as per Census of 2001, whereas Dimapur, being highly urbanized district had the lowest sex ratio of 854. It is interesting to note that Zunheboto which is backward district of Nagaland had highes. sex-ratio of 931 in the Census of 1991 and it retained first position in Nagaland in terms of sex-ratio in the Census of 2001 (Table 22.3).

Table 22.3 : Sex-Ratio of Nagaland District-wise

Districts	*1981*	*Rank*	*1991*	*Rank*	*2001*	*Rank*
Dimapur	–	–	–	–	854	8
Mokokchung	907	3	912	3	919	5
Wokha	918	2	917	2	927	3
Kohima	790	7	856	7	944	2
Phek	873	6	880	5	923	4
Zunheboto	964	1	964	1	945	1
Tuensang	892	4	889	4	913	6
Mon	870	5	872	6	881	7
Nagaland	863	–	886	–	909	–

Source: Census of India : Statistical Abstract of Nagaland, 1990-2000.

3. Density of Population District-wise

Density of Population

The density of population of Nagaland has considerably been increasing. Density of population per sq. km. in the Census of 1961, 1971, 1981, 1991 and 2001 is 22, 31, 47, 73, 120 respectively. This will have serious implication on the ability of state to meet infrastructure requirement to its people specially in fledgling urban areas. As a matter of fact changing population density mainly depends on rate of population growth and the land utilization pattern. Accordingly, the density varies from place to place and from district to district. It can be seen from the statement above that among the districts, Dimapur is most densely populated (333) followed by Mon (145). The lowest density of population per sq. km. among the district of Nagaland is Phek (73) followed by Tuensang (98). The reason is obvious. The area of land in these two districts is vast but amenities for people living are very low (Table 22.4).

Table 22.4 : Population Density District-wise

Districts	*1981*	*1991*	*2001*
Dimapur	–	–	333
Mokokchung	69	98	141
Wokha	35	51	99
Kohima	62	96	101
Phek	35	50	73
Zunheboto	49	77	123
Tuensang	36	55	98
Mon	44	84	145
Nagaland	47	73	120

Source : Census of India, 2001.

4. Conclusion and Suggestions

In Nagaland communication in the interior area is very poor and consequently providing health services and other facilities to the remote rural area is problematic. The people are untouched by modernizing influences in remote villages of Nagaland and they have no access to the means of family planning and as such, have no control over growth of population. They still continue to have 4-5 children on an average. There is lack of effort to carry the campaign of contraceptive to the doorsteps. The women of these remote areas do not know the places of its availability and methods of its applicability. Besides, the Governmental agencies seem to be indifferent to the qualitative aspects of population management.

References

State Human Development Report 2004, Government of Nagaland, pp. 14-16.

Wayne A. Cunningham and Virginia M. Cunningham (1975) "Population Control: A Technological Necessity", published in *Health Education*, September 1975.

Statistical Hand Book, Government. of Nagaland, 2004.

24 Population Growth Trend in Nagaland

A Study of Zunheboto District

R.P. Athparia and *B.F. Kulirani*

The State of Nagaland was constituted as Sixteenth State of Indian Union in December 1963. The State lies between 25° 6′ and 27° 4′ latitude north of equator and between the longitudinal lines 93° 20′E and 95° 15′ E having an area of 16,579 sq. km. The State is bounded by Assam in the north and west, by Myanmar and Arunachal Pradesh in the east and by Manipur in the south and runs more or less parallel to the bank of the Brahmaputra. The topography is very severe, full of hill ranges which break into a wide chaos of spurs and ridges. The altitudes vary between 194 metres and 3,048 metres.

There is tremendous rise of population in Nagaland from 1951 to 2001. In 1951 Census, the total population of Nagaland was 2,12,975 persons and it rose to 19,88,636 in 2001. During the decades from 1951 to 1991, Nagaland has recorded the highest growth of population in the whole of North Eastern States which was 471 per cent followed by Tripura with 330 per cent, Mizoram with 250 per cent and 178 per cent respectively as against 134 per cent in the country as a whole (*Source*: Choudhury, R.K., 2000).

It is also observed that the decadal growth rate of population in Nagaland in the decades 1951-2001 shows unequal picture in different districts. For example, Phek district recorded the highest growth rate of 58.36 per cent in 1971-81 while Kohima recorded the highest growth rate of 95.01 per cent. The lowest population growth rate was recorded in Mon district with 22.52 per cent in 1971-81 while Zunheboto recorded the lowest population growth rate of 32.68 per cent in 1981-1991. In 1991-2001, the lowest population growth rate was recorded from Mokokchung with 43.48 per cent.

The decadal growth of rural population in the state in the last four decades of 1951-1991 was at the higher side than all India rate. However, in the decade of 1951-1961 Nagaland recorded 6.9 per cent of rural growth which was lower than the decades of 1961-1971, 1971-1981 and 1981-1991. In the decade of 1961-1971, 1971-1981 and 1981-1991 the rural population growth rate was in the ranges between 33 per cent and 53.6 per cent. It may be asserted that the urban growth was the highest at 364.4 per cent in the period of 1951-1961 in the State and it is possible that there was large scale of in-migration from rural to urban areas in that decade. Again, in the decade of 1981-1991, there was no much difference of rural and urban growth rate, i.e. 53.6 per cent for rural and 74.7 per cent for urban. But the decadal growth rate of urban population in 1961-1971 and 1971-1981 was 168.3 per cent and 133.9 per cent respectively. The migration of the people from rural to urban areas in Nagaland is not that spectacular as compared to other North Eastern States.

As on 31st March, 1995 there were 28 Rural Development Blocks in the State with 1225 villages with 10,01,323 persons in 1991 Census. In 2001, the Rural Development Blocks increased to 52 with 1278 villages. The highest number of villages was recorded in Kohima district in 1991 with 318 villages with 3,12,185 persons. In 2001, two new districts, namely Dimapur and Paren have been formed by carving out twelve administrative circles of old Kohima district. Out of the twelve circles, six circles went to Paren district and six circles to Dimapur district. At present, Kohima district has four administrative circles, namely Chiephobozou, Kezocha, Jakhama and Sechu. In Zunheboto district, all the villages are placed under 4 Rural Development Blocks, Ghathashi R.D. Block has 21 villages, Zunheboto R.D. Block has 57 villages while Tokiyo has 50 and Akuluto R.D. Block has 55 villages.

The present paper aims to throw light on the population growth trend of Zunheboto district from 1951 to 2001. The study also attempts to see how far the modern amenities like education, health, drinking water, communication facility, market and power supply have developed with the growing population in the rural and urban areas of the district.

Zunheboto district was chosen for the present study because this district is fast developing in Nagaland as compared to other districts. During the British rule in India, there was no Zunheboto town or any other place by this name. The areas now known as Zunheboto were never known by a single nomenclature before. It was Sema area and so it was known as Sema country or Sema land, but more often by names of different villages or group of villages. After the Second World War which ended in 1945 there was a great awakening for education among the Nagas and so also among the Semas. As a result of their growing enthusiasm for education and consequent demand for schools, several middle schools were opened all over Naga Hills and one was opened in a place which is now known as Zunheboto town. When the second was to be set up it became necessary to give a name to it. The people did not want to give any old name which might show favouritism to any particular village or clan. To avoid all confusion the local inhabitants decided to name the place after the plants which grow abundantly there. The name of the plant is 'Zunhebo' and the place was named 'Zunheboto', meaning 'the range of Zunhebo plant'. Zunheboto is a kind of thorney flowering shrub. Its leaf is green on the obverse and whitish hairy on the reverse. Most of the names of the modern administrative outpost of Zunheboto district, such as Satakha, Atoizu, Aizuto, etc. have originated like this manner.

Zunheboto is one of the present nine districts of Nagaland and is centrally located in the State. Formally, Nagaland had only three districts, namely Kohima, Mokokchung and Tuenchang. Later in December 1973, it was divided into seven – Kohima was again divided into Kohima and Phek; Mokokchung into three such as Mokokchung, Wokha and Zunheboto and Tuenchang into Tuenchang and Mon. In 2001, Kohima was further divided into Dimapur and Paren. Thus, the total number of districts in Nagaland came to nine with a total area of 16,579 sq.km.

The total area of Zunheboto district is 1255 sq.km. Total population of the district in 1971 was 47,093 and it increased to 61,161, i.e. 29.87 per cent in 1981 Census. There were only 7678 urban population in the district in 1981 and it increased to 14.94 per cent in 1991. The total population of Zunheboto district in 1991 Census was 96,218, out of which, 84,745 lived in the rural areas and 11,473 in Zunheboto town.

In 2001, there was a record increase of 61 per cent population growth in the district as compared to 32.68 per cent in 1981-1991 and 29.87 per cent in 1971-1981. The urban population increased to 19.81 per cent in 2001. There were nine circles in the district in 1981; two more circles were added in 1991. These two circles were Pughotobo and Ghathashi. Earlier, these circles were in Kohima district. At present, the district has eleven circles. These are Pughoboto, Ghathashi, Satakha, Zunheboto Sadar, Satoi, Atoizu, V.K., Akuluto, Suruhoto, Asuto and Aghunato.

As stated above that Zunheboto was one of the three sub-divisions of Mokokchung district till 1971. In 1973, whole of Zunheboto sub-division with 147 villages bifurcated from Mokokchung district and a new district was formed. Later on, eight villages were added. Thus, in 1981 the district had 155 villages and an urban area. In 1991, two more circles, namely Pughoboto and Aghunato with 29 villages were added in the district. Thus, the district had 184 villages in the district came to 187.

It is observed that more than 50 per cent population growth was recorded in three circles, namely Sotoi, Ghathashi and Pughoboto in 1991. In was recorded the highest growth of population of 60.90 per cent followed by Ghathashi with 56.59 per cent and Pughoboto with 56.03 per cent respectively. In Aghunato circle, the growth rate was 46.18 per cent and almost similar percentage of growth rate was recorded in Suruhoto, Asuto and Zunheboto Sadar circles with 26.73 per cent and 26 per cent respectively. Satakha circle recorded an increase of 19.99 per cent population growth in 1981-1991 while Atoizu, Akuluto and V.K. recorded 16.96 per cent, 9.71 per cent and 5.56 per cent respectively.

Maximum rural villages in the district have the popolation of 200 to 500. Such villages constitute 53.60 per cent of the total 184 inhabited villages. There are 47 inhabited villages which have the population at the ranges from 500 to 2000 constituing 25.99 per cent. There are villages which have the population less than 200. Such small sized villages constitute 15.34 per cent. Two villages have the population ranging from 2000 to 5000 constituting 1.07 per cent.

The entire rural population in the district is well served by drinking water facility. Tap, tank, well and river are the main sources of drinking water in all the villages. In some villages, the inhabitants get drinking water from the spring as well. It is observed that all the rural villages are having water within their reach.

As regards to education, all the villages under Ghathashi and Akuluto R.D. Blocks having schools. These two circles are served by cent-per-cent educational facility while 98.04 per cent of the total population is served by educational facility under Zunheboto R.D. Block and 93.58 per cent of the population under Tokiye R.D. Block are served by the educational facility. 98.14 per cent of the total rural population of the district are served by more primary schools, middle schools and few high schools. The residents of two villages in the district avail the educational facility from the nearby villages of five kilometre distance. Another two villages get the facility from the villages located at a distance of 5-10 kms. while 3 villages have the same facility from the neighbouring villages located at a distance of 19 and above kilometres.

Medical facility is better served to the population under Akuluto and Ghathashi R.D. Blocks with 88.39 and 79.33 per cent respectively. Zunheboto and Tokiye R.D. Blocks are served with 57.84 and 41.13 per cent medical facilities. Overall, 66.04 per cent of the rural population in the district is served by medical facility. Out of 187 villages, 131 do not have medical facility and the residents of 30 villiges avail it from the villages located at the minimum distance of less than 5 km. and the villagers of 42 villages avail the medical facility from the neighbouring villages located at a distance of 5-10 kms. There are 59 villages where medical facility is not available even within 5-10 kms. but the villagers have to cover above 10 kms. to avail the medical facility.

Out of 187 villages in the district market facility is not available to 179 villages. Only 7.97 per cent population of Ghathashi R.D. Block is served by the market facility. While 7.21 per cent rural people of Akuluto R.D. Block could avail the market facility. As a whole the rural population of the district has 3.65 per cent market facility.

Communication facility in the district is still poor in the rural areas of the district. Only 28.27 per cent of the rural population is served by bus service in the district. There are only few *pucca* roads in the district, so 25.33 per cent of the total population is served by *pucca* approach roads in the district. Among all the Rural Development Blocks, Akuloto has the highest *pucca* roads with 41.38 per cent. It is followed by Ghathashi with 24.90 per cent, Zunheboto with 21.57 per cent and Tokiye 12.07 per cent. From the above, it is observed that Akuloto R.D. Block has better road communication facility compared to other areas. As regards to communication facility, the residents of 21 villages avail the facility of bus from the places located at a reasonable distance of less than 5 km. While for 41 villages this facility is available at the distance of 5-10 kms. But the residents of 88 villages have to cover 10 km. and above to avail the bus facility. Considering the hilly terrain of the district covering 10 km. and above to avail any type of communication facility is a difficult task. Power supply is well served to the rural population in the district. All the population under Ghathashi and Akuluto R.D. Blocks are fully served by power supply while the population of Zunheboto and Tokiye R.D. Blocks are being served by the same facility with 95.62 per cent and 96.61 per cent respectively. The total of 90.94 per cent of rural population of the district is served by power supply in Zunheboto district.

Majority of the villages in the district are situated at a distance of 16 to 50 kms. away from an urban centre which comprises 43.65 per cent to total inhabited villages in Zunheboto district. 52 (28.73 per cent) villages are situated at a distance of 51 kms. and above while 13 (7.18 per cent) and 35 (19.34 per cent) villages are located at a distance ranges from 0-5 and 6-15 kms. respectively.

To sum up it can be said that the modern amenities like educational, drinking water and power supply facilities are well served in the villages situated far and near to the urban centre. The medical facility is available only to 50 villages in the district. Out of 50 (27.62 per cent) villages, 9 (42.86 per cent) villages of Ghathashi, 13 (22.81 per cent) villages of Zunheboto, 18 (33.96 per cent) of Akuluto and 10 (20.00 per cent) villages of Tokiye R.D. Blocks possess the medical facility. Communication facility is still inadequate in the rural areas of the district. Only 31 villages are connected by bus service in the whole district, which comprises 17.13 per cent of the total villages in the district.

Every village is approachable by *kutcha* roads and even by foot-paths. There are only 22 villages which are having *pucca* approach roads which comprises 12.15 per cent of the total villages in the district.

With the increased size of population the different amenities available to the rural population are found successively higher. It is found that educational, drinking water, communication and other amenities like market, approach by *pucca* road and even power supply are served better in the villages of population size of 500 to 2000 and 2000 to 5000 than the small villages of population below 500. There are 132 small size villages of population less than 500. Out of 132 villages 94.70 per cent of them have educational facility, 24.24 per cent of villages have medical facility, 15.15 per cent have communication, 6.82 per cent have approach by *pucca* roads and 94.70 per cent have power supply. 47 medium sized villages which have population of 500 to 2000 and 2 big sized villages which have their population from 2000 to 5000. There is no village in the district which has more than 5000 population.

It is observed that the decadal growth of population in the district has increased from 29.61 per cent in 1971-1981 to 32.68 per cent in 1981-1991 and it jumped to 61 per cent in 1991-2001. More than 50 per cent of the decadal growth of 1981-1991 and 1991-2001 was recorded in 3 circles, namely Satoi, the highest growth rate of 60 per cent followed by Ghathashi and Pughoboto with 56.89 per cent and 56.03 per cent respectively. These three circles are closer to Kohima and Mokokchung districts and are much more advance in respect of education, medical and other aspects.

Reference

Growth Trend of Population and its Characteristic Features in North Eastern Region. In *Population Poverty and Environment in North East India*. Ed. by B. Dattaray, H.K. Mazhari, P.M. Passah, M.C. Pandey. Concept Publishing Company, New Delhi.

25 Population Dynamics in Arunachal Pradesh

R.P. Bhattacharjee

Introduction

In ancient times, the system of Census prevailed in many countries such, as Egypt, Babylonia, India, China, Palestine and Rome. Five thousand years ago, the Sumerians counted their population for taxation purposes. In ancient Egypt, enquiries were made about the occupations of the people. India, during the reign of Emperor Ashoka (270 B.C. to 230 B.C.) Census, operations were often undertaken (IIPS, 1994).

In the ancient history of India, a few references about collection of population data include "*Arthashastra*" of Kautilya, the Prime Minister of Chandragupta Maurya (323-300 B.C.) and the *Ain-i-Akabari* of Abdul Fazl during the reign of Akbar (1542-1605). The first population census in modern India was held in the province of Madras during 1851-52. But due to Sepoy Mutiny during 1857, there was an intervention in the collection of population data through census. The census of North West Frontier Province had been taken on 10th January, 1865 by W.C. Plowden (Mitra, 1977). Perhaps the appointment of W.W. Hunter as Director-General of Statistical Survey in 1869 speeded up the process of population census in India. The first population census was held in our country during 1952.

Systematic census operation in Arunachal Pradesh started in 1961. But before that, under Assam Government's census operation, there was partial census of the then North East Frontier Tract. According to Census of India, 1951 (Vol.XII, Part-I-A), "Tribal areas of the North East Frontier Agency were omitted from regular census operations as in the past, excepting a small fractions of its area, viz. 1372 sq.miles"

(Bhattacharjee, 1993). We find population of Arunachal Pradesh from 1901-1951 as enumerated in the Mishmi Hills, Abor Hills, Tirap Frontier, Balipara Frontier Tract and Naga Tribal area (Census of India, 1951, Vol.XII). But these are of not much use to study population dynamics in this state.

Population Dynamics in the State

The composition of population under different censuses covering age, sex, race, nationality, religion, language, marital status, literacy, educational composition and occupation, birth rate, fertility, mortality, migration and social mobility highlights the basic issues of population dynamics. As data base in North-Eastern Region in general and Arunachal Pradesh in particular is very limited, we will rely on data available through census reports, NFHS, and other survey reports are available.

Arunachal Pradesh, being a tribal state, it is a matter of concern to all that the percentage of Scheduled Tribe is decreasing. We find in Table 25.1 that the ST population of Arunachal Pradesh was 88.67 per cent during 1961 and the population percentage decreased to 79.02 per cent during 1971. The ST population during 1981 and 1991 was 79.02 per cent and 63.66 per cent respectively. There is marginal increase of ST population share during 2001 which was 64.22 per cent. This can be attributed to opening up of the administration and economy to outside people after expansion of the administration and specially after shifting of Capital from Shillong to present Itanagar. The concentration of general category population is more in the districts of West Kameng, Papum Pare, East Siang,

Table 25.1: Size of Population in Arunachal Pradesh

Census	Total Population	ST Population	P.C. of ST
1961	336,558	298439	88.67
1971	467,511	369408	79.02
1981	631,839	441167	69.82
1991	864,558	550351	63.66
2001	1097,968	705158	64.22

Source : Census of India, Arunachal Pradesh, 1961, 1971, 1981, 1991 & 2001.

Lower Dibang Valley, Dibang Valley, Lohit and Changlang districts (2001). The state can boast now of having sufficient infrastructure like road, housing facility, water access and power availability. The increasing number of total population from 3,36,558 to 10,97,968 from 1961 to 2001 indicates a high growth rate of pupulation in the State. This is shown in Table 25.2. The growth rate of population

Table 25.2: Growth Rate of Population of Arunachal Pradesh

Census Decade	*Person*	*Male*	*Female*
1961-1971	38.91	41.40	36.13
1971-1981	35.15	35.06	35.25
1981-1991	36.83	37.04	36.59
1991-2001	27.00	24.72	29.65

Source: Census of India, Arunachal Pradesh, 1961, 1971, 1981, 1991 & 2001.

during 1961-1971 was 38.91 per cent per decade which decreased to 35.15 per cent during 1971-1981 but was marginally high at 36.83 per cent during 1981-1991. The population growth substantially decreased to 27.00 per cent during 1991-2001. This can be attributed to the reservation policy of the State Government in employment increasing the number of indigenous population in both public and private jobs in the State. Similar to the total population of the State, the growth rate of male and female population also declined. Another reason of decline of population growth is the expansion of education, increase in literacy and increase in enrolment ratio in schools. These are shown in Tables 25.3 and 25.4. The literacy rate in Arunachal

Table 25. 3: Literacy rate in Arunachal Pradesh

Census Year	*Arunachal Pradesh*	*All-India*
1961	7.13	28.30
1971	11.29	34.45
1981	25.55	43.57
1991	41.59	52.21
2001	54.34	64.84

Note: Literacy for 1961 & 1971 is of age five and above while during 1981, 1991 and 2001, it is age seven and above.

*Source:-*Economic Survey, 2006-2007, GOI, P-S-114.

Table 25.4 : Gross Enrolment Ratio in Arunachal Pradesh, Classes I-VIII, (6-14 years)

State	*Total*	*Boys*	*Girls*
Arunachal Pradesh	106.70	113.47	99.63
All-India	94.23	97.56	90.61

Source: Economic Survey, 2006-07, GOI, P-S-112.

Pradesh was only 7.13 per cent during 1961 but after four decades of adiministrative expansion, the literacy has increased to 54.34 per cent during 2001. The growth of literacy in the State is high compared to all-India growth rate. The enrolment ratio of school going children from Class-I to Class VIII (6-14 years) is also very high as 106.70 per cent during 2004-05 compared to national enrolment ratio of 94.23. Similarly the enrolment of boys and girls was also high. This shows an increasing interest in human resource development in the State. The decrease in population is also due to decrease in birth rate and death rate. The birth rate in the State was 30.9 during 1991 and this has decreased to 22.2 during 2001. Similarly, the death rate was 13.5 during 1991 and this too decreased to 5.7 during 2001 (NEC, 2006). This changes in birth rate and death rate show that the natural growth of population in the State was less during the period.

The health condition has improved in the State as we find in one of the most important indicators of health development, i.e. Infant Mortality Rate (IMR). In the State, IMR was 126 (Person) during 1961 which has decreased to 34 during 2003 and 37 during 2005 (Economic Survey). Similarly, the IMR of male decreased from 141 to 29 and female IMR from 111 to 46 during the period of 1961 and 2005. There is marginal increase in IMR for females from 38 to 46 during 2003 and 2005 (Table 25.5). The IMR was 77 in this State during 2002 (APHDR, 2005).

Table 25.5 : Infant Mortality Rate (IMR) in Arunachal Pradesh

Years	*Person*	*Male*	*Female*
1961	126 (125)	141 (122)	111 (108)
2003	34 (60)	31 (57)	38 (64)
2005	37 (58)	29(56)	46 (61)

Note : Figures in brackets is of all-India.
Source: RGI. as cited in Economic Survey, 2006-2007, GoI, P-S-115.

Life expectancy is another health indicator. Life expectancy at birth has not increased substantially in this State. There is no data available on life expectancy except the estimate of the author as being 54.4 based on 1987-88 data (Bhattacharjee, 2000) and Arunachal Pradesh Human Development Report, 2005 where life expectancy is estimated as 54.05 (2001). The life expectancy, as per APHDR, was higher to state average in the districts of Lower Subansiri, Changlang, Lohit, Lower Dibang Valley, East Siang, and Papum Pare. The life expectancy for the period 1999-2003 for all-India is 62.7 and for Assam, it is 58.0 (Economic Survey, 2006-2007, P-S-111). The low life expectancy in the State on the other hand shows that the health condition of the citizens is yet to improve. In fact, there is no effort to study such data in the State. Even the existing higher educational institutes do not have any course on population or demography. However, the increasing proportion of ageing indicates that life expectancy is increasing slowly. The ageing of population is another factor which needs proper plans and programmes. Old age home and health care facilities for the aged are required in the State as 4.65 per cent of population are in the age-group 60+ as per 2001 population census. According to NFHS-1, there was 2.2 per cent of population in the age group of 60-64 and 2.6 per cent of population 65+(Total 4.8% of 60+ age) while as per NFHS-2, the percentage of aged population were 2.0 per cent and 3.1 per cent respectively. These are shown in Table 25.6 and Table 25.7. Compratively, ageing problem is less in Arunachal Pradesh with reference to other NE States.

Table 25.6 : Percentage Distribution of Ageing Population (1992-93)—a study of NER

States	*Age Group*	
	60-64	*65+*
Arunachal Pradesh	2.2 (4)	2.6 (5)
Assam	2.3 (3)	3.6 (3)
Manipur	2.7 (2)	4.1 (2)
Meghalaya	1.6 (6)	2.0 (6)
Mizoram	1.7 (5)	3.3 (4)
Nagaland	1.1 (7)	1.2 (7)
Tripura	2.9 (1)	5.5 (1)
India	3.0	4.8

Source: NFHS-1, 1992-93, Introductory Report, IIPS. Mumbai, P-16.

Table 25.7: Percentage Distribution of Ageing Population (1998-99) of six NE States

States	*Age Structure*	
	60-64	*65+*
Arunachal Pradesh	2.0 (6)	3.1 (6)
Manipur	2.4 (2)	4.7 (2)
Meghalaya	2.1 (4)	3.4 (5)
Mizoram	2.3 (3)	4.3 (4)
Nagaland	2.1 (4)	4.4 (3)
Tripura	2.5 (1)	5.2 (1)

Source: NFHS-2, 1998-99, P-18, IIPS, Mumbai.

Urbanization is another factor for change in the life-style of the people in this State. The improvement in educational and health facility inspires the populace to migrate to urban areas including State capital and district headquarters. We find that percentage of urban population is increasing in the State. The percentage of urban population was 3.79 per cent during 1971 but this has increased to 6.56 per cent during 1981, 12.14 per cent during 1991 and 20.75 per cent during 2001 (Table 25.8). This State has 227,881 urbanites out of total population of 10,97,968 (2001). The growth rate of urban population was 139.63 per cent during 1971-1981 and 153.39 per cent during 1981-1991 while it was 117.09 per cent during 1991-2001. This is remarkable. But this is also due to increase in administrative towns and declaration of more census towns in the State. During 1971, there were only 4 towns, namely Pasighat, Bomdila, Aalo (new name of Along) and Tezu. During 1981, Naharlogun and Itanagar were added as census towns as twin capital

Table 25.8 : Urbanisation in Arunachal Pradesh

Census Year	*Urban Population*	*Percentage of Urban Population*	*Growth Rate of Urban Population*
1971	17,288	3.79	-
1981	41,428	6.56	139.63
1991	104,973	12.14	153.39
2001	227,881	20.75	117.09

Source : Census of India, Arunachal Pradesh, 1961, 1971, 1981, 1991, and 2001.

towns of the State. Four more administrative centres at district level were declared as towns during 1991. These are Ziro, Khonsa, Namshai and Roing (Table 25.9). And during the last population census (2001), seven more administrative centres were declared as town. These are Tawang, Seppa, Daporijo, Basar, Changlang, Jairampur and Deomali. Thus urbanization in the State is mainly due to expansion of administration. There is negligible impact of industrialization in the State.

Table 25.9 : Population of all Towns in Arunachal Pradesh

Towns	*1971*	*1981*	*1991*	*2001*
1. Pasighat	5116	9139	14639	21965
2. Bomdila	3172	3860	5655	6693
3. Aolo	4818	8074	13239	17033
4. Tezu	4182	6239	15271	15015
5. Naharlogun	–	7710	14369	27020
6. Itanagar	–	6406	16545	35022
7. Ziro	–	–	8862	12384
8. Khonsa	–	–	7079	9233
9. Namshai	–	–	7975	11747
10. Roing	–	–	6976	8376
11. Tawang	–	–	–	8376
12. Seppa	–	–	–	15002
13. Daporijo	–	–	–	15756
14. Basar	–	–	–	4079
15. Changlang	–	–	–	6469
16. Jairampur	–	–	–	5919
17. Deomali	–	–	–	6061

Source : Census of India, Arunachal Pradesh, 1971, 1981, 1991 and 2001.

The density of the State is very low. It was 4 during 1961, 6 during 1971, 8 during 1981, 10 during 1991 and only 13 during 2001. It may be mentioned that density of the State is lowest in the country (Table 25.10). Only Mizoram (42), Andaman & Nicobar Island (43) and Sikkim (76) have density less than 100 in the country during 2001. This thinly population hinders the plans and programmes as the social overhead cost is very high because of scattered population in the State.

The respect for women is very high among the autochthors. The sex-ratio of the State (Table 25.11) was 894 during 1961 and almost constant during 2001 as 893. The sex-ratio among the ST is

Table 25.10 : Density in Arunachal Pradesh

Census Year	*Density (Person per sq.km.)*
1961	4
1971	6
1981	8
1991	10
2001	13

Source : Census of India, Arunachal Pradesh, 1961, 1971, 1981, 1991 and 2001.

Table 25.11 : Sex-Ratio in Arunachal Pradesh

Census	*Sex-Ratio of Total Population*	*Sex-Ratio of ST Population*
1961	984	1013
1971	861	1007
1981	862	1004
1991	859	998
2001	893	1003

Source : Census of India, Arunachal Pradesh, 1961, 1971, 1981, 1991 and 2001.

very high as it was 1013 during 1961 and remained 1003 during 2001. It indicates that there is no discrimination towards female birth among the indigenous people. The variation in sex-ratio can be attributed to floating population of the State who come for employment and trade or other services leaving behind the family in the home state.

The female population in politics is also increasing in the State. During last Punchayat Election (as on 1st April, 2003), the representation of women in Zilla Parishad was 33 per cent, in Anchal Samiti, it was 35 per cent and in Gram Panchayat, it was 39 per cent (Bhattacharjee, 2006). It may be mentioned that 33 per cent reservation for the women was statutory. However, it is a good indicator of women's empowerment and this will reduce population pressure on the society. Similarly, the turn out of women voters to a large extent is a part of women empowerment. During last two Lok Sabha elections, 76.3 per cent (1999) and 55.2 per cent (2004) was female turn-out compared to 69.11 per cent (1999) and 56.7 per cent (2004) of male turn-out respectively (Despande, 2004).

We found earlier that literacy has increased in the state during four decades along with increase in enrolment. This is perhaps the reason why Work Participation Rate (WPR) has decreased (Table 25.12). The WPR during 1971 was 57.65 per cent which declined to only 43.92 per cent during 2001. This is due to different baskets of option to the household and keenness of the children for education.

Table 25.12 : Workers Participation Rate (WPR) in Arunachal Pradesh

Census Year	*WPR (%) in Arunachal Pradesh*
1971	57.65
1981	52.63
1991	46.24
2001	43.92

Source : Census of India, Arunanchal Pradesh, 1971, 1981, 1991 and 2001.

The most remarkable population dynamics of Arunachal Pradesh is the transition of religious faith in the State. The State had 21.99 per cent of population as Hindus during 1971 and this has increased to 34.60 per cent during 2001 (Table 25.13). Similarly, the Christian population has increased from 0.79 per cent (1971) to 18.72 per cent (2001). The population of Buddhists had remained almost constant from 13.13 per cent (1971) to 13.03 per cent (2001). No significance difference is observed in other religious faiths including negligible Jains and Sikhs in the State. It is said that loss of culture is loss of identity. It is the society to ponder whether there is loss of any identity in the State. The ST population is at the brink of such a situation

Table 25.13 : Population by Religion (%) in Arunanchal Pradesh

Particulars	1971	1981	1991	2001
1. Hindus	21.99	29.24	37.04	34.60
2. Buddhists	13.13	13.69	12.88	13.03
3. Christians	0.79	4.32	10.29	18.72
4. Muslims	0.18	0.80	1.38	1.88
5. Sikhs, Jains, others & religion not stated.	63.91	51.95	38.41	31.77

Sources : (i) Census of India, Arunachal Pradesh, 1971, 1981, 1991 and 2001
(ii) Bhattacharjee (2000), P-60-61.

Secretary, Social Science Research Institute of Arunanchal Pradesh, Itanagar.

especially after embracement of various other religions. It may be mentioned that the per cent of Muslim population in the State was only 0.18 per cent during 1971 but this has increased to 1.88 per cent during 2001. There was no indigenous Muslim population earlier but it is reported that there is now one such organization in existence (*The Arunachal Pradesh Times* dated. 13.4.2007).

Immigration is another issue of population dynamics. The migrants to Arunachal Pradesh were 6008 during 1951 while it was 22, 849 during 1991. There has been some impact of socio-economic condition and assimilation in the State. There is migration from other States too and they are largely from Bihar as 45.60 per cent (1951) and 39.14 per cent (1991) (Bandyopadhyay & Chakraborty, 1999). The intra-regional migration in Arunachal Pradesh is mainly from the State of Assam as we find that 89.7 per cent of intra-regional migrants were from Assam during 1951 and 94.08 per cent during 1991. The reason for out migration in this State during 1991 is employment (27.76%), business (3.42%), education (1.76%), family moved (28.95%), marriage (10.65%) and other reasons (27.47%).

The reason for migration from other States of India to this State was employment (36.04%), business (11.11%), education (2.51%) 'family moved' (32.49%), marriage (9.31%), natural calamities (0.26%) and other reasons (8.28%). The reason for intra-regional migration is mainly for employment, 'family moved' and marriage. The migration in the State has not had much impact yet as it has not disturbed social, economic, cultural and political domain of the people. The only disturbing issue is the settlement of the Chakmas, the Hajongs and the Tibetans. This conflict resolution is required once and for all for speedy socio-economic development of the State.

Conclusion

The developmental programme started by the Government of India in the post-Independence period brought into being the forces of dynamism in the socio-economic and cultural realms of Arunachal Society. The thin population in a ridged geographical condition retarded the developmental efforts specially without any basic infrastructure.

The low density of population in this State increases the over-head cost for each plan and programme and as a result the benefit of each programme is not reaching the people at a grassroots level. The Centrally Sponsored Schemes (CSS) are based on population and as the population is very thin and scattered; the benefit of each dose of investment is not reaching the masses as it should be. The growth rate of the State's Gross State Domestic Product (GSDP) during 9th Plan was 3.8 per cent at 1993-94 prices and 6.0 per cent during first 4 years of 10th Plan at 1999-2000 prices (DES, AP).

The Growth rate in this State is not inclusive. The average growth rate of agriculture and allied services was 1.8 per cent from 1999-2006 while industry and allied services had a growth rate of 8.5 per cent during the same period, and contribution of construction being predominant in industry and allied sector. The growth rate of service sector during the same period was 7.1 per cent based on 1999-2000 prices. Thus economic growth in this state is not inclusive and low density of population is a hindrance to agricultural development considering the ridged topography of the state. The relocation of population is a better approach to have a high growth rate and development especially human development for each plan and programme. Poverty among the populace is a major obstacle as we find that he poverty level in the State has increased to 65 per cent as per 10th Plan BPL estimate conducted by the RD Department compared to 54 per cent of 9th Plan.

References

IIPS (1994): "Population Dynamics-I", Reading Material of MPS-02, p-19.

Mitra, Asok (1977): "The Census of India—Past and Future", in "*Population Statistics in India*" ed. by Ashish Bose, *et el.*, Vikas Publishing House Pvt.Ltd., New Delhi, p. 9-11.

Battacharjee, R.P. (1993); "Population Trend in Arunachal Pradesh, Reading Material on Population Education, series-VII," NEHU, Shillong, pp, 79-94.

Census of India, 1951, Vol. XII, Assam, Manipur and Tripura, Part-II-A, Shillong, 1953, pp, 6-10.

Directorate of Economics and Statistics, Government of Arunachal Pradesh, "Statistical Abstract of Arunachal Pradesh, 2005", Itanagar, p. 5.

Bhattacharjee, Dr. R.P. (2000): "*Economic Development of Arunachal Pradesh*", Himalayan Publisher, Delhi, Itanagar, pp. 59-61.

"GoI, Economic Survey, 2006-2007", New Delhi, pp. S-112-S-114.

Dept. of Planning, Govt. of Arunachal Pradesh, "Arunachal Pradesh Human Development Report, 2005" (2006).

International Insititute of Population Science (IIPS), National Family Health Survey-1, 1992-93, p. 16 and National Family Health Survey-2, 1998-99, p.18, Mumbai.

The Arunachal Times dt. 13.4.2007.

Census of India, Arunachal Pradesh, 1961, 1971, 1981, 1991 and 2001 (all issues).

Census of India, Arunachal Pradesh, Shillong "A Bird's eyeview of census of Arunachal Pradesh, 2001".

Bandyopadhyay, Sabari and Chakraborty, Debesh (1999): "Migration in the North-Eastern Region of India during 1901-1991: Size, Trends, Reasons and Impact" in *Demography India* Vol.28, No.1 (January-June, 1999), pp. 75-97.

Directorate of Economics and Statistics, "Reports of SDP from 1999-2000 to 2005-2006", Arunachal Pradesh, Itanagar.

Bhattacharjee, Dr.R.P.(2006) "Globalisation and its impact on women population of Arunachal Pradesh" in *SIRD-ARUN* (Annual Journal of Rural Development), Vol. I, June, 2006, p. 40.

Despande, Rajeshwari (2004): "How Gendered was women's participation in election 2004?", *EPW*, Vol.XXXIX, No.51, p. 5432.

NEC-2006, "Basic Statistics of NER, 2006", Shillong-3, pp. 166-67.

26 Demographic Profile of Arunachal Pradesh

Surojit Sen Gupta

Arunachal Pradesh earlier known as NEFA (North–East Frontier Agency) is situated on the North East extremity of India with an area of 83,743 sq. km. and has a long international border with Bhutan to the West (160 kms), China to the North and North–east east (1030 Kms.) and Myammar to East (440 Kms.). The State is bounded on the North, North-East and North-West by China (Tibet), on the South by Assam and Nagaland, on the South–east by Myanmar (Burma) and on the West by Bhutan. Arunachal Pradesh lies roughly between the latitudes 26° 28'N and 29° 30'N and the longitudes 91° 3'E and 97° 30'E on the easternmost corner of India. Arunachal Pradesh is broadly divided into two halves—east and west—by a mighty river Tsangpo, as it is called in Tibet and Siang or Dihang in Arunachal, which becomes Brahmaputra after it is joined by Dibang and Lohit in the Assam plains. The area is full of valleys, large and small, ridges and mountains rising up to 22,000 ft.

Before the coming of the British the people of Arunachal Pradesh were known for having relationship with the neighbouring people of Assam plains. The Ahom kings preferred to maintain friendly ties with them. British penetration into the North-East Frontier Areas started right from 1826 when the Burmese authority surrendered all claims upon Assam and its dependencies. The extension of British authority towards the peripheries of Assam plains was gradual and in a sense these areas were brought under British administration not before 1875.

British followed a policy of isolating the hill people from the plains. They were separated by a line called inner line prescribed under the Bengal Eastern Frontier Regulation (Regulation V of 1873). In the 1880 these areas and the people thereof were brought under Assam Frontier Tract Regulation (Regulation II of 1880) whereby Acts in operation in the plains were decided to be suspended for these areas.

In 1914 these hill areas were totally separated from the plains and North East Frontier Tract was formed. Under the Government of India Act, 1919 Section 52A(2) these same areas were named as Backward Tracts to be renamed again as Excluded Areas under Government of India Act, 1935.

In 1950 under the Constitution of India these areas were rechristened as Tribal Areas. In 1954 North East Frontier Agency (NEPA) was born and on Junuary 21st, 1972 these areas were upgraded to a Union Territory under Section 7 of North Eastern Areas (Reorganisation) Act, 1971 and named as Arunachal Pradesh. In 1987 Arunachal Pradesh become a full-fledged state with Itanagar its Capital.

Arunachal Pradesh consisted of five districts till 1980. Thereafter four more districts were added after passing of the Arunachal Pradesh Reoraganisation of Districts Act, 1980 by carving the areas of Kameng, Subansiri, Siang and Lohit districts. But Tirap district remained unaffected by the Reorganisation Act. In 1984, two new districts Tawang and Changlang were created by carving out West Kameng and Tirap districts. Till 1991 Census there were eleven districts in the State. These are Tawang, West Kameng, East Kameng, Lower Subansiri, Upper Subansiri, West Siang, East Siang, Dibang Valley, Lohit, Changlang and Tirap. It was in 1992, Papum Pare district was carved out circles from Lower Subansiri district and again in 1994, another district Upper Siang was formed, thereby increasing the number of districts to thirteen, in the State by 2001 Census.

Growth Trend of Population in Arunachal Pradesh

Arunachal Pradesh has registered the growth rate of population by 26.21 per cent during the last decade 1991–2001 as compared to 36.83 per cent in 1981–1991. This indicates that the growth rate has gone down as compared to the previous decade. Compared to the national growth rate of 21.34 per cent this rate seems to be on higher side. However, the highest growth rate of 67.21 per cent is shown by Papum Pare district where the State Capital is located. This is followed by Dibang Valley with 33.61 per cent, West Kameng 32.21 per cent, Changlang 30.84 per cent and Lohit 30.78 per cent. The lowest growth rate of 9.80 per cent is found in Upper Subansiri district. Tawang, West Kameng and East Kameng have shown lower growth rates, which can be seen from Table 26.1 below:

Table 26.1 : Population Distribution, Percentage Decadal Growth Rate, Sex-ratio and Population Density

Sl. No.	*State/Districts*	*Population 2001*			*Percentage Decadal Growth Rate*		*Sex-ratio (Number of Females per 1000 Males*		*Population Density per sq. km.*	
		Person	*Male*	*Female*	*1981–1991*	*1991–2001*	*1991*	*2001*	*1991*	*2001*
	Arunachal Pradesh	1091117	573951	517166	+ 36.83	+ 26.21	859	901	10	13
1.	Tawang	34705	17676	17029	+ 30.15	+ 22.69	844	963	13	16
2.	West Kameng	74595	42638	31957	+ 35.74	+ 32.21	822	749	8	10
3.	East Kameng	57065	28743	28322	+ 17.92	+ 13.24	962	985	12	14
4.	Papum Pare	121750	64122	57628	+ 83.24	+ 67.21	831	899	21	35
5.	Lower Subansiri	97614	49184	48430	+ 14.06	+ 17.37	957	985	9	10
6.	Upper Subansiri	54995	27873	27122	+ 27.09	+ 9.80	867	973	7	8
7.	West Siang	103575	54139	49436	+ 31.64	+ 15.17	873	913	11	13
8.	East Siang	87430	45131	42299	+ 30.26	+ 21.66	877	937	18	22
9.	Upper Siang	33146	17844	15302	+ 31.50	+ 19.32	822	858	4	5
10.	Dibang Valley	57543	31280	26263	+ 39.03	+ 33.61	788	840	3	4
11.	Lohit	143478	77252	66226	+ 57.85	+ 30.78	797	857	10	13
12.	Changlang	124994	65608	59386	+ 53.56	+ 30.84	863	905	20	27
13.	Tirap	100227	52461	47766	+ 28.70	+ 17.21	862	911	36	42

Source: Census of India.

The population density per sq.km. of the State is only 13 as against 10 in 1991 Census. The highest population density is recorded as 42 in Tirap district and the lowest being 4 in Dibang Valley District. The ranking of districts according to population density of 2001 is same as that of the 1991 Census, which can be seen from Table 26.2 below:

Table 26.2 : Ranking of Districts by Population Size in 1991 and 2001

Rank in 2001	*Districts*	*Percentage to*		*Percentage to*		*Rank in 1991*
		Population 2001	*Total Population of the State 2001*	*Population 1991*	*Total Population of the State 1991*	
1.	Lohit	143478	13.15	109706	12.69	1
2.	Changlang	124994	11.45	95530	11.05	2
3.	Papum Pare	121750	11.16	72811	8.42	6
4.	West Siang	103575	9.49	89936	10.40	3
5.	Tirap	100227	9.19	85508	9.89	4
6.	Lower Subansiri	97614	8.95	83167	9.62	5
7.	East Siang	87430	8.01	71864	8.31	7
8.	West Kameng	74595	6.84	56421	6.53	8
9.	Dibang Valley	57543	5.27	43068	4.98	8
10.	East Kameng	57065	5.23	50395	5.83	11
11.	Upper Subansiri	54995	5.04	50086	5.80	10
12.	Tawang	34705	3.18	28287	3.27	12
13.	Upper Siang	33146	3.04	27779	3.21	13

Source : Census of India.

The 2001 Census revealed a population of 1,091,117 persons in Arunachal Pradesh. Out of which 573,951 are males and 517,166 are females. The distribution of rural-urban population shows that 868,429 persons live in rural areas, out of which 453,560 are males and 414,869 are females. In urban areas 120,391 are males and 102,297 are females. Percentage of urban population comes to 20.41per cent. The highest number of 143,478 persons, is found in the Lohit district, followed by 124,994 persons in Changlang, 121,750 persons in Papum Pare, 103,575 persons in West Siang and 100,227 persons in Tirap. The lowest populated district of the State is Upper Siang with 33,146 persons only. Districts-wise share of urban population is highest in Papum Pare district where 50.83 per cent of the District population live in urban areas comprising the Capital Itanagar and Naharlagun.

Sex-Ratio

From (Table 26.3) above it can be seen that, in the State of Arunachal Pradesh sex-ratio in 2001 Census has been 901 in total, 915 in rural and 850 in urban areas as against 859 in total, 880 in rural and 728 in urban in the last Census of 1991. Among the districts, the highest sex-ratio of 985 was recorded by East Kameng and Lower Subansiri districts, followed by 973 in Upper Subansiri, 963 in Tawang, 937 in East Siang, 913 in West Siang, 911 in Tirap and Changlang with 905 females per 1000 males. The lowest sex-ratio of 749 is shown by West Kameng. In rural areas, the highest sex-ratio 1019 was recorded in East Kameng and the lowest 740 in West Kameng. Urban sex-ratio 950 was seen in West Kameng and the lowest 762 in Dibang Valley. The lowest sex-ratio of 513 has been recorded in Sinchung Circle of West Kameng district. The lowest sex-ratio of 788 in Dibang Valley district of 1991 Census has improved in 2001 Census. While looking at the sex-ratio of child population in the age group 0-6, Upper Siang and East Kameng show balanced sex-ratio of 1018 and 1011 females per 1000 males respectively, as against the State sex-ratio of 961.

Literacy Rates

The percentage of literates in the State of Arunachal Pradesh is 54.74 per cent out of this 64.07 per cent are males and 44.24 per cent are females. From the above (Table 26.4) it can be seen that in Arunachal Pradesh out of thirteen districts, the highest percentage of literates is in Papum Pare with 70.89 per cent, followed by 61.67 per cent by West Kameng, 61.22 per cent by East Siang, 60.31 per cent by West Siang and the lowest percentage of literates is shown by East Kameng with 40.89 per cent. Six districts have registered percentage of literates above the State average of 54.74 per cent and seven districts are below the State average. Among the circles, the highest percentage of literacy

Table 26.3 : Sex-Ratio since 1901 for State and Districts

Sl. No.	State/Districts	Sex-Ratio (Number of Females per 1000 Males)										
		1901	1911	1921	1931	1941	1951	1961	1971	1981	1991	2001
	Arunachal Pradesh							894	861	862	859	901
1.	Tawang							884	853	905	844	963
2.	West Kameng							586	661	834	822	749
3.	East Kameng							1017	930	943	962	985
4.	Papum Pare							832	909	754	831	899
5.	Lower Subansiri	Data not available						967	949	965	957	985
6.	Upper Subansiri							982	953	972	867	973
7.	West Siang							870	850	913	873	913
8.	East Siang							963	863	833	877	937
9.	Upper Siang							879	872	907	822	858
10.	Dibang Valley							999	806	661	788	840
11.	Lohit							854	762	781	797	857
12.	Changlang							918	855	833	863	905
13.	Tirap							961	903	899	862	911

Source : Census of India.

Table 26.4 : Population in the Age Group of 0–6, Number of Literates and Literacy Rate for State and Districts

Sl. No.	State/Districts	Total Population			Population in Age Group 0-6			Number of Literates			Literacy Rate		
		Persons	Males	Females	Persons	Males	Females	Persons	Males	Females	Persons	Males	Females
	Arunachal Pradesh	1091117	573951	517166	200055	102010	98045	487796	302371	185425	54.74	64.07	44.24
1.	Tawang	34705	17676	17029	6535	3340	3195	11589	7318	4271	41.14	51.05	30.87
2.	West Kameng	74595	42638	31957	12181	6221	5960	38488	25864	12624	61.67	71.02	48.56
3.	East Kameng	57065	28743	28322	11702	5819	5883	18548	12072	6476	40.89	52.66	28.86
4.	Papum Pare	121750	64122	57628	20160	10195	9965	72021	42602	29419	70.89	79.00	61.72
5.	Lower Subansiri	97614	49184	48430	17582	8809	8773	36025	21673	14352	45.01	53.68	36.19
6.	Upper Subansiri	54995	27873	27122	10543	5307	5236	22623	13270	9353	50.89	58.81	42.74
7.	West Siang	103575	54139	49436	17329	8913	8416	52015	30176	21839	60.31	66.72	53.24
8.	East Siang	87430	45131	42299	15243	7780	7463	44196	25779	18417	61.22	69.02	152.87
9.	Upper Siang	33146	17844	15302	6223	3084	3139	13409	8655	4754	49.80	58.64	39.09
10.	Dibang Valley	57543	31280	26263	10221	5251	4970	28131	17706	10425	59.45	68.02	48.96
11.	Lohit	143478	77252	66226	27686	14338	13348	64899	41323	23576	56.06	65.68	44.59
12.	Changlang	124994	65608	59386	24733	12691	12042	52116	33248	18868	51.98	62.83	39.85
13.	Tirap	100227	52461	47766	19917	10262	9655	33736	22686	11051	42.01	53.76	29.00

Source : Census of India.

is recorded by Naharlagun circle with 79.29 per cent literates and the lowest of 7.63 per cent by Manchal Circle under Lohit district. In rural areas, the highest literacy percentage is shown by Naharlagun Circle of Papum Pare district with 76.25 per cent and the lowest literacy per cent by Manchal Circle. Among the Seventeen Census Towns, Khonsa town with 86.73 per cent emerge as the highest literate town in the State and Seppa with 67.72 per cent is regarded as the lowest literate town.

Trends of Urbanization in Arunachal Pradesh

Till 1961 Census the State of Arunachal Pradesh was entirely rural. From 1971 Census only, urban centres came into being after the declaration of Bomdila, Along, Pasighat and Tezu as Census Towns. Two more towns, that is Naharlagun and Itanagar were added to the previous list increasing the urban areas to six in 1981. Ziro, Roing, Namsai and Khonsa were added to the earlier list raising the Towns to ten in 1991. In 2001 Census, seven more areas were added to the Town list. These are Tawang, Seppa, Daporijo, Basar, Changlang, Jairampur and Deomali. All the seventeen towns of the State taken together form 20.41 per cent of the State population in 2001.

There is no notified town in the State of Arunachal Pradesh. There are only seventeen census towns in the State. Based on the size, population, cities and towns in census are divided in six size classes. Arunachal Pradesh is without any Class I or Class II cities having no Towns with population of 1 lakh and above or 50,000 and above. Itanagar, Naharlagun and Pasighat Towns fall in the category of Class III having population in the range of 20,000–49,999. Along, Daporijo, Tezu, Seppa, Ziro, Namsai and Roing fall in the size class of category IV with population ranging between 10,000–19,999. Khonsa, Bomdila, Changlang, Deomali and Jairampur towns are categorised in Class V with population ranging between 5,000–9,999. The last category of Class VI has only two towns Tawang and Basar with less than 5,000 population.

Conclusion

From the above analysis it can be seen that the State is thinly and sparsely populated, but population growth whether positive or negative have considerable impact on the demographic and socio-economic attributes of the people in the State.

References

Datta, P.S. (1993), in Sinha, A.C. (ed)., *Hill Cities of Eastern Himalayas,* Indus Publishing Company, New Delhi.

Ganguly, J.B. (1995), *Urbanization and Development in North East India,* Deep and Deep Publications, New Delhi.

Census of India, 2001, Series 13, Arunachal Pradesh, Part–I and II.

Das, G. (1995) in Ganguly, J.B.

Mitra, A. (1995), in Ganguly, J.B.

27 Population Growth in Manipur
A Demographer's View

Elangbam Nixon Singh and *G.P. Prasain*

Introduction

Demography is a term derived from the two Greek words, Oñuog, the people, and Ýpáø€w, to draw or write. This term was first used by Guillard in 1855 and nowadays it denotes the study of human population by statistical methods. This involves primarily a measurement of the size and growth or diminution of the number of people. The change in the number of population arises from births, deaths, and migration and demographers analyze the related functions of fertility, mortality and population transfer. Intense public interest is expressed in the prospects for the future development of the population, and the demographic study can lead to some sort of forecast for, or projection into, the years to come, although it is well known that estimates made in the past have not so far been accurately borne out in the event.

Manipur is situated in the strategic North Eastern most border of India. It is bounded on the north by Nagaland, on the east by Myanmar, on the south by Mizoram and on the west by Assam. The State is located in a rectangular shape between 23.80°N and 25.68°N latitudes and 93.03°E and 94.78°E longitudes. The geographical area of the state is 22,327 sq. km. Basically, it can be divided as hill and valley. The hill region covers nine tenth of the area. Here, it is worthwhile to mention that information regarding the total land utilization of the entire state cannot be obtained since land records are available only for the valley and a small part of the hill areas. Due to the rapid growth population in the state, acute pressure is on the valley area where all the people belonging to different ethnic groups use to settle and concentrate with high density. On the hand, the region accounting for 90.00 per cent of the total land area of the state is only meant for the scheduled tribes and is sparsely populated.

The valley has reached a stage of population explosion. The density in the valley consisting of four districts has been 631 persons per sq. km as against 44 persons per sq. km. in the hill region (2001 Census). The general opinion is that Manipur Land Revenue and Land Reforms Act, 1960 should be extended to the whole of the State for proper utilization of land areas of the State. At the same time, the population of the state is composed of different religious communities like Hindus, Muslims, Christians, Sikhs, Jains, Buddhists etc. Though the majority Hindus constitute 60.00 per cent of the population, 34.00 per cent are Christians. The third majority community is the Muslims (locally known as Meitei Pangals). It is also very interesting to know that a sizeable number of persons who have faith in the tradition Meitei religion (better known as "Sanamahi") are recorded recently in the category of "other religions".

Economically, Manipur is a backward state. It is characterized by the absence of any medium and large scale industries and predominance of backward agricultural practice and allied activities accompanied by large scale shifting cultivation especially in the hill regions.

Objectives of the Paper

The present study is purely based on the census data, prepared from time to time. In fact, the First Census count in India was found to be partially conducted in 1872[1] by covering only a limited area though it was considered to be the foundation of the history of population census in the country. Then, the Second Census was conducted in 1881 covering wider areas and since then regular and periodical population census of the country are found to have been conducted every ten years. It can be pointed out that the population of Manipur was recorded as only 2,21,070 persons in 1881. Then in the year 1891, the princely State was annexed by the British. Later, the population of Manipur was recorded as 2,84,465 persons with an addition of only 63,395 persons in twenty years (1881–1901). But one of the important feature of the trend of population growth is that during the period 1901 to 1951, the population of Manipur reached 5,77,635 persons with a net addition of 2,93,170 persons during the period of 50 years. In other words, it took 50 years to complete a little more than double of the population of 1901.

In this paper, an attempt has been made to analyze the growth of population in Manipur during 1951 and 2001 with the possible effects on the economy of the state.

Growth of Population in the North Eastern States

First of all, the growth of population in the entire North Eastern States of India may be observed to make a comparative study. Table 27.1 shows that Arunachal Pradesh has more or less identical population growth, even though the first Census started in 1961 in

Table 27.1 : Decadal Growth of Population of North Eastern States of India (1951– 2001)

States	*1951*	*1961*	*1971*	*1981*	*1991*	*2001*
Arunachal Pradesh		336558	467511	631839	864558	1097968
			(38.91)	(35.15)	(36.87)	(27.00)
Assam	8028856	10837329	14625152	18041248	22414322	26655528
	(19.93)	(34.98)	(34.95)	(36.05)	(12.65)	(18.92)
Meghalaya	605674	769380	1011699	1335819	1774778	2318822
	(8.97)	(27.03)	(31.50)	(32.50)	(32.86)	(30.65)
Mizoram	196202	266063	332390	493757	689756	888573
	(28.42)	(35.61)	(24.93)	(48.55)	(39.68)	(28.82)
Nagaland	212975	369200	516449	774930	1209540	1990036
	(8.60)	(14.07)	(39.88)	(50.05)	(56.13)	(64.53)
Tripura	639029	1142005	1556342	2053058	2757205	3100203
	(24.56)	(78.71)	(36.28)	(31.92)	(34.29)	(16.03)
Sikkim	137725	162189	209843	316385	406457	540851
	N.A.	(17.76)	(29.38)	(50.77)	(28.47)	(33.06)
Manipur	577635	780037	1072753	1420953	1837149	2293896
	(12.80)	(35.04)	(37.53)	(32.46)	(29.29)	(24.86)

Note: Figures in parentheses indicate decadal growth in percentage.

Sources: (i) Census of India, 2001.
(ii) Statistical Abstract of Manipur, 2005.
(iii) Economic Review of Manipur (1994-95), Directorate of Economics and Statistics, Government of Manipur, p. 9.

this State. In Assam, the decadal growth rate of population was maximum in 1971–1981 (36.05 per cent) and minimum in 1981–91(12.65 per cent). The highest growth rate can be found in Tripura (78.71per cent) in 1951–1961 which may be due to influx of migrants from Bangladesh (erstwhile East Pakistan).

In Nagaland, the high rate of growth was observed since 1971 Census (39.88) and it attained its peak (64.53 per cent) in the 2001 Census. In short, Assam is the highest populated state (2, 66,55,528 persons) and Sikkim the least (5,40,851 persons) as per 2001 Census report.

Trend of Population Growth in Manipur

Population-wise, Manipur is a small state as compared to other states of India like U.P. or Bihar. But it can be observed from Table 27.2 that the state has been experiencing a very high population growth over the years since 1951. The population of the state was 5,77,635 persons in 1951 and it reached 7,80,037 persons in 1961 (35.04 per cent growth rate). At the national level, it was only 21.51 per cent.

Table 27.2 : Trend of Population Growth in Manipur

Years	*Population*	*Net Increase of Population*	*Decadal Growth in Percentage*		
			Manipur	*North East*	*All-India*
1951	5,77,635				
1961	7,80,037	2,02,402	35.04	41.01	21.51
1971	10,72,753	2,92,716	37.53	34.98	24.80
1981	14,20,953	3,48,200	32.46	26.52	25.00
1991	18,37,149	4,16,196	29.29	27.61	23.85
2001	22,93,896	4,56,747	24.86	22.00	21.54

Sources: 1. Census of India, 2001, Director of Census Operations, Manipur.
2. Statistical Abstract of Manipur, 2005.

The highest growth rate was in 1971 when it was recorded as high as 37.53 per cent against the all-India rate of 24.80 per cent. It is also interesting to note that the state also exceeds the overall North East rate except in the1961 Census. But the decadal growth rate started declining from 1981 Census (32.46 per cent) against 25.00 per cent of all-India rate. In the recent Census of 2001, the growth rate was observed at only 24.86 per cent against 21.54 per cent all-India rate.

This analysis shows that the trend of population growth has been not only continuously high in Manipur over the years but also significantly much higher than the national level and north east level during the last five decades under study.

District-wise Growth of Population

The uneven growth of population in the districts of Manipur is also an interesting area of discussion. Table 27.3 observes that Senapati district had, in all the censuses, all time high rates of growth which are above the state averages. Another scene can be seen in the district of Tamenglong in 1951-1961 census. The growth rate was negative (-3.10 per cent) during that period. However, it increased to 23.16 per cent, 38.50 per cent, 38.51 per cent and 29.23 per cent in 1971, 1981, 1991 and 2001 censuses respectively. In Chandel district, the maximum growth rate of 66.62 per cent was recorded in 2001 Census which had raised so many questions. The Churachandpur district also had high raised rates of growth since 1951 and it never came down below the state average. It had the highest growth rate in 1961-1971

Table 27.3 : District-wise Decadal Growth Rate of Population (1951–2001)

Districts	*1951-1961*	*1961-1971*	*1971-1981*	*1981-1991*	*1991-2001*
Senapati	66.80	44.61	49.19	34.09	36.09
Tamenglong	(-)3.10	23.16	38.50	38.51	29.23
Churachandpur	46.20	57.19	37.37	30.72	29.36
Chandel	15.09	39.90	45.76	25.81	66.62
Imphal	75.72	34.72	27.51	26.83	@
Thoubat	20.95	36.19	28.01	27.89	23.87
Bishnupur	67.87	37.35	30.33	28.07	15.27
Ukhrul	14.35	28.07	33.29	31.74	28.83
Total	35.04	37.53	32.46	29.29	24.86

Notes: Imphal District was bifurcated into Imphal East and Imphal West Districts in 1997.

@ Imphal East–19.49.

Imphal West–16.70.

Source: Statistical Abstract of Manipur, 2001 Directorate of Economics and Statistics, Government of Manipur.

period with 57.19 per cent. The rate of growth in the hill districts of Senapati, Churachandpur, Tamenglong and Chandel could be because of large scale influx of immigrants into these districts[3].

On the other-hand, the growth rates in the valley districts were more or less consistent around the state averages except in Imphal and Bishnupur districts in the 1951–1961 period. Imphal and Thoubal stood first and second in the growth rate of population with 75.72 per cent and 67.87 per cent respectively. Later on, in all other censuses, the valley districts had never exceeded the growth rate of the state averages for all the time.

Growth of Population by Religion

Another aspect of population study in Manipur is the growth of population as characterized by different ethnic and religious communities. In fact, the state is considered as the homeland of the Meiteis, who are by and large Hindus, and different tribes and Manipuri Muslims known as Meitei Pangals who had migrated a few centuries ago. Nowadays, there are also the Bengalis, Biharis, Nepalese, Jains, Sikhs etc. who had migrated and settled in the state for livelihood. The majority of the Meiteis are valley dwellers, though a few of them are also found in certain areas of the hill region. The Hindus accounted highest (61.68 per cent) in 1961 and lowest in 2001 (46.01 per cent).

Next to Hindus, the Christians are the second largest communities accounting for 11.84 per cent in 1951. But it increased to 34.11 per cent and 34.04 per cent in 1991 and 2001 respectively. They are mainly hill dwellers but now-a-days a major chuck of them is also found in the valley.

The third important religious community is the Muslims. Their numbers are less than 10.00 per cent of the total population of the state (Table 27.4). Like Meiteis, Muslims of Manipur (Meitei Pangals) are valley dwellers. All the Muslims of Manipur are not Meitei Pangals because Meitei Pangals are those who are born and brought up in Manipur. Even among the Meiteis, some of them are Scheduled Castes (2.00 per cent), viz. Lois, Yaithibi, Dhobi, etc. It is worthwhile to mention here that the population of Manipur is divided into eight religious groups, viz. Hindus, Christians, Muslims, Sikhs, Jains, Buddhists, others and religions not stated as above.

Table 27.4 : Population by Religions in Manipur (1951-2001)

Religions	1951	1961	1971	1981	1991	2001
Hindu	3,47,325 (61.13)	4,81,112 (61.68)	6,32,597 (58.97)	8,53,180 (60.04)	10,59,470 (57.67)	9,96,894 (46.01)
Christian	98,394 (11.84)	1,52,043 (19.49)	2,79,243 (26.68)	4,21,702 (29.68)	6,26,669 (34.11)	7,37,578 (34.04)
Muslim	37,197 (6.44)	48,588 (6.23)	70,969 (6.62)	99,327 (6.99)	1,33,535 (7.27)	1,90,936 (8.81)
Sikh	50*	523 (0.07)	1,028) (0.10)	992 (0.07)	1,301 (0.07)	1653 (0.07)
Buddhist	33*	325 (0.04)	495 (0.05)	473 (0.03)	711 (0.07)	1926 (0.08)
Jain	150 (0.03)	778 (0.10)	1408 (0.13)	975 (0.07)	1337 (0.07)	1461 (0.06)
Others	1,24,486 (21.55)	–	83,167 (7.75)	35,490 (2.50)	14,066 (0.77)	2,35,280 (10.86)
Religion not stated	–	96,668 (12.39)	3,846 (0.36)	8,814 (0.62)	–	1057 (0.05)
Total	5,77,635 (100.00)	7,80,037 (100.00)	10,72,753 (100.00)	14,20,953 (100.00)	18,37,149 (100.00)	21,66,788** (100.00)

Notes : Figures in parentheses indicate percentage to total.

* Negligible.

** Figures of 2001 census excludes Mao Maram, Paomata and Purul Sub-Division of Senapati District.

Sources : (i) Economic Survey of Manipur, 1999–2000, (ii) Statistical Abstract of Manipur, 2005.

Conclusion

After examining the growth of population in Manipur, two main responsible factors emerge. One is the high birth rate and declining death rate and the other is migration. The factor of high birth rate and low death rate may be considered as a natural demographic transition. But, the second factor of migration alarms the general public at the highest level. Migrants constituted about 6.00 per cent of the total increase in population during 1961–1971 in which 17,667 migrants were added to the population of the state. It was 20,399 during 1971–1981 (Economic Review of Manipur, 1994–1995). Therefore, it can be concluded that migration from other states of the country and immigration from other neighbouring countries significantly contribute to the growth of population of this state. On the other hand, the uneven growth of population among the different groups of ethnic religious communities needs the urgent attention of all. This may be due to the feeling that increase in population in their own groups might be assets to their own groups or communities.

Whatever may be the causes of growth of population, the growth rate itself has been very rapid since 1951 after it had merged with the Indian Union in 1949. The more alarming point is that the trend of population growth was significantly much above the national averages during the last five decades. Further, the distribution and density of population between the hill and the valley had shown a great difference. Though density of population in the state is not so high in comparison to the national average, the heavy concentration of the population in the small valley of the state is a matter of great concern. For example, as per the 2001 Census, the density of population in the state was 103 persons per sq.km. It was 631 in the valley and 44 in the hill regions. The national average was 325 at the same period. The relationship between population growth and economic development of a state has been the focal attention of the whole world. It may be desirable for a particular state or country to obtain growth of population upto a certain level because human beings are both means and ends of all economic activities. However, rapid growth of population will become a liability and extra burden to the state or country. Problems of unemployment, poverty, malnourishment etc. are all the example of evils of population explosion. It is worthwhile to mention here that unemployment levels reached 5,84,830 persons in Manipur as on 30th April, 2007 (Employment Exchange, Imphal). It was 5,83,653 persons as on 31st March, 2007. The rate of increase per month was 1,177 persons. Out of the total, 4,21,623 were male and 1,63,207 were female candidates searching for jobs. In this regard, a proper policy of population needs to be formulated in order to meet the challenging issues of economic development of the state.

Last but not the least, the pressure of population in the valley areas are very high, particularly in the capital town of Imphal. Imphal West district continues to be the most populous district of Manipur. There were 2,63,769 persons or 45.66 per cent of the total population of the state in Imphal district alone. The number of population in this district increased to 7,11,261 or 38.72 per cent in 1991. In 2001, after Imphal district has been bifurcated as Imphal East and Imphal West District in 1997, there were 3,94,876 persons or 17.21 per cent of population of the state in Imphal East District and 44,44,382 persons or 19.37 per cent in the Imphal West District. Density wise also, Imphal West District has the highest density (856 persons per sq.km) followed by Thoubal District (856 persons per sq.km) and Imphal East District (557 persons per sq. km). On the other hand, the most populated hill district, i.e. Senapati has a population of 283621 persons or 12.36 per cent of the total population of the state (2001 Census). The average density of the total hill region was 44 persons per sq. km against 631 persons per sq. km of the total valley region (2001 Census). Therefore, the extension of the Manipur Land Revenue and Land Reforms Act, 1960 with necessary modifications in the hill areas of the state is the need of the hour for proper utilization of land areas and equitable distribution of economic development of the state.

Notes & References

1. Mahendra K. Premi (1991): *India Population Heading Towards a Billion,* B.R. Publishing Corporation; New Delhi, p.1.
2. Dun E.W.(1975) : "Gazetteer of Manipur".
3. *Economic review of Manipur,* (1990–1991), Directorate of Economics and Statistics, Government. of Manipur.
4. Census of India (1981), Directorate of Census Operations, Manipur.
5. Agarwal, A.K. (1985). *North East India,* Chug Publication, Allahabad.
6. Chandra, R.C. (1998) : *Population,* Kalyani Publishers, Ludhiana.
7. Datt, Ruddar & Sundharam, K.P.M. (1996) : *Indian Economy,* Hand and Company Ltd., New Delhi.
8. Government of Manipur (1999–2000) : "Economy of Manipur", Directorate of Economics and Statistics.

9. Government of Manipur (2005): *Statistical Abstract of Manipur*, Directorate of Economics and Statistics.
10. Singh, L. Tombi Dr. (1990–95): "Population and Human Resources Planning for Manipur" Sponsored by Planning Department, Government of Manipur.
11. Peter R. Cox, (1998): *Demography*, Cambridge University Press, Cambridge.

28 Demographic Profile of North East India with Special Reference to Manipur

Rajmani Singh and *A.Ratan Sharma*

Introduction

Population explosion of any region or a country leads to increase in demand for food, land, fuel-wood, timber and other forest products causing large scale depletion of natural resources and forest resources. Massive growth urban population leads to various urban problems such as shortage of houses, lack of proper sanitation, lack of safe drinking water, lack of education and health care facilities, lack of drainage system, traffic congestion and environmental pollution etc. On the other hand in the rural areas, development works remain almost at a standstill and per capita availability of amenities is considerably reduced. People in rural areas suffer most from lack of proper education, medical, electricity and communication facilities are not at par with the pace of population growth in the rural areas.

According to 2001 Population Census, the Indian population was 102.87 crore (at the time of sunrise on March 2001) with males at 53.22 crore (51.72 per cent of total population) and females at 49.65 crore (48.28 per cent of total population). In the global context, India consitutes 16.87 per cent of world population. India being a developing country is also at the level of "high birth rate and high death rate" to the intermediate transition stage of "high birth rate and low death rate" which manifest in high rate of population growth, before graduating to "low birth rate low death rate". The United Nations has estimated that the world population grew at an annual growth rate of 1.4 per cent during 1990-2000, China registering a much lower annual growth rate of population of 1 per cent as compared to that of India at 1.93 per cent during 1991-2001. Thus, it is now estimated that by 2050, India will most likely overtake China to become the most populous country on the earth with 17.2 per cent population living here if the present growth rate is not controlled below 1 per cent.

Keeping in view the trend of population growth in North East India particularly Manipur, the researcher has undertaken the topic delves on three areas. The first part which demographic profile of North East India exculding, Sikkim. The second part of the paper highlights the population size and distribution in Manipur involving growth rate, density of population, sex-ratio, literacy rate, growing unemployment rate, rural-urban distribution of population, birth and death rate, and Infant Mortality Rate (IMR) and finally, it will devote on the consequence of population growth specially unemployment problems in the process of socio-economic development of Manipur in particular and North Eastern Region of India in general. It also highlights on the unemployment problems and suggests remedial measure at the end of the paper.

Overall Demographic Features of North East India

The North East India, with a land mass of 2,55,059 sq. km. (9 per cent of the country's total), hosts a population of 38,539 million as per 2001 Census. Urbanization in the North Eastern States of India has gradually increased over the last few decades. The urban population of North East India has increased significantly during the last two decades from 18.47 lakhs in 1991 to 59.72 lakhs in 2001 with the growing rate of 223.34 per cent spreading over 200 different urban centres. But in comparison to all-India percentage of urban population to total population, the North East India's percentage is very poor. It accounts only 15.51 per cent of the total population of the region against all-India percentage of 27.78.

Among the seven North Eastern States, Mizoram stood as the highest urbanized state with 49.5 per cent of its total population living in urban areas, followed by Manipur with 23.88 per cent, Arunachal Pradesh 20.41 per cent, Meghalaya 19.63 per cent, Nagaland 17.74 per cent, Tripura 17.02 per cent and Assam 12.72 per cent as per

2001 Census. It is very intersting to note that except Mizoram remaining six other states of the region were below the national average percentage of 27.78 of urban population. The highly urbanized state of Mizoram which accounts for 49.5 per cent of urban population is placed in 5th position among the different States and Union territories of the country as per 2001 Census. Delhi, the capital of the country is the highest urban population with 93.01 per cent and Himachal Pradesh remains the lowest urbanized state with 9.79 per cent of urban population against total population.

Table 28.1 represents the overall demographic features of north eastern states, levels of literacy, density of population living in per sq.km, sex-ratio of female per 1000 male population, rural and urban distribution of population etc. Total of seven North Eastern States is 2,55,028 sq. km (2001) habitat of about 38.539 million persons in 2001 and support 3.75 per cent of India's population. However, as the North Eastern States are, dominantly rural, so, out of India's total rural population of 741,660,293 in 2001 the N.E. States share of rural population is 4.38 per cent which is higher than the share of total population. Except Assam, in all the other States, the density of population is less than the national average which is an index of backwardness. In case of urbanization, all North Eastern States except Mizoram state are behind national average. Assam is the most populous state with least urbanization and Mizoram is the least populous state with highest urbanization. By literacy rate, the N.E. States are more or less same as of national average. But Mizoram outshines with nearly 91 per cent male and 86 per cent female literacy followed by Tripura. As per report of CMIE, taking the selected indicator level of development of all states and districts India is given the value of 100, rest of the states remain related to national average of 100. Developed states exceed 100 points less developed states falls below 100. The N.E. States show remarkable unifomity, values ranging 54-55 points only. However, Arunachal Pradesh is the only state having a little higher value with 66 points.

Table 28.1 also shows the trend of rural-urban settlements among the states of North Eastern Region of India for the last three decades. Mizoram was the most urbanized state in the region. Once, Mizoram

Table 28.1: Demographic Profile of North Eastern Region of India 2001

States of North East India	*Area sq.km*	*Population*			*Population*		*Literacy*	*Density per sq.km*	*Sex-Ratio per 1000 Males*
		Total	*Male*	*Female*	*Urban*	*Rural*			
Arunachal Pradesh	83743	10.98	5.80	5.18	20.81	79.19	54.3	13	893
Assam	78438	266.55	137.77	128.78	12.92	87.08	63.3	340	935
Manipur*	22327	23.89	12.07	11.82	23.88	76.12	68.8	107	978
Meghalaya	22429	23.19	11.76	11.43	19.63	80.37	62.6	103	972
Mizoram	21087	8.89	4.59	4.30	49.60	50.40	88.8	42	935
Nagaland	16579	19.90	10.47	9.43	17.24	82.76	66.6	120	900
Tripura	10486	31.99	16.42	15.57	17.12	82.88	73.2	305	848
NE Total	*255079*	*385.39*	*198.88*	*186.51*	*15.51*	*84.49*	*68.77*	*149*	*936*
All-India	*3287263*	*102.87*	*53.22*	*49.65*	*27.78*	*72.22*	*64.8*	*325*	*933*

Sources: (i) Census of India, Series Manipur 2001.
(ii) NEDFi Data Bank Quarterly, Vol. Issue-1 July 2002, p. 2.
(iii) India's Population is in crores.
(iv)* As per 2001 Census provisional figures.

was second in position as urbanized during 1981 Census after Manipur by a margin of 1.75 per cent. But it rose to first position during 1991 Census and 2001 Census. One of the main reason behind the sudden improvement in 2001 Census was due to return of peace and normalcy in the state. It is also seen from Table 28.1 that except Mizoram and Manipur all the remaining states of the region are below the national average rate of urbanization. One very interesting figure is noticed from the table that except Manipur all the remaining states have improved their level of urbanization decade by decade. But for Manipur it was 26.42 per cent in 1981 rising to 27.52 per cent in 1991 and again declined to 23.88 per cent. One of the basic reason behind the increasing and decreasing trend of urbanization in Manipur was due to delimitation of Churachandpur as urbanized in 1991 and de-recognition during 2001 Census.

Population Size and Distribution of Manipur

As recorded on the 1st March, 2001, the population of Manipur was 23,88,634,634 consisting of 12,07,388 males and 11,81,296 females population. Among the 35 different States and Union territories of India, Manipur state is 23rd in rank in term of its population. It supports about 0.23 per cent of the total population of India. Thus nearly every 413th (four hundred thirteenth) person in the country is a Manipuri. The distribution of population in the nine districts of the state is very much heterogeneous in nature showing a heavy concentration in one but thin population is another. For population in other example, Imphal West district has 18.40 per cent and Tamenglong district has 4.67 per cent of the total population.

Growth Rate

The growth rate of Manipur during 1901-1951 was more or less same corresponding to all-India rate, that is 12.1 per cent of Manipur against 12.5 per cent for all-India. But from 1952 onwards the growth rate of Manipur has been alarming as it is much above the national level. Unfortunately, the decennial growth rate of the state has increased

Table 28.2 : District-wise Demographic Status of Manipur

Districts	*Area sq.km*	*Population as per 2001 Census*			*Literacy Percentage*	*Density*	*Sex-Ratio*	*Sub-Division*	*Unemployed as on 31st Dec. 2006*
		Total	*Male*	*Female*					
Imphal West	519	439532	218947	220585	80.61	847	1007	4	201712
Imphal East	709	393780	197710	196070	76.38	555	992	4	80530
Thoubal	514	366341	183338	183003	67.90	713	998	3	83285
Bishenpur	496	205907	102772	103135	71.59	415	1004	3	53700
Churachandpur	4570	228707	114740	113967	74.67	50	993	5	52172
Ukhrul	4544	140946	73413	67553	68.96	31	920	5	23044
Senapati	3271	379214	196646	182568	50.47	116	928	6	42026
Chandel	3313	122714	61778	60936	57.38	37	986	4	20035
Tamenglong	4391	111493	57994	53499	58.46	25	922	4	16828
Total	22327	2388634	1207388	1181296	68.87	107	978	38	573,332

Sources: 1. Census of India, Series Manipur 2001.
2. Manipur General Knowledge, 2007.
3. Directorate of Employment Service, Manipur, 2007.

from 29.29 per cent in 1981-1991 to 30.02 per cent in 1991-2001. It had, however, declined from 23.84 per cent in 1981-91 to 21.34 per cent in 1991-2001 for all-India figure.

Table 28.3 : Decadal Growth of Population of Manipur by Rural and Urban Sectors

Hibitants	*1971*	*Decadal Growth %*	*1981*	*Decadal Growth %*	*1991*	*Decadal Growth %*	*2001*
Rural	9,31,261	12.27	10,45,493	27.36	13,31,504	36.55	18,18,224
Urban	1,41,492	165.36	3,75,469	34.67	5,05,645	12.81	5,70,410
Total	10,72,753	32.46	14,20,953	29.29	18,37,149	30.02	23,88,634

Source: Census of India Series Manipur 1971, 1991 and 2001.

Density of Population

One of the important indices of population concentration is the density of population. The population density of Manipur is lower than that of all-India figures, i.e. 107 persons per sq. km for Manipur against 325 for all-India and 149 for North East India according to 2001 Census. There is a uniform trend in increase of the density of population for both state and its nine different districts from 1991 to 2001. One of important feature is that the average density of population in the valley comprising four districts, viz. Imphal West, Imphal East, Thoubal and Bishenpur are above 16 times the average density in the five hilly districts, viz. Churachandpur, Ukhrul, Senapati, Chandel and Temenglong. It may be noted that Imphal West district is the only city above one lakh population with a population density of 827 per sq. km. followed by Thoubal, Imphal East and Bishenpur with 713,555 and 415 persons per sq. km. respectively. Among the five hill districts Tamenglong is the most thinly populated district with 25 persons per sq. km. in 2001 Census and Senapati district has the highest density with 116 followed by Churachandpur, Chandel, and Ukhrul with 50, 37 and 31 respectively. Senapati district having the state density of population with 107 as per 2001 Census.

Sex-Ratio

The sex-ratio of the state has increased from 958 female population per 1000 male population in 1991 compared to 978 in 2001 which is higher than the corresponding all-India figure of 927 in 1991 to 933 in 2001. The sex-ratio of North East India is 936 per 1000 male as per 2001 Census. On the other hand the urban sex ratio of Manipur is 1009 against the rural sex-ratio of 969 as per 2001 Census. Among the districts, Imphal West district is having the highest sex-ratio of 1007 of which 1018 are from urban and 994 from the rural. The highest rural sex-ratio is in the district of Bishenpur with 1015 female against 1000 male population. The increase in the state sex-ratio is relatively due to larger increase in the sex-ratio of the seven districts except Senapati and Tamenglong.

Literacy Rate

Manipur is one of the most literate state among the States and Union territories of India with 68.87 per cent covering 77.87 per cent male and 59.70 per cent female. And the literacy rate of North East India is 68.77 per cent of which 75.08 are males and 61.91 per cent are females. The literacy rate of Manipur is higher than that of all-India figures that is 65.38 per cent consisting of 75.85 per cent male and 54.16 per cent females as per 2001 Census. On the other hand the total number of illiterates of the state has continued to increase from 6,13,840 (1991) to 6,46,287 (2001). The district literacy rates are heterogeneous in nature. With 80.61 per cent Imphal West district has the highest rate of literacy followed by Imphal East district with 76.38 per cent, Churachandpur 74.67 per cent, Bishenpur 71.59 per cent, Ukhrul 68.96 per cent, Thoubal 67.90 per cent, Tamenglong 58.46 per cent and the lowest rate of 50.47 per cent is recorded in Senapati district. Thus it is observed that the three hill districts, viz. Tamenglong, Chandel and Senapati are lagging behind the national level literacy rate and other six districts are above national literacy rate. Further it is also observed from Table 28.4 that Imphal West district is having highest literacy with 80.61 per cent followed by Imphal East with 76.38 per cent and Churachandpur with 74.67 per cent, Senapati district has the lowest literacy rate with 50.47 per cent.

Table 28.4 : District-wise Literacy Rate as per 2001 Census

Districts	*Male*	*Female*	*Person*
Imphal West	89.10	72.24	80.61
Imphal East	86.44	88.30	76.38
Thoubal	80.50	55.34	67.90
Bishenpur	82.25	61.09	71.59
Churachandpur	84.98	64.40	74.67
Ukhrul	75.40	61.91	68.96
Senapati	56.39	44.04	50.47
Chandel	66.12	48.57	57.38
Tamenglong	67.04	49.11	58.46
Manipur Total	77.87	59.70	68.87
North East India	75.08	61.91	68.77
All-India	75.85	54.16	65.38

Source : Census of India 2001 Series-14 Manipur.

The above Table 28.4 also shows the district-wise male-female literacy rate for the state. Among the districts male literacy is highest in Imphal West district and lowest in Senapati district. Out of 9 districts, four districts such as Ukhrul, Senapati, Chandel and Tamenglong are below the state male literacy rate of 77.87 per cent. Further, four districts such as Thoubal, Senapati, Chandel and Tamenglong have less female literacy rate than state female literacy rate of 59.70 per cent. Only three districts have below the national average literacy rate of 65.38 per cent.

Unemployment

Manipur is one of the industrially and economically backward states among the states of North-East India. On the other hand Manipur having the highest rate of unemployment among the states of the region and in the country. The total number of unemployed has crossed more than 5,73,332 as on 31st December, 2006 and 5,84,830 as on 30th April, 2007 which is approximately 25 per cent of the total population against 12 per cent in North Eastern region and 7.7 per cent in all-India as per 2001 Census. Out of total unemployed persons 4,19,774 were male unemployed youth and remaining 1,60,110 were female unemployed youth. The main reason behind the increasing rate of unemployment in the state are lack of industrial development, lack of service sector contribution to the economy, banning on new recruitment by the government for the last one decade, slow pace of basic infrastructural development, lack of entrepreneurial skills and awareness among the youths and lack of career guidance and counseling centres which could give proper training and education to the unemployed youth. Table 28.5 given below shows the detailed information related to unemployment pattern of the state.

Table 28.5 : District-wise Unemployed Male and Female of Manipur

Districts	*Male*	*Female*	*Person*	*Total Population*	*% of Total*
Imphal West	1,40,333	61,379	2,01,712	4,39,532	45.89
Imphal East	57,364	23,166	80,530	3,93,780	20.45
Thoubal	65,639	17,646	83,285	3,66,341	22.73
Bishenpur	39,340	14,360	53,700	2,05,907	26.08
Churachandpur	39,468	12,704	52,172	2,28,707	22.81
Ukhrul	16,262	6,782	23,044	1,40,946	16.35
Senapati	31,055	10,971	42,026	3,79,214	11.08
Tamenglong	13,630	6,355	20,035	1,22,714	16.33
Chandel	12,987	3,841	16,828	1,11,493	15.09
Total	4,16,128	1,57,204	5,73,332	2388634	24.00

Source : Directorate of Employment Service, Government of Manipur.

The district-wise unemployment pattern is seen from the above Table 28.5 and it is found that Imphal West district is having the largest unemployment figure of 2,01,712 against the total population of 4,39,532 comprising 1,40,333 male and 61,379 female unemployed youth followed by Thoubal district with 83,285 against the total population of 3,66,341 and Chandel district with 16,828 against the total population of 1,11,493.

Rural-urban Distribution of Population

Growing urbanization is a recent phenomenon in developing countries. The proportion of urban population in Manipur has declined from 27.52 per cent in 1991 to 23.88 per cent in 2001. The corresponding figures of all-India are 25.72 per cent and 27.78 per cent respectively. The state is highly urbanized state among the seven sister states after Mizoram with 49.50 per cent. Demographers recognize that the increase in urban population attributed both to natural growth and mobility from rural areas because of employment opportunities, attraction to better living standard and availability of social serivices such as education, health, transport, communication and entertainment etc.

Table 28.6 : District-wise Rural-urban Population of Manipur 2001

Districts	*2001 in Percentage*	
	Urban	*Rural*
Imphal West	42.54	57.46
Thoubal	23.01	76.99
Imphal East	18.98	81.02
Bishenpur	12.85	87.15
Chandel	2.62	97.38
Total	23.88	76.12

Source : Census of India, Manipur 2001, p. 48.

Birth and Death Rate

These rates are important components of population growth. The national birth rate has declined from 39.9 in 1951 to an estimated 30.2 per 1000 population in 1990 and 20.3 in 1999 whereas the death rate has considerably declined from 27.4 in 1951 to an estimated 9.7 per 1000 population in 1990 and 6.3 in 1999. The birth rate in the state is 16.4 in 1999 which is slightly less than its national figure. However, the corresponding death rate 6.6 is above the national figure.

Infant Mortality Rate (IMR)

Demographers have rightly identified that IMR as one of the factors contributing to high population growth. It is true that unless couples are reasonably certain that two or three children born to them will survive to adulthood, they may not accept the idea of family planning, National figure shows that the crude rate has declined by 42 per cent from 16 per 1000 population in 1975 to a little over

9 in 1994, while the IMR has declined by about 48 per cent from 140 per 1000 population.

Effects on Economic Development

Faster population growth is a handicap, like extra weight carried by a racehorse. This would be clear from a brief discussion of the various problems of the growth of population in Manipur. Growth of population of any state, region or a country leads to increase in consumption for food, demand for land for construction of house, safe drinking water, increase in unemployment rate, lack of per capita infrastructural facilities such as health and education facilities. Further, massive growth of urban population leads to various urban problems such as shortage of house, lack of proper sanitation, lack of safe drinking water, lack of education and health care facilities, lack of drainage system, traffic congestion and environmental pollutions etc. On the other hand in the rural areas, development works remain almost standstill, per capita availability of amenities is considerably reduced. People in rural areas suffer most from lack of proper education facilities, lack of medical facilities, lack of electricity, lack of drinking water facility and communication facilities etc., as these amenities are not at par with the pace of population growth in the rural areas.

In spite of the rapid advancement in the crop productivity, the faster rate of populaion growth causes a great problem to agriculture in the state of Manipur. Since the increase in the net cultivated area of land has been insignificant, the pressure on land has increased tremendously. It can be said that the benefits of planned development in the state have been offset by rapid population growth as only a marginal part of the development contributed towards improving the quality of life. In this era of economic globalization, population explosion, food problem and environment have become major areas of concern and we need to act consciously and collectively to meet these challenges.

Conclusion

From the interpretative analysis it may be concluded that over population gives a tremendous pressure on land in addition to causing environmental damages and growing burden on natural resources, underutilization of labour and adverse effect on quality of production which together hamper all the development plans made by the government from time to time. The situation is more serious in developing countries like India.

References

Singh Rajmani *et al.* Growth and Development of Rural-Urban settlements in Manipur. Paper to be presented in two days regional seminar on Habitation Pattern in Manipur. Organised by Department of Geography, Manipur University on 23rd and 24th March 2007.

Yojana, A Development Monthly, December 2006.

Indian Economy 2005 General Studies, *Pratiyogita Darpan*.

The Sangai Express 9th December 2003 and 11th July 2004.

Office record of the Directorate of Employment Exchange, Government of Manipur.

Census of India 2001 Series 14, Manipur.

Dhingera, I.C. (2001) *Indian Economy: Environment and Policy*, published by Sultan Chand & Sons, New Delhi-2.

Ved Prakash Memorial Lecture, delivered by Prof. M.S.S. Swaminathan in New Delhi on May 21st, 1999.

29 Religious Minorities and Communal Harmony

The Situation in Assam

Tapan Kumar Chattopadhyay

The Assam Situation

Ethnic conflicts in Assam took a violent turn in the early 1980s when one ethnic community claimed exclusive rights over a geographical space which it regarded as its 'homeland' on the ground that it was the original inhabitants of the land. Other communities, they argued, were outsiders and had no right to settle there. The main targets of the Assamese agitators were Bengali Hindus, Bengali Muslims and Adivasis. Matters became complicated when the Bodo community began demanding a separate homeland for themselves in the western part of Assam. According to the Census Report of 2001 the Bodo community comprises the majority in the Kokrajhar district of western Assam. Kokrajhar is now the headquarters of the Bodoland Autonomous Council (BAC) formed in 1993. The present BAC covers a space spread across seven districts of Assam.

However, in a large portion of the land under the BAC there was more than 50 per cent non-Bodo population composed of a variety of ethnic groups. Since the Bodos did not constitute a simple majority in these areas, clear demarcation of the boundaries of the BAC was not possible. Assam refused to hand over the non-Bodo majority areas to the BAC. To establish their majority, therefore, the Bodo extremists chose the path of ethnic cleansing. Since October 1993, large scale attacks were made on non-Bodo communities, particularly on Muslims of Bengali origin. By the end of 1994 more than 20000 Muslims were displaced in Kokrajhar and Bongaigaon districts. The Bodo militants also attacked Bengali Hindus and Adivasis; but unlike the Muslims, the Bengali Hindus and Adivasis formed their own militant groups and started attacking the Bodo villages. The Muslims, thus, are the worst victims of internal displacement in Assam. It is precisely in this context that one can conceptualize the issue of minority rights in India (particularly, rights of religious minorities) and examine the question of communal harmony.

Human Rights and Minority Rights

On 10th December 1948 the UN General Assembly 'adopted and proclaimed the Universal Declaration of Human Rights as a common goal, realizing them for all people, all nations and every individual and every group in society.' The Preamble of the Declaration emphasizes 'the recognition of the inherent dignity and of the equal and inalienable rights of all the members of the human family.' This is considered as 'the foundation of Freedom, Justice and Peace in the World'. The enjoyment of 'freedom of speech and belief and freedom from fear and want' has been proclaimed as the highest aspiration of humankind. It also cautioned that if human rights are not protected by the rule of law, men will be 'compelled to have recourse, as a last resort, to rebellion against tyranny and oppression.'

Now, although the UN Charter recognizes the rights of all individuals as human beings, the Declaration did not sanction the rights of people as minorities within a broad nation-state. The rights of the minorities were recognized for the first time in the UN Covenant on Civil and Political Rights, which though adopted in December 1966, came into force on 23 March, 1976. Article 27 of this Covenant recognized the rights of ethnic, religious and linguistic minorities of all countries to enjoy their own culture, profess and practice their own religion or to use their own language. In 1992 the UN, through its Declaration of the Rights of Persons belonging to National or Ethnic, Religious and Linguistic Minorities, directed all member states to protect minority rights. Thus although initially the United Nations was not very much concerned with the protection of minority rights, today minority rights are enjoying a special status along with human rights in general. In a country like India, on the contrary, which has always been multi-ethnic, multi-religious and multi-linguistic, minority rights are recognized from the very beginning, i.e since the time of the framing of the Constitution.

Human Rights and Minority Rights in India

The Constitution of India contains a list of Fundamental Rights of citizens in Part III. These rights are justiciable and the State has to safeguard these rights. There is another set of rights in Part IV of the Constitution, known as the Directive Principles of State Policy, which are connected mainly with the social and economic rights of the people. Although these are 'fundamental in the governance of the country' (Article 36), they are non-justiciable.

Almost all the rights covered in the UNs—Universal Declaration of Human Rights (1948) are included in the Fundamental Rights of the Constitution of India. The Chapter on Fundamental Rights has provided a special space for minority rights also. The Fundamental Rights of the Indian citizens consist of the right to equality (Arts. 14–18), the right to freedom (Arts. 19–22), the right against exploitation (Arts. 23 and 24), the right to religion (Arts. 25–28) and cultural and educational rights (Arts. 29 and 30). The citizens also have the fundamental right to Constitutional remedies. The right to property was originally a fundamental right, but it was later deleted from Part III and introduced as a constitutional right to property under Art. 300A by the 44th Amendment Act of 1978.

Articles 29 and 30 provide protection to the interests of the minorities. These Articles give the minorities the right to establish and administer educational institutions of their choice. Constitutional provisions apart, the judiciary have played a positive role in expanding the rights of the minorities. The interpretations of the Supreme Court have strengthened the safeguards provided to religious and linguistic minorities. However, despite the safeguards provided in the Constitution and further strengthening of these by Court rulings, a feeling of inequality and discrimination persists among the minorities. Hence, for effective enforcement of these safeguards the Government of India set up a Minorities Commission on 22 February, 1978.

Subsequently, in May 1992, the Commission was renamed 'National Commission for Minorities'. The Commission consists of a Chairman, a Vice-Chairman and six members. One of the important functions of the Commission is to 'look into specific complaints regarding deprivation of rights and safeguards of the minorities and take up such matters with the appropriate authorities.' The Commission has all the powers of a civil court trying a suit.

Minority Rights and Multi-culturalism

The question of minority rights is closely related to the concept of multi-culturalism. There are three main insights of multi-culturalism. 'First, human beings are culturally embedded in the sense that they grow up and live within a culturally structured world and organize their lives and social relations in terms of a culturally derived system of meaning and significance.'[1] 'Second, different cultures represent different systems of meaning and visions of the good life. Since each realizes a limited range of human capacities and emotions and grasps only a part of the totality of human existence, it needs other cultures to help it understand itself better, expand its intellectual and moral horizon, stretch its imagination, save it from narcissism to guard it against the obvious temptation to absolutise itself, and so on.'[2] 'Third, every culture is internally plural and reflects a continuing conversation between its different traditions and strands of thought... A culture cannot appreciate the value of others unless it appreciates the plurality within it.'[3] Thus understood, multi-culturalism does not imply only equality of cultures, but also mutual tolerance and healthy interaction. The concept of multi-culturalism, which has given rise to minority rights, can be fruitfully employed to promote communal harmony. Multi-culturalism is against majoritarianism. Unlike pluralism, which only recognizes the co-existence of various religious, cultural and ethnic groups, multi-culturalism recognizes the equality of these various groups.

Today, multi-cultural policies of nation-states constitute an alternative to the assimilationist goals pursued for long by liberal States. In India there are a good number of minorities identified by factors like religion, caste, class or region. In popular perception, however, the quintessential minority is the religious minority. The Constitution of India recognizes both cultural differences and the values of equal citizenship and equal rights. The Constitution of India guarantees protection to religious, cultural and linguistic minorities. In the case of religious communities, no special privilege is granted to any religious community, not even the majority community. In a multi-cultural, multi-religious and multi-ethnic country like India, majority communities have no right, whatsoever, to offend the sentiments of minority communities.

Notes

1. Bhikhu Parekh, 'What is Multi-culturalism?', *Seminar*, December 1999, No. 484 (http : www. India–semi–nar. com 1999/1484/484%20parekh. htm)
2. *Ibid.*
3. *Ibid.*

Index